To our children

Nicola
Richard
Diane
Stephen
Rudolph
Su-Lize

The Theory and Principles of Risk Management

The Theory and Principles of Risk Management

Anthony C Valsamakis
CRM Risk Finance Consultants (Pty) Ltd

Robert W Vivian
University of the Witwatersrand
Department of Business Economics

Gawie S du Toit
University of South Africa
Department of Business Economics

This text is based in part on a DCom thesis (Business Economics) by Anthony C Valsamakis submitted to the University of South Africa

Butterworths
Durban

Butterworth Publishers (Pty) Ltd
Reg No 91/05175/07

Reprinted 1993, 1995 (twice)

ISBN 0 409 11162 7

Durban
8 Walter Place, Waterval Park
Mayville 4091

Johannesburg
Grayston 66, 2 Norwich Close
Sandton 2196

Cape Town
3 Gardens Business Village, Hope Street
Cape Town 8001

About the cover

The illustration on the front cover is William Turner's *The Slave Ship* (1840). The painting was based on an account of an event which occurred in 1783, when the captain of the salve ship Zony had a large cargo of slaves thrown overboard during an epidemic, so that insurance, payable for those lost 'at sea', but not from disease, could be claimed.

Typeset by Digma Publications
Printed and bound by Interpak Natal Pietermariitzburg

FOREWORD

Risk Management . . . who's heard of it?

Many years ago when I started my career with a large multinational insurer the discipline was unknown. Those insurers who knew about Risk Management considered it to be counter-productive in many respects while industry and commerce were unaware of its strengths.

This is no longer the case. Increasingly, insurers around the world are realising the merits of Risk Management. This growing acceptance is taking place against a backdrop of severe competition which has now placed the traditional market place for insurance in turmoil. Lloyds of London has been shaken to its foundations and some providers of insurance are withdrawing from the market. Reinsurance capacity is under strain and prices have been pushed to unprecedented heights. In the face of such market failings Risk Management must be viewed as a discipline whose time has come.

Managers of industrial and commercial organisations are becoming increasingly aware of the economic benefits that Risk Management can offer their organisations. Closer lines of communication and more intensive use of what is a legitimate management tool can only enhance the identification and control of risk itself, and thus minimise foreseeable loss. For many years organisations have formed subsidiaries for the purposes of leasing, purchasing, manufacture, selling and distribution and many other functional aspects of their business. Now, as risk becomes more pervasive, leading organisations are forming dedicated insurance subsidiaries to co-ordinate risk financing and control.

Intermediaries look upon Risk Management as an important attribute in organisational growth. They view it as an essential consideration when advising their clients and providing a professional service.

There can be little doubt that the last decade has seen substantial developments in the area of Risk Management. Indeed, the rapidity of change is virtually unprecedented. No longer is it a discipline shrouded in mystery and obscured by jargon, but exists as a response to the natural demand for more effective management, and as an academic subject in its own right. It is a new tool – in some respects a revolutionary one – the awareness of which is escalating rapidly. Those who fail to recognise its benefits and adapt to the change it could precipitate are neglecting an integral aspect of responsible business practice.

This book provides a comprehensive evaluation of Risk Management techniques, presenting methods that are fundamental in highlighting those areas of vulnerability that all organisations face and suggesting practical ways to reduce the possibility of financial loss.

Bill Hastings

ACKNOWLEDGEMENTS

Valuable interaction was achieved with colleagues of the Price Forbes Group and with many individuals involved in the discipline. The authors acknowledge their interest and assistance, and indeed, in many cases the ideas expressed in this book reflect their thinking as much as that of the authors.

A special word of thanks is due to Sieglinde for her tireless efforts in converting the manuscript to a meticulously typed document.

CONTENTS

LIST OF TABLES

LIST OF FIGURES

1 THE HISTORICAL DEVELOPMENT OF THE RISK MANAGEMENT FUNCTION

1.1 Introduction

The origins of risk-financing can be traced as far back as 1700 BC when the Babylonians established bottomry as a means to handle the risks associated with international trade.[1] Bottomry was a type of loan; a grantee issued a loan on the value of goods which were shipped between countries. Repayment of the loan was based on the safe arrival of the goods – the seller had to repay the grantee if the goods arrived safely, if not, the loan did not have to be repaid.

The first risk control measures were introduced as far back as approximately 700 BC by the Greeks and Phoenicians. They extended the bottomry principle and developed bonds with special provisions which were aimed at reducing the risk to the grantee of the bond. The bonds provided for specified loan terms, the placement of agreements in escrow, specified loan periods and specified interest rates, and included severe penalties for breach of contract. Some bonds also contained provisions which prohibited a ship from deviating from a mutually agreed upon, prespecified route, considered to be the least risky by the parties involved. These measures truly qualify as risk control measures in terms of the present-day description of the concept of risk control, since they were aimed at reducing the possibility of loss and thereby reducing the creditor's exposure.

The above developments eventually led to the establishment of the insurance industry. Insurance contracts developed which provided for indemnification of an insured against losses as a result of the occurrence due to specified perils. As the insurance industry developed, insurance contracts were extended to cover perils of the sea, fire, personal accidents, burglary, explosions, breakage of glass, loss of profits and legal liability.

The development of the insurance industry resulted in a situation where organisations relied on insurance to provide indemnification against losses. Risk management services were provided[1] by insurers and brokers. These took the form of surveys which they conducted on the premises of clients, leading to recommendations concerning limited risk control measures to be adopted. Risks were handled mainly by transferring the financial consequences of the risk to the insurance industry.

The recognition of risk management as a separate management function can be attributed to Fayol,[2] who in 1916, in his seminal article on

1 In the last century various fire insurers had their own fire mark displayed outside the insured premises. In the event of a fire, the fire-fighting teams of insurers were despatched to fight the fire. The system never really developed in South Africa, but it is known that an insurer donated fire equipment to municipalities. It is known that at least one fire insurer, the *SA Fire and Life Assurance Company*, established in 1831, had a fire mark. This company was acquired in 1894 by *The London and Lancashire*, which is one ancestor of the *Mutual and Federal*, South Africa's largest short-term insurer.

the functional approach to management identified the following six basic functions:

(i) *technical activities* such as production, manufacture and adaptation

(ii) *commercial activities* such as buying, selling and exchange

(iii) *financial activities* such as the search for an optimum use of capital

(iv) *security activities* such as the protection of property and persons

(v) *accounting activities* such as stocktaking, compiling financial statements, determination of costs and the compilation of statistics

(vi) *managerial activities* such as planning, control, organisation, command and co-ordination.

Although Fayol's perception of the security function was limited in scope, if compared to the present-day risk management function, it did give early recognition to the need for a security and loss-control function in the organisation. It was not, however, till the early 1960's that risk management really became established as a recognised management function primarily through the impetus it gained in the United States.

1.2 The development of risk management in the United States of America

It is generally accepted that the modern concept of risk management originated in the United States. The rate of technical development in that country confronted the insurance industry with a multiple of insurable risks so that insurance was arranged on an 'all risk' instead of a 'specified peril' basis.[2] The resulting fluctuating premiums focused the attention of top management on the cost of insurance. This resulted in the development of risk management actions which were aimed at containing the cost of insurance. Risk managers were also made responsible for developing ways and procedures to restrict and limit losses which resulted in the integration of the risk control and risk-financing activities.

Risk management, and in particular some of the techniques which are used in risk control in the United States, also developed from highly sophisticated techniques which were used to control macro-risks such as, for example, nuclear catastrophes. As these techniques became known they were adapted and used within business organisations.

The first indication of the importance of the insurance-buying function was in 1931 when the *American Management Association* held a conference in Boston which led to the formation of an insurance division of the association.[3]

2 See Melamet II, par 3.83 for an objection to the 'all risks' basis under the heading of 'Insurance embracing more than one class of business with composite premiums.'

The term risk management was not formally used until the early 1950's when Snider[4] complained about the lack of literature and suitable courses on this subject. In 1964 the *Insurance Journal* changed its name to *Journal of Risk and Insurance*.

The first[5] textbook on the subject of risk management, *Risk Management in the Business Enterprise* appeared in 1963, written by Mehr and Hedges and published by Irwin, Hammond. This was followed in 1964 by *Risk Management and Insurance*, authored by Williams and Heins and published by McGraw Hill.

In 1965 the *Insurance Institute of America* pioneered professional education in risk management and awarded the designation of *Associate of Risk Management* on the successful completion of a three semester course.[6]

Although risk management developed from, and because of, the insurance-buying activities of companies, the close association with insurance-buying also restricted the development of the function in the United States. The reason for this was that risk managers firstly restricted their activities to the handling of insurable risks only. Secondly, they tended to turn to insurance when they were faced with the problem of handling risk. This reliance on insurance is illustrated by the fact that employee disability claims were, for example, met by acquiring additional insurance; capacity problems in the insurance industry in the mid-seventies were resolved by establishing captive insurance companies; increasing liability claims were met by obtaining additional liability cover.[7]

Other developments confirmed the close relationship between insurance and risk management. In 1932 the insurance buyers of New York formed the *Risk Research Institute* and in 1950 the *National Insurance Buyers Association* was launched. This later became the *American Society of Insurance Management* which eventually became the *Risk and Insurance Management Society*.[8]

In the late 1960's, however, proponents of risk management submitted that the nature of the function extended beyond the management of insurable risks and insurance buying. Head,[9] for instance, points out that:

> risk managers increasingly are learning to evaluate and present their programmes in terms of their effects on the amount and timing of the organisation's cash flow and therefore are subject to increasing integration with general management

and makes the following statement regarding risk management:

> risk management is a special sub-division of the discipline of general management – a sub-division having the basic goals of preventing accidental losses and financing the restoration of those losses which cannot be prevented, to enable an organisation to fulfil its mission despite actual or potential accidental losses.

This approach emphasises the distinction between insurance-buying and risk management as a function on a general management level. Gahin[10] confirms this view in the following statement in this regard:

In the real world it is inconceivable that pure risk exists in a vacuum, independent of other activities. Treatment of pure risk should, therefore, be an integral part of the decision concerning the activity that creates pure risk.

In summary, risk management is now seen as a fully-fledged management function – a view which is totally removed from the insurance-buying approach which prevailed in the early stages of its development. Some authors like Robinson and Kunath[11], Baglini[12] and Gahin[13] are of the opinion that the risk manager of the future will also have to deal with speculative risks, particularly foreign exchange risks. Greene and Serbein[14] even express the view that activities such as quality control, market research, business forecasting and investments are within the scope of the risk management department.

These views show that risk management is developing into a management function with a much wider scope than was ever envisaged by Fayol, for instance in his rather visionary article on management.

1.3 The development of risk management in the United Kingdom

As in the United States the origins and development of risk management in the United Kingdom were also closely linked to risk-financing activities. Although original attitudes towards this new function in the early seventies were cynical,[15] brokers and underwriters began to employ risk management consultants while the financing aspects were being actively pursued by merchant bankers who were seeking new areas to serve.

The first book on risk management in the United Kingdom appeared in 1969. It was entitled *Risk, Risk Management and Insurance* and was written by Horrigan. Another major event in the development of risk management in the United Kingdom was when Kluwer published the *Handbook of Insurance* in 1973.

On the educational side, the *City University in London* and the *University of Nottingham* have been presenting courses in risk management and insurance since the early 1970's. In 1982 the *Glasgow College of Technology* started the first degree programme in risk management. Also in 1982 the *Chartered Insurance Institute* included a paper on risk management in their Fellowship examination.

The Association of Insurance Managers and Insurance Consultants (AIMIC) was formed in December 1963 when 12 major insurance and industrial companies provided a forum to discuss problems encountered in the insurance market. This organisation later changed its name to the *Association of Insurance and Risk Managers in Industry and Commerce* (AIRMIC).

In 1989 the *Institute of Risk Management* introduced a three-year non-degree programme in risk management.

1.4 The development of risk management in the Republic of South Africa

Risk management started to develop in South Africa in the 1970's. Various bodies and persons working independently were involved. Most of the broking houses such as Price Forbes Group, Bowrings and Minets were involved. The first known signed risk management statement was in 1975, by Mike Rosholt of Barlow Rand.

Persons involved in the early development included H. Spooner, B. Edmundson and J. Whetmar. Spooner was one of the earlier authors who published in this field. He reported on risk management in South Africa in 1976 and indicated that most corporations were familiar with the fundamental principles of risk management.

In 1975, Edmundson formed the *South African Risk Management Association*. The association never really gained momentum and was eventually dissolved in 1979. Various views on why the association failed exist, but Edmundson attributed its failure largely to the soft insurance market which prevailed during that time, the focus of insurance brokers and risk management consultants on loss control and insurance, the lack of education and the lack of a sound theoretical base on which risk management principles could be developed.

In 1986, a large number of the major South African companies formed the *South African Risk and Insurance Management Association* (SARIMA). Membership of SARIMA is on a corporate basis.[16]

The *Society of Risk Managers* was formed in 1990. Reg Lambert of Barlow Rand was elected as the first President of the Society. Membership is on an individual basis and the major aim is the promotion of the professional status of risk managers in South Africa.

Risk management is being taught at the formal and non-formal levels by various educational institutions in South Africa. Universities such as the *University of the Witwatersrand and the University of South Africa,* teach risk management as part of a degree programme at the undergraduate or post-graduate level, or both. The papers on risk management and insurance are usually offered as optional papers in business management. The *University of Stellenbosch* offers risk management as an optional paper in the MBA-degree programme. Chairs in risk management at the *Universities of South Africa and Stellenbosch* are sponsored by the PF-group and the *Insurance Institute* sponsors a chair in insurance at the *University of the Witwatersrand.*

In addition *The Centre for Business Economics* at the *University of South Africa* (UNISA) commenced a risk management training programme for industry in 1989. The development of the programme was sponsored by Barlow Rand. The study material includes managerial subjects as well as risk control, risk-financing and statistics. The first group of students who entered into this programme were actively involved in the establishment of the *Society of Risk Managers of South Africa.*

Most brokers in South Africa offer risk management services. In some cases separate companies were formed to provide these services and certain brokers have even extended their services to include the management of both pure and speculative risks. It seems therefore that risk management in South Africa is keeping in line with the major trends in risk management internationally, and, in certain aspects, local practice could even be ahead of overseas developments.

1.5 Summary

From its humble origins as an insurance-buying activity and a security function, risk management has developed into a fully-fledged management function which is beginning to move into areas which were originally considered unrelated.

Its impact and value have been accepted not only by the insurance buyers but also by the insurance industry.

Bibliography

Baglini, NA 1976. *Risk management in the international firm.* New York: Risk Studies Foundation.

Cockerell, HAL 1976. 'Approaches to risk management.' Education for risk management in *The Oxford Conference held at Queen's College* in April. Edited by Crockford, GN, London: Keith Shipton Developments.

Crockford, GN 1982. 'The bibliography and history of risk management; some preliminary observations.' *The Geneva Papers on Risk and Insurance.* No. 23, April.

Duffy, KJ 1978. 'Global risk management expectations.' Address delivered to *Insurance Institute of London.*

Farthing, D 1988. 'Is risk management essential to corporate survival?' *Risk Management.* February.

Fayol, H 1949. *General and industrial management.* New York: Pitman Publishing Corporation. (English translation of the French original, published in 1916.)

Gahin, FS 1984. 'Reworking classical models to fit real world decision making.' *Risk Management.* June.

Greene, MR & Serbein, ON 1983. *Risk management: Text and cases.* Virginia: Reston Publishing Co. Inc.

Head, GL 1982. 'Continuing evolution of the risk management function and education in the United States.' *The Geneva papers on Risk and Insurance.* No. 23, April.

Robinson, R & Kunath, L 1981. 'A dynamic approach to risk management.' *Risk Management.* September.

Snider, HW 1956. 'Corporate risk management: Current problems and perspectives.' *Journal of Insurance.*

Vaughan, EJ 1982. *Fundamentals of risk and insurance.* New York: Wiley, 3rd Edition.

Williams, CA & Heins, RM 1989. *Risk management and insurance.* New York: McGraw-Hill Inc.

Williams, CA & Heins, RM 1976. *Risk management and insurance.* New York: McGraw-Hill Inc.

Zadjlic, W 1986. *The future of risk management.* London: Risk Research Group.

Endnotes

[1] Zadjlic, 1986, 139.
[2] Fayol, 1949.
[3] Zajdlic, 1986, 17.
[4] Snider, 1956.
[5] Crockford, 1982. 169-179.
[6] Head, 1982, 180-186.
[7] Farthing, 1988, 34-37.
[8] Vaughan, 1982, 36.
[9] Head, 1982, 180-186.
[10] Gahin, 1984, 62-70.
[11] Robinson & Kunath, 1981, 42-50.
[12] Baglini, 1976, 4.
[13] Gahin, 1984, 68.
[14] Greene & Serbein, 1983, 4-6.
[15] Duffy, 1978.
[16] *Business Day,* 2 October 1986.

2 INTRODUCTION TO INTEGRATED RISK MANAGEMENT

2.1 Background

The process and theme of risk management is quite discernible in the fields of economic science. In a 'macro' sense, aspects of economic theory which concern optimisation and equilibrium face the challenge of achieving a balance between return and risk. In a 'micro' sense, it has been accepted that investment theory, for example, has as a central theme or aim the evaluation of investment alternatives in terms of an optimum ratio of return to risk.

At some point in the spectrum of risk, lies pure risk. With regard to the treatment of such risk, the process of risk management has become significant over the past two decades. The nature of pure risk has, however, dictated a risk management process which may be seen as divorced from traditional risk theory within which definitions of risk and return have been expounded and trade-offs between return and risk evaluated against a general financial market activity or index. Pure risk management, on the other hand, has tended to evolve piecemeal and implies in part a **physical** process of controlling risk, as well as a **financing** process for funding the consequences of risk, where the insurance mechanism has traditionally played the most significant rôle.

2.2 Integrated risk management

The challenge facing contemporary risk managers is simply whether or not risk management as it pertains to pure risk situations can be approached in a structured and integrated manner. An examination of the relevant statistics reveals the substantial impact that various risks have in terms not only of economic loss, but also of human suffering.[1] Whilst no further attempt is needed to put risk in perspective, there is no doubt that a need exists for the effective management of risk – a **total approach** to the problem of risk – which encompasses more than simply prudent insurance management.

1 Various sources of South African statistics need to be consulted in order to summarise the total costs of losses arising from the variety of pure risks. In order to illustrate the point, reference can be made to the UK experience. The following estimates are given (Dickson, 1989, 17-18):

- Fire losses amount to more than £1 000 every minute.
- Thirty-five people are injured or killed in road accidents every hour. The costs of these incidents are measured in terms of tens of millions of pounds.
- Two people are killed in their workplace every day, and over £800 000 is paid out every day to those who are injured at work.

Insurance does represent an effective means of risk **cost** transfer and this fact constitutes the source of a fundamental problem. The preoccupation with insurance as a means of risk treatment, and more particularly as a means of 'risk transfer' militates against a strictly integrated approach to the management of risk: one that subscribes to both elements of **physical** and **financial** risk management, and which recognises the responsibility for controlling risk, as well as the latter's interface with the question of financing risk in an optimal manner.

Whilst a decline in the use of insurance is in evidence, there still exists a significant orientation toward it as a means of financing the consequences of risk which has diverted attention from otherwise competing sources of finance. Thus, in considering these financing options, the problem to be addressed is that of placing the financing issue within a structured financial framework that evaluates both the investment and financing decision and which also considers an optimal mix of finance – specifically the optimal mix between insurance, self-insurance and risk control expenditure.

2.3 The case for risk management

The preceding section summarised the problems to be addressed. Attention has been directed to the specific issues of integration of the risk management process and optimisation of risk-financing options. Naturally, these problems have been crystallised from what can be considered a multitude of issues facing risk management as it has evolved to date. To place in perspective the importance of the study of risk management it will be useful to examine the general case or motivation for risk management, and to inquire into the trends that are already apparent and which will become more so in the future.

As a point of departure, it is appropriate to consider first what is meant by the term *risk management*. Dickson[1] offers one definition as:

> the identification, analysis and economic control of those risks which threaten the assets or earning capacity of an organisation.

Such a definition displays a significant orientation toward a general management function.

In reviewing the roots of present-day risk management, Kloman[2] points out that one set of roots lies in the development of management itself as a professional function. In 1916, Fayol[3] argued that management comprised a number of elements, one of which was 'security'. The emphasis which Fayol placed on the responsibility of management for the security or well-being of revenue-generating assets seems to have been overlooked in modern management texts. It is submitted however, that Fayol's emphasis on 'security management' is correct. Risk management is a response to the view that an organisation's leaders have a generally recognised responsibility for securing and protecting against pure risks threatening its assets and earning capacity.

However management-orientated the definition may be, it becomes an academic issue with little meaning unless what is implied is put into practice. The underlying implication of the definition is that a systematic approach to the management of risk is, indeed, necessary. This becomes more pertinent when one attempts to consider the risk challenges of the future.

There is no doubt that, today, the general world is steeped in uncertainty, and to identify clear trends for the future is indeed difficult and even subjective. Nevertheless, a cursory reflection on such issues as, for example, environmental pollution, terrorism, and the age of bio-technology leaves one with little doubt as to the existence of potential exposures – hence the importance of trying to understand the present and ever-changing interrelationships of events, institutions and trends.

In this era of rapid and indeed accelerating change, one should view the discipline of risk management as a mechanism for coping with the effects of change. From such efforts a range of possible or probable futures can be constructed, leading to better decisions and more effective management of organisations.

For reasons that will become evident further in the text, the definition of risk management adopted in this book is as follows:

> Risk management is a managerial function aimed at protecting the organisation, its people, assets, and profits, against the consequences (adverse) of pure risk, more particularly aimed at reducing the severity and variability of losses.

The case for a systematised approach to managing risk becomes more prominent when the following trends are considered:

The increasing sophistication of risk

Risk has become more sophisticated over recent years through increased automation, extensive use of robotics, the discovery of new chemicals, treatments and processes, all of which spell potential new risks. The danger exists that the effective management of risk is sacrificed in the quest for progress. Dickson[4] argues that there exists a leapfrog mentality concerning risk – progress and change is left unchecked until a major incident occurs, prompting risk management to leapfrog into the forefront of attention.

The increasing concentration of risk

This concentration can take place in a number of ways, although one of the most obvious is the concentration of complex functions inherent in the momentous advances in silicon-chip technology. This concentration entails added risk, as does the concentration resulting from the size of buildings, manufacturing plants and organisations, generally. Individual values and potential liabilities have increased enormously over recent years.

The increasing awareness of risk

The public is more aware of risk and safety today. The impact of major disasters has tended to accelerate the move toward what could be termed *risk consumerism*. Particularly in the USA, social and political forces have moulded, what Kloman[5] describes as an *entitlement society* in which citizens suffering misfortune refuse to accept personal accountability, turning instead, to others and to the state for reimbursement or reward.

The decline of insurance as a risk-financing technique

There has been a steady decline in the use of insurance in that the expenditure on insurance, compared to expenditure on risk control and risk retention, has reduced. In 1977, for some 500 United States corporations, insurance comprised 65,3 percent of the 'cost of risk' (expenditure on risk control, self-funded losses, other funding for catastrophe, insurance and administration). By 1980, this figure had dropped to 52,6 percent. Although the 1982 figures indicated an increase to 61,2 percent, primarily as a result of recession-induced reductions in risk control expenditure and the greater use of insurance in a soft market, the long-term trend is toward a lower percentage. It is anticipated that in the 1990's some 75 to 90 percent of predictable losses will be funded internally, and that, moreover, what is predictable will be larger, due to the use of more sophisticated assessment techniques.[6] This trend in itself dictates that the risk control and risk-financing aspects be integrated and that trade-offs between risk retained and self-funded on the one hand, and risk insured, on the other, be understood and managed optimally.

2.4 The present status of risk management

Against such a backdrop, an examination of the present status of the discipline will identify any differences between risk management reality, and objectives to be attained for coping with risk needs of the future.

Over the years during which risk management has evolved there has developed a substantial body of literature aiming to provide a routine, if not a discipline, to ensure corporate survival in the face of risk. Such thinking has led to the present understanding of risk management as a process comprising four discrete stages, as follows:

(i) risk identification
(ii) risk quantification

(iii) risk control directed at loss elimination, or more usually, loss reduction
(iv) risk financing, via transfer.

Strutt[7] makes the following observations, *inter alia*, concerning the risk management process (model):

- ☐ The model can be described as a static one, envisaging discrete stages followed in a predetermined and logical sequence. There is a weakness in that it does not allude to the possibility of a dynamic interrelationship between the components. It is suggested that the static nature has resulted in many risk management companies organising themselves into two distinct divisions – one for risk control, the other for risk finance – unfortunately with a limited direct working relationship between the two.

- ☐ A considerable body of literature relating to each of the four stages exists, with advice on the preferred methods of approach to each subject. Texts dedicated to risk management *per se*, lack the required integration and are, in the main, written from an insurance point of view.

This assertion is not altogether unexpected. The concept of risk management is extensively marketed by insurance brokers, who, by the nature of their business, have a strong leaning toward insurance. What seems unfortunate however, is that the concept is often presented as a new management approach, which, of course, it is not, when one takes cognisance of the management discipline proposed by Fayol, in 1916. If indeed the concept is being regarded as a novel management approach, then this naivety could explain the shortcoming that risk management presently faces: one of dis-aggregation and divorce from the broader management (including financial management) science. In this respect, Kloman[8] states:

> so long as risk managers over-emphasize insurance-buying and managing, they will be incapable of responding to the real needs of their organisations.[2]

These differences can be addressed by adopting a broader definition of strategic risk management. Risk management must become more proactive, holistic and systemic. In this way, risk management becomes an integral part of general management as opposed to a set of isolated functions comprising risk control and risk financing. In adopting such a broader definition of risk management, it is suggested that definitions such as *pure*

---

2 It is interesting to note that some USA firms have deliberately extended the function of risk management beyond the realms of pure risks. Under the title of 'risk management advisor', at senior level, macro-issues including currency, commodity and economic risks, are being addressed. Such consultants are trained economists who advise on major financial issues. (Kloman, 1987, 58.)

and speculative and *static and dynamic* risk obscure, rather than assist, in the development of a holistic view.

> These definitions have forced us for too long to look inwardly at those risks that are or have been conventionally insurable, rather than allowing us to look outwardly at the risks that are of increasing significance to society.[9]

2.5 Objectives

In helping to achieve a broader and more strategic definition of risk management, as implied in the preceding section, this text argues in favour of an integrated view of risk management that considers both elements of **physical** risk control and **financing** of risk.

Specifically, the objectives are as follows:

- ☐ to present an integrated or holistic approach to the effective management of pure risks
- ☐ to view the risk financing function within a broader financial context, which evaluates the mechanisms of insurance and retention funding against developed financial objectives.

In aiming to attain these goals, the text develops along the following broad lines:

- ☐ the discussion of the concept of risk and uncertainty and the definition of risk
- ☐ an examination of the fundamentals of pure risk management
- ☐ the development of the risk control function
- ☐ the development of the risk financing function
- ☐ the integration of the risk control and risk financing functions
- ☐ the integration of the risk financing function as it pertains to the elements of risk insured and risk retained (self-insured).

The objectives and nature of this text dictate that the discipline of risk management be reviewed as a holistic concept within which the problems of integration and optimisation are examined. Whilst a strong case for such an approach can be made, the approach itself entails one important limitation.

Of necessity, the elements comprising the function of risk control and those comprising the function of risk financing need to be explored. However, since the task is accomplished with the specific purpose of showing and promoting their inter-relationship, discussion of the separate elements in the risk management process must not be seen as exhaustive. This aspect represents a major limitation. Particularly with regard to the elements pertaining to risk control, these are regarded as separate disciplines, mainly within the science of engineering.

However, as was mentioned earlier, there does exist an extensive body of literature and research relating to the individual stages of risk management, to which reference can be made should an in-depth understanding be required.

Bibliography

Dickson, G 1989. 'Risk Management: what does the future hold?' *Journal of Society of Fellows*. London: Chartered Insurance Institute, Vol. 4, July.

Fayol, H 1949. *General and industrial management*. New York: Pitman Publishing corporation. (English translation of the French original, published in 1916.)

Kloman, HF 1984. 'Risk management: 1990 and beyond.' *Risk Management*. March.

Kloman, HF 1987. 'Risk management . . . by many other names.' *Risk Management*. June.

Strutt, RSG 1989. 'The reality of risk management.' Paper prepared for the Institute of Risk Management and presented to the AIRMIC Conference, Robinson College, Cambridge, April.

Endnotes

[1] Dickson, 1989, 18.

[2] Kloman, 1984, 33.

[3] Fayol, 1949, 3-6.

[4] Dickson, 1989, 20.

[5] Kloman, 1984, 34.

[6] Kloman, 1984, 38.

[7] Strutt, 1989, 3-6.

[8] Kloman, 1987, 62.

[9] Kloman, 1987, 60.

3 THE CONCEPT OF RISK

We are not certain, we are never certain. If we were, we could reach some conclusions, and we could, at last, make others take us seriously.

Albert Camus, The Fall 1956

3.1 Introduction

The logical departure point for this book is to describe the milieu of risk and to provide a definition so that some form of perspective is gained of the business of managing risk. This chapter begins by describing the condition of uncertainty and its inter-relationship with risk. It concentrates on defining risk where the classification of risk and the concepts of peril and hazard are also given consideration.

Managing risk requires an understanding of its dimensional expression so as to facilitate decision-making under conditions of uncertainty; but at the same time, recognising the qualitative and often psychological facet. In this chapter therefore, the theory of probability and its application to risk measurement is introduced, and for illustrative purposes, a relatively simple model for decision-making under pure risk conditions, is described.

A central theme of this book is the integration of the activities which collectively represent the risk management process and discipline. The fundamental principles governing risk management, which are translated into a simple integrated model, are discussed in the chapter which follows. This model identifies, *ab initio*, the two underlying facets in the risk management process, namely:

- ☐ the physical management or control of risk
- ☐ the financing of risk, where the insurance market is an important mechanism for financing the consequences of risk.

In line with this integrated approach, this chapter also considers the definition of risk from a financing perspective – particularly, the question of risk as applicable to an insurer. Finally, in the more general context, particular aspects relevant to the formation of a market for treating risk, are described.

3.2 The concepts of risk and uncertainty

Uncertainty, being a condition that results from an inability to foresee future events, has been recognised as pervasive in its influence in all walks of life. The finite nature of our minds denies us the ability to foresee, and hence control, the multitude of happenings that affect our lives and those of others. In interpreting the notion of uncertainty, Shackle[1] offers the following:

> The word uncertainty can convey either the mind's consciousness of ignorance and its consequent willingness to entertain an array of diverse hypotheses, or

> alternatively the mind's hesitant contact with any hypothesis which has not a complete case in its favour or has some partial case against it.

Whilst many statisticians and philosophers believe that there are laws which precipitate change, be it in attitudes, perceptions or business environment, such laws and governing principles are too vast to be regarded as charted knowledge. In his effort to understand or minimise uncertainty, man has attempted to determine causation, unfold patterns and give meaning to unexplained events, possibly in terms of a controlling power.[2]

Notwithstanding such attempts and the aversion to yield to domination, man's milieu will ever be fraught with the presence of uncertainty.

In a literal sense, the concepts of risk and uncertainty are regarded as inter-related. The perception is that uncertainty gives rise to risk. This is because where the outcome of events are subjected to, or surrounded by, uncertainty, risk will be present. It would seem necessary to subject risk and uncertainty to a more precise interpretation, for reference to uncertainty is made when considering events whose outcomes display lack of predictability, albeit that such outcomes may be assigned objective associated probabilities. In such cases, the assigning of objective probabilities may be seen as being incongruent with the concept of uncertainty.

Willett[3] draws the following distinction between risk and uncertainty:

> My only reason for mentioning it here is to show why it seems necessary to define risk with reference to the degree of uncertainty about the occurrence of a loss, and not with reference to the degree of probability that it will occur. Risk in this sense is the objective correlative of the subjective uncertainty. It is the uncertainty considered as embodied in the course of events in the external world, of which subjective uncertainty is a more or less faithful interpretation.

The distinction between risk and uncertainty then, is in the **objective** and **subjective** aspects of variability in the outcome of events.

The interpretation offered by Knight[4] may also be seen to hinge on a similar objective-subjective distinction. Knight distinguished between measurable and immeasurable risk. More particularly, in the cases where possible outcomes and associated probabilities are known and therefore the spread of values can be subjected to mathematical measurement, such variability is defined as risk by Knight. When the distribution of possible values and probabilities is not known, the situation is described as uncertain.

Thus, where so many uncertainties (technical, political and economic) surrounding a value exist, implying that the number be viewed as a random value, uncertainty is deemed present. However, this interpretation implies that in situations where objective probabilities surrounding outcomes cannot be assigned, but where subjectively one may impose a range on the possible magnitude of outcomes, then risk is present, but it cannot be measured so conveniently.

In distinguishing between uncertainty and risk in the definitions offered by Willett and Knight, attention should be focused more on the important similarities, rather than on any differences that may be perceived. The modern-day precept is to interpret **risk** as the **absence of certainty**. Hence, a risky outcome is one which can assume a number of values, but the particular value is not known in advance.

3.3 The definition of risk

Given the fact that contemporary finance theory has not become deeply involved in semantics and that the technical usage of the term *uncertainty* has, to a degree, been limited, it is not surprising to find in risk and insurance literature, varying definitions of risk.

- Pfeffer,[5] for example, defines risk as a combination of hazards measured by probability.
- Denenberg, *et al.*,[6] define risk as uncertainty of loss, where the term *risk* is implicitly understood as uncertainty of financial loss – and, where the definition denies that the degree of uncertainty needs be measurable or the probability of loss determinable.
- Greene & Serbein[7] qualify the existence of many usages of the term *risk* and therefore no single definition which is universally employed. Nevertheless, it is stated that the term is understood to mean mainly the uncertainty of the occurrence of economic loss.
- Athearn & Pritchett[8] define risk simply as a condition in which loss or losses are possible. Risk (pure), it is stated, involves only the possibilities of loss or no loss.

One of the problems in defining risk in a universally accepted manner is that the contexts within which risk can be viewed, are so diverse. This gives rise to interpretations and definitions suited only to specific areas of study or disciplines. Hence, in an actuarial context for example, risk is given a statistical interpretation; whilst in the world of insurance, the term *risk* may be used to describe the subject of the policy (the property or liability that is insured) or the peril that is insured under the contract.

Certainly in determining the definitions cited above, authors have been careful to qualify that interpretation depends to some extent on the particular orientation of the discussion of risk. Notwithstanding such qualifications however, there is still evidence of non-uniformity, rather than disagreement, concerning certain fundamental tenets when defining risk in the context of pure risk management and insurance.

With the emergence and growing importance of risk management as a systematised discipline, it becomes pertinent to provide a more rigorous definition of risk by enlarging on the early concepts developed, and by so doing adding clarity to the more contemporary definitions and interpretations. The following is proposed:

> Without necessarily introducing a superfluous semantic distinction between risk and uncertainty, the condition that **risk implies the presence of uncertainty**, should be reinforced. This condition then becomes the foundation of any discussion of risk in a risk management context, which imposes a stricture on risk analysis, which is appropriate when one considers the objective of **managing** risk.[1]

In a sense, such definition removes any dichotomy between risk and uncertainty. Uncertainty prevails because outcomes of situations are not known in advance. Consequently, such situations display risk. To the extent that associated probabilities are assigned (objectively or subjectively) to possible outcomes, risk is measurable to a degree. Where situations dictate that associated probabilities cannot be assigned (objectively or subjectively), risk is immeasurable and thus, from a risk management perspective, whether one regards these situations as uncertain as opposed to risky, becomes immaterial.

> The degree of uncertainty surrounding the event determines the extent of risk.

This distinction seems to be somewhat ignored in the definitions provided. The tendency in the definitions is towards the negative financial consequences associated with the event, which, although it must be seen as an important consideration, somewhat blurs the question of whether uncertainty, and hence risk, is present. For example, it is maintained that insurers carry risk since they are involved in funding the economic loss which is the consequence when an insured event does occur. In the extreme, it could be argued that, given a sufficiently large number of exposure units, the insurer's aggregate loss is known with some degree of certainty and thus, notwithstanding the economic loss implied, there exists little or no risk to the insurance market. The **variability** surrounding the **expected aggregate loss** is small under these conditions and therefore the risk is limited – the insurer theoretically carries little risk and is merely a mechanism for funding the financial consequences of the insured events.[2]

1 This merely reinforces Willett's early rationale of distinguishing between risk and uncertainty with the explicit view to defining risk, or the extent of risk, with reference to the degree of **uncertainty** about the occurrence of a loss, and not with reference to the **probability of loss**.

2 Under these conditions, the insurer theoretically faces only the liquidity or solvency risk. However, systematic risk may be inherent. For example, in the life insurance industry the effect of Acquired Immune Deficiency Syndrome (AIDS) has been to increase insurers' risk, (possibly in the shorter term). The overall uncertainty surrounding the event of death (in the books of the insurer) has increased.

Obviously, from the viewpoints of the individual insureds, there does exist uncertainty and hence risk; each exposure viewed independently displays considerable variability in outcome. The act of insuring has the effect of pooling the exposures and as the number of exposures pooled increases, so the variability in the aggregate outcome diminishes.

It is contended that the degree of risk is solely dependent upon the **variability** rather than upon the probability value surrounding an event or its outcome. Such an interpretation refutes the viewpoint of those who consider risk in terms of **probability** of occurrence and who often measure risk on a scale with certainty of occurrence at one end and certainty of non-occurrence at the other end. The assumption that risk exists in varying degrees between these extremes, and that risk is thus greatest where the probability of occurrence or non-occurrence is equal, is incongruent with the basic tenet that risk refers to the degree of uncertainty or variability about the occurrence, and not to the degree of probability that it will occur.

From a risk management perspective there exists the uncertainty concerning:

- ☐ whether the **event** or occurrence will take place, and,
- ☐ if it does, what the **outcome** (financial) of the event will be.[3]

The definition, for example, that risk is uncertainty concerning loss is indicative of the orientation towards insurance, rather than towards risk management: one which concerns itself more with the financial treatment of the consequences of the event, than with the business of managing risk. Managing risk implies not only the financial provision for the consequences of an event, but the effort to:

- ☐ reduce or minimise the likelihood of the loss-producing event occurring
- ☐ reduce or minimise the adverse effects (mostly financial) once the event has occurred.

3 Simplistically, the situation is analogous to that of throwing a die. The uncertainty not only concerns the *value* of the thrown die, but also whether the die *will be thrown at all.* There are instances of course, where one is more concerned with how often the event will occur as opposed to whether it will occur. For instance, in the case of a motor fleet, the event, defined as an accident, is not uncertain. What is uncertain is how many vehicles will be damaged by accidents. If the national annual accident rate is, say, 13% and if the fleet comprises 200 vehicles, one could expect 26 vehicles to be damaged each year. The concern is not with the probability of a vehicle being involved in an accident – it is almost certain that an accident will take place. The concern in this instance is about the number of accidents that will occur and about the outcome (annual costs) of such accidents.

Taking cognisance of the points offered above, the following definition is proposed:

> Risk is defined as the presence of uncertainty, where there may be uncertainty as to the occurrence of an **event** producing a loss, and uncertainty as regards the **outcome** of the event; where the degree of risk is interpreted with reference to the degree of variability and not with reference to the frequency with which the event will occur or to the probability that it will display a particular outcome.[4]

3.4 The classification of risk

Risks may be classified in various ways. These classifications are of course arbitrary and by no means exhaustive. From a risk management perspective, the terms *risk* and *management* imply, in a sense, that only some risks inherent in corporate activity will concern this discipline. This class of risks has distinguishing characteristics that differentiate it from other forms of risks.

Doherty[9] identifies four types affecting an organisation. These are:

- ☐ marketing risk
- ☐ financial risk
- ☐ resource management risk
- ☐ environmental risk.

Greene & Serbein[10] classify risks along quite similar lines, namely:

- ☐ property and personnel
- ☐ marketing
- ☐ finance
- ☐ personnel and production
- ☐ environment.

An organisation, in seeking to earn a profit for its owners, is susceptible to the collective effect of these various risks. But the firm is also exposed to, for example, the possibility of fire loss to its plant and equipment, to liability claims due to defective products, and to possible theft of assets and fraud perpetrated by its officers. These risks are primarily the concern of the risk management activity; they hold only the prospect of reducing profit and are termed *pure* risks. Against this backdrop therefore,

4 Outcome in itself can assume various forms, for example, criminal prosecution arising from an accident, emotional stress due to the loss of a limb, and many others. In this study, however, the concern is primarily about the financial outcomes of risk.

further classification of risk is sought by drawing a distinction between pure and speculative risks.[5]

> Pure risks concern the possibility of either loss or no loss.

As already mentioned, the damage or destruction of an asset by a peril such as fire creates a loss; if the asset is not damaged or destroyed then no loss occurs.

> Speculative risks on the other hand are those that offer a chance of gain or loss.

Marketing risks are usually speculative, as changes in demand can either decrease or increase corporate earnings. Similarly, capital gains or losses in the organisation's holdings of physical or financial assets represents another speculative risk area.

The methods of treating these two categories of risk differ. The financial consequences associated with pure risks can often be mitigated by risk management techniques, while speculative risk (which is conventionally an uninsurable risk) may be treated by techniques such as hedging.[6]

One may further categorise risk by distinguishing between fundamental and particular risk.

> Fundamental risks arise from losses that are impersonal in origin and in consequence.

Fundamental risks affect large parts of society or even the world, rather than individuals. Thus, the risk of damage to assets due to wear and tear, or corrosion, is fundamental.[7]

Most fundamental risks such as, for example, war and recession originate in the economic, political or social interdependency of society,

---

5 The distinction between these two classes is attributed to Mowbray (1930, 4-5).

6 The reader is referred to Chapter Thirteen, section 13.5, which debates the financial treatment of speculative risk. Further descriptive parameters for speculative, or economic risk are conceptualised, which assist in determining whether, theoretically, insurance is possible. As a matter of interest, it has been stated (Robinson & Kunath, 1981, 43) that:

> ... the future risk managers will not limit their activities to the analysis and surmounting of pure risk situations, but will extend them to embrace many aspects of speculative risk.

Whilst such projections have been mooted, no explanation has been offered as to how this extension of risk management activity will be achieved. It is believed that the rationalisation set out in the afore-mentioned section, offers at least a starting point for developing a broader front of risk management activity and involvement by insurers.

7 Most exclusions from insurance policies referring to land-based risks, relate to fundamental risks, such as for example, war and nuclear exclusions.

although they may also arise from purely physical occurrences, such as, for example, pollution, or even the Irish famine experienced during the previous century and which was caused by the destruction of the potato crop. A further example, is damage due to the accidental nuclear release which happened at Chernobyl. Fundamental risks are regarded as commercially uninsurable.

Particular risks give rise to losses that have their origin in discrete events, which are essentially personal in cause. Such risks would include the explosion of a boiler or fire damage to a building.

The distinction between fundamental and particular risks is not, however, definitive. The classification of risk as either fundamental or particular, depends on judgement. For example, while it was previously readily accepted that unemployment was a particular risk (caused by a person's lack of ability or work ethic) it is more widely accepted today that in most cases unemployment is a result of the economic system – a responsibility of society rather than of the individual, and therefore a fundamental risk as opposed to a particular one.

One reason for determining whether a given risk is particular or fundamental is to establish whether commercial insurance may be appropriate, or in fact available, as a means of financing the consequences of such risk. Losses arising from fundamental risks cannot be prevented, particularly by an individual. Such losses are frequently catastrophic, and therefore 'social insurance' may need to be established in order to mitigate their effects, instead of commercial insurance.

Changes in attitudes, knowledge, technology and social conditions, and other factors, sometimes political in nature, make it difficult to determine whether the risk is fundamental or particular and thus whether the cost of such risks should be borne by society or remain the responsibility of the individual. However, the relevance of such a classification or categorisation is real.[8]

3.5 Risk-related concepts of peril and hazard

The term *risk* and *peril* are often confused and used synonymously. A peril has been defined as the **cause** of a loss;[11] it has also been defined

8 It can be argued that the legal liability crisis (the increase in liability litigation and the consequent spiralling of the price of insurance and even the withdrawal of capacity) has arisen because risks such as personal injury, which used to be seen as particular risks, are now in fact treated as fundamental risks. As a logical consequence of classifying a risk as fundamental, the negligence system of delictual liability is inappropriate as a legal remedy. Viewed from a different perspective, judicial systems have tried to use private financing systems (insurance) to fund what the judiciary perceive as social responsibilities; hence the liability crisis. This aspect is discussed more fully in Chapter Nine.

as the **source** of loss.[12] For reasons that will become evident when considering the definition for hazard, it is preferable to consider peril as the **source** of loss.

> Peril is defined as the *source* of loss.

Peril, therefore, is quite distinct from risk, which has been defined as the absence of certainty relative to both the occurrence of a loss-producing event, and its outcome. Typical perils are fire, explosion, storm and earthquake. These perils give rise to risk, but are not defined as risks themselves.

> Hazard relates to the environ surrounding the **cause** of loss.

Thus, for example, a fire in a warehouse is the peril against which insurance may be purchased, whilst the oil drums stored on the warehouse floor represent a fundamental loss-causing environ. This definition coincides reasonably with that provided by Mehr,[13] who states that behind the ostensible cause of loss (peril), is hazard – except that it purports to differentiate between risk as the source of loss and hazard as the fundamental loss-causing environ or agent.[9]

Intuitively then, one situation *vis-à-vis* another may be described as more hazardous if that environ is fundamentally considered more loss-causing; the term *hazardous* should not be interpreted as describing the degree of risk, for the latter refers to the degree of uncertainty (variability).

A distinction can be drawn between physical and moral hazards.

> The material or physical aspects in the environ surrounding the cause of loss are termed **physical hazards**; the personal aspects or characteristics are termed **moral hazards**.[10]

9 It has been stated that hazard represents a condition which increases the likelihood or chance of loss (Denenberg, *et al.*, 1974, 8; Mehr, 1986, 28). Paradoxically, when considering the definition of risk and in particular the interpretation of the degree of risk proposed in the previous section, hazard may imply (strictly) that uncertainty is reduced and hence risk is reduced. It is unlikely that, in defining hazard in such a manner, the authors' intentions have been to point to this ambivalence. As mentioned earlier, there has developed a literal sense in the definition of risk and this, it is contended, is also evidenced in the definitions of the risk- related concepts of peril and hazard.

10 In the literal sense, moral hazard connotes the possible existence of a dishonest tendency. Reference is also made to morale hazard (Mehr, 1986, 28) where the intention is to denote broader characteristics of carelessness or indifference to loss. Objectively, the term should refer broadly to a behavioural characteristic (not necessarily unethical), concerning the level of effort devoted to loss-reducing activity. This aspect is further debated in Chapter Thirteen.

The preceding sections aimed at providing a definition and classification of risk and to distinguish between risk-related concepts of peril and hazard. Any discussion of risk should, however, embrace both qualitative and quantitative aspects. The concern is to place risk and particularly the management of risk in an overall framework within which it can be understood and managed. Managing risk implies not only the qualitative understanding and perception of risk, but the application of developed quantitative techniques to arrive at some dimensional expression of the concept.

Hence, the sections that follow aim to give perspective to:

- ☐ the quantification of at least some aspects of risk through the use of quantitative techniques
- ☐ the psychology of risk and decision-making under pure risk conditions
- ☐ market considerations for the financial treatment of risk.

3.6 The theory of probability and its application to risk measurement

Risk was defined as the uncertainty surrounding an event and outcome in a specific situation. Thus, when an outcome is not certain to occur, then risk is present. But clearly not all events or resultant possible outcomes are as uncertain as others.

In attempting to formulate a dimensional expression of the concept of chance, and to facilitate decision-making under conditions of uncertainty, probability theory plays a significant rôle. However, probability should be distinguished from risk, and as a result, the analysis of problems involving both risk and probability are somewhat restricted. Risk, it should be recalled, is a concept of variability and reflects the uncertainty of an event rather than its underlying probability.

There are various techniques of determining probabilities,[11] namely:

- ☐ *a priori* probabilities
- ☐ subjective probabilities
- ☐ objective probabilities.

> **A priori** probabilities or objective probabilities are those that can be determined when in the long run all possible outcomes are known.

11 A famous definition of probability is that given by Pierre Simon, Marquis de Laplace, as quoted by Sheldon (1984, vii):

> We see that the theory of probability is at bottom only common sense reduced to calculation; it makes us appreciate with exactitude what reasonable minds feel by a sort of instinct, often without being able to account for it.

Probability statements of such a nature are made without observing the actual frequency of occurrence; the probability estimates are made on the basis of deductive reasoning and assuming that the occurrence of the event is due to chance alone, that is, subject to randomness alone. *A priori* probabilities of outcomes are thus determined for problems associated with games of chance such as, for example, dice-rolling, and coin-spinning.

However, it is not possible to estimate most probabilities on a deductive basis, but rather by estimation after experimentation and observation. This is particularly true of future probabilities of outcome of events which can change in the future. One can generalise an estimate of an outcome of a future event by observing its relative frequency of occurrence in the past. Such probability statements are referred to as statistical or inductive probabilities.[12] The underlying assumptions upon which reliance of these estimates are based are that, firstly a sufficiently large number of past events has been observed and, secondly that casual influences will remain the same as those in the past. Naturally, the future is seldom a perfect repeat of the past, and hence margins of error in estimates must be anticipated. Statistical techniques have been developed to measure the probable range of deviation of actual, from expected, outcomes.

> To the extent that these measure variability of outcome, they become a measure of risk in the correct sense.

It can be seen therefore, that statistical probabilities can alter either on account of changes in our condition of knowledge of causes (affecting deductive reasoning) or because of changes in underlying forces (affecting inductive probabilities).

However, for the purposes of this text, probability is regarded as the relative frequency with which an event occurs in the long run.

3.7 Long-term expected loss and pure risk to an insurer

The contribution of probability theory to the theory of insurance is well recognised. Significant progress has been achieved by actuaries and insurance theoreticians[13] in developing amongst other aspects, mortality tables and statistical data, so as to refine the process of prediction. Although this aspect is dealt with in more detail in forthcoming sections, a brief discussion of expected loss and pure risk will achieve the desired introductory resumé of the contribution of quantitative reasoning to the

12 Where such statements are based, in part, on known tendencies or on subjective guesses, they may be termed *subjective probabilities*.

13 Mainly in the life insurance industry.

understanding and management of risk. On the assumption that alternative courses of action exist, and that probabilities can be assigned to (and derived from) each, then meaning can be given to statistical expectation of loss (or gain).

With a large number of events, the expected monetary value (EMV) of an event is the sum of the product of the probability of each possible outcome of the event multiplied by the possible financial loss (or gain).

Mathematically, expected monetary value can be expressed as follows:

$$EMV = \sum_{i=1}^{n} p_i . x_i$$

where:

EMV = expected monetary value

p_i = probability of the ith outcome

x_i = monetary value of outcome i

n = number of possible outcomes

In computing an insurer's expected loss per exposure unit, one is concerned not only with the probability that the event insured against will occur, but also with the average severity or size of loss. The probability that an insured event will occur implies the calculation of the number of times that the given event will occur in a given period of time. Hence, an insurer's expectation of loss becomes: the **average frequency** times the **average severity** of losses.

The following example, taken from actual data relating to motor fleet losses[14] over the period 1986/87 to 1989/90 illustrates expected costs to an insurer.

Table 3.1
Summary of the number of exposure units

Insurance period	No of exposure units
1986/87	3 013
1987/88	3 045
1988/89	3 291
1989/90	3 119

14 *These losses represent the actual loss experience (inflation adjusted) of a leading South African haulier. The losses relate to accidental damage, fire and theft and exclude losses of a liability nature.*

Table 3.2 Frequency and loss costs per exposure, for sample motor fleet per severity interval

			Severity interval (R)									
Period	**Total cost (R) and total frequency**	**0**	**1 1 000**	**1 001 2 500**	**2 501 5 000**	**5 001 10 000**	**10 001 25 000**	**25 001 50 000**	**50 001 75 000**	**75 001 100 000**	**100 001 200 000**	**> 200 000**
86/87												
Loss costs	3 208 695	0	25 892	117 218	138 711	302 957	541 277	386 812	428 400	87 068	563 332	617 028
Frequency	3 013	2 753	51	68	39	42	35	11	7	1	4	2
87/88												
Loss costs	3 412 208	0	41 496	98 931	181 037	285 338	623 314	491 666	238 049	807 307	257 986	387 084
Frequency	3 045	2 753	69	62	50	40	40	14	4	10	2	1
88/89												
Loss costs	3 817 155	0	45 018	111 921	127 048	259 181	685 546	611 526	363 446	243 830	804 194	565 445
Frequency	3 291	2 999	80	65	34	34	45	18	6	3	5	2
89/90												
Loss costs	5 280 595	0	24 589	93 603	177 792	311 396	581 647	746 690	242 305	357 044	723 687	2 021 842
Frequency	3 119	2 837	52	56	50	47	36	21	4	4	5	7

Midpoint of severity (x_i)	0	500	1 750	3 750	7 500	17 500	37 500	62 500	87 500	150 000	300 000
Total frequency for the periods 86/87 to 89/90	11 342	252	251	173	163	156	64	21	18	16	12
Relative loss frequency (p_i)	0,9097	0,0202	0,0201	0,0139	0,0131	0,0125	0,0051	0,0017	0,0014	0,0013	0,0010
$p_i.x_i$	0	10,10	35,18	52,13	98,25	218,75	191,25	106,25	122,50	195,00	300,00

Therefore, EMV, or average per exposure $= \Sigma p_i.x_i$
$= \underline{\underline{R1\ 329,41}}$

The loss severity distribution is depicted graphically in Figure 3.1.

Figure 3.1
Loss severity distribution curve.[15]

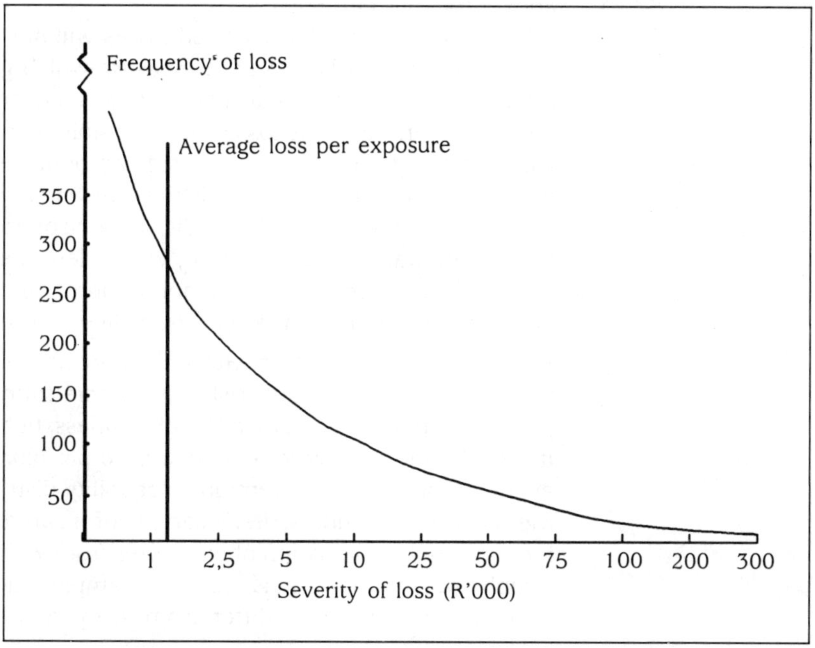

Then, the **expected loss per exposure** is R1 329,41, and the total loss R4 146 430. Expected loss is also referred to as an insurer's *pure* premium as it represents the amount that would be just sufficient to pay for expected losses. To the pure premium, an amount is 'loaded' by the insurer to take account of administration, facility and other expenses and also to allow for insurer's profit. The loading for profit to arrive at the premium actually paid by the insured takes cognisance of in the first instance, that notwithstanding the predictive process, the insurer faces risks for which return is sought. The intention is not to examine or debate in this section the other factors and forces which may impinge upon the concept of profit-loading.

An insurer faces many types of risks. The most significant of these is the **insolvency risk**: the risk that at a particular moment, liabilities exceed assets.[16] This risk is the consequence of other risks:

- ☐ The risk that the expected loss per exposure unit will be greater than the pure premium charged for the exposure, that is, the uncertainty that incurred losses will not equate to expected losses. It is conceivable that in a particular line of insurance there is an underlying **pure premium** probability distribution (rand losses per exposure unit) which

15 It is clear that even when no losses occur, the insurer incurs administrative costs.
16 The equation for solvency takes into consideration minimum statutory surpluses.

is in itself reflective of frequency and severity distributions (as described above) for that particular line.

The insurer's risk that incurred losses will not equate to expected losses can be translated into a measure which gives the dispersion around the mean; it is clear that although an exposure is assumed to incur long-term average losses, it is possible that losses may take on values ranging from zero to very high amounts. Hence, any underlying pure premium probability distribution with a mean pure premium per exposure unit of say X, will display a dispersion around X, calculated as its standard deviation σ_p, which describes this aspect of the insurer's risk, namely, the variation of pure premium from the average pure premium for that particular line of insurance business.[17]

- ☐ In addition to the variation **within** the pure premium distribution, the insurer faces an additional risk. All insurers cannot insure the entire population of exposures (of a line of business) but only a sample from it. Should an underwriter charge a pure premium X, derived as the average from the pure premium probability distribution, there exists the risk that the underwriter's sample of insureds (exposures) is not identical to the population of exposures from which X was estimated. Simply stated, the risk is that the sample's **actual** average pure premium, say X_s, may differ from X by more than an expected amount.

Having recognised that the insurer faces an additional sampling risk one can now describe the risk in a mathematical form that combines both elements of risk, that is, the variation in the pure premium distribution (σ_p) and the measure of sampling error.[18]

It is significant to note that such a mathematical expression elucidates the principle of risk-reduction through pooling. The insurer's risk will vary inversely with the square root of the number of exposures insured (sample size).[19] Therefore, it is the combination of a large number of exposures

17 The standard deviation may be mathematically defined as follows:

$$\sigma_{pp} = \sqrt{\frac{\Sigma(pp - \mu)^2}{n}}$$

where

σ_{pp} = standard deviation of the pure premium distribution
pp = all possible pure premium values
μ = mean pure premium
n = number of pure premiums

18 The discussion follows closely the definition of risk to an insurer as stated by Houston (1964, 511-538).

19 This is per the Central Limit Theorem which states that:

> The distribution of the mean value of a set of n independent and identically distributed random variables each having mean μ and variance σ^2 approaches a normal distribution with mean μ and variance σ^2/n as n tends towards infinity.

See Freund, Williams & Perles (1988, 299-301).
This aspect is dealt with further in Chapter Fourteen.

that enables an insurer to act as underwriter and reduce risk by increasing the predictability of average losses.

The sum of what we have provided under this section is the rationale that propositions based on statistical theory refine our understanding and management of an insurer's risk. The more fundamental aspects in particular, have been examined; other risk aspects do, of course, exist so that the risk borne by the insurer can assume a multiplicity of meanings. What is relevant is that whilst the theories of probability and sampling have greatly contributed towards approaching risk from a more rigorous viewpoint, their inherent assumptions present major limitations, so that it becomes necessary to adjust one's approximations of expected outcomes by factors which are non-quantitative in nature.

3.8 The psychological nature of risk

The understanding of human behaviour and the development of a recognised area of study has for some time preoccupied the minds of many an academic and practitioner in the discipline of psychology. This has lead to the development of sub-disciplines or specialisations such as social psychology, clinical psychology, psychology of education and others. In contrast however, the psychology of risk (human behaviour under conditions of risk or uncertainty) has been comparatively neglected.

Interest has been directed at the influence of risk on decision-making – more particularly on determining surrogates for risk and incorporating these in decision-making techniques, almost always quantitative ones, so as to reflect the effects of uncertainty more accurately. Unfortunately, little attention has been directed otherwise, as to how individuals or entities react to conditions of risk. Nevertheless, their perception of risk is critical to the study of risk management and insurance; situations of risk are perceived differently and such perceptions are often contingent upon an individual's reaction to risk or even dictated to by the entities' cultural preferences towards risk treatment. Simplistically, one person's reaction towards risk which could be described as aggressive, might be contrasted with another's whose psyche dictates the purchase of insurance merely as an effort not 'to tempt providence'.

An individual's reaction to risk is influenced by many factors. Family background, wealth, previous experience, position or status and geographical location are but a few of what seem to be an endless list of factors. Not only have psychologists not identified all such factors, but the effects of those already identified on decisions made under conditions of uncertainty have not been satisfactorily quantified.

It is interesting to note that research has shown the attitudes towards risk to be unstable in that the individuals' prior attitudes can change when he/she is being subjected or exposed to the attitudes of a group.[14] The implication that group decisions are less risky than individual ones may be inaccurate. This influence of group attitudes is particularly relevant when placed in the context of organisational behaviour towards risk and its overall profile. This often dictates what is an acceptable level of risk to be borne and hence, as a corollary, what level of risk should be insured. It is likely that the perceptions and attitudes of those individuals responsible for insurance are swayed to coincide with those portrayed by the group as a whole. Organisational culture or ethos, therefore, pervades the specific arena of risk-perception and management.

Personal or group characteristics are not the only influences on reaction to risk. The **type** of risk (pure as opposed to speculative) may also exert an influence. Williams[15] argues that speculative risk situations are frequently desirable and pure risk situations undesirable. Again, it is not uncommon to evidence the decision by individuals or organisations to purchase insurance whilst simultaneously engaging in speculative risks – a decision which appears contradictory since both situations may indeed have the same objective probability of occurring.[20]

3.9 Economic principles of decision-making under pure risk conditions

Whilst there has been considerable research conducted in the area of decision-making under risk conditions in relation to speculative risks,[21] what may prove to be a rational theory in this context may prove inappropriate in a pure risk scenario. Nevertheless, one may derive some rationale in arriving at a decision whether, for example, to buy insurance. The following illustration purports to show how one could rationally select one of several courses of action, given a pure risk situation.[22]

The situation under consideration is summarised in table 3.3. It is assumed that any loss will be a total loss and that four alternative and plausible courses of action exist for protection against the risk of such a loss:

(i) retain the risk entirely

(ii) purchase insurance

(iii) purchase insurance with say a R5 000 deductible (that is, with an element of retained risk and a commensurate premium reduction)

20 A rational explanation for this has been offered by means of utility theory. See Friedman & Savage (1948, 279-304).

21 See, for example, Francis (1986, 204-235; 592- 617).
Further references can be found in Valsamakis (1983, 103-111).

22 This illustration has been taken from Denenberg, *et al.*, (1974, 50).

(iv) retain the risk but implement certain loss prevention measures – the latter will cost R20 000 and is depreciated over a 10 year period.

Table 3.3
Hypothetical situation of risk: data for decision rules

	Value (R)
Assets	150 000
Consequential Loss (indirect and uninsured)	60 000
Insurance premium	12 000
Insurance premium with a R5 000 deductible	9 000
Probability of loss	
without prevention devices	0,05
with prevention devices	0,03

Table 3.4
Assumed financial impact resulting from courses of action under loss and no-loss outcomes

Course of action	Monetary outcomes (R)	
	Loss	No loss
1. Retain risk entirely		
Insurable loss	150 000	0
Indirect loss	60 000	
Total	210 000	
2. Purchase insurance		
Premium	12 000	12 000
Indirect loss	60 000	
Total	72 000	
3. Purchase insurance with deductible		
Premium	9 000	9 000
Cost of deductible	5 000	
Indirect loss	60 000	
Total	74 000	
4. Retain risk but expend on loss prevention measures		
Insurable loss	120 000[23]	
Consequential loss	50 000	
Cost of prevention measures	20 000	2 000[24]
Total	190 000	

23 The maximum insurable loss is less under this course of action, since the safety devices are expected to reduce the loss severity.

24 It is assumed that in the event of loss, the loss prevention measures/devices will be destroyed. In the event of no loss, the prevention measures/devices will be depreciated in equal amounts over a 10 year period.

Table 3.4 sets out the assumed financial impact resulting from the courses of action under loss and no loss outcomes. Although it is recognised that there may in fact be numerous objectives to be satisfied, this illustration refers to four specified objectives around which decision rules may be applied:

- ☐ to minimise the maximum potential monetary loss (minimax)
- ☐ to minimise the minimum potential monetary loss (minimin)
- ☐ to minimise the expected monetary loss
- ☐ to minimise the expected monetary regret.

3.9.1 Minimax

This objective is characterised by extreme pessimism where the possibility of no-loss becomes non-pertinent to the decision. Obviously the minimax solution is to buy insurance (course of action 2) where the advantage is perceived solely as the relative low premium outlay in relation to the potential monetary loss. It is interesting to note that this strategy underlies an assumption that the possibility of loss is 1,0 – yet (although unrealistic) those situations that closely resemble such a probability are not amenable to insurance in view of the relatively high administration and other costs involved in the insurance process.[25] Nevertheless, it is difficult to perceive a situation in which the minimax objective will not result in the purchase of insurance.

3.9.2 Minimin

Conversely to the minimax, the minimin objective is characterised by extreme optimism, where the course of action to be adopted is to retain the risk in its entirety (course of action 1) with a resultant minimum monetary loss (zero) in the event of no loss occurring. Suffice to say that the minimin objective suffers from the same shortcomings as that of the minimax, but at the other extreme.

3.9.3 Minimise expected monetary loss

A more appropriate method than assuming either loss or no loss certainty, is to assign some weight to possible outcomes – such weighting reflects somewhat on the chance of a loss occurring or not occurring. The resultant loss then becomes the expected monetary loss and represents the average period loss over a large number of periods.

Using the probabilities of losses assigned as per table 3.3 and applying these to the monetary outcomes as listed in table 3.4, the expected losses are computed in respect to the four courses of action, as shown in table 3.5.

25 Included in such costs is the 'normal' profit expected by the insurer.

Table 3.5 Expected losses associated with each respective course of action

Action	Expected loss (R)				
1	– 210 000(0,05)	+	[0(0,95)]	=	– 10 500
2	– 72 000(0,05)	+	[– 12 000(0,95)]	=	– 15 000
3	– 74 000(0,05)	+	[– 9 000(0,95)]	=	– 12 250
4	– 190 000(0,03)[26]	+	[– 2 000(0,97)]	=	– 7 640

The above results indicate that in order to minimise the expected monetary loss, the appropriate course of action to adopt would be to retain the risk but to institute loss prevention measures. If the probabilities assigned, **absolutely** reflect the possibility of loss and if one assumes these to be the same as those relied upon by insurers, then, theoretically insurance would never be purchased. Insurers' premiums would reflect those same probabilities in addition to their administrative and other costs, resulting in a premium higher than the expected value of loss. The probabilities assigned by individuals seldom coincide with those assigned by insurers. Access to relevant and sufficient data is a major consideration and in the final analysis it is more likely that individuals would assign probabilities which are arrived at subjectively, rather than objectively. It is argued that such probability evaluations, based on belief, judgement and the like, may vary widely from the underlying mathematical probabilities and hence may be considered irrational.[27]

3.9.4 Minimise expected monetary regret

Regret may be defined and quantified as the difference between the monetary loss of a course of action selected, and the value of the final outcome. It is a practical parameter for consideration, since often after the action has been selected and an outcome materialises, some regret may be experienced for having selected the 'incorrect' course of action. It can also be seen as a performance yardstick in the short term – it is not inconceivable that decision-makers' performance is evaluated either consciously or unconsciously by the application of this measure of regret. Indeed it can be argued that the measure of regret (and concomitant consequences) exerts influences, often irrational in nature, on the decisions of organisations concerning pure risk situations.

Possible regrets associated with each course of action according to the illustration are set out in table 3.6.[28]

26 0,03 assumed as a result of loss prevention measures.

27 The study of subjective probability is still in its infancy. Nevertheless, studies have indicated that this divergence between probabilities is 'normal' and furthermore predictable within limits. See Cohen (1960, 114) and Edwards (1961, 478).

28 The regret is based upon the difference between the best possible course of action under each outcome and the various courses of action available.

Table 3.6
Possible monetary regrets associated with each course of action

Action	Regret (R)	
	Assuming a loss outcome	Assuming a no-loss outcome
1	210 000 – 72 000 = – 138 000	No regret
2	72 000 – 72 000 = No regret	– 12 000
3	74 000 – 72 000 = – 2 000	– 9 000
4	190 000 – 72 000 = – 118 000	– 2 000

The minimax and minimin objective applied in the context of regret analysis would result in the purchasing of insurance (action 2) and the retention of the entire risk (action 1) respectively.

As noted previously this set of decision rules take no cognisance of the probability of loss and therefore once applied, the **expected** monetary regrets associated with each course of action become those indicated in table 3.7.

Table 3.7
Expected monetary regret associated with each course of action

Action	Expected monetary regret (R)
1	– 138 000(0,05) + [0(0,95)] = – 6 900
2	– 0(0,05) + [– 12 000(0,95)] = – 11 400
3	– 2 000(0,05) + [– 9 000(0,95)] = – 8 650
4	– 118 000(0,03) + [– 2 000(0,97)] = – 5 480

In the longer term the course of retention of risk with loss prevention measures (action 4) will yield the least average expected regret.

As mentioned earlier, the objective has been to define and develop a set of decision criteria and thereby to offer a framework within which one may rationalise decision-making as far as risk taking is concerned. Resultant monetary values as measures of potential loss have their shortcomings nevertheless, for they may have varying effects for different individuals.

The expression of expected loss or regret in absolute terms may not necessarily suffice, so that it becomes necessary to consider the decision in the context of utility.

3.9.5 Concept of utility

The concept of utility[29] purports to characterise an individual's preference for goods and services. Generally, more goods and services are preferred to less and generally the more one has, the less satisfaction

29 The concept of utility has become basic for the current micro-economic theory of individual economic behaviour. Reference can be made to the pioneering article by Friedman & Savage (1948, 279-304).

(measured in utils) one derives from an extra unit of income (denominator for the acquisition of goods and services referred to). Hence the concept displays diminishing marginal utility.

Figure 3.2
Hypothetical utility curve

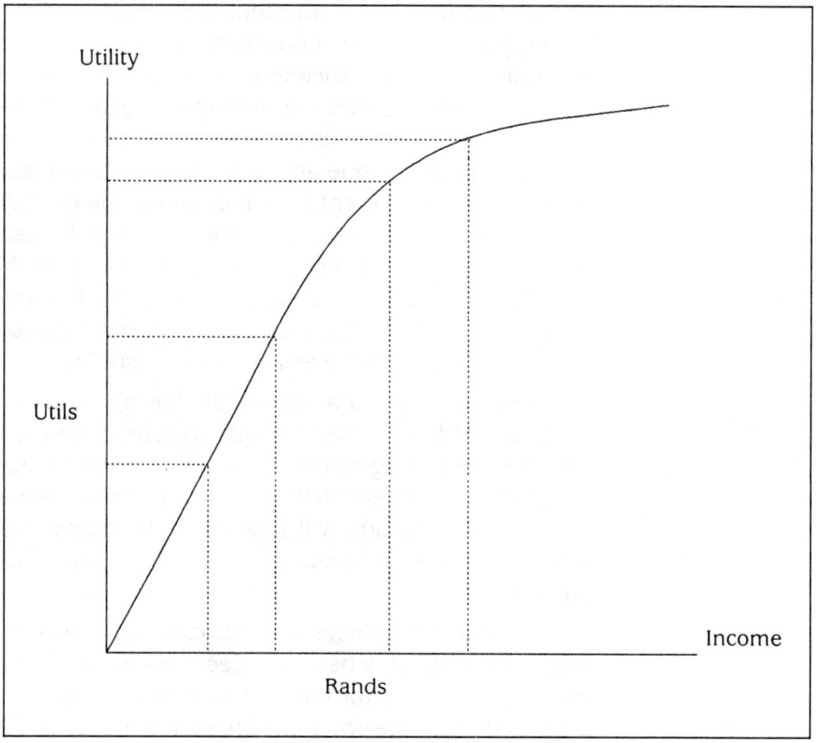

The set of decision rules defined in sections 3.9.1 through 3.9.4 describe outcomes in terms of losses and not gains. The concept of diminishing marginal utility implies that greater possible losses will result in even greater than proportional loss of utility, that is, increasing marginal disutility. This explains why mathematical probabilities alone do not control the purchase of insurance. Plainly, the disutility accompanying a premium payment may be less than that associated with an uninsured loss, even after making allowances for the assigned probabilities of loss.

Utility is of course personalised in nature and consequently each person or group has its own utility function, based on a myriad of factors such as, for example, age (or life cycle), income (or earnings), savings (or retention capacity). A utility function could nevertheless be conceptualised, and disutilities to potential monetary loss subjectively assigned in order to examine the resultant decision rules; given the same objectives previously described, that is, minimax, minimin, minimum expected disutility and minimum expected regret. Although the utility function would necessarily be only hypothetical, the exercise or modus of arriving at an appropriate course of action would not be dissimilar to that discussed earlier, using monetary values.

Under the minimax or minimin objective the resultant decision would be the selection of the same course of action as with the use of monetary values, given the fact that normally a person would not be adverse to having additional 'rands'. Therefore, when probabilities are ignored, the action selected will be the same regardless of the unit of measure. On the other hand, when probabilities of occurrence are assigned to the various outcomes (expected monetary loss/disutility) the course of action selected may indeed be different to that of which the objective was to minimise expected monetary loss. This could result in the decision rules pointing towards the purchasing of insurance rather than to the retention (to varying degrees) of risk. This emerges from the fact that there is a greater increase in disutility associated with a given increase in potential monetary loss, that is, increasing marginal disutility.

The same course of action of purchasing insurance cover would most likely be chosen if it were sought to satisfy the objective of minimising expected regret. Again this would be because the regret (or as a further extension, the anxiety factor) associated with the expenditure of premium when no loss occurs, will most-likely be outweighed by the regret (or anxiety) experienced when a loss occurs and when no insurance had been purchased.

It is significant to note that this latter comparison of regrets becomes more meaningful when the decision-maker is the professional risk manager whose performance may well be measured in the light of actual events. Thus, in the practical context the anxiety factor, although difficult to quantify, becomes an important influence in the decision-making process.

3.10 Market considerations for the financial treatment of risk

The preoccupation thus far has been to define and characterise risk – to provide some framework within which uncertainty may be conceptualised in an attempt to deal with it. Both quantitative and qualitative considerations have been discussed. The problem in the economic and management sense is to develop a rationale – a model of choice for uncertain situations which will help outline the relevant considerations for the creation of a market (insurance).

The model that economists have developed revolves around the concept of utility, as introduced in the preceding section. It characterises the preferences of individuals for goods and services. The model itself, however, is purely an academic exercise but it does explain the workings of a market for insurance. Importantly, it allows one to conclude that in an uncertain world an insurance market will arise and hence will mitigate the effects of risk on society as a whole; a prime consideration for economists.

The premise underlying the theory of utility is that generally more goods, income etc. is preferred to less; an individual therefore receives a level of utility or satisfaction in relation to the extent of his 'package'. Secondly, the more the individual already has, the less satisfaction the individual receives from an extra unit (goods, service and income).

To illustrate the economist's basic model of decision-making under uncertainty, the assumption is made that the following utility curve applies to a consumer, whose preferences for income are represented by OU.[30]

Figure 3.3
Hypothetical utility curve (OU)

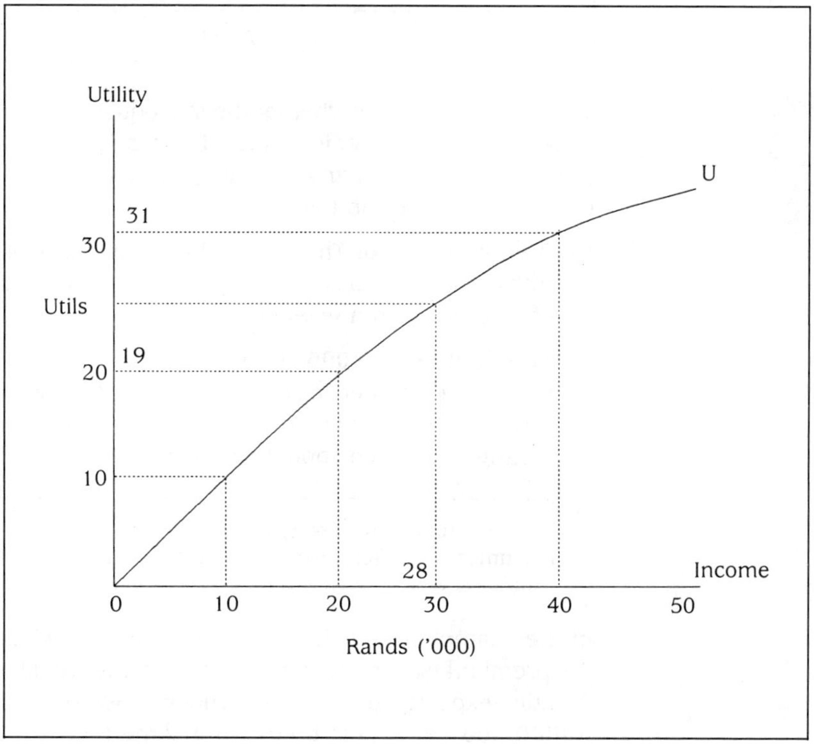

30 Insurance consumers, in this model, will always display a diminishing marginal utility of income and gamblers will display an increasing marginal utility of income. Individuals who neither gamble nor insure will have a straight utility curve [constant marginal utility of income].

Assuming further that the following risk situation prevails:

Present income	R40 000
Own dwelling valued	R20 000
Probability of house burning down	0,50

The following conclusions may be drawn:

No Insurance	**Income**	**Utils per OU**
No event of fire	R40 000	31
Certain event of fire	R20 000	19
Expected utils (0.50)(19) + (0.50)(31)		25

The question posed is whether the individual can ameliorate his situation through the purchase of insurance. The answer is dependent upon whether the cover is offered at an acceptable premium. The limits (hypothetically) can be said to be the following:

- ☐ **Premium = R 0.** The financial consequences of the risk have been transferred at zero cost so that the individual is guaranteed an income of R40 000 and a level of utils of 31.
- ☐ **Premium = R40 000.** Total income is spent on insurance. There is no income and hence zero utility, compared with 19 utils should the house be destroyed by fire where the individual carries no insurance. Clearly, insurance should not be purchased.

> A consumer's **indifference premium** is that premium at which a consumer is indifferent to buying or not buying insurance.

In the example cited, this would be at a level where having expended the premium (say x) the consumer's income would represent a utility of 25 utils (expected utils derived under conditions of no insurance), that is (R40 000 $-\, x$) = post premium income (y)

= utility of 25 utils.

From the curve OU one can see that:

- ☐ income representing 25 utils = approximately R28 000, hence
- ☐ premium (x) to arrive at post premium income (y) of R28 000 = R12 000.

3.10.1 Market viability

It is clear that the economist's basic model of decision-making under uncertainty dictates that if an insurer asks for premium greater than R12 000, the consumer will reject the offer, but if the offered premium is less than R12 000 the consumer's post premium income will be greater than R28 000, his utility (with insurance) will exceed 25 utils and he will purchase the cover.

The next fundamental principle to address is the viability of a market forming, given the above criteria for acceptance and non-acceptance of insurance. The criteria apply equally to the insurer who will obviously be a supplier of insurance if the possibility of profit exists. It can be shown that a market can exist for the benefit of both buyer (consumer) and seller (underwriter) provided there is a reasonably large number of other potential consumers whose utility curves are similar.

Assuming there are, for example, 100 such consumers, then the insurer may charge a premium of say R11 500 (below the indifference premium of R12 000). The insurer's cost can be expected to be:

- ☐ claim payments resulting from fires:

  (number of exposure units)(loss)(probability of loss)
  100(20 000)(0,50) = R1 000 000

- ☐ insurer's administrative expenses (assumed) = R50 000
  Total costs = R1 050 000

  Insurers revenue = 100(11 500) = R1 150 000

  Expected profit = R 100 000

The above shows a break-even price for the insurer of R10 500. Hence, for a market to exist there needs to be a premium price struck between the two limits of R10 500 and R12 000. This is achievable and both parties benefit: the insurer earns a profit by removing uncertainty for the consumer, even though the premium charged is greater than the consumer's expected monetary benefits from insurance (R20 000)(0,50) = R10 000.

3.10.2 Reasons for market failure

Although simplistic, the above example illustrates that market formation is possible, provided that the crucial element of compensation for risk-bearing is inherent. It is important, however, to examine the possible sources of market failures as well, for there are risky situations where insurance is desirable but where a market will not arise through the natural functioning of the private economy. Having briefly categorised such situations one can examine the rôle of the public sector in an effort to 'correct' such market inability/failure, the latter being defined as the existence of pure risks without the possibility of insurance.[31]

Specialised risks

Firstly, the risks may be too **specialised** making pooling by underwriters not possible. In these circumstances there does not exist a reasonably large number of such specialised risks. Therefore, no insurer can enjoy the risk-spreading advantages of pooling, where any individual's uncertain situation is turned into an approximately certain loss to the insurer but at the same time allowing a profit residual.

The difficulty of pooling may also arise from less contrived conditions. Organisation of a market (meeting of supply and demand) is not costless. Factors such as geographical and informational barriers and the like, may entail an overall cost structure, which includes market acquisition costs for the underwriter and which may exceed the indifference premium and thus fail to produce a market. Under these conditions of marketing costs the public sector may fulfill a rôle of central marketer by disseminating and distributing relevant information through a central information centre, thus making market creation possible. Such marketing costs could then be defrayed by the imposition of a tax, for example, on insurance sales.

Adverse selection

A second source of market failure is the process of **adverse selection** of insureds. This implies heterogeneity of insureds concerning their utility curves and hence indifference premiums. The lack of information by insurers surrounding true probabilities of loss may mean that insurance is offered at premium levels which cannot support any profit to underwriters. This being the case, premium levels are then adjusted upwards, but, because of the diversity of the groups insured, certain consumers' indifference premiums may be surpassed and hence total revenue to insurers declines, notwithstanding the increase in the price of cover. The process of adverse selection, therefore, entails the purchase of cover by those who are increasingly certain that they will need insurance once premium levels rise. Thus, as premiums increase, the better risks no longer buy cover, leaving a higher proportion of relatively poorer risks to share the costs of benefit payments. The process continues and the final outcome may be that no insurance is offered at any price. The principal difficulty is the **asymmetrical information** subsisting between supply and demand – if the insurer knew the true probability of loss for each group of buyers, differential premiums could be charged and profit earned in each market segment.

31 The presence of pure risks without the opportunity to buy insurance does not always mean market failure. There are, for example, gamblers who might be prepared to take the risk.

As in the case where information costs are expensive, the public sector may be able to provide the information needed to allow the insurer to rate differentially and thereby achieve market viability. However, when information is too expensive or indeed impossible to retrieve, an alternative method may be to impose a compulsory insurance plan at a premium level which allows underwriting profits. Clearly such a scheme will inevitably penalise the low risk market participants and favour the high risk participants. This, then, merely suggests an income redistribution which society will need to evaluate.

Public goods

A further source of failure can arise when one considers **public goods**. In this instance, the reduction of an individual's loss from risk may not only offer satisfaction to the insured but to others in society as well. The reduction in loss from risk *per se* is a public good. Programmes which, for example, offer disability benefits to veterans, training for the handicapped, or life and disability cover for military servicemen, are usually approved of because it is deemed unfair that some other third party must suffer these hardships. Hence, the more fortunate derive satisfaction from witnessing a reduction in the losses of the less fortunate. The benefits enjoyed by the more fortunate, who in fact do not directly receive the insurance coverage, are a public good.

Paradoxically, therefore, because everyone benefits from everyone else's purchase of the good, no one has the **private** incentive to buy the insurance service, since one could enjoy the benefits of the coverage free of charge. In such situations it may be necessary for society to buy such commodities/services collectively and payment may be made by the collection of taxes.

Inadequate compensation

Finally, there is the consideration of the prerequisite of the private economy for handling risk, namely added compensation for bearing risk. Market formation and a smooth functioning of a decentralised pricing system is only possible if the crucial element of compensation is recognised.

The economic system rarely guarantees an outcome so that ultimately, profit is characterised as the reward or lure that draws entrepreneurs into taking risks and achieving economic progress. Generally, the greater the added profits required, the larger the risk. Evidence shows that risk, measured by the variability of a firm's profits through a period of time, is positively related to average profits through a period of time, and that a negative relationship between the skewness (asymmetry) of the profit distribution and its mean (required returns) exists.[16]

As the asymmetry in the profit distribution becomes more positively skewed, there are fewer chances of very large losses – and hence less risk. Therefore as skewness becomes more positive, average rates of return decline, indicating a fall in risk-compensation as risk declines.[17]

Ordinarily then, market formation is possible if the return to compensate for the risk is adequate. This premise applies equally well, of course, when considering insurance market formation, although one may qualify that high risk-deterring investments may require public policy intervention. Catastrophic and remote perils such as floods, urban riots and the like, entail very large benefit payments. Losses associated with catastrophes of this type are large albeit unlikely, and insurance companies will need to pool these risks to avoid the danger of a very large one-time payout. Thus, public policy or even regulation may be required in these instances so as to encourage private investment.

3.11 Conclusion

The objective of this chapter has been to provide a general background to risk management by examining, in the first instance, the concept of uncertainty and the definition (and classification) of risk. With regard to the latter, a degree of rigour was imposed, whilst elucidating, from a risk management point of view, the two distinct elements of event and outcome, inherent in uncertainty.

The discussion has, of necessity, considered the question of risk quantification and decision-making under uncertain conditions, taking cognisance of the financial mechanism of an insurance market to fund the possible financial outcomes resulting from risk.

Having reviewed what may be regarded as the salient features relative to the environment of uncertainty or risk, attention is now focused, in the chapter that follows, on the **fundamental** principles governing the management of pure risk.

Bibliography

Athearn, JL & Pritchett, ST 1984. *Risk and insurance*. St. Paul, Minnesota: West Publishing Co.

Cohen, J 1960. *Chance, skill and luck*. Baltimore: Penquin Books Ltd.

Denenberg, HS, Eilers, RD, Melone, JJ & Zelten, RA 1974. *Risk and insurance*. Englewood Cliffs, New Jersey: Prentice-Hall Inc.

Doherty, NA 1985. *Corporate risk management - A financial exposition*. New York: McGraw-Hill Inc.

Edwards, W 1961. 'Behavioral decision theory.' *Annual Review of Psychology*. Vol. XII.

Fisher, IN & Hall, GR 1969. 'Risk and corporate rates of return.' *Quarterly Journal of Economics*. Vol. LXXXIII, No. 1, February.

'Risk and corporate rates of return: reply.' *Quarterly Journal of Economics*. Vol. LXXXV, August 1971.

Francis, JC 1986. *Investments: Analysis and management*. New York: McGraw-Hill Inc.

Freund, JE, Williams, FJ & Perles, BM 1988. *Elementary business statistics. The Modern Approach*. Englewood Cliffs, New Jersey: Prentice-Hall Inc.

Friedman, M & Savage, LJ 1948. The utility analysis of choices involving risk. *Journal of Political Economy*. Vol. LVI, No 4, August.

Greene, MR & Serbein, ON 1983. *Risk management: Text and cases*. Reston, Virginia: Reston Publishing Co. Inc.

Houston, D 1964. 'Risk, insurance and sampling.' *Journal of Risk and Insurance*. Volume XXXI, No. 4, December.

Knight, FH 1921. *Risk, uncertainty, and profit*. Boston: Houghton Mifflin Co.

Mehr, RI 1986. *Fundamentals of insurance*. Homewood, Illinois: Richard D. Irwin Inc.

Mowbray, AH 1930. *Insurance: Its theory and practice in the United States*. New York: McGraw-Hill Inc.

Pfeffer, I 1956. *Insurance and economic theory*. Homewood, Illinois: Richard D. Irwin Inc.

Rim, Y 1968. 'Personality and group decisions involving risk.' reprinted in Hammond, JD *Essays in the theory of risk and insurance*. Glenview, Illinois: Scott, Foresman and Co.

Robinson, R & Kunath, L 1981. 'A dynamic approach to risk management.' *Risk Management*. September.

Shackle, GLS 1961. *Decision, order and time in human affairs*. Cambridge, England: Cambridge Press.

Sheldon, R 1984. *A first course in probability*. New York: The MacMillan Co.

Valsamakis, AC 1983. *The investment policies and practices of South African long and short-term insurers.* Unpublished M.Com. Dissertation, University of the Witwatersrand.

Willett, AH 1951. *The economic theory of risk and insurance.* (1901) reprinted Philadelphia: University of Pennsylvania Press.

Williams, CA Jr. 1966. 'Attitudes toward speculative risks as an indicator of attitudes toward pure risk.' *Journal of Risk and Insurance.* Vol. XXXIII, No. 4, December. Reprinted in Hammond, JD *Essays in the theories of risk and insurance.*

Endnotes

[1] Shackle, 1961, 109.

[2] Denenberg, et al., 1974. 15-16.

[3] Willett, 1951, 8.

[4] Knight, 1921, 233.

[5] Pfeffer, 1956, 42.

[6] Denenberg, et al., 1974, 4-5.

[7] Greene & Serbein, 1983, 24.

[8] Athearn & Pritchett, 1984, 4-5.

[9] Doherty, 1985, 2.

[10] Greene & Serbein, 1983, 20.

[11] Mehr, 1986, 27.

[12] Denenberg, et al., 1974, 8.

[13] Mehr, 1986, 28.

[14] Rim, 1968, 70-79.

[15] Williams, 1966, 579.

[16] Fisher & Hall, 1969, 79-91; 1971, 518-522.

[17] Fisher & Hall, 1969, 79-91; 1971, 518-522.

4 THE FUNDAMENTAL PRINCIPLES OF RISK MANAGEMENT

4.1 Introduction

The preceding chapter provided an introduction and a context within which the discipline of risk management can be placed. In essence, it described the milieu of risk and offered some definition. The examination of the underlying principles surrounding the quantification of risk led to the brief discussion of what is meant by pure risk to an insurer. Qualitative considerations were recognised as being relevant in the process of decision-making under conditions of risk. Finally, the rationale of treating risk financially via the formation of a market was examined; the concept of managing risk by rationalising decision-making (both quantitatively and qualitatively) and by 'transfer of risk' (deriving the benefits of pooling) was thus introduced *ab initio*.

Against this background, this chapter presents the **fundamental** principles of risk management. In particular, it addresses the question of providing an integrated model for risk management, which then represents an underlying rationale, from which the techniques for managing pure risks can be developed and discussed more fully in the ensuing chapters. This, then is also the objective of the chapter.

In pursuing this objective, however, the weaknesses as evidenced in the present approaches to risk management, which are described in the contemporary texts, are addressed. It is felt that the present view of risk management does not display the requisite integration of principles governing the discipline, and this provides a major motivation for laying down the relevant fundamental issues early in the text.

In arriving at a simple model for risk management, the chapter first considers the meaning of risk management, and the reasons for managing pure risk from an organisational standpoint.

4.2 The meaning of risk management

Various definitions of risk management have been offered. Dickson[1] defines risk management as:

> the identification, analysis and economic control of those risks which threaten the assets or earning capacity of an organisation.

In a similar vein, Greene & Serbein[2] describe risk management as:

> the process for conserving the earning power and assets of the firm by minimising the financial effect of accidental losses.[1]

Implicit in these definitions is the fact that risk management entails the control of pure risks facing the organisation, **and** the minimisation of the

1 Reference to some of these definitions can be found in Morkel (1988, 10-11).

adverse financial effect of such risk consequences.[2] Although the financial aspect, (financial provision/recovery from adverse effects of risk) is implied, it is interesting to note that the risk management process as presented in most texts does not provide an explicit model which shows clearly enough the interrelationship between these two management concerns, or activities.[3]

Risk and the management thereof is mostly viewed within the context and field of insurance, and in those cases which also embody the processes relevant to the control of risk, even a simplified model showing the interaction between control and financing is generally lacking. Hence, it is not surprising that, when commenting on the future of risk management, writers have been critical of the present process, which they describe as static – a process which envisages discrete (rather than interactive) stages followed in a predetermined and logical sequence, and which is excessively orientated towards insurance.[3]

A further consideration, in assessing the meaning and extent of risk management in the future, is whether the discipline should encompass speculative risk situations. Kloman,[4] for example, states that definitions such as *pure* and *speculative* risks obscure rather than assist in the development of an holistic or integrated view of the discipline. Robinson & Kunath[5] point towards the possibility of risk management extending to embrace aspects of speculative risk.

This extension of activity may well map out the future of risk management; indeed there is evidence of principles of risk management and insurance funding being presently applied to particular aspects of speculative (economic) risk.[4]

---

2 In practice, the risk manager's line responsibility is concerned with the financial consequences of risk. The entity as a whole, however, is concerned with the practical totality of risk. If, for example, a factory is destroyed or damaged by fire, it is the cost and other overt consequences of the fire which is of concern; in practice therefore it is seldom deemed necessary to be overly concerned with the theoretical nature or philosophy of risk. See Vivian (1986, 44-45).

3 This point is discussed under section 4.4. Other writers, notably, Strutt (1989, 2-5), Kloman (1987, 59) and Robinson & Kunath (1981, 42-43) have referred to this lack of integration and have pointed to the piecemeal development of the discipline of risk management. Reference to the texts, listed at the end of the chapter, will show that even a simple model connecting the constituent risk management activities is lacking. Also, whilst attention is focused on insurance and self-funding, the question of any interrelationship between these two financing techniques is not adequately addressed. There seems to be a general disregard for the fundamental issue of the 'financing mix' in the risk financing activity. Doherty (1985, 334-349), whose approach to risk management is mainly from a financial investment perspective, does provide a model which shows the criteria for risk management and which addresses the financial techniques of insurance and self-funding, one *vis-à-vis* the other.

4 Reference here is made to a recent development with regard to the management of currency risks, where, in support of an underlying risk management process, insurance capacity has been offered to finance any nett resultant loss following adverse fluctuations.

Critically, one may state, however, that whilst attempts are made to project the discipline of risk management in a more structured manner in order to cope with the complex requirements of the future, little is offered by way of how such structuring and growth of involvement will be achieved.

The tendency, it seems, is to 'elevate' the discipline to risk areas that have traditionally been outside the ambit of risk management; without addressing, first, the fundamental issues at stake.[6] Paradoxically, deliberate introspection (by risk managers), and the integration of pure risk management activities will assist in providing the growth path for the future. Firstly, by adopting, as a starting point, a more rigorous definition of risk (as proposed in Chapter Three), a clearer appreciation and delineation will be gained as to which risks are amenable to treatment through a risk management process. Secondly, the strict view that the overall activities encompassing control and financing of risk are interwoven, will encourage greater discipline and self-responsibility. This, in turn, will lead to the availability of financial capacity (from insurers, who should be regarded as financial intermediaries) to deal with hitherto unconventional risk situations.

This text therefore is preoccupied with the management of pure risk, without refuting that its future development may well be in risk areas presently regarded as being outside the province of the discipline.

With this in mind, risk management is defined as follows:

> **Risk management** is a managerial function aimed at protecting the organisation against the consequences (adverse) of pure risk, more particularly aimed at reducing the severity and variability of losses.

Management of risk explicitly **includes** the activity of financial recovery or provision for losses.

Furthermore, in recognising the existence of the two elements of uncertainty, namely,

(i) the uncertainty as to whether the event or occurrence will take place

(ii) the uncertainty surrounding the outcome (financial) of the event when it takes place.

The management of risk specifically entails the effort to reduce or minimise the likelihood of the loss-producing event occurring, as well as to reduce or minimise the adverse effects (including financial) once the event has occurred.

Although one could claim that the field of risk management is rather definite in scope, its entailed activities are both broad and complex. Successful risk management implies the employment of qualified personnel, usually specialists in the varied techniques of risk management (control and financing).

4.3 Reasons for managing risks

Before describing the fundamental principles of risk management it is opportune, first, to consider the reasoning behind the managing of pure risk. The reasons offered for managing risk are linked to such aspects as the corporate objectives of growth and survival. Corporate policy, good citizenship and freedom from anxiety, are also stated as reasons for risk management in an organisation.[7]

The grounds that are offered are of course valid, although presented under the general guise of risk management objectives. In discussing these reasons, the practical question of why pure risks are actually managed, is addressed, rather than the more normative question of why pure risks ought to be managed. It is appropriate, therefore, to approach the question by firstly seeking to justify pure risk management action, and thereafter identifying why certain action is in fact taken.

4.3.1 A normative justification for risk management

The concepts of risk and return are by nature interrelated. Under such premise, there exists the underlying rationale that the trade-off is managed best when consideration is given to both elements.

It is feasible to assume that the overall performance of an organisation, or economic unit, and the evaluation of such as an investment by the market, is a function of that unit's understanding and management of risk. Given the distinction in Chapter Three between pure and speculative risk, any reduction in the pure risk profile of an organisation (against a given expected return) following a deliberate risk management programme, will result in a more efficient risk-return trade-off.[5]

This, then, can be seen as the fundamental (normative) reasoning supporting risk management. Because, in theory, investment decisions entail the achievement of efficient risk to return trade-offs, this dictates that in the pure risk context, risk, *per se*, should be considered as equally fundamental and significant as return, *per se*. This rationale can now be translated into more practical reasoning, suggesting the following reasons for managing pure risks.

5 For a discussion of the effect of insurance on the value of the share price of the firm see Main (1982, 237-247).

4.3.2 Practical reasons for managing risk

4.3.2.1 *The steps taken are cost-beneficial*

This is the most common reason given;[6] it supports the risk to return premise outlined above and finds favour particularly amongst risk managers who are, in the organisational context, finance orientated. Simplistically, the decision rule would hinge upon whether the return/benefit derived from risk management measures outweigh the expenditure incurred.

Clearly evident in this approach is the risk-return valuation process. However, an important qualification needs to be made. Although the principle is sound in logic, the emphasis should be on maximising or achieving risk-return trade-off efficiency in the **longer term**. Emphasis should not necessarily be placed on short-term cost to benefit relationships; the error in this practice is the disregard of the **principle** and its substitution for a short-term accept or reject **criterion**.

Nevertheless, considering that expenditure on and benefit derived from risk management cannot always be evaluated in the shorter term, the aim of minimising the long-term cost of risk and thereby attaining an efficient long-term risk to return relationship remains the fundamental principle of risk management.

4.3.2.2 *Risk aversion*

The preceding chapter introduced the concept of utility as one means of characterising risk. The concept was presented to describe decision-making criteria under conditions of risk. It should be noted that the concept of diminishing marginal utility, which implies that greater possible losses would result in even greater than proportional utility loss, confirms that man is averse to risk.

Hence, even under given cost-to-benefit conditions, an aversion to risk, *per se*, often dictates what the risk management programme will be. One finds that, notwithstanding possible inefficiencies of, for example, purchasing insurance, organisations will tend towards such a 'transfer of

6 Most literature refer to *cost-to-benefit* being the main reason or at the least implies this, judging from the structure of the work. For example, Doherty (1985, 365) states:

> The criteria for making loss reduction decisions are the same as those used for loss financing. The common yardstick is the value of the firm; loss reduction decisions can be made according to their impact on the value of the firm's existing equity.

Greene & Serbein (1983, 102) recognise two criteria for the rationale of loss control: (i) economic, (ii) non-economic.

Mehr & Hedges (1974, 439) recognise cost-to-benefit and non-monetary criteria. Within the latter, legislative requirements are considered.

risk'.[7] Such behaviour reinforces the view that risk aversion is indeed a major motive influencing the risk manager, whether in the form of risk 'transfer' to the insurance market, or the implementation of a deliberate retention funding or reserve programme which will ensure that the effects of major losses are minimised.

Significant too, is the fact that risk management activities involve expenditure of funds rather than the creation of income; even excellent performance by the risk manager is often unidentified, but, a failure to recognise a source of loss or failure to arrange adequate financial cover or a similar error, becomes readily apparent to top management and shareholders. Individuals' risk aversion, therefore, also has a bearing on how and why risks are managed.

4.3.2.3 *Policy-based decisions*

In practice, many decisions to implement risk management programmes are simply based on organisational policy. Quite often, however, the decision which reduces risk, may not be motivated by risk management concerns at all. For instance, a company may be motivated to design and implement a quality assurance programme because it strives for excellence, rather than a concern for the liability exposure of its products. Similarly, the decision to follow a NOSA (National Occupational Safety Association) programme may well be a policy-based decision arising out of the organisation's concern about occupational injuries, despite the fact that in terms of section 7 of the *Workmen's Compensation Act* (30 of 1941) it has no liability exposure. It is not suggested of course, that this attitude is wrong or in fact ineffectual; but that deliberate company policy dictates or decisions sometimes have an unintentional impact on the risk management function. The risk manager should support, encourage and monitor the implementation of any corporate programme which reduces the risk.[8]

4.3.2.4 *Authoritative reasons*[9]

Finally, with regard to certain risks, for example products liability or fire and occupational safety, there are authoritative reasons why risk management measures are implemented. Commonly, these are imposed through legislation and accepted codes of practice.[10]

---

7 The influence of risk aversion in the decision-making process of purchasing insurance has been researched by numerous writers.
The seminal work on the attitude towards risk appears to be by Grayson (1960). See also, Williams (1966, 577-586), Gordon & Dickson (1982, 89), Smith & Buser (1987, 225) and sources quoted by Kihlstrom & Roth (1982, 361).

8 See, for example, Vernon (1988).

9 The reader is referred to Chapter Eight, section 8.6 for a list of Statutory Enactments.

10 For example, in the field of safety and occupational health, the leading legislation in South Africa is the Machinery and Occupational Safety Act (MOSACT) (6 of 1983). In the USA safety and occupational health is covered under *Occupational Safety and Health Administration (OSHA) Standards* (29 CFR 1910).

4.4 The risk management model

4.4.1 An integrated approach

In discussing the meaning of risk management, it was established that the risk management process entails, basically, the control of risk (in the context of the two elements of uncertainty surrounding pure risk situations) and the financing of risk consequences. It is immediately evident, therefore, that the risk management process comprises two fundamental activities. Understandably, each fundamental activity in turn can be seen to entail or incorporate separate disciplines, often very complex in nature. For example, risk control may involve expertise in chemical engineering, whilst the financing aspect may require the appreciation and use of insurance markets, specialising in, say, energy risks.

Notwithstanding the obvious necessity of various disciplines which may be individually required for the managing of risk, when the conceptualisation and formulation of an overall discipline is considered, it is necessary firstly to lay down a foundation on which individual activities and even disciplines can be based. This will achieve not only clarity in so far as what the objectives of the discipline are, but also clarity as to how activities may be integrated to help achieve the objectives.

The lack of such an integrated model for risk management becomes evident when reference is made to the texts covering the discipline. In the main, definitions of risk are provided first and the scope and objectives of risk management are discussed only then. The strong historical links with insurance and loss prevention measures are accentuated, but this leads, mostly, to what may be seen as separate discussions of aspects relating to loss prevention on the one hand, and insurance and self-financing, on the other.

These shortfalls have been identified by various writers. Strutt,[8] as mentioned earlier, is critical of the view that the risk management process comprises discrete stages (described as static and which lack integration), and points to the disregard of the subjects of risk identification and quantification in the texts. Kloman[9] is critical of what he calls risk management's 'umbilical cord to insurance', and suggests a more holistic approach – in other words, considering the whole rather than dealing with specialities only. Robinson & Kunath[10] state that:

> because the underlying philosophy and application of risk management has often not been thoroughly thought through, it has tended to evolve piecemeal. If, instead, responsibilities were developed from a simple set of fundamental guidelines, it is more likely that the importance of the risk management principle would be recognised as a whole concept and as a profession.

Although some models for risk management have been designed, these can still be seen to address **specific** interests rather than addressing the more fundamental issues as identified above. Head[11] describes the typical **steps** involved in the risk management process, and elaborates on these in chart-form. Robinson & Kunath[12] developed a model showing **exoteric** influences on risk; their perspective is the extension of the boundaries of the total risk management system. The need, therefore, is to describe the fundamental principles, with the aim of highlighting the integration between the risk management activities of control and financing, and the integration within the financing activity of insurance funding and self-funding.

The fundamental principles for the management of risk can be explained best by means of a diagram, as depicted in figure 4.1.

In terms of this model, risk is managed by refering to two intrinsic activities:

(i) risk control[11]

(ii) risk financing.[12]

The model identifies the two related management activities of risk control and risk financing.

Risk control broadly aims to:[13]

- ☐ prevent losses from occurring
- ☐ minimise the magnitude of loss, should the event occur
- ☐ deal (physically) with the event while it is occurring, in an attempt to recover from the loss with the least possible economic consequence.

Since there does not exist a physical risk management programme which can effectively prevent all events or consequences of pure risk exposures, provision must be made for access to financial resources in order to finance

11 The list of risk control programmes as shown in the figure is not exhaustive. These risk control programmes could be categorised generally under the following headings:
- assets programmes
- consequential loss programmes
- liability programmes
- personnel.

12 Today captives represent a significant and unique financing option. Thus, this financing source has been identified separately in the model and is discussed in further detail in Chapter Twelve.

13 Greene & Serbein (1983, 93), Denenberg, *et al.*, (1974, 80) for example, refer to this activity as *loss control/prevention*, recognising the purpose as being to reduce the frequency and severity of losses. It is more suitable to refer to the activity as *risk control*, as such a definition could encompass the broader scope of managing the environment of risk, rather than the control of losses only.

Figure 4.1
The risk management model

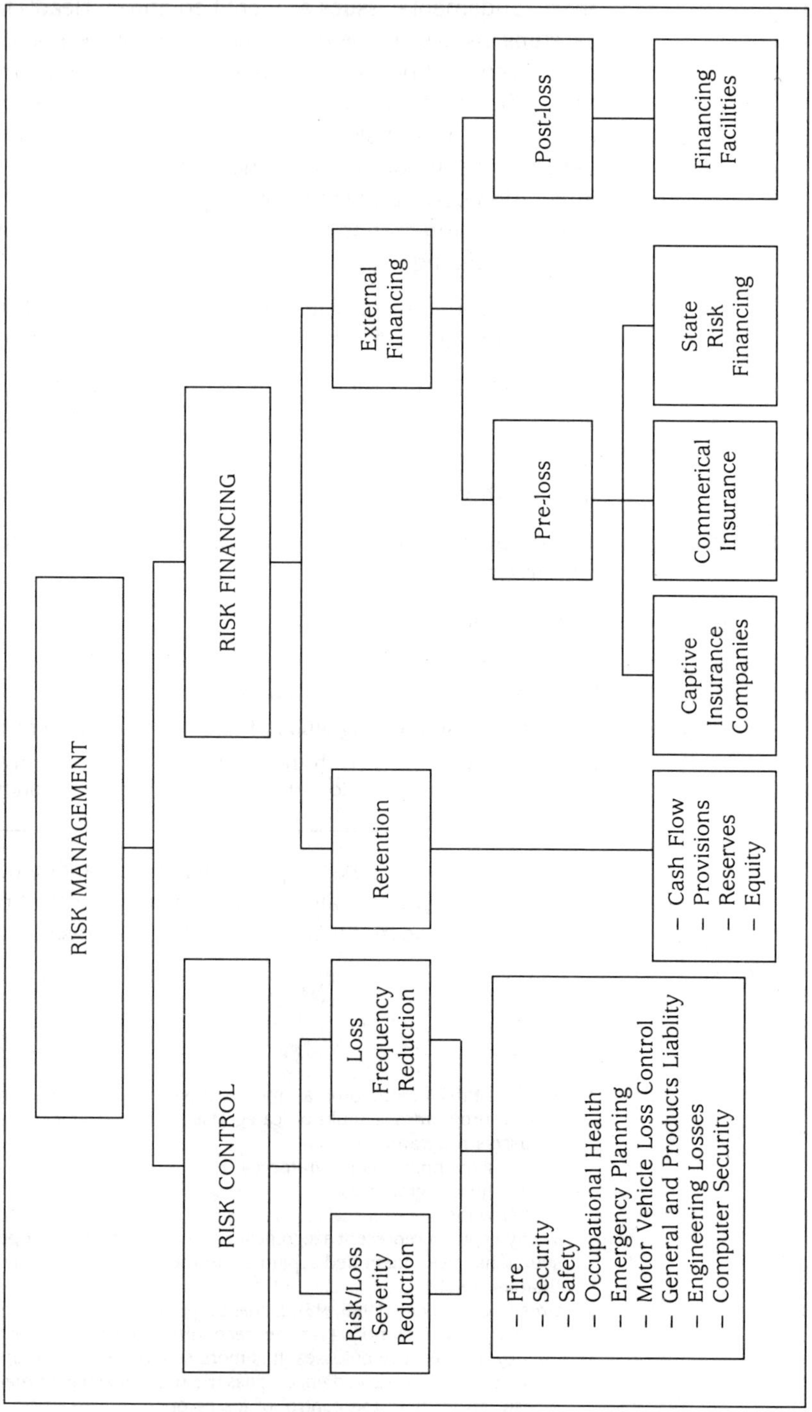

or fund losses should they occur. This, then, is the preserve of risk financing, which basically identifies accessibility to funds via:

- ☐ an organisation's own resources (self-funding)
- ☐ the resources of some other third party, the latter usually being the private insurance market and State/Government funds.[14]

Having identified the internal and external sources of finance, risk financing also includes consideration of the most efficient 'mix' of finance.

The model as described, highlights the integration of control and financing, and the further integration within financing of external and internal sources. The model has been recognised as both realistic and practical,[15] and purports to represent the **process** by which risks are managed.[16] It is significant to note that as such, it should be considered as dynamic and progressive; in deriving the fundamental steps it is relevant to view the process not as an event, but as a programme within an organisation that must be continually monitored and evaluated.

4.4.2 Steps in the risk management process

The process fundamentally entails the following steps:

- ☐ risk identification (discovering the sources from which losses may arise)
- ☐ risk evaluation[17] (evaluating the impact on an organisation or individual should a loss occur)

---

14 In South Africa, the two most important funds are those established in terms of the *Workmen's Compensation Act* (30 of 1941) used for the purpose of financing claims as a result of industrial accidents, and the *Multilateral Motor Vehicle Accidents Fund Act* (93 of 1989) used for financing claims resulting from personal injuries following motor vehicle accidents.

15 As an example of the model being applied to South Africa's largest industrial company, see *Barlows '88* (Number One. Journal of the Barlow Group. 8-9).

16 In the context of this research, risk management is considered a professional discipline. During the past fifteen to twenty years both American and European scholars have been developing quantitative methods of risk management. These may be used by both buyers and sellers of insurance. Notwithstanding what has been accomplished, the techniques set forth are, however, little understood and little used by risk managers. The concepts have related more to the problems besetting insurers and the methods are applicable mostly only to certain situations. Moreover, their application is not a simple matter and the mathematical language is difficult for most people to understand. See Williams & Heins (1981, 26) and Allen (1972, 2).

17 This process should also include **assessment** of the risk; it is often convenient to consolidate all the data into a relatively shorter synopsis providing a 'subjective' assessment of the risk, where one can discount certain risks and emphasise the exposure to others. As an example of the assessment being applied to politically motivated risks, see Vivian (1986, 1-25).

- ☐ risk control (selecting the most effective and efficient techniques to minimise the risk)[18]
- ☐ risk financing (making financial provision to fund or finance the loss, should it occur).

The sections that follow provide a brief description of the steps identified above.

4.4.2.1 *Risk identification*

Logically, before any attention can be focused on the management of risk, the source of risk must be identified. Identification, in many instances, is self evident. In other instances, the identification requires more insight. Often, consultation with professional personnel/bodies is required to identify all risk sources which may give rise to multiple risk situations. Risk identification can be more systematically achieved when viewed separately from a macro- and micro-identification perspective.

Macro-identification

Macro-identification implies the identification of major perils within an organisation. From a risk financing point of view this process is important. An appropriate means of financing the losses arising from such perils, is the provision of insurance or suretyship. Essentially, the traditional area of cover provided by the short-term insurance markets are against:

- ☐ sudden and **accidental** events, resulting in
- ☐ financial loss.

Thus, macro-identification involves a review which is directed at discovering risks that are normally treated by insurance, namely those risks which give rise to the following:

- ☐ loss or damage to assets
- ☐ the consequential losses which arise from loss or damage to assets
- ☐ legal liability claims in circumstances where a court of law would hold the company liable to pay compensation[19]
- ☐ losses suffered by personnel
- ☐ pure financial losses (by exception).

---

18 Most references to risk management identify three fundamental steps, these being:
- **discovery** of the sources from which losses may arise
- **evaluation** of the possible impact of losses
- **selection** of the most efficient methods of treating the selection risks identified.

It is obvious that the selection of the most effective and efficient methods of risk treatment encompasses both physical (risk control) and financial risk management techniques. The model adopted in this paper and depicted in Figure 4.1 differs only in that it accentuates the two distinct sub-elements in the total process. It is felt that the separate 'disciplines' have in time developed to an extent which warrants some distinction and therefore the reference to four fundamental steps in this process.

19 Historically, the grounds were also for sudden and accidental events causing loss or damage and physical injury.

These losses can arise from various perils, for example, fire, crime, and the sale of products. Consequently, macro-identification should follow a pattern which aims to identify the above consequences from identified perils, bearing in mind the requirements of the insurance market.

Micro-identification

Having identified the major perils through the process of macro-identification, the next step is one of micro-identification, which entails the identification of sub-perils and hazards **within** the macro-class.

Although the risk management texts do not differentiate between these two steps, as proposed in this book, this differentiation does offer more rigour and system to the process of risk identification. It provides a sequential system for identifying, firstly, major perils, where insurance plays a significant rôle, and secondly, derivative perils, the identification of which is fundamental to the activity of physical risk management, or risk control. Arguably, such a systematised approach will ensure a more encompassing and precise identification of risk sources facing the organisation.

Micro-identification thus aims to identify derivative perils within the main perils class. For example, this means the identification of the various and possibly numerous sources of fire and the steps to be taken to avoid or mitigate the risk. The micro-identification process is therefore fundamental to physical risk management (risk control).

4.4.2.2 *Risk evaluation and assessment*

This step is most important in the overall process, as together with identification of possible sources of loss, it represents the foundation for planning, organising and managing the risk to reduce the impact of possible losses.

Risk evaluation entails quantifying the risk and determining its possible impact on the organisation. Head[13] refers to the process of risk evaluation as the analysis of loss exposures, where attention is focused on:

> how frequent and how severe accidents are likely to be and how they may interfere with the organisation's success.

More particularly, risk evaluation and assessment concerns the following:

- ☐ The evaluation of both loss frequency and loss severity – an analysis of which will provide, *inter alia*, the two significant measures of **expected average loss** and **maximum possible loss**. Since the characteristics of risks, and the frequency and severity of losses are all constantly changing, the evaluation thereof becomes a continuous process.
- ☐ An analysis of the financial strength of the organisation, which basically entails the assessment of the firm's risk retention capacity. The objective is to ascertain what the impact of a given risk might be relative to the financial strength of the firm.

The evaluation process does require expertise in several disciplines and use of techniques, which by nature necessitate interface with numerous organisational units. For example, in evaluating liabilities emanating from contractual agreements, or in evaluating possible losses from a liability viewpoint of a new product, input from both the legal and research-and-development departments is required.

4.4.2.3 *Risk control*

Having identified the various risks and evaluated their possible impacts, the next step is to minimise the risk practically through design and implementation of a physical risk management programme.

Such programmes would aim to achieve the following goals:

- ☐ the reduction of the magnitude of the exposure
- ☐ the reduction of the frequency of the loss-producing events
- ☐ the dealing (physically) with loss-producing events
- ☐ the recovery (physically) from loss-producing events.

Risk control programmes may be referred to as practical, in the sense that they are conducted at the source of the risk. Whilst, to a large degree, the responsibility for risk management in an organisation can be viewed as a staff function, the practical implementation and monitoring of loss control programmes is conducted by line management.[20]

4.4.2.4 *Risk financing*

The final step in the process of risk management entails the financial provision for losses that may occur. It is therefore in the selection of the most efficient method of financially providing for the consequences of risk, that the following choices become evident:

- ☐ the retention of risk under a deliberate self-insurance or some other retention
- ☐ the combination of risks (diversifying or hedging) to obtain the benefit of greater certainty in predicting the loss occurrences through the use of the law of large numbers
- ☐ the transfer of risk cost to other third parties, through such techniques as insurance.[21]

---

20 One of the more significant aspects of successful risk management however, is the understanding and commitment of top management to any such programmes.

21 Reference to the concept of *risk transferral* to other third parties can be traced back to the old writers on Roman-Dutch law. Grotius Th 712. (3.24.1), for example, defines insurance as

> an agreement whereby one person takes upon himself the risk of uncertain danger apprehended by another, and the latter in his turn binds himself to pay the former a premium.

(*Continued on page 63*)

The combination method of risk treatment may be used by business firms, individuals or indeed insurers. It has its limitations however, since the scope of combination or diversification may be limited.[22]

Risk retention and risk transfer to third parties is discussed in detail in the ensuing chapters and therefore not commented on further here. Nevertheless, it should be pointed out that the evaluation of the advantages and costs of alternative methods and the selection of the most efficient method or technique is a difficult task. Prudent risk retention is underpinned by relatively complex quantitative analyses aimed at determining probable quantums of loss which are to be self-financed. Other aspects to consider include for example, whether a given risk should be 'transferred' by insurance, or self-retained; if retained as self-insurance whether there should be a limit beyond which the risk should be 'transferred' by purchase of excess insurance.

4.5 Conclusion

The major thrust of this chapter is to provide at the outset, the fundamental principles of risk management, which are easily illustrated by means of a model. In order to achieve this, attention is firstly focused on the meaning of, and reasons for, risk management. This not only provides a definition for the discipline being studied, but also prompts a degree of introspection, which identifies as a shortfall the general lack of integration between the activities constituting the risk management process.

The definition offered, identifies the two broad and interrelated activities of risk control and risk financing. The design of the model for risk management is influenced by the necessity to integrate the two broad risk management activities on the one hand, and the two sources of risk financing, namely insurance and self-insurance, on the other.

The concept of risk transferral therefore is one embedded in legal literature and referred to in most contemporary writings. However, it should be noted that **conceptually** risk cannot be transferred *per se*. As pointed out by Channell, J. in *Prudential Insurance Company Ltd. v Inland Revenue Commissioners* (1904) 2 KB 658:

> Where you insure a ship or a house, you cannot insure that the ship shall not be lost or the house burnt, but what you do insure is that a sum of money shall be paid upon the happening of a certain event.

See Getz & Davis (1983, 77-78), Williams & Heins (1981, 187; 200) and Vivian (1990, 26).

22 Apart from the fact that the ways in which the risk manager can 'spread' or 'diversify' risk across several exposures is limited, it is pertinent also to consider their attitude toward individual risk. For shareholders, the effect of pure risk may be lost within their investment portfolios. If shareholders hold efficiently diversified investment portfolios, the effect of pure risk on a particular stock in the portfolio will have an insignificant effect on the riskiness of the whole portfolio. However, risk managers cannot diversify away their **employment risk** so easily. Consequently, they may adopt more risk-averse postures in making corporate decisions. See Elliott (1972, 1309-1320).

Emphasis is placed on the fact that the model purports to represent a dynamic process by which risks should be managed – one which must be continually monitored and evaluated. The fundamental steps in the risk management process are identified as the following: risk identification, risk evaluation, risk control, and risk financing. These are then broadly described, and form the foundation for the more detailed discussion that follows in the ensuing chapters.

However, the process of risk management, as described, is one performed within an organisation, and hence one needs to examine risk management in this context, first. This is the objective of Chapter Five.

Bibliography

Allen, TC 1972. 'Quantitative risk management methodology – A historical perspective.' *Journal of Commerce*. New York, March.

Barlows '88. Number One. Journal of the Barlow Group.

Dickson, G 1989. 'Risk management: what does the future hold?' *Journal of the Society of Fellows*. London: Chartered Insurance Institute, Vol. 4, July.

Doherty, NA 1985. *Corporate risk management – A financial exposition*. New York: McGraw-Hill Inc.

Elliott, JW 1972. 'Control, size, growth and financial performance in the firm.' *Journal of Financial and Quantitative Analysis*. Vol. 7.

General Industry. 1978. U.S. Government Printing Office.

Getz, WS & Davis, DM 1983. *The South African law of insurance*. Cape Town: Juta & Co. Ltd.

Gordon, CA & Dickson, G 1982. 'A comparison of attitudes towards risk amongst business managers.' *The Geneva Papers on Risk and Insurance*. April.

Grayson, CJ Jr. 1960. 'Decisions under uncertainty: Drilling decisions by oil and gas operators.' Boston: Harvard Business School.

Greene, MR & Serbein, ON 1983. *Risk management: Text and cases*. Virginia: Reston Publishing Co. Inc.

Grotius, H 1631. *Inleiding tot de Hollandsche rechtgeleertheyt*. The Hague. Translation by Maasdorp A.F.S., Cape Town, 1903, 3rd Edition.

Head, GL 1986. 'Updating the ABCs of risk management.' *Risk Management*. October.

Kihlstrom, RE & Roth, AE 1982. 'Risk aversion and the negotiation of insurance contracts.' *Journal of Risk and Insurance*. Vol. XLIX, No. 3.

Kloman, HF 1987. 'Risk management . . . by many other names.' *Risk Management*. June.

Main, BGM 1982. 'Business insurance and large, widely-held corporations'. *The Geneva Papers on Risk and Insurance*. July.

Mehr, RI & Hedges, RA 1974. *Risk management: Concepts and applications*. Homewood, Illinois: Richard D. Irwin Inc.

Morkel, P 1988. *Strategies for managing corporate risk in the mining and industrial sectors*. Unpublished MBL Dissertation, University of South Africa.

Robinson, R & Kunath, L 1981. 'A dynamic approach to risk management.' *Risk Management*. September.

Smith, ML & Buser, SA 1987. 'Risk aversion, insurance costs and optimal property-liability coverages.' *Journal of Risk and Insurance*. Vol. LIV, No. 2, June.

Strutt, RSG 1989. 'The reality of risk management.' Paper prepared for the Institute of Risk Management and presented to the AIRMIC Conference, Robinson College, Cambridge. April.

Vernon, D 1988. 'Encouragement of the NOSA programme.' *Barlows 88*.

Vivian, RW 1990. 'Risk transfer – fact or fancy.' *Cover*.

Vivian, RW 1986. 'Is insurance the solution?' *Safety Management*. October.

Vivian, RW 1986. 'The application of the fundamental principles of risk management, to manage the risk in politically motivated acts.' *Engineers' Association of South Africa*. Professional Security Conference.

Vivian, RW 1985. 'The fundamental principles of risk management.' *The South African Treasurer*. May.

Williams, AC & Heins, RM 1981. *Risk management and insurance*. New York: McGraw-Hill Inc.

Williams, AC 1966. 'Attitudes toward speculative risk as an indicator of attitudes towards pure risk.' *Journal of Risk and Insurance*. December.

4.7 Endnotes

[1] Dickson, 1989, 18.

[2] Greene & Serbein, 1983, 3.

[3] Strutt, 1989, 2-5.

[4] Kloman, 1987, 60.

[5] Robinson & Kunath, 1981, 43.

[6] Robinson & Kunath, 1981, 44.

[7] Mehr & Hedges, 1974, 29-37.

[8] Strutt, 1989, 2-5.

[9] Kloman, 1987, 56-62.

[10] Robinson & Kunath, 1981, 42.

[11] Head, 1986, 50-51.

[12] Robinson & Kunath, 1981, 50.

[13] Head, 1986, 50.

5 THE RISK MANAGEMENT FUNCTION IN AN ORGANISATION

5.1 Introduction

The definition of risk management offered in the preceding chapter implies that such management is performed in the organisational context. The term *risk management* may of course be applied to the control and minimisation of the risks facing individuals, but even in this respect, in our society today, the organisation plays a significant rôle in assisting with, or even assuming the responsibility for personal risk management.[1]

The challenges surrounding the integration and formalisation of risk management, therefore, will need to be met by corporate risk management practitioners. It is consequently opportune, to review the rôle and position of risk management in a corporate context, with the aim of appraising it and to determine what possible future course should be adopted. These are the objectives of this chapter, which then also provide the background, in a corporate sense, for discussing in the chapters which follow, the risk management activities as identified in the model.

5.2 The rôle and position of risk management in a corporate context

5.2.1 The rôle of risk management in an organisation

The title *risk manager* is becoming acceptable for job title purposes by large corporations.[2] It is not uncommon however, to find risk managers also carrying other titles of an entirely different nature. The management of pure risk is also assigned to executives under whose control and responsibility falls the corporate treasury function, where actually a pure risk manager should be reporting.[3] With the formalisation of risk management as a management function, it is also becoming evident that

1 To a large extent the responsibility for managing personal risk has shifted from the individual or family unit to the business organisation. Such a shift can be evidenced by the development of employee benefit plans (retirement, medical aid, group schemes and personal accident). The importance of such a shift of responsibility is further supported by the success and growth of risk management consultancy firms offering specialist employee benefit consultancy to organisations.

2 The title *risk manager* is becoming more widely used by South African organisations. As for the relevant experience in America, Greene & Serbein (1983, 7) can be referred to.
The extent to which the risk management practice is viewed formally as a corporate management activity in South Africa can be gauged from the membership criteria of the *South African Risk and Insurance Association* (SARIMA). Persons elected as representatives of a corporate body are required to be managers or heads of insurance or risk management departments, or have at least 5 years' experience in insurance or risk management activity. Organisations which spend R1 million or more on insurance annually, are eligible to become members of the Association.

3 For examples of titles of risk managers, see Parrott (1969).

there is a proliferation of outside specialist consultancy concerns aiming to provide this service to organisations in return for a fee.[1]

When discussing the functions of the risk manager there is, presently, a debate over the types of risks to be managed. Should the risk manager's function be confined to insurable risks only, or to all pure risks? How far does the scope of fundamental risk extend? The distinction between pure and speculative risks, as made in Chapter Three, may obscure rather than assist in developing an holistic risk management approach, and the boundaries of risk management could be extended.[2]

It still remains unclear as to how such a progressive course for risk management will be followed.

It is generally believed that all pure risk situations should be included in the ambit of the risk manager and that risk management should be regarded as a specialist function, as should the treatment of speculative risk within the organisation.[3] In efficiently carrying out such a function it may well be required that a wider approach to risk definition be adopted, but the starting point must be the implementation of a risk management process along the lines described by the model.

There is of course no single method of applying risk management within an organisation, as each is different and thus the method of implementation must suit the needs of the particular entity. Nevertheless, the purpose or object of the risk management department could be, simply stated, to ensure that the functions of risk management are implemented; that the risks facing the corporate entity are being managed.

Within the framework of what has been deduced in the preceding chapter, the organisation must ensure that the risk management model is effectively implemented, namely:

- ☐ that steps are taken to manage risk physically
- ☐ that adequate provision, where appropriate, is made to finance losses which may arise.

In order to achieve the risk management objectives, organisations deploy the requisite resources and establish risk management departments for this purpose. The complexity of the risk management departments varies widely, depending on the organisation's size and scope of activity, but these departments are mostly divided into a risk finance and insurance division, and a risk control division.[4] Whilst there is an obvious interrelationship in the activities of these two divisions, there is also an apparent difference in emphasis.[4]

---

4 Whilst there is obvious need to examine the two elements separately, the model developed in this study stresses the integration of these two programmes so as to achieve an encompassing risk management rationale, or holistic approach.

5.2.1.1 *The risk financing responsibility*

Traditionally, the purchase of insurance cover and the implementation of other risk financing strategies have been regarded as the main functional responsibilities of the risk manager. This has originated primarily from the interpretation of the function of risk management as serving to insulate the organisation from the negative financial consequences of pure risk situations.

The activity entails the structuring, purchasing and administration of the appropriate risk financing programme (usually insurance) for the organisation. Thus, *inter alia*, the risk manager needs to be familiar with the scope of the cover afforded by each respective policy covering the major perils as identified through the macro-identification process.

The responsibility of risk financing in the organisation is far-reaching. In major organisations these financing programmes can be complex and hence this function is specialised. It is not uncommon for the risk manager to devote most of his time and energy to the risk financing responsibility.

5.2.1.2 *The risk control responsibility*

There is a significant organisational difference between the financial and risk control responsibilities entailed in risk management. Whereas, even in a multi-faceted organisation, a centralised risk finance department can ensure that appropriate risk financing programmes are implemented, this is not possible with physical risk control programmes. These programmes which, for instance, include detailed risk inspections, demand a far higher man-power intensity so that day-to-day risk control remains a line management responsibility. The risk management department could be used in a consultative rôle (fulfilling a staff function) to assist and give guidance to line management.

There are various methods of implementing physical risk control programmes depending on the type of organisation. The fundamentals as well as the level of sophistication will differ when one compares risk control programmes implemented for a multiple site company, to those that have, for example, one or two major sites (with concomitantly higher relative asset values). The latter may employ a highly qualified risk control complement of engineers, safety officers and even medical practitioners, directing attention to the psychological or sociological aspects of risk control.

5.2.1.3 *External consultancy*

The risk management department is also charged with the responsibility of procuring, where appropriate, the expertise and services of external risk management consultants.[5] The extent of the use of external specialist consultancies is evidenced by examining the number of employees typically employed in American risk management departments, shown in table 5.1.

Table 5.1
Survey of American risk management departments in terms of number of employees

Number of employees	Percentage
0 – 1	18,50
1 – 2	23,30
2 – 5	34,60
5 – 10	15,80
10 – 20	5,50
>20	2,30
Total	100,00

Source: *Cost-of-Risk Survey*, 1990

The table shows that only 2 % of American companies engage more than twenty employees in their risk management departments. The vast majority of others engage less than five. It is characteristic therefore for risk management departments to be relatively small in size as these departments usually contract external consultants for the more specialised risk control aspects. This is not surprising when one considers the multitude and diversity of risks facing an organisation.

5.2.2 The position of risk management in the organisation

The development of a formal programme of risk management in an organisation is of relatively recent origin. In the United States of America it was only during the late 1920's and early 1930's that industry began to formalise the responsibility for treating pure risks.[6] Today, risk management departments are common, particularly in the USA,[7] and a survey of these proves interesting in the understanding of their position and indeed their limitations.

In 1990, the *Cost-of-Risk Survey* examined a number of functional aspects of the risk manager as pertains to the organisation. These findings are summarised in the following tables 5.2 and 5.3. Table 5.2 specifically shows risk management reporting relationships, while table 5.3 indicates the risk manager's functional responsibilities within an organisation.

It is evident that the majority of risk managers (approximately 65 %) report to the finance section (taken as finance and treasury in table 5.2) of the organisation.

Table 5.2
Risk manager reporting relationship

Function to which risk manager reports	Percentage of total
Finance	35,66
Treasury	23,90
CEO/President	9,63
Administration	8,76
Legal	6,38
Other	10,88
Human resources	4,75
Total	100,00

Source: *Cost-of-Risk Survey*, 1990

This is in line with prior investigations conducted by Miller[8] and Cerveny,[9] who found that approximately 70% of risk managers reported to the head of finance although they had access to the general manager.

This is not surprising, since the major functional responsibility of the corporate risk manager is regarded as the purchase of insurance cover. Naturally, in terms of impact on the operations and general survival of the business, appropriate insurance cover, especially to protect against catastrophe-type risks, cannot be underestimated. However, this narrow functional preoccupation with insurance matters does prompt the risk management philosophy to be biased towards a cost-to-benefit and cost-to-risk approach, and negates the full contribution that the discipline can make to attaining the objectives of the organisation.

In interpreting the results summarised in tables 5.2 and 5.3, various conclusions may be drawn, depending on the perspective of the approach. However, from the standpoint of this study, the following observations are relevant:

- ☐ The vast majority of risk managers are involved in aspects of a financial nature. The functional preoccupation with property and liability matters, coupled with the reporting lines as per table 5.2, indicates that such activity refers predominantly to insurance.
- ☐ An equal percentage of risk managers report to either the organisation's chief executive or to administration. This, coupled with the relatively thin spread of functional responsibilities, as summarised in table 5.3, leads to the conclusion that risk management, as a management function, is restricted by the limited rôle played by the function in business decision-making, and displays a misplaced position in the corporate structure.[5]

5 This point is alluded to by Farthing (1988, 37) who, in addressing the risk management department's rôle in the challenge of corporate survival, states:

> . . . that risk managers will have to be more closely involved in the strategic planning of business in the future.

Table 5.3
Risk manager responsibilities

Functional area	Responsibility level: General authority	Shared authority	Recom-mend only	Not respon-sible	Total
Property & Liability Insurance Purchase	82,3%	10,8%	6,8%	0,1%	100%
Liability Claims Management	63,0%	27,2%	5,0%	4,8%	100%
Workers' Compensation Insurance Purchase	70,7%	12,3%	7,7%	9,3%	100%
Workers' Compensation Claim Management	46,3%	26,3%	7,1%	20,3%	100%
Property Loss Prevention	43,6%	36,6%	14,9%	4,9%	100%
Employee/Public Safety	23,8%	37,7%	22,7%	15,6%	100%
Environmental Affairs	11,3%	35,3%	26,7%	26,7%	100%
Employee Benefits – Welfare Plans	12,3%	18,6%	10,1%	59,0%	100%
Pension/Profit sharing – Deferred Compensation Plans	7,2%	13,1%	7,7%	72,0%	100%
Security	7,8%	18,1%	24,2%	49,9%	100%
Selection of Brokers/ Agents	78,2%	13,5%	6,4%	1,9%	100%

Source: *Cost-of-Risk Survey*, 1990

In profit-seeking organisations, management aims at maximising shareholders' wealth, which implies the maximising of long-term profit *vis-à-vis* risk considerations. This objective is ultimately the responsibility of the organisation's chief executive. As risk plays a major rôle in this objective, the chief executive could be labelled the ultimate risk manager. Hence, it is not unreasonable to expect the pure risk manager to report to the chief executive, and to be consulted when considering the investment decisions of the organisation. In contrast to this viewpoint are the results of practical investigations conducted by Miller[10] and Cerveny,[11] who found that risk managers are usually positioned at about the third level of management in the organisational hierarchy.

In all, it seems that the risk management function does not fulfil its entire potential within the corporate context. If the objective is for the risk management profession to be more fully appreciated and accepted in the future, then there are certain challenges to be met, which, arguably, will assist in forging a more desirous future path for this management discipline.

5.3 Future challenges

5.3.1 Cutting the umbilical cord to insurance

There has been a natural and historical association between risk management and insurance. The rôle of risk managers has to a large extent, been perceived as revolving around the provision of insurance cover, and insurance in relation to other financing techniques, has been afforded a rather privileged and irreplaceable status.[12]

This means that risk management is still approached by certain practitioners from the narrower perspective of insurance. Therefore, the pervasiveness of the discipline has still not gained acceptance. In order risk management to reach its full potential as a management function within the business context, it is argued[13] that

> . . . risk managers should make a conscious effort to break free from their entangling alliances with the practice of insurance-buying.

One could argue that such a recommended course for the future is made with the explicit aim of forcing general attitudes toward risk management and control responsibility, as opposed to an insurance or 'risk transfer' responsibility. This, in itself is very desirable, since it lends support to the fundamental (normative) reasoning behind the discipline of risk management.

5.3.2 Placing greater emphasis on the management and decision-making aspects of risk management

The nature of risk management is both technical and diverse. There is a tendency, therefore, to describe the discipline in terms of separately identifiable processes, phases and steps (as is done in this study). These methods do, of course, contribute to the understanding of the diverse subjects, but this often leads to the neglect of the functional management tasks which accompany the risk management function. According to Church,[14] the greatest part of the risk manager's time is spent on operational aspects, and as his investigations showed, only 11 per cent of their time was devoted to management activities.

The possible conceptualisation of risk management along the discrete lines mentioned above and the preoccupation with the separate operational aspects, militate against an holistic treatment of risk. In the introductory section of this chapter, it was said that present errors in thinking, and other inconsistencies needed to be addressed. The most significant starting point is to practise **management** and decision-making in relation to risk in an integrated manner; whereby the objectives, activities and results pertaining to the relevant risk management processes and steps are recognised as interrelated. Their possible cause-and-effect relationship must be recognised. These, collectively, should form the input for effective risk management decision-making.

The greater emphasis on management and decision-making thus represents an important challenge for the future. In striving to achieve such a management emphasis, the suggestion has also been made[15] for risk management to be regarded as a profit centre; as opposed to a costing centre,[6] whereby managers redefine their function in terms of the wider management elements of planning, organising, directing, co-ordinating and control.

Moreover, as with management, risk management is needed at all levels. As Crockford[16] points out:

> No one man is likely to have the range of knowledge and skill necessary to undertake the management of the whole of the company's vast range of risk himself. Even if such a polymath could be found, he might well have difficulty in communicating his ideas to all the many managers, all busy with their own problems, and in persuading them that risk management was something they should be aware of and care about.

The task, therefore, is to introduce and integrate risk management thinking and skills at all levels of an organisation.

5.3.3 Extending the scope of the discipline

In the preceding chapters, a distinction was made between pure and speculative risk, and risk management was assumed to mean the management of pure risks. Logically, such a limitation can be seen to contribute towards the establishment of risk management as a business function, which entails the combination and interaction of expertise from various disciplines.

Hence, in this regard the limitation constituted by the 'handling of pure risks' fulfilled the useful purpose of preventing any invasion of the other functions of the organisation.

However, business is exposed to both pure and speculative risk, and these constitute important components of the total risk exposure. The question, therefore, of extending the boundaries of risk management to encompass speculative risk is not unexpected. Baglini[17] argues, for example, that political and foreign exchange rate risks should form part of the risk management function; Robinson & Kunath[18] and Gahin[19] propose that all speculative risks should be included in the ambit of risk management.

---

6 The general approach has been to regard the risk management department as a cost centre. Church (1984, 3), found that only 14 per cent of risk managers regard their function as profit-orientated, and of these, 41 per cent do not transform their budgets into business plans which identify specific objectives for their departments. Resulting from this is the fact that the relative contribution and importance of the risk management function is not adequately understood. Temple (1983, 82), suggests that the negative connotations of 'risk' and 'loss' have often worked against the risk manager, and proposes using a product as a basis for strategy in developing a positive image of the risk management department as a profit, rather than cost, centre.

To some extent these points of view may arguably be motivated by the desire to place risk within a more dynamic environment, in reaction to an overly introspective and insulated treatment of risk, which may possibly be evident. There seems to be no doubt that the future course of risk management is in the 'delimitation' of the discipline, but the challenge is also in trying to overcome the structural implications that arise. The inclusion of all speculative risks, for example, would, strictly speaking, make the risk manager responsible for all business decisions, and therefore by implication, an overlapping of functions within the business entity would arise.

One possibility,[20] which this study proposes, is that risk management should be differentiated at functional management level into pure risk and speculative risk, with the functions represented at top management level by the corporate risk manager. This method would recognise the specialist, but different skills involved in the management of pure and speculative risk, without removing the possible interaction, influence or integration of the two activities. In the final analysis, although the respective risk management activities may differ vastly, the aspects of risk control and financial provision for the consequences of risk, are common to both risk classes.

Another factor which may support the structure is the possibility that the insurance industry will break out of its more traditional perimeters of operation, and by redefining its rôle as a financial intermediary, will start to offer financial instruments that are appropriate for speculative risk situations. Such an eventuality would enhance the commonality of the two risk management functions in the organisation.

5.4 Conclusion

In considering risk management as a corporate function, attention was directed to its rôle and overall position within the organisation. The rôle of the corporate risk management department was defined in terms of the two major responsibilities as described in the model, namely the physical risk management responsibility and the risk financing responsibility.

The examination of the risk management position in the organisation leads to the conclusion that as a management function, risk management does not fulfil its entire potential.

This results basically from an over-emphasis on insurance-purchasing as a function, a misplaced position of risk management in the organisational hierarchy, and the lesser emphasis placed on management and decision-making *vis-à-vis* operational risk management aspects.

These factors, together with the extension of the risk management discipline into the realms of speculative risk, are regarded as the future challenges facing the discipline. In overcoming structural implications resulting from such delimitation, the proposal is made that risk management is differentiated at functional management level (pure and speculative) and these functions represented at top level by the corporate risk manager. This would enhance further the integration of activities and achieve a more holistic approach to the management of risk.

In Chapter Six the physical risk management responsibilities of risk identification will now be considered.

Bibliography

Baglini, NA 1976. *Risk management in the international firm.* New York: Risk Studies Foundation.

Berlonghi, A & Mattman, JW 1987. 'A new understanding of risk management.' *Risk Management.* April.

Cerveny, RP 1979. 'How risk managers use information.' *Risk Management.* July.

Church, FC 1984. 'The "compleat" risk manager.' *Risk Management.* July.

Cost-of-Risk Survey. 1990. Connecticut: Risk Planning Group Inc.

Denenberg, HS, Eilers, RD, Melone, JJ & Zelten, RA 1974. *Risk and insurance.* Englewood Cliffs, New Jersey: Prentice-Hall Inc.

Du Toit, GS 1989. *Inaugural lecture.* Pretoria: UNISA.

Farthing, D 1988. 'Is risk management essential to corporate survival?' *Risk Management.* February.

Gahin, FS 1984. 'Reworking classic models to fit real world decision-making.' *Risk Management.* June.

Girard, L 1981. 'L' Assurance francaise.' as quoted by Charbonnier in Carter, RL, Crockford, GN & Doherty, NA (eds.) 1974-1988. *Handbook of Risk Management.* London: Kluwer Publishing.

Greene, MR & Serbein, ON 1983. *Risk management: Text and cases.* Virginia: Reston Publishing Co. Inc.

Head, GL 1986. 'Updating the ABCs of risk management.' *Risk Management.* October.

Kloman, HF 1987. 'Risk management . . . by many other names.' *Risk Management.* June.

Miller, JN 1981. 'A close-up shot on risk management.' *Risk Management.* April.

Parrott, JT 1969. 'Practices in risk management (selected readings).' *Insurance Institute of America.* Pennsylvania: Bryn Mawr.

Richards, RM 1985. 'Analyzing speculative risks with the RMIS.' *Risk Management.* April.

Robinson, R & Kunath, L 1981. 'A dynamic approach to risk management.' *Risk Management.* September.

Temple, DM 1983. 'Risk manager or insurance buyer.' *Risk Management.* April.

The Post Magazine. 1983. December.

Endnotes

[1] Denenberg, *et al.*, 1974, 66.

[2] Kloman, 1987, 60.
Robinson & Kunath, 1981, 42.

[3] Head, 1986, 50.
Richards, 1985, 54-56.

[4] Greene & Serbein, 1983, 8-9.

[5] Greene & Serbein, 1983, 80.

[6] Denenberg, *et al.*, 1974, 72.

[7] Farthing, 1988, 34-35.

[8] Miller, 1981, 12.

[9] Cerveny, 1979, 10.

[10] Miller, 1981, 12.

[11] Cerveny, 1979, 10.

[12] Girard, 1981, 1.4.1-02.

[13] Kloman, 1987, 56.

[14] Church, 1984, 38.

[15] Temple, 1983, 84.

[16] *The Post Magazine*, 1983, 2936.

[17] Baglini, 1976, 4.

[18] Robinson & Kunath, 1981, 43.

[19] Gahin, 1984, 68.

[20] du Toit, 1989, 13.

6 RISK IDENTIFICATION

6.1 Introduction

In Chapter Four, the fundamental principles of risk management were addressed, the objective being to provide an underlying framework for managing pure risks. The model developed, suggested a process which entailed:

Figure 6.1
The risk management process

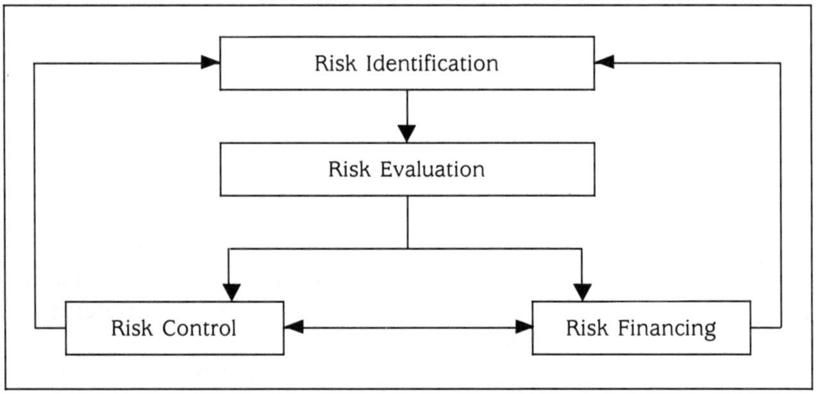

Whilst reference is made to identifiable elements within the overall risk management process, it must be reiterated that risk management must be viewed as an ongoing process, and not as a single event. The explanation of this risk management process by means of a model does assist, however, in providing a structure for further discussion.

The risk management model dictates that the study proceeds by examining the process of risk identification and evaluation as a prelude to physically managing risk and finally providing financially for the consequences of risk. This chapter can be seen, therefore, as the introduction to that section of the overall study which concerns itself with the techniques of risk management, developed and expounded in the physical as well as the financial realms of the discipline.

In Chapter Four (section 4.4.1) mention was made of the general shortcoming in contemporary risk management texts, in that generally, no evidence is found of a model for risk management which adequately illustrates the constituent elements and their interrelationships. The model as propounded in Chapter Four and further enhanced in Chapter Ten (figure 10.3) purports to overcome this deficiency.

Although risk identification can be said to be the most important step in the risk management process, it has generally been neglected in the relevant literature. A number of factors may be said to contribute to the relative neglect of this subject (in general risk management texts). One factor is the preoccupation of risk managers with the financial consequences of risk, and hence the major orientation toward insurance. The interaction of the insurance market (risk cost transfer to third parties) means that the aspect of risk identification and evaluation tends to be viewed within the context of insurance provision and coverage limits. The evaluation of risk is thus dealt with through the description of risk exposures made known to the insurance market by organisations' risk managers and their insurance intermediaries.

The second factor, and possibly the more significant, is that the techniques and general methodology underlying risk identification can be diverse and complex, requiring specialised skills pertaining to specific disciplines, particularly the engineering disciplines. It is not unexpected therefore, that particular risk identification techniques are developed by specialist consultants in, for example, the chemical engineering profession from whom the risk management departments obtain advice. This aspect can also be said to apply to the question of risk evaluation, which may require specialised input by consultants with the requisite mathematical/statistical or actuarial background.

A third factor is that, in practice, an overlap exists between risk identification/evaluation and risk control.[1]

It may hence be argued that the subjects of identification and evaluation of risk, warrant separate study and consideration, because they are, in their own right, diverse and complex subjects. It is nevertheless unfortunate that they are not usually integrated into risk management since they represent intrinsic elements in the overall process. The intention in this chapter is not to provide an exhaustive study of risk identification and evaluation methods, but rather to provide a more encompassing insight so as to achieve an holistic approach to risk management which practitioners can consider.

6.2 Risk identification

It can be said that every risk management programme must necessarily be put in motion by the process of risk identification, for obviously a risk cannot be managed if it is not identified. Hence this process must be

1 A number of examples may illustrate the point:
- A risk manager notices welding taking place in a warehouse containing flammable goods. He will immediately identify this as a major hazard. In making this immediate assessment he realises that a fire will cause substantial financial loss. Part of the identification was to estimate the possible magnitude of loss.
- Similarly, a risk manager for a chain store may be concerned about damage caused by politically motivated persons. One possibility that he will investigate is arson, and he will design a risk control programme for this possibility. A further possibility is a mortar attack. Intuitively however, without assessment, the risk manager may regard this possibility as being so remote, as not to warrant any further action. His assessment of the probability would cause him to abandon any further identification or risk control procedures.

viewed as the single most important function of the risk management programme and should not be entertained in a spurious fashion, but in as systematic a manner as possible.[1]

A systematised approach to risk identification may be achieved by first considering what risks the organisation faces on a macro- and micro-front.

> Macro-identification concerns the identification of major risk sources, the consequences of which may have a very significant negative financial impact on the organisation.

> Micro-identification aims to identify sub-risks within the major risk class, such activity being pivotal to physical risk management or risk control objectives.

6.2.1 Macro-risk identification

Macro-risk identification concern the identification of the major risk sources facing the organisation. In Chapter Three, the classification of risk was discussed and broad risk classes such as marketing, finance, property and personnel were identified. Some risk classes, for instance, financial and marketing, however, entail an element of speculative or business risk, so that from the perspective of pure risk management, such classes would ordinarily fall outside the ambit of the macro-identification process.

The principal concern following macro-identification is to insulate the firm as far as possible from the major negative financial consequences of loss arising from the major risk sources. In most instances the financial provision for such consequences is made by the purchase of insurance cover. The insurance market represents an efficient financing mechanism, facilitated by the pooling effect which is evident where such risks are concerned. Hence, macro-identification and classification should logically follow accepted insurance classifications.

Macro-identification also involves identifying the impact of environmental (or dynamic) changes that can affect pure risks. These changes are outside the control of the company. An example of this is the liability crisis discussed in Chapter Nine.

6.2.1.1 *Insurance reviews*

Generally, macro-identification is mostly conducted by carrying out an insurance review. The insurance market, or industry has for centuries been a mechanism for handling pure risks and has thus developed comprehensive risk reviews which, with the assistance of a reputable insurance intermediary, can avail the organisation.

Insurance classifications of risks/perils are therefore useful. The following is a typical classification list:[2]

Fire; explosion	
Natural perils	Earthquake, storms, floods, hail, snow, and others
Crime	Theft, burglary, fraud, fidelity, arson, sabotage, terrorism, and others
Engineering	Breakdown, loss of, or damage to machinery and utilities
Transit	Loss of, or damage to goods in transit
Legal liability	Environmental impairment, products liability and employers liability

It is relevant to note that such insurance reviews will embrace uninsured perils as well as perils for which no insurance cover is available, or available only at a very high premium due to a restricted insurance market which may prevail.

6.2.1.2 *Organisational and flow charts*

To the list of perils identified by the typical insurance review, the risk manager can also append other risks facing the organisation. Such an identification can be achieved by drawing an organisational chart which illustrates the different aspects of the organisation's activities and structure. For example, the chart shown in figure 6.2, may indicate the main aspects of the organisation's activities under such headings as contracts, retail and specialised subsidiaries.

2 Unfortunately, classifications of this nature offer limited benefit to those risk managers who bear the responsibility for all pure risks, some of which may not be readily handled by means of insurance. Nevertheless, some do provide comprehensive lists of loss sources, including information which assists in evaluating risks and the adoption of preventative measures. See Williams & Heins (1981, 45-49).

Figure 6.2
Organisational chart: ABC Manufacturing Company

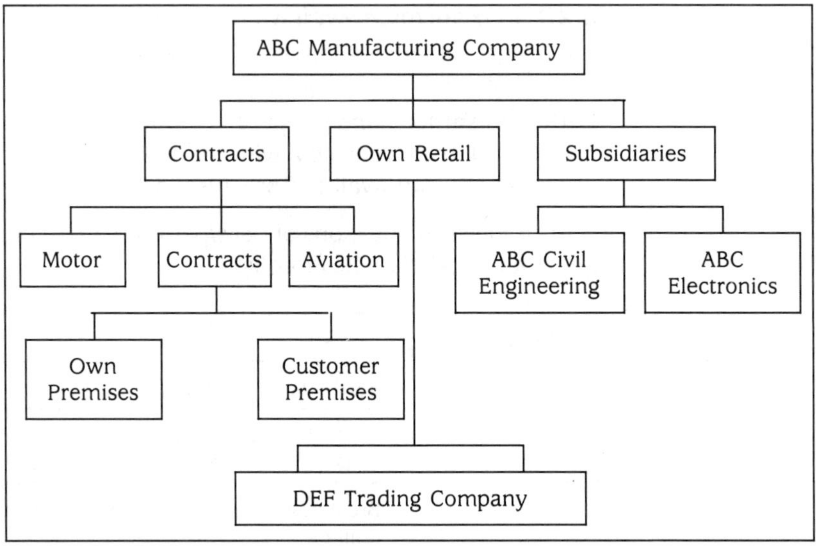

The chart in figure 6.2 depicts the structure of the organisation as a whole. It is also possible to construct a chart which could, for example, show the management and administration set up, as shown in figure 6.3.

Figure 6.3
Organisational chart: management and administration of ABC Manufacturing Company

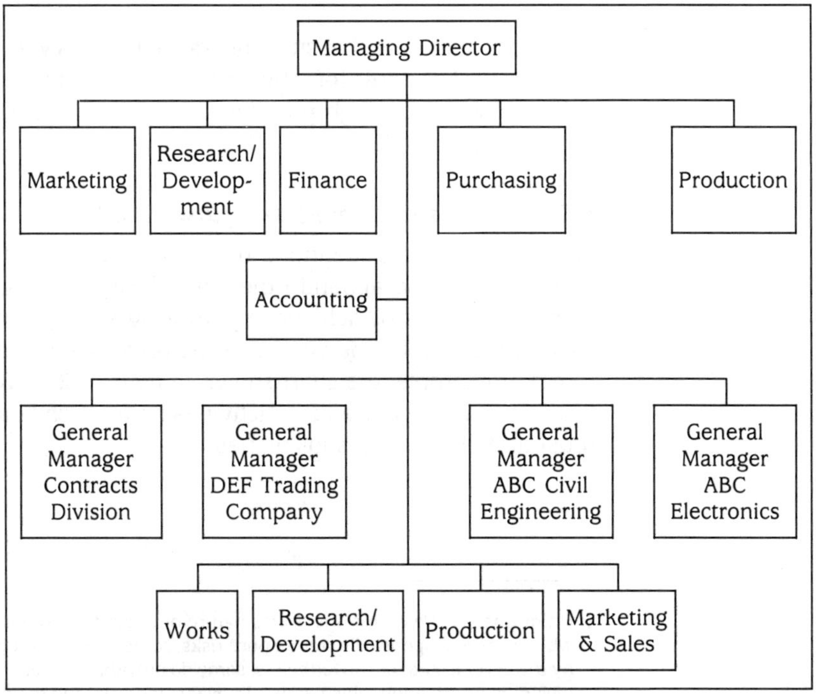

There are numerous ways in which the organisational chart may be drawn, but the salient point is that all the areas of activity should be shown. The organisational chart endeavours to identify 'areas' of risk and to highlight duplications, dependencies and risk concentrations.[2]

In contrast to organisational charts, flow charts are not restricted to the organisational structure of the firm. These charts can be used to describe any 'form' of flow within the firm, for example, the production flow, whereby raw materials are converted into the finished product. As an example, a simplified flow chart is shown in figure 6.4, which identifies broad areas of risk. From such a flow chart a more detailed chart can be compiled which considers each stage of the production process and describes likely loss-producing events, likely causes and possible consequences.

Figure 6.4
Production flow chart

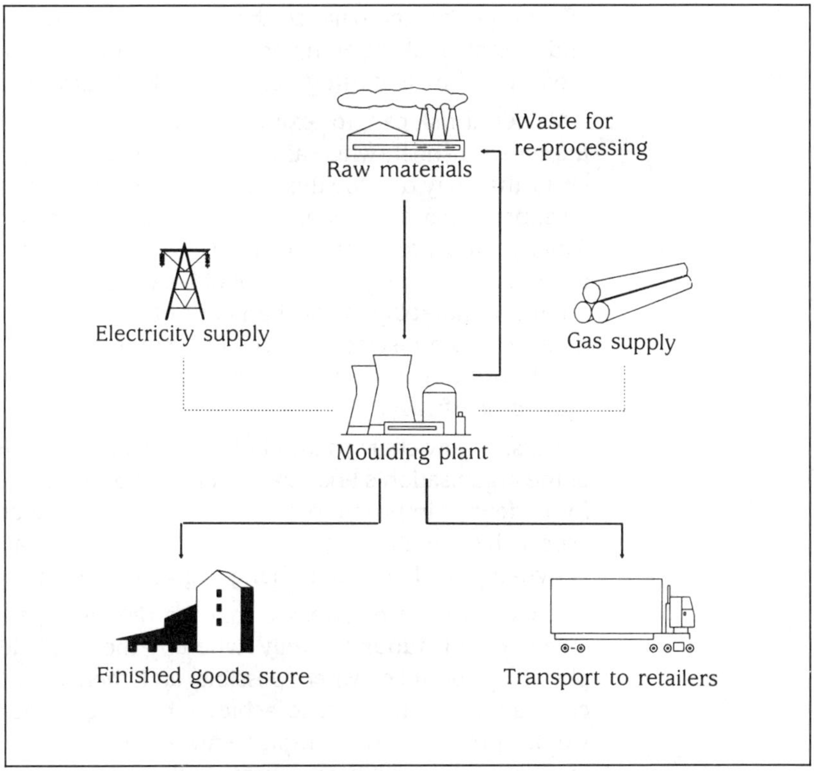

A flow chart (as depicted in figure 6.4) therefore facilitates, for example, the **identification** and **interdependency** of the various **processes** and **stages of production**, which proves useful to the risk manager in identifying risks and interpreting potential risk exposures.

Although this will, in all probability, introduce an element of business risk to the risks identified, for which no cover is available or sought, it does engender the requisite rigour and a systematic strategy. *Inter alia* this process can accomplish the following:

- ☐ the identification of risks that are extraordinary to the organisation
- ☐ the identification of a broad set of risks, for example general liability, and the focus on a sub-set within the broad set, for which cover may be sought, for example public liability
- ☐ the opportunity to discover any inter-relationship between pure and business risk where it occurs.

6.2.1.3 *Analysis of financial statements*

Another approach, more recently applied (and which is relevant to pure and business risk inter-relationships) is to identify risk by means of an analysis of **financial statements**.[3] All financial losses have an adverse effect on either the balance sheet or income (profit and loss) statement, and thus an analysis of the organisation's financial statements can prove most useful as a starting point for risk identification.

Values at risk can, for example, be readily established by reference to the balance sheet, whereafter it could be established which perils could occur that may destroy this value. The income statement may show rental expense payments which may indicate the possibility of a contractual liability exposure; or the income statement may indicate a hidden asset if, for instance, long-term rental obligations under a current lease agreement are markedly lower than current market rates. The income statement will also disclose sources of income and thereby processes from which losses may arise; such as liability to third parties in the event of product inefficacy.

Thus, a flow-chart method of identification coupled with an analysis of the organisation's financial statements provide a systematic procedure for reviewing in proper order, the company's operations. However, one aspect that should always be borne in mind, is that the business entity is dynamic and constant changes give rise to new and added risks.

Finally, it must be stressed that the risk management process should follow a **continuous strategy**, whereby the risk is identified, evaluated, physically controlled where possible, and, then provided for, from a financial standpoint. In order to achieve this, it is necessary to structure the various processes in a complementary way. If a list were compiled of the various perils which pose a threat to the organisation, without due regard to the manner in which such risk is to be financed, or without reference

3 It could be argued that this approach represents a micro-risk identification technique. Without wishing to refute this point of view, the aim of discussing accounting statement analysis under the macro-identification process, is to allow a more easy flow, or progression, of the discussion developed so far; and purports that the analysis of accounting statements is but one means of identifying macro-risk exposures facing an organisation.

to the existing insurance cover – the risk identification process will be of little use in considering additional insurance cover.

6.2.2 Micro-risk identification

As the term implies, micro-risk identification refers to the process of discovery of those risks (micro in nature) which ordinarily do not prejudice the insurance cover.[4] By way of contrast, whilst macro-risk identification 'impacts' on the insurance portfolio of an organisation, micro-risk identification is pivotal to physical risk control.[5]

Numerous methods are employed by the risk manager to identify the various risks. Dickson[3] points out that identification methods have their origins in the solving of problems within an organisation or even industry, and that the identification process requires an element of imagination. The task of matching the method to the risks is important, although it must be recognised that it is not possible to lay down firm guidelines as to how this is to be achieved. Nevertheless, having classified these broadly under macro- and micro-identification methods, the following micro-identification methods can be considered.

6.2.2.1 *Risk inspections*

The obvious and most commonly-used method to identify risks is to conduct a physical inspection.[6] This in itself represents the main advantage of this method; the sites/plants are seen firsthand and importantly, such a visit brings one into contact with those people on whom reliance is placed for much of the information concerning risks and hazards on the shop floor.

Apparent in this method are a number of drawbacks however.

- One obvious drawback is that it is time-consuming apart from the distance which may have to be travelled. Before embarking on an inspection therefore, it is essential that as much preparatory work as possible is done. This preparatory work relates primarily to preplanning or programming to ensure that the visit will coincide with other tasks to be performed. A logical approach to risk identification incorporating, for instance, the design and use of a report which is to be completed while the site is being inspected, will minimise the chance of overlooking important aspects.

---

4 By way of an example, a micro-risk situation such as failure of the water sprinkler device will not, ordinarily, prejudice insurance cover in the event of a fire, although obviously correct functioning of the system may have avoided or mitigated the loss.

5 If, for example, the danger of an inoperative water supply is identified, then risk control steps can be implemented, such as the procurement of a permit system or the installation of water gauges.

6 'Inspections', as forming an integral part of the risk management process, has been recognised by most writers in the field of risk management. See, for example, Greene & Serbein (1983, 70) and Colletta & Mayer (1984, 28).

- ☐ Another drawback arises from the fact that the effectiveness of any inspection is directly related to the competence and expertise of the individual carrying out the survey. The requisite expertise, especially for multi-faceted operations, is far-reaching indeed, and could cover many disciplines, for instance: mechanical, electrical and chemical engineering, fire prevention and security.[7]
- ☐ Significant as well, is the fact that these inspections focus on physical observations, whereas often the problems are **systems** related. For example, an inspection will not reveal loose design controls nor unsatisfactory product markings which could generate product's liability claims. Techniques such as HAZOP, FMEA, FTA, safety audits discussed below, have been developed to overcome this drawback.

6.2.2.2 *Hazard and operability studies (HAZOP)*

A *HAZOP* study has been described by Ozog[4] [8] as

> a systematic technique for identifying hazards or operability problems throughout an entire facility.

The study is a qualitative approach to risk identification which can be employed at the planning stages of projects. These studies are used most often in the chemical industry.

In essence, the *HAZOP* study is a critical enquiry into the operations of a plant, from a hazard perspective. The study follows the basic precept that those problems which are extremely complex should be broken down into manageable parts, which are then examined extensively so as to identify all associated hazards. Dickson[5] states that there are four main questions with which the *HAZOP* study is concerned:

- ☐ what the part examined is intended for?
- ☐ what the deviations from the declared intention are?
- ☐ what the causes of the deviations are?
- ☐ what the consequences of the deviations could be?

Simplistically, each segment of a process is studied to ascertain the intention of each. Lists are then compiled, showing all possible deviations from the normal operating conditions, as well as, how (cause) these deviations might arise and what the consequences of these might be.

---

7 As mentioned before, companies engage the services of professional risk management organisations who employ experts in these fields. By virtue of their specialisation, they are in a position to draw comparisons between one company and another and thereby achieve compliance standards.

It should also be noted that for those companies whose land-based asset values necessitate the absorption of worldwide insurance capacity, often the direct and the reinsurance market will require surveys to be conducted by their in-house risk surveyors.

8 Ozog refers to an earlier work by Lawley (1974).

HAZOP studies have become popular in practice, especially in the USA where it is estimated that at least half of the chemical industry has utilised the technique for new facilities or processes. With existing facilities, a typical interval between reviews is from one to five years. These studies have been found to be effectual in micro-risk identification.[6]

The main advantage of the study is that identification is carried out in an extensive manner allowing each part of a complicated system to be examined in detail. In view also, of the diverse skills required to conduct the *HAZOP* study correctly, it is necessary to involve a team of people, and this in itself has its advantages. Such a team approach encourages communication and is synergetic, which is a proven positive attribute in any risk management department.

Its main disadvantage is the time involved in carrying out the *HAZOP* study. It calls for a considerable investment in time and resources.

Probably the most famous example of where a *HAZOP* study could have prevented a disaster, is the Flixborough Disaster which occurred on the 1st of June 1974. In this case alterations were carried out at a chemical plant. The alterations involved pipework of which the support gave way causing the pipework to fail and releasing 36 tons of cyclohexane into the atmosphere, which caused an unconfined vapour cloud. The cloud ignited, resulting in an explosion killing 28 people and causing millions of rands of damage. The possible causes and consequences of the alterations could have been determined and the appropriate risk control steps taken to avoid the disaster.

The *HAZOP* is applied to each item of equipment and is carried out by addressing standard questions or considerations to the equipment. These considerations include:

- ☐ what deviations could arise?
- ☐ how can these arise?
- ☐ what are the implications?
- ☐ any further implications.

Applied to the Flixborough situation:

- ☐ the pipe could break if the supports were not adequate
- ☐ cyclohexane will escape
- ☐ a massive explosion will ensue.

6.2.2.3 *Failure mode and effect analysis (FMEA)*

Ozog[7] describes the primary function of an *FMEA* study as:

> . . . to evaluate the frequency and consequences of component failures on the process.

This method, whilst identifying risk sources, concentrates more on the effect of failure, with the objective of minimising its consequences. *FMEA* is therefore usually applied to designated equipment.[9] The analysis is thus primarily concerned with the evaluation of consequences, and the frequency of failures. The desired objective is to attain a fail-safe failure mode.

The major disadvantage of this technique is that the analysis does not extend to operational procedures. Because *FMEA* concentrates on component failures and not on errors in operating and other procedures, it has a limited application. The method is also tedious to apply to complex installations.

6.2.2.4 *Fault-tree analysis (FTA)*

FTA is not a means of identifying risk, but primarily a technique of analysing risk.[8] [10] It is consequently used only after some other technique or risk inspection has been carried out, and a major risk or hazard been identified.

The fault-tree is a diagrammatical representation of all events which may give rise to some major event. Fault-tree analysis concentrates on ascertaining all the possible combinations of individual failures that can lead to, what is termed, the *top event* or *ultimate risk*. For example, if the risk of a major toxic release (seen as the top event) has been identified by some other means, *FTA* is applied to analyse the factors or combinations which could result in the top event occurring.

These combinations are shown in a sequential arrangement on a fault tree which indicates the probability of failure of each individual event. By estimating the individual failure probabilities, and then applying the appropriate probability theory to the expressions, the probability or frequency of the top event can be determined. Having determined the top event probability, sensitivity analysis can be performed, by altering the various constituent factors to gauge the effect of alterations to the system, or to bring the top event frequency to a desired level.

Figure 6.5 shows a fault tree with the top event indicated as a tank explosion of which the frequency of explosion is 0,0002 per year (or 1 explosion every 5 000 years). The top event is contingent on both pressure

9 *FMEA* can be applied, for instance, when considering the installation of overhead electrical conductors; should any of these detach and fall to the ground they may pose a serious risk to the public. To overcome this threat one might position catch wires below the overhead conductors in an attempt to achieve a fail-safe failure mode.

10 The view taken in this study, and one adopted by Dickson (1987, 27) is that the debate on whether identification of risk is distinctly separate from analysis of risk, is irrelevant. Hence, *FTA*, which is a risk-analysis technique is included in the risk-identification methods. Such a rationale also promotes the integration of such activities as identification and analysis, as opposed to presenting these activities as being discrete and possibly unrelated.

rising **and** the relief valve failing to operate. Pressure will rise if either the pump fails **or** there is an excessive input of the raw material. The relative frequency or probability of failure of each individual event is also shown, which collectively ascertains the probability of the top event occurring.

Figure 6.5
Fault tree illustrating individual failures leading to a top event occurring[11]

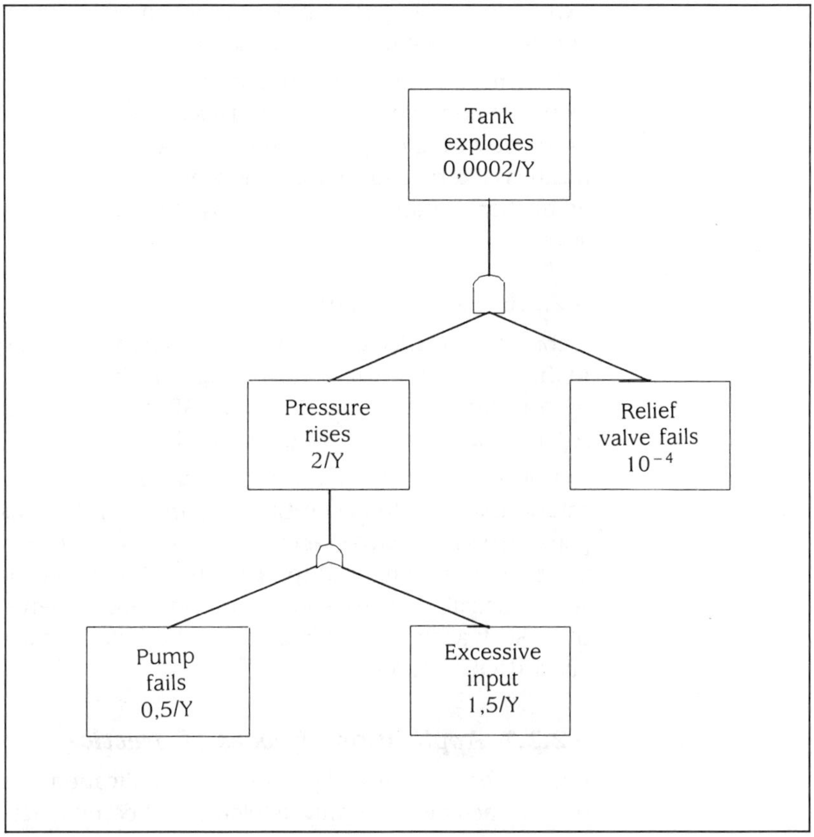

The main advantages of *FTA* stem from the fact that this method represents a structured approach to risk identification. It simplifies analysis of complex systems and traces causes and impacts. Apart from the relatively long time it takes to correctly carry out the study, it suffers from one major problem (not apparent in the other methods described): the derivation of probabilities. Should the relevant probabilities not be accurate, then the ensuing calculation, particularly the measurement of the likelihood of the top event, will be suspect.

11 This example has been taken from Dickson (1987, 72).

6.2.2.5 *Hazard indices*

Dickson[9] describes the hazard index as a technique which attempts to express the degree of hazard by using a number. In doing so, indices can be used to identify process areas with significant loss potential. The basic philosophy entails the measurement of the likelihood of loss and the expression of the result as a number to which others can be compared and annual changes monitored.

The most common method of expressing the degree of hazard is the Dow Fire and Explosion Index. This index is used primarily for insurance or underwriting purposes. The Dow Index has been expanded to include business interruption losses, and whilst various attempts have been made at further expansion and improvement, they have met with limited success.[12]

6.2.2.6 *Safety audits*

A common practice used to identify safety risks is the general safety audit. In the course of the year most industrial plants are inspected and audited by a number of people. In South Africa it is mandatory for the safety representative to inspect the workplace.

A very important aspect in the field of risk management is personnel safety (particularly in the USA and the UK). Various systems to ensure personnel safety have been devised, including the use of specially designed safety audit sheets used to facilitate risk identification. The safety audit sheets usually include some statutory requirements and defined objectives, such as those stipulated by the National Occupational Safety Association (NOSA) *MBO* system.

6.2.2.7 *Application of codes of practice*

Application of codes of practice The application of established codes of practice achieves not only an element of compliance with standards, and hence risk control, **but** also serves as a means of identifying risks.

In the manufacturing process, for example, risk identification techniques may not identify all the numerous sources which could give rise to a product liability claim. Often the risk source is only really identified when the product is returned and a claim arising out of the risk source, is presented.

Systematic compliance with legislative and other authoritative codes of practice will clearly mitigate the risks, since the sources have in effect already been identified and treated as specified. As an example, the use of status markings, and quarantine criteria (standard requirements in terms

12 See Dickson (1987, 77-83) where, using the Dow Index, an illustration is provided of how a hazard index is constructed.

of SABS code 0157 for Quality Management Systems) will treat the **risk of incorrect release** of the product simply because it is covered by the code.

6.2.2.8 *Research*

Naturally, situations do exist where the identification of risk cannot be readily accomplished. The intricacy of the product, for example, may dictate that observation, however systematised, will fail to identify the associated risk.[13]

Under circumstances such as these, specialist research, often on an ongoing basis, is required to identify and evaluate the effects of associated risk. Moreover, the complexity of situations of this type should not be underestimated, as there may be a time relationship between the circumstance and the risk,[14] and even the occasion where application of the product engenders risk in certain conditions or environments, and not in others. Unfortunately, these aspects more often than not, mean that research is conducted after the loss has occurred, which renders research not an identifying process, but one concerned with understanding the risk and perhaps mitigating its effects.

6.2.3 Features in the risk-identification process

In concluding this section on risk identification, it is pertinent to enumerate certain features of importance.

- ☐ It is unlikely that one particular method or technique of identification will be sufficient to identify all the risk exposures and address all the problems associated with such risks. It is more opportune to consider a combination of methods in order to ensure that identification is as complete and encompassing as possible.
- ☐ Since the various methods themselves have developed in response to solving problems within particular industries, certain methods are found more useful in some industries than others.[15]
- ☐ The process of identification is greatly assisted and enhanced by consultation with as many people outside the risk management department as possible. This implies consulting with various line managers

---

13 As an example, it is known today that asbestos can cause occupational disease (asbestosis). Observation of the product will not reveal this associated risk, and hence specialist research is required to correlate the substance with the disease.

14 Reference to a time relationship implies in this context that the risk factor might not exist *ab initio* but that over time it might develop. An example may be the risk of metal fatigue or stress corrosion.

15 A flow chart, for example, is an appropriate method of identifying risk in an industrial process which involves goods or materials moving through the different stages. Where, however, flow is not the main activity, another method of identification would be more suitable.

and others in the workforce who know the organisation and who possibly also have their own views on the risks which exist.

- ☐ Risk identification is an on-going process, and should not be regarded as an isolated or once-off exercise. It is essential that risks, which have been identified, are monitored and new risks highlighted.
- ☐ Finally, risk identification entails a certain degree of imagination. Whilst past routines used in risk identification do provide some system and rigour to the activity, there should be no limit imposed on any lateral approach to identification.

6.3 Summary

The model for risk management developed in Chapter Four identified the relevant steps in the risk management process. Risk identification and risk evaluation were shown as the preparatory steps to risk control and the financing of losses. The aim of this chapter was to provide insight into the identification and evaluation of risk.

In so doing the intention was also to address the relative neglect, in the general risk management texts, of these aspects of the discipline. Since risk identification and evaluation represent integral parts of the total risk management process, any holistic approach to the subject requires that these steps be understood and their rôle appreciated.

The emphasis is on developing a structured and integrated process of risk management. Hence, the question of risk identification was itself viewed from a reasonably rigorous standpoint; by first describing a macro-identification process, and thereafter a micro-identification process.

The various methodologies constituting such macro- and micro-identification were referred to and described. Important features of risk identification were also enumerated. It was stressed that the various risk identification methods must not be seen in isolation. Risk identification, it was stated, is a dynamic process in which it is essential that risks which have been identified are evaluated and monitored, and new risks highlighted.

Bibliography

Allen, TC 1972. 'Quantitative risk management methodology – A historical perspective.' *The Journal of Commerce.* New York, March.

Colletta, C & Mayer, JH 1984. 'A case study in risk control.' *Risk Management.* October.

Dickson, GCA 1987. 'Risk analysis.' *Institute of Risk Management.*

Greene, MR & Serbein, ON 1983. *Risk management: Text and cases.* Virginia: Reston Publishing Co. Inc.

Lawley, HG 1974. 'Operability studies and hazard analysis.' *Loss Prevention.* New York, Vol 8, AIChE.

O'Connell, JJ 1976. 'The environment-systematic risk identification.' *Risk Management.* March.

Ozog, H 1985. 'Hazard identification, analysis and control.' *Chemical Engineering.* February.

Williams, CA & Heins, RM 1981. *Risk management and insurance.* New York: McGraw-Hill Inc.

Endnotes

[1] O'Connell, 1976, 34.

[2] Dickson, 1987, 43-46.

[3] Dickson, 1987, 28.

[4] Ozog, 1985, 161.

[5] Dickson, 1987, 57.

[6] Dickson, 1987, 57-66.

[7] Ozog, 1985, 161.

[8] Ozog, 1985, 161.

[9] Dickson, 1987, 77.

7 RISK EVALUATION AND RISK ASSESSMENT

7.1 Introduction

> Risk evaluation can be defined as the appraisal, the assessment or the finding of the numerical expression for risk.

In a practical sense, risk evaluation becomes the conduit, per the model developed, between risk identification and risk treatment.

Risk evaluation fulfils a dual rôle: one of facilitating the method of treatment (physical and financial), the other of measuring effect or degree of success following implementation. If one describes the relevance of risk evaluation thus, then it becomes understandable that most academic research has been conducted in this area.[1] [1]

The purpose of examining risk evaluation in this section is to achieve the desired sequence of thought in developing a methodology for risk management. This section introduces further evaluation parameters, as an extension to those discussed under Chapter Three which provided a definition of risk and where consideration was given to the quantification of risk. Also, the intention is to lay the foundation for the development of specific evaluation techniques which will be considered in depth in Chapter Fourteen.

The aim in this chapter is to provide insight into the following:

- ☐ loss dimensions
- ☐ loss frequencies and probabilities
- ☐ loss/frequency distributions
- ☐ variability as a measure of risk.

7.2 Loss dimensions

From a risk management perspective, one of the most important considerations is determining the **size** or **quantum** of a possible loss. The consideration transcends all aspects of risk management. Viewed 'internally' it provides one with a backdrop against which efforts to manage the risk can be placed. And viewed 'externally' it becomes a departure point from which the insurance market (or other financing mechanism) gauges the risk.

---

1 See Chapter Fourteen where a review is provided of the statistical risk evaluation theories and techniques.

By way of illustration consider an organisation which has three operational locations as follows:

Table 7.1
Hypothetical asset values per location

Location	Asset value (R m)
A	25
B	15
C	10
Total	50

It is clear that an insurer who for example has underwritten the risk of fire is **exposed** to a **possible** claim of R50m. It is of course unlikely that all locations will suffer a fire and that all will consequently burn to the ground in the same time period; in all probability the largest exposure will emanate from location A.[2]

Whilst the largest exposure may emanate from location A, one might find that this location itself comprises separate asset elements and that it is therefore unlikely that the insurer's probable exposure from fire is location A's full asset value of R25m. In determining more accurately the loss dimension the following measures are developed:[3]

- ☐ maximum foreseeable loss (*MFL*)[4]
- ☐ estimated maximum loss (*EML*)
- ☐ normal loss expectancy (*NLE*)

7.2.1 Maximum foreseeable loss (MFL)

The **maximum foreseeable loss** (*MFL*) is defined as the value of the **largest** possible loss from a single event which is reasonably foreseeable under the most adverse conditions.

In the case of a single asset (for example, a building or a vessel) the *MFL* would probably be the value of the asset, since it is conceivable that the

2 All the information as depicted in the table is nevertheless important, for the insurer may for instance need to arrange reinsurance protection for itself should the company not be in a position to carry the entire exposure.

3 Little has been written concerning these measures and consequently agreement does not always exist amongst various writers on the terminology used. This text adopts the terminology and definition provided by Friedlander (1977, 26 *et seq.*), which has found wide acceptance in British and South African insurance practice.

See also, Berliner (1985, 314-321).

The MPY (maximum probable yearly aggregate loss) and EML (estimated maximum loss) are discussed from a statistical standpoint in Chapter Fourteen.

4 A synonym for MFL is MPL (maximum possible loss). It is suggested that, since a great deal of confusion exists concerning the interpretation of these and other terms describing loss dimensions, the two main measures used to describe severity of loss should be confined to MFL and EML.

entire asset could be destroyed (as a result, of fire, for example). In those situations where there exists a concentration of single assets (location of buildings) the *MFL* is not **necessarily** the combined asset value should the single assets be 'designed' to contain the peril from spreading. Nevertheless, it should be emphasised that the *MFL* as a measure, is the **pessimistic** forecast of loss size.

It should be noted that different *EML* and *MFL* values exist for the different perils, and that the determination of these values is largely subjective.

7.2.2 Estimated maximum loss (EML)[5]

> The **estimated maximum loss** (*EML*) is defined as the reasonably estimated loss size from a single event, *given* that risk control measures instituted do not entirely perform the task of loss containment or loss reduction attributed to them.[2] It is generally less than a total loss.

The *EML* therefore, as a measure of loss, is usually smaller than the *MFL*. Often insurers will adopt the *EML* figure as the reasonable limit of maximum exposure faced, although recognising that a higher maximum loss may indeed eventuate.

Usually *MFL* and *EML* measures relate to the material damage resulting from fire and explosion perils, although such measures may also incorporate consequential losses due to business interruption.

In determining the fire and explosion *MFL/EML*, for example, it is necessary to do the following:

- ☐ divide the risk into fire areas, that is, an area formed by one or more buildings/compartments not separated structurally or spatially
- ☐ determine the fire area with the highest potential loss, taking into consideration the fireload (quantity of combustible materials within the fire area) and the likelihood of explosion and susceptibility of plant/goods to smoke, water, corrosion damage and the like
- ☐ estimate the *MFL/EML* that could be sustained. The *MFL* would be the maximum monetary loss which could be sustained on a risk exposure as a result of a single fire or explosion when the most unfavourable circumstances combine and when, as a consequence, the fire is not at all or not satisfactorily fought against and is therefore only stopped by impassable obstacles or by the lack of physical property. The *EML* would be an estimate of the monetary loss which could be sustained as a result of a single fire or explosion considered to be within the

5 The American literature usually makes reference to PML (probable maximum loss), being the maximum amount of loss foreseeable under ordinary circumstances.

bounds of probability. The estimate ignores such remote co-incidents and catastrophes as may be possibilities but which still remain unlikely.

7.2.3 Normal loss expectancy (NLE)

The measures of loss defined hitherto purport to give a dimension to **maximum** losses possible, expected or probable under varying conditions and assumptions. There is therefore a 'catastrophe loss-type' connotation associated with these measures. Fortunately however, the vast majority of losses do not fall into catastrophe categorisation; these relatively minor-type loss quantums make up the *normal loss expectancy* (*NLE*) measure.[3]

> The **normal loss expectancy** (*NLE*) is the average loss that could result from a single event given that all risk control measures operate as expected.

7.3 Loss frequencies and probabilities

The process of risk evaluation, as has been shown, entails the numeric assessment of risk exposure. The section on loss dimensions concentrated on providing various definitions of loss **quantums** which find use in the field of risk management.

Interrelated with loss dimension is the question of **likelihood** of loss, which expressed in a numerical manner implies **frequency** and **probability** of loss. Reference to this concept has of course been made: in defining *normal loss expectancy*, for example, the qualification was expressed that, ordinarily, the majority of losses experienced do not fall into the catastrophe-type categorisation. Simply, this states that ordinarily there is a low frequency of catastrophe losses (high quantum, or severity) evidenced.

The added dimension of frequency or probability of loss becomes the remaining component in the evaluation process of assessing the risk.[6]

7.3.1 Loss frequency

The loss frequency is the measure of the number of events which occur in a defined interval. The frequency may relate, for example, to the number of motor accidents per year, the frequency of industrial accidents per hundred man-hours worked, and the like.

Since risk management's concern is also with the consequences of events one could, by way of illustration, observe the frequency of motor loss costs arranged in cost intervals, as depicted in table 7.2.

6 The section on the theory of probability and its application to risk measurement in Chapter Three, section 3.7, showed that in computing the pure premium, average loss frequency was combined with average loss severity to arrive at the expected loss.

Table 7.2
Frequency: motor loss cost interval

Cost interval (R)	Number of times the loss falls in the interval
1 – 250	6
251 – 500	11
501 – 750	20
751 – 1 000	8
1 001 – 1 250	5
1 251 – 1 500	4
1 501 – 1 750	3
1 751 – 2 000	2
2 001 – 2 250	1
2 251 – 2 500	0
2 501 – 2 750	1
Total	61

Table 7.2 shows that the motor fleet under review experienced 61 accidents during the period defined, and that there is a relatively low frequency of large losses and conversely, a relatively high frequency of smaller magnitude losses.

The tabulation of the frequency of events against respective intervals of loss costs, as depicted in the table, is useful when transforming the results into a graphical representation (distribution curves). Such distributions, have properties that are used for predictive purposes in the field of risk management.

7.3.2 Loss probability

The notion of probability and its applicability to the discipline of risk management was discussed in Chapter Three, where the definition given was that probability is the relative frequency with which an event occurs, as the number of observations tend towards infinity. More specifically, it was stated that relative frequency is the proportion of time an event takes place, and that the relative frequency with which it takes place in the long run is its probability.

There is a close association therefore between frequency and the concept of probability; both represent expressions of, or surrogates for, **likelihood**.

It is not the intention, in this section, to expound further upon the concept of probability. Rather, the intention is to reinforce its application in the process of loss predictability and hence risk evaluation.

However, it is important to point to an area of confusion which is often apparent among risk management practitioners. Inductive probability theory suggests the estimation of an outcome of a future event by observing its relative frequency of occurrence in the past.

There must be clarity of definition and full understanding of the terms *event*, *outcome*, *frequency of occurrence*, *relative frequency* and *probability*. The contention is not that such terms are generally not clearly understood, but that ill-defined reference is made to these, so that probabilities are sometimes 'assigned' to events which do not display a probability of occurrence but **certainty** of occurrence.[7]

Consequently, reference is made for instance to a probability of an accident occurring, when there is certainty that an accident (**event**) will occur – whereas the intention is to refer to the probability of an accident or occurrence having an **outcome** of, say, **X loss value**, where such probability is estimated by observing the outcome's relative **frequency of occurrence**.

7.4 Loss/frequency distributions

Table 7.2 summarised a loss experience pertaining to a motor fleet: it showed the number of accidents against costs (expressed in intervals). It is useful to depict such findings graphically. The data in table 7.2 plots what is referred to as a *frequency distribution*, illustrated below.

Figure 7.1 Frequency distribution for motor loss costs

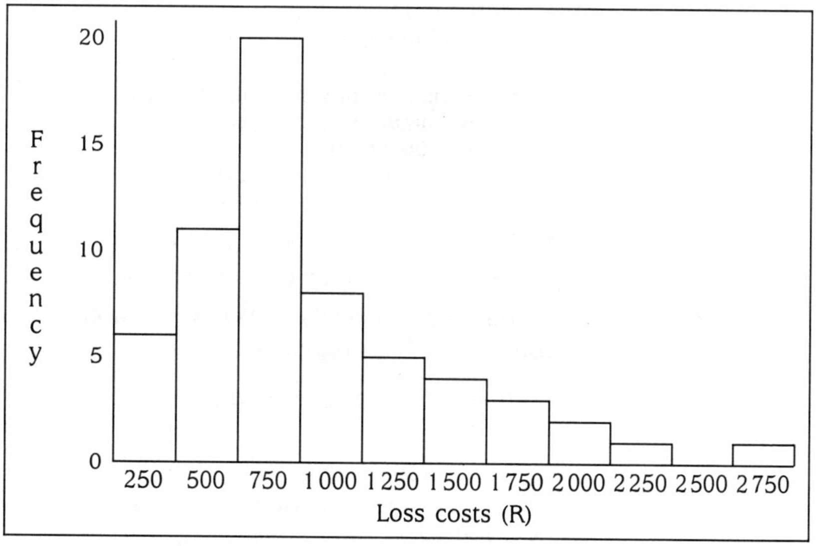

7 Reference to **certain** events not displaying a probability is made loosely in this context, since certainty can be assigned to a probability – viz. 1.

The loss tendency is clearly discernible from the diagram. The larger quantum losses are experienced less frequently than the relatively lower quantum losses.

There exist various curves which describe similar loss tendencies (and other tendencies) which have been studied and whose properties, for example find predictive use in the field of risk management.[4] This latter aspect is dealt with further in Chapter Fourteen. Suffice it to say here that distribution curves are significant as instruments in the valuation process in the management of risk. Three distributions are of particular importance.

- ☐ The *Normal distribution* is of importance because of the Central Limit Theorem,[8] and its application[9] to sampling theory to determine the mean from the sample.
- ☐ The *Binomial distribution* is of interest to the risk manager because it deals with situations where the outcome could be either a success or a failure. In a risk management context, it is interpreted as a loss-producing event or no loss-producing event occurring.

  Thus, a risk manager who has a fleet of *n* vehicles may wish to know what the probability is that no or at least one loss-event will occur during the year of insurance.

  The *Binomial distribution* is expressed as follows:[5]

The probability of getting x accidents out of a fleet size of n is:

$$f(x) = \frac{n!}{x!\,(n-x)!} \cdot p^x \cdot (1-p)^{n-x} \qquad \text{for } x = 0, 1, 2, \ldots n$$

where

n = number of vehicles in the fleet

x = number of accidents

x! = x.(x-1).(x-2) . . . 1

p = constant probability that a vehicle will be involved in an accident

Typically 90% of vehicles are not involved in accidents during a year,[10] or 10% are involved in one or more accidents each year.[11]

Thus, the probability of having zero accidents in one year in a fleet consisting of n vehicles, is:

$$f(0) = \frac{n!}{0!(n-0)!} (0.1)^0 \, (1\text{-}0.1)^{n-0}$$

$$= 0.9^n$$

8 Refer to Chapter Three, section 3.7 for a summary of the Central Limit Theorem.

9 See section 7.5.

10 See table 3.2 in Chapter Three.

11 Williams & Heins (1986, 651) impose a restriction that no vehicle can be involved in more than one accident in a year. The approach in this example differs slightly, in that this restriction is not imposed. Either the vehicle is involved in an accident or it is not.

From the above equation, it can be seen that, as n (the size of the motor fleet) increases, the probability of having no accidents [f(0)] tends towards zero.

For any fleet of reasonable size, the risk manager is faced with an almost certainty that a loss will occur.

The question thus becomes not if a loss will take place, but simply one of how large the aggregate loss will be, rather than whether a loss will take place. The risk which faces the risk manager is the variation around the estimated aggregate cost of losses.

- ☐ The *Poisson distribution* is of importance because if *n* is large and *p* is small, the *Binomial distribution* approximates the *Poisson distribution* and the *Poisson distribution* is easier to deal with since it has only one parameter which needs to be estimated, namely λ, the mean or expected value. The *Poisson distribution* can be expressed as follows:[6]

$$f(x) = \frac{\lambda^x . e^{-\lambda}}{x!} \qquad \text{for } x = 0, 1, 2, 3, \ldots n$$

where

λ = mean or expected value[12]

e = 2.71828

x = number of accidents

x! = x.(x-1).(x-2) . . . 1

To apply this distribution to the above problem λ is interpreted as the *expected*, or average number of accidents given a fleet size of *n*. Therefore, with a fleet size of *n*, one would expect (0.1.n) vehicles to be involved in an accident.

The probability of having no accident is thus:

$$f(0) = \frac{(0.1.n)^0 . e^{-(0.1.n)}}{0!}$$

$$= e^{-0.1n}$$

Again, as n increases f(0) decreases; or the probability of having no accident tends towards zero.

7.5 Variability as a measure of risk

Risk implies that actual outcomes are likely to differ from expected or anticipated outcomes. The evaluation process is concerned primarily with the measurement of risk, which process can then assist in decision-making concerning how the risk will be treated, both via risk control and financially.

12 An estimate for λ is *n.p* where *n* equals the fleet size and *p* equals the probability that a vehicle will be involved in an accident.

In risk management, one end-objective is the estimation of the total loss amount (aggregate) which an exposure or group of exposure units is likely to suffer during a one-year period.[13] What is sought is an estimate of the probability distributions (as described in the previous section) of losses of various types that face the firm, which can then be aggregated to estimate the distribution of total loss costs. The model for evaluating risk focuses on such probability distribution(s) of possible outcomes for total annual losses.

Supposing that there are *n* number of possible outcomes for total annual losses, then the 'weighted average' value can be calculated to give the expected value of annual loss costs, E(x), which mathematically is defined as:

$$E(x) = \sum_{i=1}^{n} p_i . x_i$$

where:

$E(x)$ = expected value of annual loss costs
p_i = probability of the ith outcome
x_i = monetary value of outcome i
n = number of possible outcomes

Figure 7.2 shows a probability distribution of loss costs, where E(x) is the mean or expected value of loss costs, and $Pr(x_i)$ is the probability assigned to particular loss outcomes, (x_i).

Figure 7.2 Probability distribution of loss costs

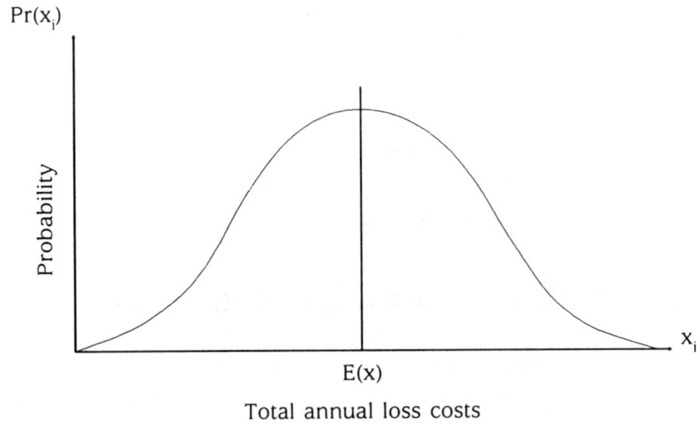

13 This value is termed the *maximum probable yearly aggregate loss* (*MPY*). Chapter Fourteen, section 14.2 deals with the estimation of the *MPY*, using past loss data.

Risk can be defined as the expected **dispersion** of the loss outcomes. Thus, risk is measured by the **dispersion** around the expected loss outcome E(x). The variance or standard deviation measures this dispersion. Mathematically, the variance $\sigma^2(x)$ is:

$$\sigma^2(x) = \sum_{i=1}^{n}(x_i - E(x))^2 . p_i$$

where

$\sigma^2(x)$ = variance

$E(x)$ = expected value of annual loss costs

p_i = probability of the ith outcome

x_i = monetary value of outcome i

n = number of possible outcomes

The standard deviation is simply the square root of the variance. Thus, the variance or standard deviation is the surrogate for risk; it is equivalent to defining risk as the variability of loss outcomes, where the greater the variability, the greater the risk. Such mathematical expression of risk can be seen to coincide with the definition of risk afforded in Chapter Three which contended that the degree of risk is solely dependent upon the variability rather than upon the probability value surrounding an event or its outcome.

7.6 Summary

Risk is amenable to expression in numerical terms. The insurer is primarily interested in the magnitude of the exposure which he has agreed to insure. This magnitude is expressed in concepts such as *MFL*, *EML* and *NFL*.

When probability theory is applied to individual losses it quickly becomes apparent that, as the exposure units increase, the risk which the risk manager faces, is not whether or not an individual event will take place, but rather the variation around the expected aggregate loss.

Bibliography

Allen, TC 1972. 'Quantitative risk management methodology – A historical perspective.' *The Journal of Commerce.* New York, March.

Berliner, B 1985. 'Large risks and limits of insurability.' *The Geneva Papers on Risk and Insurance.* Vol. 10, No. 37, October.

Cummins, JD & Freifelder, LR 1979. 'Statistical analysis in risk management: Analyzing loss severity.' *Risk Management.* March.

Cummins, JD & Freifelder, LR 1979. 'Statistical analysis in risk management: Analyzing loss frequency.' *Risk Management.* February.

Freund, JE, Williams, FJ & Perles, BM 1988. *Elementary business statistics: The modern approach.* New Jersey: Prentice-Hall, Inc.

Friedlander, AW 1977. 'Assessing fire loss potentials.' *Risk Management.* October.

Endnotes

[1] Allen, 1972, 2.

[2] Friedlander, 1977, 27.

[3] Friedlander, 1977, 27.

[4] Cummins & Freifelder, 1979, 20-26; 32-36.

[5] Freund, Williams & Perles, 1988, 213.

[6] Freund, Williams & Perles, 1988, 224.

8 RISK CONTROL

8.1 Introduction

As the title suggests, this chapter concerns itself with issues related to the physical control of risk, or as it is referred to in most instances, the prevention and control of losses, or risk control.[1] That which has preceded this chapter has in effect set the background against which this section and those that follow, should be viewed. Having identified and evaluated risk, the stage now has been reached where it has to be treated.

The direction followed will be to describe the meaning of risk control and, by reference to its development, to set out its principles and objectives. Approaches to loss prevention and control are discussed, and specific programmes and authoritative requirements designed to control risk in certain areas, are described.

It must be noted that the professional disciplines encompassed within the risk control activity are both broad and specialised.[2] The intention is not, therefore, to provide an authoritative discussion of such risk control disciplines or programmes, but to describe the risk control activity within the context of the overall risk management discipline, so as to achieve the necessary integration of elements constituting risk management.[3]

Risks can be differentiated broadly as those being related to assets (property) and those that give rise to liabilities. In view of some

1 The aspect of prevention or control is referred to by various terms and consensus does not always exist as to their exact meaning. Earlier South African risk management models used the term *physical risk management* (Vivian, R.W., 1985, 109). British writers also use the term *physical risk control* (Diacon, S.R. & Carter, R.L., 1984, 73; 1988, 78).

Historically, the emphasis on managing risks has been on the purchase of insurance ie, a financial technique. In the late 1970's and early 1980's the integrated or holistic model, which includes preventative measures, began to be applied in South Africa. In order to distinguish preventative from financial measures, the former were referred to as physical risk management steps, and were depicted as such in various articles published at the time.

See Vivian (1985, 108-109) and Vivian (1987, 10-13).

The term *Physical Risk Management* also appears in English literature (Carter, 1982, 5). The term also appears, for example, in the 1984 B.A. Curriculum of the Glasgow College of Technology and the Prospectus of the Institute of Risk Management. The American literature refers mainly to *loss control* and sometimes *risk control.*

2 In this regard it is appropriate to consider the observations reported by Crockford (1982, 171):

> The theories of risk management which have emerged from the insurance world have very largely ignored, and have been ignored by, the forms of risk management which have been developed in the engineering world. It would be necessary to decide whether or not the literature from this area forms part of the literature of risk management to be studied. A possible solution would be to treat this literature as that of a specialist field of loss control and to subject it to the same criteria for admission as the literature of, say, fire prevention.

3 See Chapter Ten, figure 10.3, which depicts the integrated risk management process, having given consideration to the risk financing element and to the process of risk management in the context of the corporate objective of shareholders' wealth maximisation.

fundamental differences between these two categories, a separate discussion on the legal basis of the latter risks and the means of countering them is dealt with in the chapter which follows (Chapter Nine).

8.2 The meaning of risk control

It is not too difficult to define what is meant by risk control; literature abounds with examples categorising actions by individuals and organisations which aim towards preventing and controlling risks and resultant losses.[4]

Depending on the depth of analysis however, public perception of risk control ranges from it being defined as any process which prevents losses, or curtails their effects; to it being a complex philosophy which incorporates a number of subtle definitions and disciplines. It may of course be suggested that complexity of definition is often the result of an attempt to highlight a concept or phenomenon which is not normally readily recognised. It can be said that this precept applies to the definition of risk control.

Today, in risk management circles, debates are held regarding the differences, if indeed any, between loss control and risk control, and whether these concepts constitute what is termed *physical risk management*. The reaction is not altogether unexpected; non-financial aspects of risk management have been traditionally fragmented within an organisation, being treated as separate activities. Thus, in an effort to integrate, subtle differences in definition are bound to arise.

For the purpose of this discussion the following course is adopted. Risk control entails any activity which is aimed at preventing losses or minimising the consequence of losses that may arise from all pure risks facing the organisation; even those which are relatively unpredictable and which pose a threat to the organisation's existence. The aim is to treat risk control as pervasive in the business environment and not to limit it to the activities of prevention of losses which are seen as inevitable – those activities which can be described as loss control activities.

Clearly, the concept which is being emphasised is that risk management is a holistic discipline: loss control must be viewed within the context of risk control; risk control must be viewed within the discipline of physical risk management; which when integrated with the discipline of financial risk management constitutes the science of risk management.

---

4 The seminal comprehensive work in the field of risk control appears to be MacDonald (1966, 22 *et seq.*).

Risk control is therefore defined as a method of countering risk. In the broader sense (as intended), it includes all activities conducted for the purpose of:

- ☐ eliminating or reducing the factors that may cause loss to a person or organisation, and
- ☐ minimising the actual loss that occurs when preventative methods have not been fully effective.

It was stated in Chapter Three that risk (pure) implies uncertainty surrounding:

- ☐ the magnitude of losses
- ☐ the frequency of losses.

In order to achieve consistency, and notwithstanding the broader definition provided above, risk control should be directed at controlling the two uncertainties of severity and frequency.[5] However, since risk management is concerned with the management of risk, risk control is not only directed at the elements of uncertainty but also encompasses management planning, even before an event occurs. As will be seen, contingency and emergency plans are preformulated plans designed to deal with events, if and when they occur, and these fall within the ambit of risk control.

Most risk control activities are therefore directed towards the minimisation of future losses, and these may be seen as falling into two categories. Firstly, there are those pointing toward **controlling** the (previously identified or detected) possible adverse occurrence and then endeavouring to eliminate it, and secondly, those directed towards **minimising the loss** after the occurrence has taken place (the loss control activities).[6]

Risk control may be measured in economic terms or in humanitarian terms. The former is generally applied when prevention of property losses is considered, whilst the latter measure is relevant to the loss of human life values. There are cases where both measures coincide as, for instance, in the prevention of industrial accidents.

Risk control is, by implication, mostly possible and effective in relation to particular risks, which as defined in Chapter Three, section 3.4, are risks which the exposed person or organisation has considerable control over the causes thereof. Control activities are effective in handling the

5 This emphasis is quite significant in the risk evaluation stage.

6 By means of an example, risk and loss control can be focused on:
- designing contingency plans to deal with the eventuality of a fire
- developing fire detection and fire extinguishing techniques
- dealing with the fire while it is occurring
- once the fire has ceased to burn, endeavouring to recover as rapidly as possible and as much as possible through salvage, and minimising the disruption caused by the fire.

risks of fire, burglary, boiler explosion, and the like. Their effectiveness can be said to be directly proportional to the degree of control that can be exercised. Conversely, such activities are not as effective as regards fundamental risks, which are essentially economic, social, political or natural in their origin.

8.3 Development of risk control

8.3.1 Introduction

In understanding current risk control activities it is appropriate to describe briefly their historical development. Attention will be given to the development of loss control in the areas of fire, explosion and industrial accidents.[7]

Early risk control programmes were directed at specific perils and did not comprise a holistic manner of handling risk by management techniques. The first organised loss- prevention activities were directed toward the prevention of property losses resulting from fire.[1] The nature of fire perils dictates the following:

- ☐ everyone is exposed to this risk
- ☐ losses occur relatively frequently
- ☐ a considerable number of these losses are severe, even catastrophic
- ☐ losses may be difficult to prevent since in many instances they are due to the actions or negligence of others.

These factors naturally suggest that fire and its prevention have a very important bearing on the economy and particularly on the insurance sector, which has traditionally been the medium to meet the financial consequences of this risk. It is not surprising therefore that early fire prevention developments were originated by insurers, who began appointing surveyors to inspect and report on all properties to be insured, and who stipulated that certain requirements and standards be met before insurance was offered.[8]

Thus, from early times, the practice of careful inspection of property and insistence on periodic follow-up of these inspections developed.

---

7 Discussion is centred around these perils on account of the fact that early attention was focused on these specifically; as they represented the perils to which most people were exposed. Obviously present activities encompass a much wider area, where notably the prevention of mortality and morbidity display marked accomplishments. In the USA for example, the average lifetime in 1900 was 49.2 years (Spiegelman, 1962, 34). Presently this figure is approximately 70 years (Denenberg, *et al.*, 1974, 81).
The intention is not to provide a detailed chronological account. For a more detailed historical development of loss control/prevention, see Allen (1943), Heinrich (1950) and Blake (1963).

8 See Valsamakis (1983, 20-27) for a summary of the development of fire insurance in England.

8.3.2 Fire risk control

As fire insurance developed there was also a growing realisation that the most effective prevention technique involved the understanding of the **causes** of loss and their elimination. Consequently, records of the circumstances of loss began to be kept, which in turn prompted research into, for instance, the causes of spontaneous combustion and the effects of friction.[2]

The preoccupation with risk control coupled with increasing sophistication meant that the industry began employing people with varied but specialised knowledge of engineering. Today the scientists of numerous manufacturing, service and research organisations are constantly developing apparatus and techniques aimed at preventing fire, explosion and similar loss-producing perils.[9]

The present pace of technology has resulted in a higher concentration of assets and new fire hazards are created, with the result that prevention specialists are continually required to research and combat the new special hazards posed by modern-day equipment and materials. Specialised management techniques are required to ensure modern fire technology is brought to bear and minimising the risk from fire.

8.3.3 Engineering risk control

Parallel with fire prevention, the development of **boiler explosion** prevention came about. For example, losses caused by boiler explosion began receiving attention during the early 1860's from state and local governments in the USA.[3]

Appointments of engine and boiler inspectors were made by insurance companies specialising in flywheel, engine breakdown, turbine and electrical insurance; which ultimately were combined under the general classification of machinery insurance.

The emphasis was on the prevention of loss rather than providing an indemnity subsequent to the loss – an objective evidenced by the fact that loss payments generally were, and continue to be, less than the amounts paid out for prevention.

---

9 As an example, insurance companies such as Allianz and the American mutual insurer *Factory Mutual* display specialised risk control expertise which has developed to prevent a wide range of losses. These insurers produce authoratative publications in the field of risk control, distilling the considerable practical experience gained by the industry. See for example *Allianz handbook of loss prevention* and the comprehensive Factory Mutual publications.

8.3.4 Occupational accidents

8.3.4.1 *Accident control – background*

Although, like fire perils, **industrial accidents** have a widespread effect on persons, the development of industrial accident prevention historically took a somewhat different perspective.

The growth of industry naturally drew attention to the increasing number and the severity of industrial accidents. However, in those early times they were considered to be a result of the socio-economic conditions under which the worker operated. It was assumed that a reduction in the number of accidents could be achieved by the consideration of contributing factors such as working hours, pay, lighting, heat, sanitation and other working conditions. It was commonly believed that the wages of the workers were too low and that not only the working conditions, but also the non-working environment, needed improvement.[4]

Early efforts in industrial accident prevention were made in Russia, which was one of the first nations to pass comprehensive occupational safety legislation.[10]

8.3.4.2 *Accident control – South Africa*

South African industry has a standardised approach to accident control in the form of the NOSA programme discussed below. Similarly the mining industry has the MSMS system. These systems are essentially based on the concept of *Management by Objectives* and have been very successful. Interest in these programmes has been shown by a number of other countries.

The emphasis during the earlier stages of development in South Africa was on legislation and supervision by government officials. Safety, and to a limited extent, occupational health in industry was governed by the *Factories, Machinery and Building Works Act* (22 of 1941), usually referred as the *Factories Act*,[11] and in the mining industry by the *Minerals Act* (50 of 1991). Specialised industries such as the explosives industry has its own legislation, such as the *Explosives Act* (26 of 1956).

Despite the legislative approach, an emphasis on management techniques has always been evident. For instance, the *Factories Act* required the appointment of a responsible engineer to oversee machinery. The management approach is very evident in the *Machinery and Occupational*

---

10 It is interesting to note that this legislation, although passed in 1835, was not in fact enforced. See Pascoe (1981, 486).

11 The use of the shortened title had the unfortunate consequence that the erroneous views that the act only applied to factories developed. In fact three separate issues were regulated: Factories, Machinery and Building Works. In this regard see part IV of the Wiehahn Report, Chapter 3, par. 3.4.

Safety Act (6 of 1983), usually referred to as *MOSACT*, which repealed the *Factories Act*.

Workmen's Compensation Act in South Africa[12]

☐ Employees' rights in the previous century

Closely allied to the question of compensation for occupational injuries, is the right of the employee to sue his employer and hence the exposure of the employer to the so-called employer's liability risk. This risk is covered by an employer's liability policy and the Workmen's Compensation Schemes (WCA).[13] The position regarding employers' liability must be viewed against the historical development of these actions.

In the previous century an employee injured in the course of employment had little chance of recovering damages for these injuries sustained at work.[14] His remedies were confined to the common law which, as a study of English cases clearly indicates, was not kindly disposed to this kind of action. Essentially he had to prove negligence on the part of the employer. Even worse, during 1837, in the well-known and often criticised[15] case of *Priestly v Fowler* (1837 3M and W1) the English courts set a precedent when the court ruled that an employer was not liable for the negligence of a fellow employee. This established the so-called doctrine of common employment. The doctrine of assumption of risk also applied and hence the injured worker was presumed to run the risk of being injured. The employer was free to contract out of the liability.

It is now clear that, whatever the theory may have been, in reality the rights of injured employees to recover damages by common law during the previous century, were very limited indeed.

☐ Development of workmen's compensation in South Africa

At the turn of the century South Africa's legal system depended heavily on developments in England and, as was the case there, only a

---

12 The history of the Workmen's Compensation legislation in South Africa has been researched by Budlender (1979).
See also South African Labour Bulletin (Vol. 9, February 1984, and Vol. 8, August 1983).
It appears that the emphasis for improved safety standards and a compensation system originated from employer groups and government, and not employees. Even today, until recently, organised labour has not taken much interest in these matters.

13 Section 7, in particular, which limits the employee's and his dependants' rights to sue his employer.

14 The position of employers' liability and compensation in England, during the last century is succinctly covered by Ruegg (1901, 268-279). At this time South African law was strongly influenced by the position in England and most writers commenting on the development of South African law rely on English law. See for example Budlender (1979, 157).

15 This case is often used as the point of departure in legal theory as, for example, by Dworkin (1986, 2).

limited right of recovery for injury existed. Big companies, such as those in the mining industry, were, however, not satisfied with this state of affairs and a scheme to compensate injured workers was introduced. As early as 1894, the mining industry established the *Rand Mutual Assurance Company*.[5] Since the mining industry had established its own fund, it was mostly unconcerned with the efforts of others to develop a statutory scheme.

In 1914 a consolidating act was passed.[16] The 1914 act, based on the British act of 1906 and the New Zealand Workmen's Compensation Act, altered the common law. The new act provided for compensation in the case of all accidents 'arising out of, or in the course of employment' and where the accident was not due to the 'serious and wilful misconduct of the employee'.

Under the 1914 Act an injured worker could choose between claiming under the common law or under the new statutory provisions. The worker did not, however, have recourse to both. In 1917 the act was extended to provide compensation for certain industrial diseases as well.

In the early form of the act, the obligation was on the employer to pay the compensation. There was, however, no guarantee that the employer would be able to pay the compensation. The next step was to make the purchase of insurance cover against this risk compulsory.

☐ The *Workmen's Compensation Act* of 1941

The *Workmen's Compensation Act* (25 of 1914)[17] was repealed by the *Workmen's Compensation Act* (38 of 1934),[18] which in turn was repealed and replaced by the *Workmen's Compensation Act* (30 of 1941).

Insofar as the risk manager is concerned, the WCA is an important act which has, to-date, largely prevented many of the liability crises which have occurred in the rest of the Western world,[6] as an injured workman cannot sue his employer[19] but must seek compensation in terms of the legal mechanism set up by the act.

☐ An overview of the act

The Act is divided into 11 chapters and contains two schedules. Regulations have been promulgated in terms of the act and rules for making applications for increased compensation were promulgated in 1956.

16 Act 25 of 1914 which consolidated acts promulgated in the Cape, Transvaal and Natal. For a commentary on this act Barry *et al.* (1914) can be consulted.

17 A commentary by Barry *et al.* (1914) was published on the 1914 act.

18 A commentary by Nathan (1935) on this act was published.

19 Section 7 of Act 30 of 1941.

Table 8.1 Overview of the WCA

Chapter I	Definitions	s 2-11
Chapter II	Administration	s 12-26
Chapter III	Right to compensation	s 27-36
Chapter IV	Liability for compensation	s 37
Chapter V	Amount & method of compensation	s 38-49
Chapter VI	Recovery of compensation	
	(A) Notice of accidents	s 50-53
	(B) Lodging of claims	s 54-55
	(C) Procedure for determination of claims	s 56-63
Chapter VII	The accident & reserve funds	
	(A) Establishment of funds	s 64-67
	(B) Rendering of wage returns by employers	s 68
	(C) Levying & recovery of assessments & other charges	s 68-74
Chapter VIII	Medical Aid	s 75-81
Chapter XI	Compensation for blacks	s 82-88
Chapter X	Industrial diseases	s 89-94
Chapter XI	Miscellaneous	s 95-100
First schedule		
Second schedule		

Chapter One deals with definitions and the application of the act. Chapter Two deals with administrative issues, Three with the right to compensation and Chapter Four, consisting of one short section, specifies the persons liable to pay the compensation. Chapter Five deals with the amount of and method of compensation payable, while Chapter Six deals with the requirements of giving notice of accidents, lodging of claims and the procedure for the determination of claims. Chapter Seven deals with the establishment of the accident and reserve funds, the rendering of wage returns by employers and the levying and recovery of assessments. Chapter Eight deals with medical aid to injured workmen. Chapter Nine, an outdated and outmoded chapter, deals with compensation payable to blacks. Chapter Ten is of increasing importance and deals with industrial diseases. Miscellaneous issues are covered in the final chapter.

Workmen's compensation – other countries

☐ Britain

England has a long history of employment legislation.[20] In 1802,[21] the first *Factory Act* (42 Geo III c 73) was passed, followed by a number of other acts which were consolidated in 1878. The Act of 1844 allowed the inspector to bring an action for damages on behalf of a workman injured by factory machinery. This was the first step in granting compensation to the injured workman and was the precursor to the

20 The history that follows is taken from Ruegg (1901, 241 *et seq.*).

21 It is interesting to note that the first act mentioned by Pascoe (1974, 474) is the 1825 Act.

Employers' Liability Act (43 and 44 Vict c 42) of 1880. A *Workmen's Compensation Act* was passed in 1897 based on the German system and a further act passed in 1900, but did not displace the doctrine of common employment. In 1877 a Select Committee of the House of Commons was appointed to consider the subject, but did not go so far as to recommend that the doctrine of common employment be abolished. It rather advised that the master be liable for the negligence of certain persons to whom he had delegated his rights as master over the workmen. These persons were called vice-masters in the report.

Although the act imposed liability, it was established soon thereafter that the employer may contract out of this liability.[22]

By 1900 the legislation passed by the Conservative Government of the day had established that the employer would be liable, not only for injury caused by fellow workmen but also that he should pay compensation for every accident arising out of the work, whether caused by negligence or not.

Other acts were also applicable to accidents, as for example the *Fatal Accidents Act* (9 and 10 Vict c 93 of 1845).

□ Other countries

Germany was one of the first countries to pass workmen's compensation legislation. In the USA industrial accident prevention reflected the earlier English and German efforts. These efforts began by the passing of laws requiring factory inspections and the setting up of central bureaux of labour statistics to assist in determining the nature and causes of industrial accidents.[7]

Subsequent legislation followed, requiring for example, the guarding of dangerous moving machinery, but more importantly, in time the modification and expansion of the common law rights and duties of employers and employees in the event of industrial accidents followed. Under these circumstances, the employer had little incentive, other than a moral one, to pursue preventative practices.

As was the case in England and South Africa, three principal defences, were pursued:[23] The *contributory negligence* defence maintained that the worker, by an act of omission contributed to the occurrence of the accident. The second, the *fellow servant* defence allowed the employer to show that a fellow employee contributed to the accident, and the third defence, the *assumption of risk* enabled an employer to claim that when an

22 *Griffiths v Earl Dudley* 9 QBD 357.

23 For a detailed discussion on these defences any textbook on delict or tort can be consulted. In South Africa the leading works are McKerron (1971), Boberg (1984), Van der Walt (1979) and Neethling, Potgieter & Visser (1990).

employee accepted employment, he also accepted the risk of injury which was associated with the job.[24]

Clearly, the legal position of employers defending themselves against claims brought against them by employees was inordinately strong. The laws, narrowing and defining more clearly their liability, did not achieve much in encouraging loss prevention. It was costly for employees to pursue legal recourse and this encouraged employers to resist claims, rather than to attempt to reduce them through loss prevention.[8] In tracing the development of industrial accident prevention in the USA, the dissatisfaction with the negligence system acted as a catalyst for the passing of workmen's compensation laws.[25] These provided specifically for compensation to the injured worker and his dependants when injury arose out of, or in connection with his employment. These laws prompted an increase in the number of claims and in the amounts claimed, which in turn precipitated the production of more data regarding accidents and their causes. As a result, the development of industrial accident prevention was greatly stimulated.

Today, largely because of the great improvement in plant facilities, and the fact that the more important causes of industrial accidents have been identified as being human rather than physical, a greater emphasis is placed on safety and remedies that are non-physical in nature. Significant too, is the tendency to include within the scope of preventative efforts the aspect of rehabilitation. These efforts are regarded as endeavours to minimise loss through maximum recovery of physical, emotional and occupational potential following injury or occupational disease.

It is interesting to note that in the USA rehabilitation centres receive support from insurance companies, particularly those involved with workmen's compensation.[9] There is also evidence presently that efforts are being made by some companies to establish rehabilitation centres for claimants arising from motor accidents.

This concern, which has as its underlying objective the rehabilitation of the handicapped person for gainful re-employment, reinforces the importance which is being placed on the question of risk control.[26] There is a rate of increase in the adoption of loss control activities (resulting in legislative controls being introduced), which has been described as geometric rather than arithmetic; because at present this topic is receiving

24 See, *Priestley v Fowler* [1837] 3M & W1.

25 The first of these laws was passed by the United States Congress in 1903 and applied to certain hazardous types of federal employment. By 1921, 42 states had enacted such laws; today all the states have them.

26 This is also true of some other countries. In Australia for example, all companies with more than 20 employees must appoint an accredited rehabilitation firm to handle any workplace-based occupational rehabilitation training. See Skully (1989, 28).

front page exposure in the media. This phenomenon is not, of course, altogether unexpected. Largely because of the business boom experienced in the developed economies, particularly post 1960 and following large (frequent and severe) losses from, for example, fires and mine disasters, there has been a resurgence of interest in this concern.[10] Pressure has also been exerted by the consumer movement.[27]

8.4 General principles and objectives of risk control

8.4.1 General principles of risk control

Having traced some of the historical developments, consideration is now given to the fundamental principles of risk control.

Briefly stated, these principles express a philosophy that prescribes:

- the identification and application of **management** principles to risk control[28]
- the recognition that risk exposures and their associated losses should be deliberately assessed
- the meaningful endeavour of loss prevention, recognising the impact of losses on the organisation and the economy as a whole
- the recognition that the process is an ongoing one which is facing the challenge of the pace of technological development
- the recognition that approaches to risk control must be integrated with the other activities within the organisation, thereby acknowledging the inter-relationships that exist.

8.4.2 Objectives of risk control programmes

More specifically, the objectives and principles of a risk control programme (after having identified and evaluated the risk) can be described as follows:

8.4.2.1 *The reduction of the magnitude of the exposure*

This entails the careful assessment of the exposure *per se* with a view to identifying and implementing action plans that will reduce the **quantum** of the exposure. From a practical viewpoint such action may mean, for example, the purchase of back-up equipment which would result in diminishing the vulnerability following a break-down. Another example

27 There has been considerable questioning by consumers of risk control measures and the protective legislative controls imposed. See Hood (1990, 42 *et seq.*) who indicates that safety legislation designed to protect children from hazardous medicines has not resulted in the number of harmful incidents decreasing.

28 This is one aspect where South African companies have succeeded more than those of other countries. See Vernon (1989, 142-143).

is the installation of party-perfect fire walls to divide buildings into separate compartments.

8.4.2.2 *The reduction of the frequency of loss-producing events*

Independently from reducing the magnitude of an exposure or loss, there exists the possibility of reducing the **frequency** of loss-producing events. This entails a critical analysis of the causes of loss, followed by implementation of plans and procedures to eliminate such causes. For instance, the frequent cause of transformer failure may be identified as the result of the overheating of connections. The frequency of losses for this source may be reduced by periodical infra-red inspections which should detect such a possibility.

8.4.3 Planning and recovery from losses

Risk control, in meeting its objectives, is also concerned with planning in order to deal with loss situations.

8.4.3.1 *Recovering from loss-producing events (contingency planning)*

Contingency planning can be compared closely with emergency planning, in that it also adopts a preconceived plan, on the assumption of a particular type of loss. The objective is to have a contingent plan of action in place which will ensure recovery from the loss in the shortest and most economical manner. Contingency planning thus encompasses both pecuniary and non-pecuniary aspects of recovery.

An example of contingency planning is planning to identify alternative suppliers of materials to deal with the event of the loss of a critical supplier.

8.4.3.2 *Dealing with loss-producing events (emergency planning)*

These are preconceived specific designs or emergency plans implemented on the assumption of a particular type of loss, and with a view to reducing the effect of such a loss. Such plans may, for instance, entail communicating the potential risk exposure to all those who could be affected. Instruction and information concerning the potential risk, coupled with an emergency plan of action will, generally, prompt a greater understanding by, say, customers of an organisation and will reduce the negative impact in the event of a loss. This also achieves the desired integration of the risk programme with the other areas of operations and with other participants (often outside the organisation) in the economic equation.

An example of an emergency plan is the drafting of evacuation plans for high-rise buildings, or plans to deal with a major toxic spill, or nuclear release. It is often necessary to draft emergency plans in conjunction with other bodies such as, the civil defence and local authorities.[29] In some centres, as a result of major industrial disasters such as that which occurred in Bhopal, emergency planning is becoming mandatory.

8.5 Approaches to loss prevention

Loss prevention generally necessitates first the identification of the source or cause of loss and then its elimination or the reduction of its effect. In summarising the various approaches to loss prevention one should recognise that causes of loss are either animate or inanimate in nature, and that it is this distinction that determines, generally, the approach taken to prevent and control losses.

Denenberg, *et al.*,[11] refer to two customary approaches: the *engineering approach*, and the *human or personal approach*. The former takes cognisance of the physical or mechanical (inanimate) properties of the risk situation, whilst in the latter's case, the personal (or animate) aspects are considered.

Approaches such as the *educational approach*, the *statistical approach* and the *enforcement approach* are also referred to.[30] Although some degree of delineation may be desirable, these approaches may in fact be seen as complementary to the basic engineering and human approaches to loss prevention.

8.5.1 The engineering approach

The objective of the engineering approach is to control the physical aspects of the risk situation, that is, the risk is confronted through an engineering perspective. It involves the knowledge and use of the physical sciences to prevent loss-producing events from occurring, and to minimise the loss should they occur.

Attention is thus directed at such physical factors as construction design, materials, apparatus, amenities supplies, protective devices, machine

29 Holistic industrial plans are formulated as Mutual Aid Plans. Because of possible liability problems, which became apparent after the 1976 unrest, the Workmen's Compensation Act was amended to facilitate Mutual Aid and Emergency arrangements. See *Workmen's Compensation Act* (30 of 1941), section 28.

30 The actual approach adopted by individual organisations and societies differs from time to time. For the better part of the last century and this century, the emphasis has been on enforcement. As a result of the Robbens Commission of Inquiry a more enlightened self-regulatory approach was adopted in the UK. South Africa, with the National Occupational Safety Association (NOSA) approach has always been self-regulatory. The same approach forms the basis of the *Machinery and Occupational Safety Act* (MOSACT).

maintenance, and even the physical factors of adjacent locations (risk exposures).

Generally, the engineering approach to loss prevention is the first to be considered and implemented. In most risk situations, many inanimate factors which may cause losses can be eliminated (or their effects reduced) relatively inexpensively, and moreover, these efforts remain effective over a considerable period of time. The complexity of the loss-prevention approach is obviously a function of the risk which may, at one extreme, require a simple remedy but, at the other, necessitate intricate knowledge of physics, chemistry, electricity, mathematics and so forth. The trend is, nevertheless, toward more complex and technical prevention techniques in trying to keep abreast of new technology.

Under the broader definition of the engineering approach, one can also incorporate a relatively recent approach to prevention, labelled the *systems safety* approach.[31]

Systems safety was primarily developed and is still used mainly by the U.S. Department of Defence, although its application has also been used in attempts to solve social problems.[12]

Lederer[13] defines the systems safety approach as the following:

> a systemized approach used to identify and correct hazards continually from the early conceptional stage of a product right on through a detailed design and operation.

Therefore, it envelops the complete ambit of operations and testing procedures, inspections, even reviews by top level management and motivation of workers, so as to ensure a systematised and integrated approach to safety.

The objective of this particular approach cannot be said to differ from that of conventional approaches, but it does accentuate the identification of possible causes of losses before they occur. Conventional loss prevention often analyses losses or accidents to identify causes, but understandably, in the sectors in which systems safety application is needed, the cost in property and indeed life values is inestimable. Hence, this approach requires the use of the expensive and most advanced management skills, mathematics, computer science (simulation etc.) in order to attain the set objectives. It follows, therefore, that because of the costs involved, systems safety is usually possible only in state or government projects; its success has however prompted the formation of a number of private enterprises offering systems safety services to private sector participants.

---

31 Some authors, for example Denenberg, *et al.*, (1974, 100-101), refer to *systems safety* as a novel approach and treat it as supplementary to the engineering and human approach. Systems safety practices do encompass most comprehensively, the engineering and human sciences – hence the reference to it as being 'systematised' and integrated.

8.5.2 The human or personal approach

> The human or personal approach is based on the fact that losses are caused in part by physical factors, but postulates that the most important causes of loss are human-fault related, or at least can be traced to the actions of humans.[14]

Consequently, prevention of losses entails the study and the remedying of people's habits, faults and any maladjustments of people to their environment, both personal and work.

The nature of the approach also indicates that it finds its most practical application in the field of industrial accident prevention. It was principally after World War One that in the industrial accident field, it became apparent that physical causes of loss to property were in most instances easily corrected provided that attention was paid to the actions of people.

Human causes of accidents include complacency, irresponsibility, ignorance, boredom, defiance, timidity, fatigue, misunderstanding, alcoholism, communication barriers, emotional stress, and others. Some of these causes often do not appear on loss reports and, as has been pointed out,[15] remedial steps aimed at avoiding repetition might therefore not go far enough.

The focus of attention on the human element was largely attributed to the research of Heinrich, who developed, what has been described or labelled the *Personnel Administration Approach*.[16]

The research by Heinrich led to three basic conclusions or premises:[17] [32]

(i) 88 percent of all accidents were primarily the result of unsafe actions by people.

(ii) The causes of major injuries were the same as those for minor injuries. Since it was rationalised that the severity of the injury was in fact a matter of chance or providence, efforts to prevent accidents should be directed toward the prevention of **all** causes of loss.

(iii) Indirect losses from industrial accidents amounted to four times the direct losses; and this phenomenon drew attention to the managerial type of loss control.

The principles subscribed to by the human approach to loss prevention have been significantly extended. Accident cause analysis has been further developed and modified so that efforts are channelled to identifying underlying causes (heredity and environment) which could parade in the

32 The research of Heinrich still forms the cornerstone of modern accident prevention. See Baker & Coetzee (1983, 168).

guise of workers' faults. The use of the human sciences (psychology and sociology) has become increasingly popular.

Today, in a risk management discourse one also finds references to the humanitarian approach or view to prevention. Again, further delineation is not deemed necessary as it can be seen as a contemporary extension to the basic human approach. In general, the humanitarian viewpoint considers the preservation of life values as the key objective. The term *humanics* has been adopted to describe the principal theme of this approach; which is not only concerned with the prevention of accidents, but also with the effective reduction of suffering and expense of injury through the use of medical and rehabilitation services.

8.5.3 Educational, statistical and enforcement approaches

Mention was made earlier to the educational, statistical and enforcement approaches to risk control. It was stated that the view adopted was that these could logically be seen as complementary, rather than separate strategies.

The increasing importance of risk management as a science and its applicability in practice needs no further emphasis – evidence of this claim is plentiful. This type of trend obviously dictates that a commensurate advance in education is necessary.

This education should extend beyond the established training and awareness programmes and general prevention activities. The fact is recognised that for risk management to be successfully implemented there must be a requisite appreciation of concept, philosophy and policy which originate from the top level of management. In addition, theoretical endeavours are presently gaining ground, as the subject is likewise gaining recognition as a discipline for study and research at University level.

The use of statistics, when developed properly, includes the formulation of statistical techniques for the collection and analysis of facts relating to losses. Although considerable progress has been made in this respect, effective application of statistics is often regrettably absent, particularly in the private sector.[33]

This state of affairs can be traced to a lack of education and an, as yet, less than fully developed policy toward risk management. Again, in many instances, because of the mechanism of insurance and the misconception that risk transfer is thus effectively achieved, sufficient emphasis is not being placed (at the risk source) on statistics. There is rather an undue

33 See Denenberg, *et al.*, (1974, 533) and Hurley (1962, 186-188).

reliance on the statistics which are collected and collated by insurers and their intermediaries.[34]

When one considers enforcement, one basically hypothesises that human nature is fallible and prone to procrastination, forgetfulness and other such weaknesses. Thus, in order to render prevention measures effective, it is argued, these should be used carefully and moreover consistently. Naturally this means strict enforcement through statutes and safety codes.

In some situations, where for example, there exists an employer-employee relationship, such enforcement is achievable by pressure on the employee. Many risk control programmes incorporate a penalty and reward system which may induce proper and consistent use of prevention methods.[35]

However, in the wider sense of the term one may encounter varying degrees of enforcement. At one end of the continuum one could view a deliberate policy laid down by top management, constituting its enforcement of risk control. At the other extreme, one looks to legislation as its means of enforcement.

It is therefore evident that the degree of enforcement increases progressively from:

- ☐ a motivation to control risk due to a natural **aversion to risk** (evident in most people)
- ☐ the subscribing to a well-developed and specific **risk control programme**
- ☐ the insistence on the application of standard **codes of practice**, to
- ☐ **authoritative** risk control **requirements**, prescribed by law.

Turning to the South African context, specific risk control programmes, codes of practice and authoritative requirements will now be considered.

8.6 Authoritative risk control requirements

As mentioned earlier, one may view the extreme case of enforcement as requirements prescribed by legislation. In South Africa there are numerous such risk control measures, the most important of which are contained in the acts listed in table 8.2.

---

34 A significant number of organisations 'subcontract' the responsibility concerning statistics to the insurance market and its participants. As a result, their managements have insufficient appreciation of the direct or indirect costs resulting from losses. Mostly, this attitude is prevalent with those organisations which do not subscribe to any deliberate risk management philosophy or programme, except to the extent of purchasing insurance.

35 For example, in the National Occupational Safety Association (NOSA) system, results are measured against defined criteria, and those organisations which comply, are awarded star ratings.

Table 8.2
Some South African legislation impacting on risk control measures

Legislation	Reference
Machinery and Occupational Safety Act [MOSACT]	6 of 1983
Minerals Act	50 of 1991
Nuclear Energy Act	92 of 1982
Environment Conservation Act	73 of 1989
Atmospheric Pollution Prevention Act	45 of 1965
Water Act	54 of 1956
National Building Regulations and Building Standards Act	103 of 1973
Hazardous Substances Act	15 of 1956
Explosives Act	26 of 1956

In addition to stipulated risk control measures, each act also contains numerous regulations, all with the purpose of providing the legal framework within which risk is to be managed and controlled.

With such a plethora of enactments it is not surprising that some risk management commentators[18] voice some apprehension when the opinion is expressed that further authoritative regulation may be necessary. This apprehension may well not be intended as criticism of the enforcement approach to risk control, but rather to stress that the problem is not the interpretation of the stipulated requirements, but the question of how an organisation will ensure that the law is complied with.

The view that ought to be espoused is that, notwithstanding any governing legislation, the most effective risk control is achieved when a deliberate and integrated risk management philosophy is entrenched in the overall policy of an organisation.

8.7 Specific risk control programmes and codes of practice

8.7.1 Safety

8.7.1.1 *Introduction*

Table 8.3 indicates the number of accidents reported each year while table 8.4 indicates the direct costs of compensation.

Table 8.3
South African reported accidents: 1981-1986

Year	Total number of accidents reported	Number of accidents per 1 000 workmen
1982	301 721	46,70
1983	271 052	42,70
1984	271 659	40,16
1985	255 890	39,15
1986	242 755	38,09
1987	238 419	35,96
1988	265 854	—
1989	281 580	—

Source: *Workmen's Compensation Reports*, 1982-1990

Table 8.4
Estimated income and expenditure of the Accident Fund

Year	Total income (R m)	Expenditure (R m)	Unappropriated surplus (R m)
1983/84	111,68	78,14	33,54
1984/85	114,57	92,64	21,93
1985/86	161,89	109,08	52,81
1986/87	149,99	121,68	28,31
1987/88	185,88	148,80	37,08
1988/89	215,56	175,12	40,44
1989/90	317,69	233,91	83,78

Source: *Workmen's Compensation Reports,* 1985-1990

Against a background of rapidly changing industrial relations and increasing participation by employees and employee organisations in, what may be termed the 'new' industrial society, greater awareness and planning in the area of occupational safety and health is required.

8.7.1.2 *Statutory requirements*

Apart from humanitarian, moral and social responsibilities on the part of management to provide a safe working environment for employees, there are onerous statutory duties in this regard. In South Africa statutory intervention in working conditions is regulated mainly by the *MOSACT* (6 of 1983) (as amended by Act 40 of 1989 and *Minerals Act* (50 of 1991) to the *SATS* (9 of 1989), the *Minerals Act* (50 of 1991), and the *Explosives Act* (26 of 1956). These acts provide for the registration and control of factories and mines. They also make provision for supervision of the use of machinery and precautions against accidents and occupational diseases.

Penalties which may be imposed on a company for non-compliance with statutory requirements are severe. Consequently, it is essential that a risk manager, or whoever is responsible for safety (for example, the factory engineer), should keep abreast of the changing legislation in safety matters; familiarise himself with legislation covering the organisation's activities, and ensure that all legislation is complied with.

8.7.1.3 *Responsibility*

Responsibilities for safe working conditions and practices extend from top management down to the shop floor. It is not sufficient for management merely to supply safety equipment and clothing; it must take steps to ensure that it is used by employees. Likewise, safe working practices must be enforced, and employees must be clearly warned of the penalties that will be imposed for failure to comply with safety instructions.

8.7.1.4 *Safety programmes and organisations*

Three main safety programmes are used in industry to manage safety and occupational health risks and as such supplement the legislation:

(i) The *Mine Safety Management System* (MSMS) of the Chamber of Mines.

(ii) The *International Mine Safety Rating* (ISR) programme introduced by the *International Loss Control Institute* (IICI), developed by Frank Bird.

(iii) The *National Occupational Safety Association* programme (NOSA).

While the MSMS and ILCI programmes are designed specifically for the mining industry, the NOSA programme applies to commerce and industry in general.

8.7.1.5 *The National Occupational Safety Association (NOSA)*[36]

The *National Occupational Safety Association* is registered under section 21 of the Companies Act as an association not for gain, and was established in 1951. It is modelled on the pattern of the *Industrial Accident Prevention Association of Ontario*. The bulk of the funds came from the Workmen's Compensation Commissioner. The Association's objective is the guidance, education, training and motivation of management and the workforce in the techniques of accident and occupational disease prevention. The NOSA five-star objective setting, grading and recognition programme aims at accident prevention. South Africa has achieved a high degree of success in the prevention of injuries. The programme also resulted in a reduction in damage to property and disruption of business activities.[19] The *modus operandi* for achieving its objectives is the NOSA management by objectives accident prevention programme, training courses, publicity material and safety promotional activities.

8.7.1.6 *Accident prevention – definitions and concepts*

> An accident is an undesired event that results in physical harm to a person and/or damage to property. It is usually the result of a fortuitous contact with a source of energy above the threshold limit of the body or structure.

Measurement

☐ **Disabling injury frequency rate**

The disabling injury frequency rate relates the injuries to the hours worked during the period and expresses them in terms of a million hour unit by means of the following formula:

$$\text{DIFR} = \frac{\text{Number of disabling injuries} * 1\,000\,000}{\text{Total number of man hours worked}}$$

36 For a discussion of the NOSA system consult Matthysen (1983, 164) and the commemorative edition of *Safety Management* (June 1991).

The above formula can be modified to show the approximate percentage of the workforce injured annually, the so-called *incidence rate* (IR).

Simplified

$$IR = \frac{\text{Disabling injuries} * 200\,000}{\text{Total number of man hours worked}}$$

$$IR = \frac{DIFR}{5}$$

- ☐ **Disabling injury severity rate**
  The disabling injury severity rate relates the days charged to the hours worked during the period and expresses them in terms of a million hour unit by means of the following formula:

$$DISR = \frac{\text{Total days charged} * 1\,000\,000}{\text{Total number of man hours worked}}$$

The basic principles of accident prevention

The unsafe acts of persons are responsible for the majority of accidents. Research has found that out of every 100 accidents:

- ☐ 88% are caused by unsafe acts
- ☐ 10% are caused by unsafe environmental and mechanical conditions
- ☐ 2% are caused by acts of providence.

From the above the conclusion can be drawn that 98% of all industrial accidents can be prevented.

The four basic reasons for the occurrence of unsafe acts provide a guide to the selection of appropriate corrective measures. Briefly, the reasons for the unsafe acts of persons may be:

- ☐ improper attitude
- ☐ lack of knowledge or skill
- ☐ physical unsuitability
- ☐ improper mechanical or work environment.

The following are the basic methods available for preventing accidents:

- ☐ engineering revision
- ☐ education, training, persuasion and appeal
- ☐ personnel selection, placement and adjustment
- ☐ enforcement (discipline).

The most valuable methods of accident prevention are analogous with the methods required for the control of the quality, cost and quantity of production. The control of quality and quantity of production and of the frequency and severity of accident occurrence have much in common. In many cases the same faulty practice is involved, and the reason for the existence of the fault is similar for both accident occurrence and unsatisfactory production.

The employer and user of machinery, usually a company, is legally responsible for supplying a safe environment, tools and safe methods of working, as is laid down in *MOSACT* and the *Mines and Works Act*. This responsibility must, of necessity, be discharged by the management of the company.

8.7.1.7 *Machinery and Occupational Safety Act*

Of greater importance to risk control are the specific regulations promulgated in terms of *MOSACT*. These include:

Regulation	Reference
Diving Regulations (DR)	RGN12/12953
Driven Machinery Regulations (DMR)	GN295/88
Electrical Installations (EI)	GN2272/85 & 2270/85
Electrical Machinery Regulations (EMR)	
Environmental Regulations for Work-places (ERW)	GN2281/87
Facilities Regulations	RGN2362/12777
General Administrative Regulations (GAR)	GN2206/84
General Machinery Regulations (GMR)	
General Safety Regulations (GSR)	GN1031/84
General Safety Regulations – Incorporation of Safety Standards	GG13082
Lead Regulations	GG13082
Lead Regulations: Incorporation of Safety Standards	GG13077

Application of MOSACT

This act is the principal act for the protection of employees in the workplace, other than mines. It replaced the *Factories, Machinery and Building Works Act* of 1941. Many of its provisions are universal in application.[37] It applies not only to persons engaged or employed in factories, buildings and certain other works, but to all persons in employment, including the public sector, agriculture, commerce, local government and domestic service. It is excluded from application only on premises where the *Minerals Act* 50 of 1991, and the *Explosives Act* of 1956, apply.

37 In particular the machinery provisions, which are not confined to the occupational situation.

The objective of the act is: to provide for the safety of persons at a workplace or in the course of their employment or in connection with the use of machinery and to establish an advisory council for occupational safety.

The act is mainly enabling legislation which allows the relevant Cabinet minister to set safety standards through the promulgation of regulations.

The act also identifies certain specific duties of employers, users of machinery, safety representatives and inspectors.

Safety standards

An innovation of MOSACT is the ability to use legislation to promulgate safety standards.[38] Regulations promulgated under the *Factories, Machinery and Building Work Act*, 1941, are deemed as having been promulgated under MOSACT and remain in force until they are repealed.[39]

Exemptions

The relevant minister may grant exemptions from all or any of the provisions of the act and regulations or from any prescribed safety standard.

Safety organisation

All operations falling under the jurisdiction of MOSACT are required, in terms of the act, to have certain persons responsible for various aspects of safety at the workplace.

Persons responsible for safety:

MOSACT imposes substantial responsibility on employers and users of machinery.

- ☐ The employer has the overall duty of ensuring compliance with much of the safety legislation. Where the employer is a corporate body, the chief executive officer (CEO) of the corporate body will have overall responsibility.[40] Corporate CEOs and all other employers, who are not personally involved in the day-to-day running of the operation, shall designate in writing the senior full-time manager or person at the operation as having that responsibility. In turn senior managers may delegate some or all of their safety duties to employees under their authority. The delegation of duties does not relieve an employer of any responsibility or any liability under MOSACT (see MOSACT section 10A; GAR reg. 4).

---

38 See for example, *Incorporation of Safety Standards – Electrical* (GN2271/85).

39 Extensive use has been made of the power to incorporate safety standards.

40 Section 1 of *Machinery and Occupational Safety Amendment Act* (40 of 1989), which came into force on 9 July 1991 Proc R65/1991.

Before the introduction of section 10A of MOSACT the requirement of the Department of Manpower was that the managing director of a company shall be designated, by a written resolution of the board of directors in terms of regulation 4(1) GAR. He may then, and in terms of Regulation 4(4) GAR, delegate these duties to the manager(s) in charge of operating sites.[41]

- ☐ **Users of machinery**
  User is defined in MOSACT and it should be noted the definition does not restrict the scope to the employment situation.
- ☐ **Designated safety representatives**
  With the promulgation of MOSACT the emphasis moved to self-regulation. One of the measures of self-regulation was the appointment of safety representatives. The safety representative is absolved of any civil liability for failing to do anything he may be required to do, in terms of MOSACT.
- ☐ **Safety committees**
  A further innovation is the appointment of safety committees. Members of the committee are absolved of civil liability (section 12(3)).

8.7.1.8 *NOSA standards*

The NOSA standards also require persons with specific training to be available as follows:

- ☐ a fire officer to co-ordinate and control the fire protection and prevention programme
- ☐ fire-fighting teams
- ☐ security staff, who should have received safety training
- ☐ an emergency controller who will be able to handle emergencies.

8.7.1.9 *Risk control organisation for safety*

Where the size of the operation warrants a risk control organisation, it is recommended that the safety organisation be included in the risk control structure. This department should systematically implement and audit the safety systems.

8.7.2 Occupational health

> Occupational health is concerned with any substance, process or circumstance which may affect a person's health or safety in the work place.

41 For an opinion on regulation 4, see Stuart CE 'General administrative regulation 4 of MOSACT.' *Association of Legal Advisers of South Africa.*

Table 8.5
Reported cases of occupational diseases

Year	Number of cases reported
1982	Ca. 10
1983	Ca. 95
1984	Ca. 130
1985	635
1986	Ca. 95
1987	144

Source: Extrapolated from graphs published by the Workmen's Compensation Commissioner

(Note: The high figure for 1985 is attributed to the results of the campaign launched by certain organisations to trace persons suffering from occupational diseases.)

It is not always possible to maintain a close distinction between occupational health and occupational safety. Some authors have expressed the view that no such distinction should exist.[42]

Occupational health can be subdivided into the following disciplines:[43]

- ☐ Occupational safety
- ☐ Occupational hygiene
- ☐ Occupational medicine.

8.7.2.1 *Historical background*[44]

Occupational health, in its narrow sense of occupational safety, was initially and quite rightly, concerned with the prevention of accidents, particularly personal injury arising from mechanisation and the use of new and powerful forms of energy such as steam and electricity. As the industrial safety movement expanded, it was realised that certain job-related environmental conditions, such as dust, fumes and chemicals, have a detrimental effect on the health and well-being of the persons exposed to it. It became increasingly clear that it was necessary to monitor and treat the environment and the people in the environment.

The legislative emphasis was also put on the prevention of accidents, although many of the regulations promulgated in terms of the *Factories Act* dealt with occupational health issues.

Concern about the position of occupational health issues resulted in the appointment of the *Erasmus Commission of Enquiry on Occupational Health* (RP55/1976). The Commission considered its terms of reference to relate

42 See for example, Benatar (1983, 952-953).
43 Piek (1986, 119) states: 'occupational medicine is one of two legs of occupational health, the other being occupational hygiene.'
44 For a discussion on some historical issues see Baker (1986, 5).

specifically to occupational diseases only, but clearly, its findings could have an indirect effect on the field of industrial accidents.[45] The Commission noted that the Gold Mining Industry had little to be ashamed of. The Commission made a number of recommendations, including the establishment of a single body to control industrial health, which should be vested in the Department of Health, and one principal industrial health act to be promulgated.

The recommendations were not immediately implemented, because of *inter alia* the appointment of the Wiehahn Commission.[46] Eventually MOSACT was promulgated, the ambit of which is broad enough to include occupational health and safety and the emphasis shifted away from the Erasmus Commission.[47]

A further commission, the *Niewenhuizen Commission of Inquiry into Compensation for Occupational Diseases in the Republic of South Africa* (RP100/1981) was appointed. A number of bills were promulgated including *Occupational Medicine Bill* (Notice 20/1984; GG9029 1984) and a *Draft Compensation for Occupational Diseases Bill.*

8.7.2.2 *Occupational safety*

> Occupational safety covers physical safety from an accident prevention perspective.

It constitutes the major thrust of the well-known NOSA programme, and broad subjects include housekeeping, safe working practices, mechanical, electrical and personal safeguarding, safety organisation, and administrative and legal requirements. It should be noted that in the MOSACT 'safe' means free from any threat which may cause bodily injury, illness or death; and 'safety' has a corresponding meaning (section 1(1) (xxiii)).

8.7.2.3 *Occupational hygiene*

Occupational hygiene is sometimes called industrial hygiene or environmental health and according to Piek[20] deals with identification, evaluation and control of potential hazards in the workplace.

> Occupational hygiene may be defined as a science devoted to the identification, evaluation and control of those environmental factors arising in or from the workplace, which cause disease, damage health or impair the faculties of workers and other members of the community.

45 Paragraph 2.38 of the report.

46 Paragraph 2.4, part 4, of the Wiehahn Report.

47 Considerable discussion did however continue. See for example:
- Metz & Benatar (1987, 72)
- the response from the former Director-General of Health (1988, 313)
- Baker (1986, 103).

The causal issues are generally clearcut in an accident, but this is not the case with occupational diseases. Environmental issues are therefore of greater importance where occupational health is concerned.

To determine the environmental factors or stresses which influence health and well-being, the processes and work procedures must be known. The main environmental factors are stated below:

Chemical Fluid, dust, smoke, mist, fumes, fog, vapour or gas and hazardous substances.[48]

Physical Electromagnetic and ionising radiation, noise,[49] vibration and extreme temperatures and pressures, and non-ionising radiation, such as that produced by welding and video display units.[50]

Biological Insects, mites, fungis, moulds, bacteria and viruses (bad handling of waste, sewage and food and lack of personal hygiene).

Ergonomical[21] Body attitude and work position, continuous repetitious movement, high work demands and mental fatigue.

The occupational hygienist recognises the above factors as threats to health and as the cause of stress and significant discomfort.

8.7.2.4 *Occupational medicine*

> Whereas occupational hygiene concerns the monitoring and treatment of the workplace environment, occupational medicine, in general terms, concerns the monitoring and treatment of persons in that environment.

In this case a knowledge of substances and work processes which could adversely affect the health of a person, as well as methods to eliminate or reduce such hazards, is required.

8.7.3 Products liability

Products can be the source of extensive liability claims. One of the well-known examples is the Thalidomide disaster of the 1960's. The drug Thalidomide caused babies to be born with deformities. In Britain 452 children were brain damaged by the drug. It took a long time to resolve

48 Common substances include lead and mercury.

49 A risk control measure is audiometric screening. For a comment on the limitations see Metz (1987, 35) and Hessel & Sluis-Cremer (1987, 364).

50 The issue of video display units is controversial. Even though billions of dollars have been spent on research there is still no proof of any danger. For a discussion on the issue consult 'The controversy over VDUs.' 1984. *Risk Management Reports.*

the issue of compensation and in Britain, eventually, the Thalidomide Trust was established. The manufacturer and the government contributed towards the funding of this Trust.[22]

After this disaster there has been a dramatic escalation in products liability claims in various parts of the world.

The approach adopted in the following section is to illustrate the various forms of products liability by referring to practical examples.

8.7.3.1 *Types of liability exposures*

Liability for latent defects

In the event of a product containing a latent defect the purchaser can suffer consequential losses as well as material damage. It is possible for a product to be manufactured with a latent defect in it.

Consider the following case:

> ***Holmdene Brickworks v Roberts Construction Company Limited***[51]
>
> A manufacturer did not bake its bricks long enough, resulting in the retention of magnesium sulphate in the bricks. As a consequence a white powdery substance formed and the bricks tended to crumble. The bricks were thus unsuitable and had to be replaced, with the result that sections of the building had to be demolished. Roberts Construction, the main contractor, sued the brick manufacturer for the consequential losses it had suffered. These damages were awarded.

The court laid down the following as the law in regard to the liability of sellers, who are also manufacturers, for consequential losses caused by latent defects in their products:

> A merchant who sells goods of his own manufacture or goods in relation to which he publicly professes to have attributes of skill and expert knowledge, is liable to the purchaser for consequential damages caused to the latter by reason of any latent defects in the goods. Ignorance of the defect does not excuse the seller. Once it is established that he falls into one of the above-mentioned categories, the law irrebuttably attaches this liability to him, unless he has expressly or impliedly contracted out of it.

From this statement it should be clear that, under certain circumstances, if a product contains a latent defect the manufacturer has virtually no defence. The basis of liability is strict liability.[52]

Thus liability also attaches to a merchant who sells goods in relation to which he publicly professes to have attributes of skill and expert knowledge, even if he did not manufacture the goods. This implies that the origin of the goods is unimportant. Hereby liability can attach to a

51 1977 (3) SA 679 (A).

52 A number of important legal issues remain unanswered. For example, is this strict liability remedy available to anyone who suffers a loss or only to the purchaser? Another issue which is not clear is when exactly is a defect a latent defect?

seller, for example, for imported goods as well as locally manufactured goods. The seller can be liable even though he did not manufacture the goods himself.

Liability arising out of suitability for purpose

It is possible that although a product has no defects, it nevertheless causes harm or loss. In such a case, depending on the specific circumstances, it can be argued that the seller is in breach of contract. In terms of statute, British law recognises that a seller is liable if a product is not suitable for the purpose for which it was sold. This also appears to be part of our common law, which has long recognised an implied term to this effect.

> ***Minister van Landbou-Tegniese Dienste v Scholtz***[53]
>
> A purchaser had bought a bull for stud purposes. After a considerable period it became clear that the bull was in fact sterile. The legal nature of the transaction was important and on this point the court ruled:
>
> The parties had concluded the agreement on the basis that the (seller) had undertaken to deliver a bull for stud purposes and that an implied term to this effect was a term in the agreement.The exact nature and extent of the implied term will depend on the factual position surrounding the contract and in particular the discussions which gave rise to the contract.

Liability for words

Another example where liability can attach despite the absence of any specific defect in the product is for words and not because of anything in the product.

> ***Sealand of the Pacific Limited v Ocean Cement***[54]
>
> In this case the plaintiff, wishing to raise the level of its sea-life display vessel, ordered concrete which it had been told by the defendant's sales representative, was a light-weight concrete which turned out to be much heavier than represented; with the result that the vessel settled below its former level. The purchaser then sued the seller. The British Columbia Supreme Court granted judgement in favour of the plaintiff, and this judgement was subsequently confirmed on appeal.

In this case there was nothing wrong with the concrete. The defendant was liable because the information or advice which was given on its behalf was incorrect.

Our courts also regard words which are negligently spoken as actionable. This is an important risk area in regard to the marketing and technical activities of a company.

---

53 1971 (3) SA 188 (A).
54 (1973) 33 CLR (3d) 625.

Liability for manufacturing defects

A manufacturing process may result in manufacturing defects.

> ***Grant v Australian Knitting Mills Limited*** [55]
>
> In this case a large number of garments had been made without mishap, with the exception of a pair of underpants which had not been properly rinsed. This caused the plaintiff a serious skin disorder. The manufacturer produced evidence of high quality control standards employed at the factory. The court rejected that this proved lack of negligence, ruling that the mere fact that the garment was put on the market place was evidence of negligence.[56] The court evoked the so-called 'res ipsa loquitur' doctrine.

This type of court case suggests that if a product is admittedly defective, the manufacturer has little defence.

Liability for incorrect despatch

It is possible for an error to be made in the despatch department of a company and the wrong product could be dispatched.[57] The receiver does not detect the error and uses the wrong product with detrimental effects.

> ***Marais v Commercial General Agency Limited*** [58]
>
> A seed merchant inadvertently supplied a farmer with seeds of a character different from that supposedly purchased and was held liable for the resultant loss of the value of the crop. The decision turned on breach of contract. The court however, said that the case may also have succeeded on other grounds, such as negligence.

8.7.3.2 *Recent examples of product liability claims*

Most people are under the impression that South Africa has not had many products liability claims.[59] This is not entirely correct. South African law has historically treated products liability claims as normal delictual or contractual claims and dealt with them accordingly.

The majority of these claims which have been settled out of court, are dealt with as insurance claims. It is only in exceptional instances that the cases do go to court. Notwithstanding this, in recent years a number of product liability cases have been mentioned in the media and some have gone to court.

55 (1936) AC 85.

56 The application of this doctrine has long been criticised as imposing negligence where none in fact exists.

57 Product liability surveys carried out on numerous companies by one of the authors have indicated that virtually every company has, at one time or another, incorrectly dispatched products. Incorrect dispatch is a common error.

58 1922 TPD 440.

59 The doctrines of products liability have been researched in South Africa. See De Jager (1978, 347); De Jager (1979, 81; 1980, 114; 1980, 83. 1980, 234).

The following are examples:

- ☐ A surgeon sued the car and tyre manufacturing firms for R1 million in loss of earnings, arising out of an accident, which occurred when one of his vehicle's rear tyres burst.[23]
- ☐ In another case an animal feed manufacturer was successfully sued, when a number of racehorses died because their feed contained a substance dangerous to horses.[24]

In addition to court cases, other claims are reported in the media. There have been numerous incidents which could have given rise to product liability claims and also incidents which indicated the concern of commerce and industry for possible product liability claims. For example, a major supermarket chain withdrew a baby teat from the market because of the danger that the teat might disintegrate in the mouth of a baby. Similar concerns caused Rooibos tea to be removed from the market. There have also been incidents of motor cars being involved in accidents and bursting into flames and killing the occupants, which have given rise to a number of court cases overseas for defective design.[60]

8.7.3.3 *Risk control steps*

Existing quality assurance or control programmes

The objective of a product liability risk control programme is the prevention of product liability claims. If the product is carefully designed, manufactured and distributed, the frequency and severity of losses should decrease dramatically.

- ☐ A product liability risk control programme should be integrated into existing programmes which are designed to ensure that product quality is of a high standard. These quality assurance and quality control programmes are already well established.
- ☐ Product design, manufacture and distribution affects virtually every department in a company and, therefore, one person should be responsible for product quality or the product risk control programme. If the raw materials which are received are, for example, defective, the final product could well be defective; this is a supplier problem. So, too, if the manufacturing dye which is used in the manufacturing process is defective, the product could be defective; this is a manufacturing problem. If the advertising material incorrectly describes the product, a products liability claim could arise; this is a marketing problem.
- ☐ In the one case, it is the storeman who is involved, the other the manufacturing department and in yet another the marketing department. When designing a products liability risk control programme it

60 The most famous of which is the American case *Grimshaw v Ford Motor Co.*

is therefore necessary to ensure that it covers all the departments and that it is a system which can be understood and is also communicated to all persons in the organisation.

SABS 0157 and a product liability programme

The standard code which defines the requirements of quality assurance programmes in South Africa is SABS 0157 which has, in recent times, incorporated the ISO 9000 series. Details of the various parts of SABS 0157 are shown in table 8.6.

Table 8.6
Details of sections of SABS 0157

Part	ISO	Title
0 – 1987	9000 – 1987	Quality management and quality assurance standards – guidelines for selection and use.
I – 1987	9001 – 1987	Model for quality assurance in design/development, production, installation and servicing.
II – 1987	9002 – 1987	Model for quality assurance in production and installation.
III – 1987	9003 – 1987	Model for quality assurance in final inspection and testing.
IV – 1987	9004 – 1987	Quality management and quality system elements – guidelines.

The risk manager, in designing a product liability risk control programme, should work closely with the quality assurance manager and his quality assurance programme. In accordance with the general philosophy of risk management, the risk manager plays a consultative rôle and can therefore never be responsible for the implementation of the quality assurance programme.

The purpose and intention of this section is to consider the major elements of SABS 0157 and to indicate those areas of the code which concern the product liability risk control programme.

The SABS 0157 consists of 20 elements, which are dealt with hereunder. In addition to these 20 elements, there are two further aspects which are important from a product liability point of view, namely a product recall programme and liability for mere words. It is necessary to ensure that the product liability programme covers these two additional elements.

It is usually the responsibility of the quality assurance manager to co-ordinate the SABS code. A product liability programme should not duplicate this programme but rather use the SABS elements to minimise the risk of product liability claims. Accordingly, the requirements of the SABS will not be discussed from a quality assurance point of view, but rather how the SABS elements can be used to minimise product liability risks.

The use of the elements of SABS 0157 to minimise risk

The aspects found in SABS 0157 Part I can be used as follows to minimise risk:

- ☐ **Management responsibility**
  To minimise the risk of product liability claims it is essential that a holistic quality assurance programme be implemented. Senior management therefore has to ensure that such a programme does exist and that responsibility has been assigned to one person in the organisation for the programme and to various other persons for individual sections within the programme.

- ☐ **The quality system**
  It is essential that a properly defined quality assurance organisation be established within the company and that various persons be assigned the responsibility for the prevention of products liability claims. One person appointed by the general manager of the site, must be given the overall responsibility for the programme. This person must ensure that the programme is kept up to date. It should also not be possible to alter documentation pertaining to the programme without his specific consent.

  It is not sufficient simply to implement a system; provision should be made for the system to be reviewed from time to time. The system should be reviewed on a regular basis by internal as well as external auditors. Two aspects in particular should be reviewed, namely whether the regulations of the system is being complied with and whether the system itself is adequate. In practice it is found that while compliance is audited, the system itself is often not revised.

- ☐ **Contract review**
  It is essential that when a new product is placed on the market, the product liability aspects be taken into consideration. Requirements and planning for these aspects should not be neglected, as the oversight could prove to be costly indeed.

> A manufacturer produced a very inexpensive item. After making tens of thousands of these items the manufacturing dye was worn out and needed to be replaced. When the dyes had been replaced, they were found to be too small. As a result of the incorrect manufacturing dyes, the products being manufactured were slightly too big. The product was put into operation and resulted in a multi-million rand claim. It could have been a very simple matter to prevent the claim and the testing equipment concerned would have cost R5,00 at the most. The only reason the necessary testing instrument was not purchased, was that when the company received the order and designed the product, nobody determined the necessary quality tests needed to establish whether the product quality was suitable.

A detailed quality plan must therefore be drawn up for every product manufactured.

☐ **Design control**
The most critical aspect of any consumer product from a liability point of view is the design. If the design is incorrect, all products which are manufactured from the design will be incorrect. Indeed, the quality assurance will ensure that all products conform to the faulty design.

> The case of the BIC disposable lighter can illustrate this problem. Approximately 250 million lighters per annum are sold in the USA alone. If the design is defective it can result in millions of claims. In America BIC paid R6,5 million to one woman because a lighter ignited in her pocket causing burns to her body.[25] One small error of design could result in a company incurring sufficient claims to render it insolvent.

The design control programme should include a design review, field testing, reliability testing, incorporation of safety codes and standards and so forth.

☐ **Document control**
The quality assurance programme is essentially a programme defined by means of documents. It is accordingly very important that these documents be kept up to date. It is also important that changes not be made except by properly authorised persons who are clearly designated to perform the task. The system should also be designed in such a way that it is obvious from the document itself whether it is up to date.

> **An example of the danger of changes**
> One of the largest industrial disasters was caused at Flixcbough when alterations were carried out to the piping arrangements of a chemical plant. The temporary supporting structure collapsed causing an explosive vapour to be released. This ignited, causing an unconfined vapour cloud explosion.

Installation, manufacturing, repairs and alterations should all be carried out in accordance with the standards set out in the approved documentation. Strict control over the documentation and control over changes to the documentation is needed.

However, documentation can also be a two-edged sword and could be used against the person who prepared the document.[26]

☐ **Purchasing**
If the inputs, materials and services are defective, the final product could be defective. It is therefore necessary that all incoming materials

and services be carefully inspected. In order to do so, it is necessary to draw up specifications against which the incoming materials can be checked.

> **Incorrect supply of materials**
>
> The importance of inspecting raw materials cannot be overemphasised. All raw materials must be inspected by an approved statistical sampling programme. The integrity and identity of the materials should be confirmed and recorded. The Kinross mining disaster is an example of what can happen if the incorrect material is supplied. In the Kinross case the mine contracted for the supply and installation of a substance called polyisocyanurate.[61]
>
> Although the mine had ordered polyisocyanurate, it was supplied with polyurethane.
>
> It is therefore essential that the identity at least, of products be confirmed and all products which could cause injury to people and all safety critical products be carefully inspected.

☐ **Purchaser supplied products**

In practice, the purchaser may often supply some of the materials for the manufacture of a product himself. In this case the quality assurance programme should take this factor into consideration in the determination of the final standards and integrity of the product. Purchaser-supplied materials should be subject to the same controls as any other material. However, liability for defects in the final product as a result of purchaser-supplied materials should be determined and agreed upon beforehand.

☐ **Product identification and traceability**

If a product is defective, it is essential that remedial action be taken as soon as possible so as to minimise the extent of the damage. Identification and traceability may be necessary to prove whether a defect is involved. Therefore it should be possible to identify and trace products to the correct manufacturer.

> **Product traceability**
>
> In one case it was alleged that a certain product was defective and had caused the death of some animals. Fortunately the bag which had contained the so-called defective feed was found and returned to the manufacturer. From the label the manufacturer could establish which day, line and batch was involved. Since the so-called defective feed was also supplied to other customers on the same day and who did not suffer any ill effects, this was a good indication that the feed was not defective. Indeed, when the relevant batching instructions were examined, it became clear that the product was not defective.

61 Unpublished judgement, 1045 of the judgement handed down by Magistrate V.R. Pieterson.

- **Process control**

  The steps required during the manufacturing process can be defined via work instructions.

  The product liability programme functions in terms of work instructions, which indicate the steps required to manufacture the product according to the design specification. Therefore a section dealing with manufacturing control should be established. In practice, the manufacturing controls and procedures are probably the most widely used and understood aspect of any system. Although many companies do not have a defined quality system, they do operate according to specified manufacturing instructions.

  Once the work instructions have been determined, the manufacturing process must be programmed for implementation. Normally this will consist of defining the steps one should take to ensure that the product is manufactured correctly. This plan is put into action by means of the drawing up of specific instructions for various employees on the procedure of manufacturing the product. It therefore concerns the issuing of work instructions. The work instructions should be comprehensive and cover all aspects relating not only to the product, but also to safety.

  For example, assume that a work instruction has been issued for the inspection of raw materials. This should include the method to be adopted to inspect raw materials. If this material is a dangerous chemical, the work instruction should also include safety instructions, such as that protective clothing must be worn.

  The specific work instructions should integrate the requirements of other systems as well as the statutory requirements. Thus the NOSA MBO requirement for protective clothing should be incorporated into the document, as should the requirements in terms of the *Machinery and Occupational Safety Act* (6 of 1983). In this way all the different requirements can be integrated into one document, namely the work instructions.

- **Inspection and testing**

  A well-designed quality system incorporates inspection and testing requirements and should define which inspections and tests should be carried out to ensure product integrity. These tests may be expensive to carry out and add to the cost of the product. Unfortunately, in recent years, cases came to light where the defined tests were not carried out and the test documents were falsified.[27] This is not only obviously fraudulent but it is also dangerous.

- **Inspecting, measuring and testing equipment**

  In most cases the product is subjected to a number of inspections and tests during the manufacturing process. These testing stages are conducted with the aid of testing equipment. The equipment could be very simple, ranging from a simple spring balance or a go-no-go gauge, to multi-million rand electronic equipment. If the equipment is defective or incorrectly calibrated, the tests will be misleading. Therefore a clearly defined programme is needed to ensure that all testing and measuring instruments are accurate. The programme must also define the right type of instrument and correct margins of error for each instrument.

It appears that one of the great nuclear disasters, the Three Mile Island disaster, was caused by a faulty instrument. The importance of correct instrumentation, and checking that the instrumentation is accurate, cannot be overemphasised. In some instances, the specifications are laid down by law.

☐ **Inspection and test status**

As has already been indicated, a significant portion of the quality assurance programme is devoted to inspections and tests of one kind or another. These start with the receipt of the raw materials and continue through the different stages of manufacture. Some indication must therefore exist to indicate that the material has been inspected and, if inspected, whether it has passed the inspection or not. The test status should be indicated.

If a product is found to be defective, this should be indicated and it should be isolated. Once identified as defective, the suspect product should be dealt with as defined in the **control of non-conforming material**, specification of the code of practice.

> In one case defective products were withdrawn from the market, but because the test status was not indicated, the products were accidentally released back onto the market.

☐ **Control of non-conforming products**

Specific provision should be made in the quality assurance programme to control materials which do not comply with specifications.

> In one case a defective product was detected but adequate procedures did not exist for its control. The unmarked defective product was stored next to the production line, and placed with the marketable products. Any quality assurance programme should therefore specify how non-conforming material is to be controlled.

Once non-conforming material has been identified, the programme should specify which person has authority to deal with the material and also record what action was taken. The decision-maker should not be a member of the production department.

The decision to declare material as non-conforming could be very expensive, and it is not inconceivable that a production manager may decide to 'take a chance' and release non-conforming material onto the market in the hope that there will not be any returns.

> For example, it was reported that drugs were being sold to the public which had nearly reached the end of their shelf life. Rather than destroy the drugs, they were sold at a discount.[28]

☐ **Corrective action**

The programme should specify that corrective action be taken and which person has the authority to take such corrective action, should the product be defective or something go wrong with the manufacturing process.

It is important that the person making the decision for this corrective action not be a member of the manufacturing staff, but under the control of the quality assurance staff. Thus if a product is defective, somebody must make the decision whether the degree of defectiveness is so severe that the product should be abandoned, which could cause extensive losses; or whether the product process should be continued.

☐ **Handling, storage, packaging and delivery**

Once a product has been manufactured, the code should specify procedures to ensure that the integrity of the product remains intact until it is in the hands of the consumer.

This is particularly important in industries such as the pharmaceutical industry where it is necessary to mark the expiry date of the product on the product itself, so that the consumer who eventually buys it, can ensure that it is still safe and effective. If the expiry date is not indicated, the product may be manufactured correctly but because its shelf-life has expired, it may have lost its effectiveness. This type of claim does not arise from the manufacturing process itself, but from preservation aspects of the product.

Labelling, too, is an important product liability aspect. Labels must be accurate and disclose sufficient information to warn against any dangers associated with the product.

☐ **Quality records**

A number of documents are generated by the quality assurance system.

The different records should be defined and controlled in terms of the requirement relating to product records. The records should be comprehensive, starting at the raw material stage, and continue to include work instructions, all quality inspections and tests and finally the despatch and sales documents. It should therefore be possible to trace the total history of the product from its records.

The quality assurance programme should also indicate for how long the records should be kept and the methods available for locating the various records.

- ☐ **Internal quality audits**
  The system must make provision for an audit of the compliance with the requirements of the system. These internal audits should be conducted on a regular basis.

- ☐ **Training**
  Because a quality assurance programme is comprehensive and complicated, it normally takes three to four years to implement it from the day that the decision is made to the final implementation thereof. Thus an adequate training programme must form an integral part of the programme, so that the employees are adequately trained to operate the system.

Services

A large section of commerce and industry is not devoted to the provision of products but to the provision of services. Special procedures should be drawn up to minimise liability claims arising from the provision of services. These procedures will obviously differ, depending on the type of service provided.

> **An example of faulty service**
> In one case a contractor supplied transportation services. He delivered products to various manufacturers which were pumped into storage tanks. One day he discharged product A into the storage tank containing product B, instead of discharging it into tank A.

- ☐ **Statistical techniques**
  It is not always necessary to inspect every incoming item, particularly if these are not safety critical, as this can be expensive. In such a case it is possible to develop a sampling plan using statistical techniques. Sampling then takes place in accordance with the plan and deviations from the sample can be used as an indication of the integrity of the entire batch of raw material. The quality assurance programme should therefore define the sampling plan in terms of which the product will be inspected.

Products recall programme

The products recall programme generally does not form part of the quality assurance programme, although it does form part of a programme such as the *Good Manufacturing Practices* of the pharmaceutical industry. This is an area of particular concern and interest to the risk manager and in product liability literature this is often the main or only element of the quality assurance programme which is dealt with, in the products recall programme.

Since this aspect is normally dealt with as part of the quality assurance programme, the risk manager should ensure that adequate provision exists for the recall of defective products.

Liability for words

The quality assurance programme is generally aimed at ensuring that the product is manufactured according to the specifications. If it meets the specifications, the quality assurance manager is satisfied that his programme is functioning adequately. As was seen from the discussion on legal cases which gave rise to products liability claims, a product liability claim could be made even though the product is not defective. A liability claim could, for example, arise if the consumer has been mislead by the company concerning the purpose and effectiveness of the product. Therefore the product liability risk control programme should also include a programme aimed at training employees (as well as other techniques) to ensure that liability does not attach because of words.

> **Liability for words**
>
> In one case a company representative was asked if the product would be suitable for purpose A. He assured the buyer that it was. After the product was manufactured, it was found to be unsuitable. The company was held liable.

Sales representatives should therefore be trained concerning the consequences of using incorrect words and promises concerning the product.

The sales and technical literature should also be thoroughly checked as part of the quality assurance programme to ensure that the information contained therein is correct.

8.7.4 Liability for gradually developing environmental impairment

8.7.4.1 *Environmental concern*

One of the recent exceptions to a general liability insurance policy is liability attributable to gradual or ongoing release of pollutants.[29] It is therefore advisable to treat gradual pollution separately from pollution caused by sudden and accidental events.

The types of cost involved in environmental impairment are also unusual. Generally it does not concern the damage caused, but the rehabilitation of the environment. These costs could, however, run into billions of rand.

In America the *Consumer Movement*, which gave rise to the products liability crisis, was ushered in by a book by Ralph Nader entitled *Unsafe at any speed*. The other well-known consumer movement is the Environmental Movement which was ushered in with Rachel Carson's (1907-1964) book, entitled *Silent Spring* (1962). Since the 1960s world-wide concern has developed concerning the environment, and South Africa is no exception. Public opinion is against parties such as large companies who are perceived as damaging to the environment.

8.7.4.2 *South African case law*

Liability for impairment recognised in principle

In South Africa very few actions for damages arising from gradually developing environmental impairment have been instituted. In fact, until fairly recently very little had even been written on the subject.[30]

However, our courts would not approach the claims for environmental impairment as something different or unique, simply because it is an action involving the environment. It would simply apply the general principles of delict, which were dicussed earlier.

An early case in which the general principles were applied to an environmental problem was ***Regal v African Superslate (Pty) Limited*** 1963 1 SA 102 (A). In this leading case, in which liability for an omission was recognised, a previous owner (a company) of a piece of land had been liquidated. The company had used the land for quarrying purposes and it had left slate waste in a position where the flood waters of the Elands River could reach it. Under these circumstances the flood waters would wash the slate downstream and cause harm to a neighbour. The neighbour sought a court interdict against the previous owner but since the owner had been liquidated, the action came to naught. When a new owner bought the property, the neighbour instituted an action against this new owner. Clearly the new owner had not created the nuisance or danger that the slate would wash downstream, as it was already in existence when he bought the property.

The action failed on these facts but the court held:[62]

> . . . that if it was reasonably practicable to avert the still threatened damage . . . then the failure to do so would be unlawful, and then the appellant would have a basis for a petition for an interdict and possibly also for a claim for compensation for damage which he might suffer . . .
>
> and
>
> . . . the only acceptable basis of liability was a failure to take reasonably practicable steps to prevent the situation complained of . . .

The court thus recognised that a claim for compensation could succeed[63] if the actions of one person caused damage to another as a result of environmental impairment.

62 Quoting from the headnote 103 FH.

63 The court also recognised that liability could attach for omissions, a point which was developed in later judgements and which culminated in the Ewels case.

It should be clear that these quotations and the developments which have taken place in the SA common law since 1963, that if a person suffers damage which arises from gradually developing environmental impairment, he may very well succeed with an action at law.

The *Rylands v Fletcher (1868)* rule

Many industrial sites store a wide range of dangerous substances and even water could, under certain circumstances, be classified as a dangerous substance.

It is quite possible that damage could be caused by the dangerous substance, including water, escaping from a premise. In such cases the South African courts could possibly evoke the so-called *Rylands v Fletcher* rule. This rule imposes strict liability upon occupiers of dangerous property and states that:

> . . . a person who for his own purposes brings on his lands and collects and keeps there anything likely to do mischief if it escapes, must keep it in at his peril, and, if he does not do so, is *prima facie* answerable for all the damage which is the natural consequence of its escape.[31]

If this rule is applied, negligence is not required and it need only be shown that the damage or loss was caused by the dangerous substance which escaped.

It is generally accepted that the *Rylands* rule does not form part of our law, but in view of the changes to our common law in recent years, the court may, given the opportunity, indeed decide to make this rule applicable.

Liability may also attach because of the following:

- ☐ solid waste disposal
- ☐ ground water contamination.

Examples of environmental impairment

- ☐ A number of vegetable farmers in Tala Valley and in other parts of Natal issued summons to obtain a court interdict against manufacturers of agricultural chemicals, on the basis that the chemicals that they were using contained a substance known as 2,4D herbicide, which could conceivably damage crops.[32]
- ☐ The Witbank Town Council had pumped water into an underground mine and had started this action a number of years ago, apparently to put out an underground fire. As a result, it is alleged that the properties in the area are beginning to crumble.[33] An action for R100 million damages was instituted.
- ☐ Johannesburg-based property developer is to sue the Palaborwa Mining Company after its stud cattle died from copper poisoning. The developer is alleging that copper dust settled on the grass or fodder in the area and that the cattle died as a result of eating this. The farm, incidently, was situated some 15 km downwind from the mine[34] illustrating how wide the affected area of danger could be.

Continued

Continued

- ☐ A municipal dump has been in existence for a number of years outside of Limbro Park and water from the refuse dump has seeped into the water table, contaminating the nearby water boreholes.[35] This is a possible example of ground water pollution and illustrates the question of environmental harmony. The dump was established long before the residential area, but as people moved into the area they became dissatisfied with the refuse dump and petitioned to have it moved. The dump site and a residential area could not exist in harmony.
- ☐ A Vereeniging school boy was walking across an ash dump when he fell into the hot dump and was severely burnt. As a result, he instituted a claim against the owners and controllers of the dump and turned down an offer of R200 000[36] for settlement. This is an example of someone being injured as a result of the location of a solid waste disposal site.

8.7.4.3 *Risk control steps*

Structuring the risk identification audit

Again, the point of departure for an environmental impairment risk control programme is the identification of the risk. Indeed, a large percentage of the literature[64] on the subject of environmental impairment in the risk control field concerns the structuring of a risk identification audit. This audit is somewhat more difficult to structure and carry out than the audit of, say, the identification of an event such as a possible accident, since the causes of the environmental impairment are not that obvious to the person carrying out the audit.

For example, in the Witbank case mentioned above, the dangers of pumping water into an underground mine were not self-evident. Even if noted, the person conducting the audit may not realise that this could be the source of a R100 million lawsuit. It is therefore so much more difficult to identify the possible sources and consequences of actions in the case of risks of this nature.

While there are a number of ways of structuring an audit, a logical way of going about it would be to examine the areas which could be affected by environmental impairment agents and then to identify the agents which could affect that particular aspect of the environment. The areas which are normally affected by environmental impairment are the surrounding land, air, running water and ground water.

☐ **Surrounding land**

The most obvious group of people who may be affected by environmental issues are the persons on surrounding properties. A description and profile of surrounding properties should be drawn up.

64 On environment auditing the following articles can be read: Pizza (1982, 253) and Russell (1985, 27, *et seq.*).

Persons on neighbouring land may be affected by the activities of an industrial company and by various impairment agents. These need not be dangerous or hazardous, but may simply be a nuisance or cause discomfort, as in the case of noise and odours. While neither of these two agents pose any particular health hazard or health threat it is a cause for concern and so an audit should determine whether any problems are known to have arisen from this particular source.

Another way in which the surrounding areas can be affected is by the disharmony caused by the activities of an industrial site. It often happens that people move into the area long after an industrial site has been developed and sooner or later pressure groups develop which aim at having the industrial site removed. A record should thus be kept of developments in the area and township developments in particular, should be carefully monitored.

☐ **Air**

Air can be contaminated by the activities carried out at an industrial site and pollution agents can be dangerous to health and property. Atmospheric pollution is controlled in terms of legislation and the audit should ensure that the necessary permits and monitoring procedures are in order. The audit should then concentrate on identifying the sources or agents which pollute the atmosphere and risk control steps should be directed at those particular sources.

☐ **Water**

Water is controlled in terms of the *Water Act* (54 of 1956), which has very strict provisions and stringent monitoring requirements. Again, some sort of statutory risk control programme should be implemented to ensure that the requirements of legislation on water have been met. The audit should concentrate on identifying the source of the water, its discharge point and also whether and where any contaminants are let into the water. Once it is determined that the water is or can be contaminated, the risk control steps aimed at those specific aspects of contamination should be implemented.

It should also be borne in mind that the contamination need not be of a chemical nature. It could be something as innocuous as heat. Often factories draw water for cooling purposes and then return the heated water to the streams. Such heated water could be the cause of changes or damage to the ecology.

☐ **Ground water**

Ground water pollution is much more serious in that the pollution can take place without anyone being aware of it. Ground water is also controlled by legislation and the requirements for the legislation, particularly the regulations promulgated in terms of the *Water Act* (54 of 1956), should be complied with.

On a large industrial site boreholes should be sunk around the site and samples taken at regular intervals to determine whether the ground water has been contaminated. The identification audit should, in addition, be aimed at monitoring the ground water condition if contamination is detected. The next step of the audit should be to concentrate on determining which aspects do, or could, cause the contamination of the ground water.

Aspects which usually cause contamination should be identified. These include items such as dams, particularly cooling or holding dams, underground storage tanks, etc. In the case of dams, contaminated water and chemicals are often pumped into the dam and as the water evaporates, the concentration of the chemical rises and then seep into the ground water. Eventually the contaminated ground water could surface several kilometres away from the site.

Another source of ground water contamination is underground tanks. If there are underground tanks on site which contain chemicals, these should be identified and the type of chemicals as well as their possible effects listed.

Closely allied to underground tanks are underground pipes.

Solid waste is another source of ground water contamination. Often waste buried years ago decomposes and seeps into the ground water. For this reason solid waste dumps and tips should also contain leaching points or boreholes from which the water which is flowing from the dumps can be monitored.

Franschoekse Wynkelder (Ko-operatief) Beperk v SAR & H[65]

In this case the SAR & H employed a contractor, Union Weedkiller Services (Pty) Limited, to spray the undergrowth alongside the railway line with weedkiller. The weedkiller apparently seeped into the water table and caused damage to vines on nearby farms. Because of damage the grapes could not be sold to the co-operative society, the society suffered a financial loss of R975 664 which it sought to recover from the SAR & H.

However, because the action was brought by the co-operative society and not the individual farmers, the exception by the SAR & H was upheld, on the basis that the damage it suffered was too remote. The basis of the action was negligence and had the individual farmers sued, the result may have been different.

Solid waste

Contaminated solid waste is becoming a world-wide problem. In some well-publicised cases ships loaded with waste have travelled around the world in search of a country which would accept the waste. The

65 1981 (3) SA 36 (C).

type of waste should be investigated and any waste sites carefully recorded on a plan.

- ☐ **Transportation**

Environmental impairment need not only originate on the site itself but can come from activities conducted off-site. For this reason it is necessary to carefully investigate the transportation activities of a company. It should be identified whether the company transports any substances which could contaminate or impair the environment. If such a situation exists, this means that if an accident occurs, the contamination of the environment can take place off-site. In South Africa a number of hazardous substances have fallen off trucks and ended up in rivers.

- ☐ **Dams**

Storage dams can be the source of environmental impairment, particularly to the ground water. If storage dams are used and have been identified in accordance with the above-mentioned risk identification programme, steps should be taken to ensure that they are not the source of contamination.

Monitoring systems should be installed on the dam to detect or monitor any leaks. The condition of the ground water in the vicinity of the dam should also be monitored. If a dam develops a leak, the detection system should pick this up and steps should be taken to seal the leak in such a way that further leaks will not occur. Special linings may have to be installed for this purpose.

- ☐ **Underground tanks**

Underground tanks are a further possible source of ground water pollution and hold the potential for economic disaster.[37] In the USA the United States Congress amended the *Resource Conservation and Recovery Act* (RCRA) in 1984 and gave the United States Environmental Protection Agency (EPA) broad new areas to regulate together with unusually specific legislative directives. Among the new items that Congress targeted for regulation are underground storage tanks, in effect changing the way that such tanks may be managed.

The new legislation in the United States specifies how tanks are to be installed and monitored. These regulations, which include the following, give a good indication of the risk control steps that one should consider with regard to underground tanks:

- The discouragement of single wall tanks and encouraging the construction of tanks with spill containment systems.
- The tanks and piping should be designed so that they can be visually inspected on a frequent basis. Tanks which cannot be visually inspected require secondary containment and alarm systems, capable of rapidly detecting a leak.

- The main emphasis of the programme is the prevention of leaks from tanks and pipelines.
- Regular tank inspection and testing. The inspection frequency should not be less than once per year. The testing programmes should form part of the plant maintenance system.
- Underground or ground water monitoring is a prerequisite of the underground storage tank programme.[66]
- All new underground tanks must be installed to a recognised, approved standard of construction.
- A detailed tank management plan which addresses operator training, emergency response procedures, and operation and inspection procedures must be drawn up and kept up to date.
- Underground tanks and pipes must have corrosion protection and make use of non-corrosive backfill materials, installed in accordance with the requirements of a properly qualified professional engineer.

It is clear from this list that the USA takes the possibility of environmental impairment from underground tanks very seriously indeed.

☐ **Underground pipes**

Underground pipes can also be the source of pollution and detailed requirements must be drawn up for the installation of these pipes.[67]

The programme is similar to the programme for underground tanks.

☐ **Solid waste**

Solid waste can be another source of environmental impairment. The waste could lie undetected for many years and then only start to pollute the environment. The problem of solid waste is international and various countries throughout the world have been trying to find ways to dispose of this waste.

Where possible this type of waste should be disposed of through the services of a properly qualified hazardous waste contractor. The contractor should then take the waste of a specially designated disposal site. When this disposal takes place it is important to ensure that all liability passes to the contractor and the contract conditions should thus be examined very carefully. The location of any buried waste should be carefully recorded on site plans.

The recently promulgated regulations for solid waste sites can be used to develop a statutory risk control programme.[38]

66 Details of an underground monitoring system can be found in Russell (1987).

67 Details of underground piping can be found in *Chemical Engineering* (7 December 1987, 22).

> ***Smit v Suid-Afrikaanse Vervoerdienste***[68]
>
> An employee of the SATS dumped some carbide in a rubbish bin at a station, a place which was readily accessible to the public. Willy Smit, who was 12 years old found the carbide and used it to make a bomb by placing it in a bottle with water. The bomb was buried and subsequently exploded, injuring the boy.

- **Atmospheric pollution**

  Atmospheric pollution is controlled in terms of the *Atmospheric Pollution Prevention Act* (45 of 1965) and the statutory risk control programme should be drawn up to comply with the requirements of this act. The necessary permits should also be obtained and the permit conditions be strictly adhered to.

- **Surface water**

  In many instances pollution from a site falls on the ground and is washed into rivers during a rainstorm. Where this is identified as a problem, the storm water system should be set up in such a way that substances are treated before leaving the sites.

- **Water**

  Water pollution is also controlled by legislation and the necessary statutory risk control programmes should be drawn up in accordance with legislation. The water authorities in this country are very strict but also co-operative and if the programme is drawn up in consultation with these bodies, the legislative requirements are, as a general rule, complied with.

8.7.5 Fire risk control

8.7.5.1 *Nature and extent of the risk*

The nature and extent of the damage caused by accidental fire and explosion is not always realised even by many of those who are relatively closely involved in this aspect of risk control.

Annual direct property damage losses in South Africa run into hundreds of millions of rand. For instance, in 1987 the direct loss was estimated at R320 m. This figure does not include consequential losses which probably total three times the direct loss amount.

In addition to the monetary loss of property or assets, the loss of life resulting from fires and explosions must also be taken into consideration. In 1987, the number of deaths reported and directly attributable to fire was 248. However, this number actually only reflects deaths which

68 1984 (1) SA 246 (C).

occurred in urban areas and figures compiled by the Department of Statistics reflect an annual average in excess of 800.

Fire also causes unemployment and loss of business opportunities. Notwithstanding insurance cover, it is estimated that in excess of 50% of all businesses which suffer a major fire never recover sufficiently to resume their business.

8.7.5.2 *Legal requirements, codes of practice and standards*

Many aspects of fire and explosion prevention and protection are prescribed by law. The most important of these are to be found in the *National Building Regulations and Building Standards Act* (103 of 1977), the *Fire Brigade Services Act* (99 of 1987) and the *Machinery and Occupational Safety Act* (6 of 1983).

Other legislation also applies to a varying extent and includes, *inter alia*, the *Hazardous Substances Act* (15 of 1973), the *Explosives Act* (26 of 1956) and local authority fire by-laws. In addition to the above, the numerous regulations pertaining thereto also apply.

Numerous codes of practice are also published by the South African Bureau of Standards. While these codes are not legal requirements in the strictest sense, the majority have become that by their adoption and incorporation into fire by-laws.

These codes of practice are extremely valuable and important documents which were drawn up by committees of experts in their respective fields and who were co-opted by the SABS for this purpose.

Another very valuable source of excellent information is the *National Fire Code* published by the *National Fire Protection Association of America* (NFPA). This is a comprehensive guide which is updated annually.

In South Africa, the *Automatic Sprinkler Inspection Bureau* (ASIB) is the body with the responsibility not only to monitor sprinklers on behalf of both the insured and the insurer, but also to publish and update the rules for automatic sprinkler installations. This rulebook is also a fully comprehensive document, which has been developed over more than a century of fire engineering experience and is an indispensable tool for those engaged in fire risk control.

In recent times, the need for effective risk control has prompted some businesses, mainly corporate groups, to formulate tailor-made risk control standards of their own.

8.7.5.3 *Requirements of insurance companies*

Depending upon the wording of the policy, the insurance company may impose certain requirements on the insured. These requirements usually apply to fire fighting equipment and systems such as automatic sprinklers, and compliance with the ASIB rules is normally a pre-requisite.

In some cases, especially where hazardous materials such as liquified petroleum gas or flammable liquids are being used, handled or stored, the insured will be required to comply with the relevant SABS code of practice.

The insured will, in all cases, be expected to comply with statutory requirements as they apply to the particular premises or business being conducted. These include *inter alia* MOSACT and the *National Building Regulations*.

In those rare cases where legislation is unclear or where no provision is made as such for a particular process or activity, the insurance company may determine the requirements it deems necessary. These requirements are generally not made conditions of the policy.

It is of particular importance to note that once the terms of a policy have been agreed upon, any loss which may occur and which can be proven attributable to the non-compliance by the insured with a warranty, may result in the repudiation of a claim by the insurer.

8.7.5.4 *Fire risk control*

Inspection programmes

By far the most important aspect of fire and explosion risk control is an adequate preventative inspection programme. No business undertaking is too small to derive benefit from this and in most cases the results are extremely cost effective in the long term. Better insurance rates are obtainable and business interruption costs are eliminated or at least minimised.

Emergency procedures

The absence of a pre-determined and formalised fire or emergency procedure is often the direct cause of a fire developing into a major loss. An almost universal necessity is that every business must have an effective plan of action in the event of fire, explosion or other emergency. One of the prerequisites of such an action plan is that it should be simple, effective and understandable to all employees.

In all business undertakings an authoritative person should be charged with the overall responsibility for risk control and also for the formulation of a fire procedure. In small operations one person would, no doubt, accomplish the task on his own but in larger organisations he would require the assistance of a nominated or elected committee.

Depending again on the size of the business, an essential part of any fire procedure is the nomination of fire teams, team leaders and fire wardens or marshals. In these people are vested the responsibility of initially taking charge in the event of an emergency, until the arrival of the public fire service or the person holding overall responsibility.

Fire-safe building design

Among the many prerequisites of any building is fire safety. This can be broken down into the following:

- **Life safety**
  Every building should be designed so that in the event of fire, persons inhabiting that building may have free and unimpeded access to safe escape routes.

- **Building protection**
  Buildings should be designed and constructed in such a way that in the event of fire, the building affords the maximum protection to itself and its contents until fire-fighting operations can begin and also during such operations.

- **Building survival**
  High value structures require that the building skeleton be capable of suffering a major fire without collapse or serious structural damage. Rehabilitation of such a building is far less expensive than demolition and reconstruction, while business interruption costs are also minimised.

Site planning and layout

It is vital that fire protection be perceived as one of the priority items to be dealt with by the design team. Possible future expansion must be kept in mind.

In all cases, the *National Building Regulations* and *SABS Code of Practice 0400* should be referred to and the former must in all cases be applied.

Construction methods

While it is possible to construct an entirely fire-resistant building, such a structure would have no practical use. Buildings must be habitable and useful and in the provision of these attributes, the resultant fire risk must be dealt with.

Non-combustible materials should be used as far as is practicable. The term non-combustible does not of necessity mean that it is fire resistant. In this way steel requires a protective covering if it is to carry a load through a fire reliably, while glass has very little or no resistance to fire.

The structure itself should ideally be designed in such a way that it adds as little as possible to the ultimate fire load.

Fire detection

One of the most important facets of prevention of loss as a result of fire is an early warning that a fire has started. Modern fire-detection systems, if properly engineered, installed and maintained can be extremely valuable in raising the alarm at an early stage.

In order to determine the type of system best suited to a particular building, it is essential to have a thorough knowledge of the nature of the risk against which it is to be protected.

Other fire-risk control measures

Other fire-risk control measures include alarm systems, portable and fixed fire extinguishers, the identification of hazardous materials and fire investigations.

8.7.6 Natural perils

8.7.6.1 *Definition*

> Natural perils may be defined as those hazards or pure risks which generally arise from natural causes, as opposed to losses brought about by the intervention of man.

For this reason damage caused by natural perils are often referred to as acts of God. Through the ages natural perils have been responsible for many of the worst losses in history, and well-known examples include fire, flood, storm and earthquake.

Because of the large scale destructive power of natural perils, the term catastrophe has come to be associated with natural perils, especially from an insurance point of view.

Virtually all natural perils are insurable:[69] in fact, modern short-term insurance practice has its origin in the need to spread the risk of losses brought about, in the main, by natural perils in the maritime industry.

In the context of conventional short-term insurance, there are two main forms of natural perils coverage:

(i) **Fire and allied perils**

Fire and 'allied perils' is a popular form of insurance cover. In this context allied perils are those which have historically been associated with fire insurance and against which cover is effected by adding them to a fire policy. The following are the usual allied perils:

- ☐ earthquake
- ☐ explosion
- ☐ riot and strike
- ☐ malicious damage
- ☐ special perils
- ☐ spontaneous combustion
- ☐ sprinkler leakage.

Special perils generally constitute an extension to a fire or profits policy. These special perils usually include the following:

- ☐ storm, wind, water, hail or snow

69 See Chapter 13, section 13.7 for a discussion of short-term insurance on natural perils.

- ☐ aircraft, aerial devices or articles dropped from it
- ☐ impact by animals or road vehicles.

(ii) **Assets all risks**

In this type of policy natural perils are covered in the property damage section. The actual perils covered are generally specified, as are those specifically excluded from the policy.

Although it is impossible to control the advent of the natural peril concerned, there are tried and tested risk control techniques and measures which can reduce the loss of life and damage to property which so often characterises these perils.

8.7.6.2 *Risk control techniques and measures*

Risk avoidance

Even a cursory knowledge of natural perils brings the realisation that many of these perils are not evenly distributed. While some perils, such as fire and lightning, occur widely, others, such as earthquake and severe storm, are governed by natural phenomena which result in area-bound perils. In South Africa, for instance, damaging earthquakes are rare events for the country as a whole and even then they are generally restricted to specific areas. This characteristic of natural perils leads directly to the risk-avoidance technique of risk control.

In accordance with this technique, areas prone to the occurrence of one or more perils will be avoided where possible. For example, given reasonable alternatives it is better to avoid sites which are subject to regular riverine flooding or tornadoes. This is easier to accomplish for certain perils than for others. In many cases the location of the premises is contingent on factors beyond management control, for example, thermal power stations near sources of coal, or sugar mills near cane farms.

Risk elimination

This technique has the same final result as risk avoidance except that in the case of elimination, the particular risk already exists and elimination will generally require a relocation to an area which is free from the natural peril that is to be eliminated.

Legislation

It is obviously in the interests of government and the local authority to avoid or eliminate, as far as possible, natural perils affecting the people for whom these authorities are responsible. For this reason, there are a number of statutes designed with the objective of avoiding unnecessary exposure to natural perils. An example of this legislation is the *Water Act* (54 of 1956), which states in Section 169(a) that no township may be established or extended without the flood levels expected at prescribed flood recurrence intervals being indicated on the layout plan. This alerts the authorities, empowered to approve the establishment or extension concerned, to the vulnerability of certain areas.

Risk reduction

This technique is aimed at the reduction of loss or damage brought about by one or more natural perils. Risk reduction starts at government level with certain legislation such as the *National Building Regulations* where the minimum standards laid down in those regulations are aimed at protecting the safety and well-being of society, by regulating the nature of buildings being constructed. Many of the features required serve to protect these buildings against water, storm, hail and earthquakes. It will be noted that earthquake-resistant buildings are being developed in Japan and California, and similar guidelines apply in South Africa.

Emergency planning

Natural perils such as floods, storms and earthquakes will often constitute emergency situations where and when they strike. Emergency planning is an important risk-control measure aimed at reducing the severity of the impact.

8.7.7 Crime perils

8.7.7.1 *Definition*

> Security, as a business management risk-control discipline, is concerned with the provision of appropriate standards of protection for people, property and other assets against the security risks to which they are exposed.

This definition correctly implies that security risks must first be identified and evaluated in the organisation concerned, before appropriate standards of protection can be considered.

Security risks in a business setting include not only criminal acts, but also so-called mischievous acts, negligence, carelessness and certain public liability risks, all of which result in downgrading incidents.

Security risks are classified into the following four main categories:

- criminal acts
- negligence, carelessness and mischief
- public liability losses
- unconventional threats and mischief.

Many of these threats, particularly conventional criminal acts, are commonplace and of long standing. Crimes such as theft, fraud, robbery and burglary have been around for ages. The protective measures relating to these traditional or conventional threats are generally in place and form part and parcel of existing security programmes. More recently, attention is being directed at some of the later, unconventional criminal threats and those arising in the socio-economic arena.

8.7.7.2 *Levels of security risks*

The range of security risks as outlined above is so wide that it is useful to consider them at three levels. The three levels of security risks are generally considered to be the following:

(i) Risks to personal security – these are risks which affect the individual in his private capacity.

(ii) Security risks to business organisations – these risks are aimed at the industrial, commercial and other private-sector undertakings.

(iii) National security risks – these are security risks which directly or indirectly threaten national assets or the nation as a whole.

8.7.7.3 *Security in the risk control context*

Security as a risk control discipline cannot be isolated into a totally separate field as it has implications for a number of other risk control disciplines such as safety and fire. For example, certain measures which may be desirable from a security point of view may not be acceptable in a fire protection context, such as the locking of exits and other means of escape from buildings.

8.7.8 Motor vehicle risk control

8.7.8.1 *Nature and extent of the problem*

Motor vehicles represent a significant part of the capital and operating expenditure of any organisation, not only because of high running costs but also because of costs associated with fortuitous losses such as accidents. Such losses can be attributed mainly to a lack of effective risk control measures.

8.7.8.2 *Consequential losses*

The opinion that accident costs are adequately covered by insurance, and that the company would not suffer any financial loss, is grossly misleading. Apart from the cost of repairs or replacement and the payment of third party claims, other factors must also be taken into consideration. These include the policy excess, loss of use of the vehicle, management time in investigation, retrieval of the damaged vehicle, hire of a replacement vehicle and loss of productivity.

Insurance premiums are linked to claims payments, and the higher the number of claims in a given year, the higher the premiums will be the following year. Properly implemented risk control measures may therefore favourably affect insurance premiums.

8.7.8.3 *Scope of vehicle risk control*

Motor vehicle risk control measures can be applied in every operating location, whether the organisation has a scooter only, or a fleet of many and varied motor vehicles. The elements of a risk control programme are the following:

Company policy Regardless of size, every organisation should have a defined motor vehicle risk control policy and a policy statement, signed by the chief executive, should be issued to all members of staff concerned with the use and operation of company or allowance scheme vehicles.

Responsibilities The responsibility for the co-ordination, decision-making and daily control of the motor vehicle risk control progamme should be delegated to a member of management either on a full or part-time basis.

Driver-selection Guidelines should be compiled for the selection of drivers and minimum standards should be detailed.

Driver induction and training A continuing programme of education, evaluation, training and re-training of drivers should be maintained.

Driver motivation A programme to encourage discipline and motivation and to provide opportunities for advancement should be introduced.

Vehicle maintenance A programme to ensure that the vehicles are maintained in a roadworthy condition is essential.

Accident reporting and investigation A procedure for reporting and investigating accidents in order to determine causes and to reduce the frequency of recurrence should be established.

Effective cost control A method for ensuring that effective cost control is achieved should be developed and maintained.

The annual accident frequency and vehicle accident loss rate should be determined on a continuous basis. Separate figures should be recorded for the different types of vehicles owned by the organisation. These rates should also be calculated in respect of each driver for control and supervision purposes.

8.7.8.4 *Fleet types*

In most organisations the various types of vehicles being used will invariably be categorised according to the different operating conditions, procedures and instructions which will apply. The following four classifications would be applicable to the majority of organisations:

(i) Commercial and industrial vehicles (comprising goods-carrying and passenger vehicles).

(ii) Allocated and allowance vehicles (comprising motor vehicles assigned on a permanent basis to a company official, or vehicles owned by the driver who receives an allowance from the company).

(iii) Pool vehicles (comprising vehicles not allocated to designated persons but which are available to authorised employees).

(iv) Off-road vehicles (comprising vehicles used exclusively on-site by appointed or authorised employees).

8.7.8.5 *Freight*

The nature of freight being transported influences the type of risk control measures that need to be applied. The following may be considered:

Explosives and hazardous substances

If explosives are transported, the relevant provisions of the *Explosives Act* (26 of 1956) and Chapter Six of the regulations must be complied with.

The regulations governing the conveyance of hazardous substances promulgated in terms of the *Hazardous Substances Act* (15 of 1972) must be complied with.

Passengers

The provisions relating to passenger-carrying vehicles in the road traffic ordinances, *Road Traffic Act* (29 of 1989) and the *Road Transportation Act* (74 of 1977) must be studied if employees are to be conveyed by company transport.

Extra-heavy loads

The vehicle must be custom-designed for the load being transported and the pre-trip checklist should include checking the stability of the load. The *SABS Code of Practice for Cargo Securement on Vehicles* (SABS 0187 – 1983) is a useful reference guide in this regard.

8.7.9 Consequential loss (business interruption)

One of the major exposures facing any company is the exposure to loss of profits as a result of some incident which interrupts or interferes with normal business activities.

It will be recalled that one of the classifications of risk was in accordance with the financial consequences of the risk. When an analysis was done on this basis, it was indicated that the following five classes of financial consequences exist:

(i) the costs of the damage to assets

(ii) the consequential losses which result from the damage to those assets

(iii) pure financial losses

(iv) legal liability claims

(v) employee benefit costs.

The consequential loss programme deals mainly with the second category, namely financial consequences associated with damage to assets.

It is important to keep this classification in mind because, otherwise, confusion will result between classes (ii) and (iii) above. The main difference is that generally, pure financial losses are not insurable.

There are many instances where a company can incur pure financial losses, as for example in the case of a strike which may bring production to a halt. This results in losses in the form of loss of sales or income which are generally not an insurable loss. Measures to prevent and deal with strikes are, however, the responsibility of the industrial manager and not the risk manager.

If one designs a consequential loss programme without taking into consideration the clear distinction between category (ii) and (iii) above, it is possible that the programme will encroach upon speculative risks. Indeed, if the distinction is not borne in mind at all times, the risk control programme will encroach on all activities of the firm.

8.7.9.1 *The nature of the interruption risk control programme*

A risk control programme is in many ways similar to the legal liability risk control programme, in that both are aimed at managing the consequences of an event. The control of the event itself will often be dealt with according to another risk control programme. Thus, extensive consequential losses can be suffered if a factory is destroyed by fire, but the prevention of fire is the function of a fire-risk control programme.

A consequential risk control programme has its own objectives. For example, the purchase of a spare transformer with the specific objective of limiting consequential losses, cannot be viewed as part of a fire risk control programme.

8.7.9.2 *Sources of consequential losses*

Loss of aggregate assets

It is important to identify those loss situations which could result in consequential losses. It is obvious that the destruction of assets can be a major source of consequential losses, because, if an asset which is normally used in the production of income is destroyed, then consequential losses can follow.

Current assets

Loss of current assets such as raw materials and finished goods can also result in consequential losses. If raw materials are damaged, say in a fire, production time may be lost. If finished goods are destroyed, loss of sales can result which could also cause a loss of market share.

Production assets

Consequential losses can arise if production equipment is damaged. Various types of machinery are the most common examples of production equipment machinery.

Testing equipment

Production can also be lost if other items of equipment, such as testing and quality assurance equipment, are damaged.

Damage to internal services

Consequential losses can occur if services such as the electrical, mechanical, steam, compressed air or computer services are damaged.

Utilities

Consequential losses are not only caused by damage to owned assets. If a business is dependent on third parties it may also arise if there is damage to such third-party assets. It follows that a business may be affected by losses occurring on suppliers' premises.

Production can also be interrupted as a result of damage to utilities such as electricity, water, gas, roads and steam. Another source of consequential loss is the loss of a distribution facility.

From the above it is clear that interruption losses can arise from a wide range of events.

8.7.9.3 *Consequential losses are time-related*

The nature of interruption losses

Consequential losses are time-related because the longer production is halted for any reason, the longer the loss of income will exist, or the longer additional working costs will be incurred, to keep the products or services in the market place.

Indemnity period

Since consequential losses are time-related, the insurance industry imposes a time limit to such losses. The period for which losses are covered is called the indemnity period and the consequence is that long-term losses (that is, extending beyond the indemnity period) will not be covered by insurance.

Danger of loss of market share

One of the most serious consequences of a long halt in production is that it may result in the company losing its share of the market. This is further aggravated by the fact that because this is a long-term consequence, it is not insurable. In cases where long-term losses may occur it is important that an adequate risk control programme, with the specific aim of preventing long-term losses be installed. Insurance is not the solution to loss of market share.

8.7.9.4 *The accounting and insurance aspects of interruption losses*

Some forms of interruption losses are insurable by means of specialised insurance.

In some instances consequential losses exceed the cost of material damage.[70] Interruption insurance cover will generally only respond to claims for damage to assets from insurable perils. Consequential loss insurance is thus not a free-standing insurance against consequential loss; it is intimately tied to physical damage to assets as a result of insured perils. This point is made very clear by Atkins.[39]

> By what ever name it is known (and for the present purpose it will be called 'profits' insurance), its basic function is to pay for the financial loss that may be sustained by a business undertaking should its operation be interrupted or interfered with as a result of 'insured damage' to the physical assets of the undertaking occurring . . .
>
> Usually, the insured damage is that which would be covered by a 'fire and allied perils' policy, but there are other forms of policy, such as 'engineering' and 'marine policies' to which profits insurance, in one form or another may be related.

Therefore, the interruption or profits policy is activated by damage to physical assets which are normally covered by another policy such as fire and engineering policies. If this distinction is not borne in mind, risk control programmes will tend to deal with management and engineering problems which might often be quite unrelated to pure risks, but rather to increased business efficiency.

The way in which the sum insured is calculated (and what this in fact means) is important if a risk is to be evaluated. However, rather than deal with it as part of this course, it should be dealt with in an insurance course on loss of profits insurance. In appendix A three articles by Atkins are noted which may be consulted to determine how the sum insured is calculated and what is meant by loss of profits from an insurance point of view.

8.7.9.5 *Risk identification*

By nature the loss is intangible

When one deals with losses which arise from damage to assets, risk identification is both important and difficult. Regarding damage to assets, all that is needed is first to identify the assets which can be damaged and then the perils to which these assets are exposed. Once it has been determined which assets are at risk, the cost of the assets can be calculated and an indication of the exposure due to loss or damage to assets can be made.

The determination of the exposure for interruption losses is much more difficult. While consequential losses have a financial implication, it is not possible simply to examine the asset and then to determine what the consequential losses, due to the loss of that asset, may be. For example, if

---

70 McDonald DL 1966. *Corporate Risk Control*. 221. In this work it is pointed out that a group of affiliated insurance companies found that in 15 of 21 cases of damage to steel plants, the consequential losses were greater than the material damage losses.

a company has a transformer, the loss of that transformer may have minimal consequences if a spare transformer is available. On the other hand, the loss of the transformer may result in catastrophic financial losses particularly if a spare is not available and the transformer is unique and cannot be replaced.

The problem is accentuated if it is borne in mind that not only individual but also groups of assets can be damaged and even total conglomerates of assets. For example, an entire factory may be devastated as a result of a fire or earthquake. On the other hand, individual buildings within that complex may be damaged or even individual items, such as an electric motor or transformer within the building may be damaged. From this it is clear that in designing an interruption loss programme one needs to start by looking at the impact that the loss of composite assets will have, then work towards assessing the impact of the individual items which could be damaged. Table 8.7 lists some of the assets which are normally involved in an analysis to determine what the consequences of loss of these assets will be.

Table 8.7
Assets from which consequential losses can arise

Item	Peril	Consequence
COMPOSITE ASSETS		
BUILDINGS		
1. Administration		
2. Production		
3. Storage		
(1) Raw materials		
(2) Finished goods		
4. Services		
5. Transport		
EQUIPMENT		
1. Production machinery		
2. Services		
3. Testing		
4. Transport		
ASSETS BELONGING TO UTILITIES		
1. Water		
2. Electricity		
3. Steam		
ASSETS BELONGING TO SUPPLIERS		
1. Materials		
2. Services		

From table 8.7 it is clear that assets which do not belong to the business are included in the analysis. The point is again emphasised that it is possible to insure against the loss of profits which can occur as a consequence of a business interruption caused by a supplier due to damage to his assets. The insurance is not actually against the loss of the supplier's materials, but against loss of supplier's material due to damage to the supplier's assets.

As was indicated in table 8.7, the impact of various perils on the assets must be assessed. The perils include fire, impact, internal breakdown and theft and in order to complete table 8.7 an estimate of repair and replacement costs must be made. The downtime will also be related to the spares kept or available.

Each item used in the production process must be identified and carefully considered. At the same time any special features such as PCB insulation in transformers or unique features, which makes a machine difficult to replace, will be discovered and the impact on downtime estimated.

If it becomes clear that the downtime is unacceptable as is the case of replacement times which exceed a few weeks, contingency plans should be developed.

Flow diagrams

Since consequential losses are intangible, it helps considerably if the potential loss sources are expressed in some tangible form such as a diagrammatic representation.

It is for this reason that extensive use is made of flow diagrams in the determination of the interruption loss exposure. These diagrams indicate the flow of materials from raw materials through to the delivery of the finished goods to the customer. The diagrams indicate the various items of equipment required for production purposes and other inputs, including the distribution system. An analysis of the flow diagrams can then be done and the consequence of an interruption from any single item, such as a machine, on the total flow of goods can be determined.

Once probabibilities and marginal contributions are included on the diagram, the flow diagram lends itself to a systematic analysis.

Use of financial and management accounts

The most useful tool for the analysis of consequential loss values is the company's financial and management accounts.

By using the income and expenditure statements, a 'what if' analysis can be undertaken. If the financial statements are available on a computer spread sheet, the analysis becomes that much easier. So, for example, the impact of loss of an item of equipment can be estimated and changes made to the spreadsheet. The income and expenditure figures affected by the loss or damage to the equipment can be adjusted and the final projected impact on the gross profit estimated with a reasonable degree of certainty.

8.7.9.6 *Risk evaluation*

Time periods used in the evaluation

Interruption loss analysis, together with the flow diagrams, lend themselves to the concept of risk evaluation by means of various forms of probability analysis. This is particularly true of items such as electrical distribution works which lend themselves to a great deal of analysis and which lead to the field of reliability studies and value engineering.

To avoid unnecessary complexity in the evaluation, one should remember that the exposure is time-related and that the evaluation has mainly two limits of concern. In the first instance, the evaluation is not concerned with small, short-duration breakdowns which can normally be funded in terms of a maintenance budget. One could, in general, therefore comfortably work on a lower limit of up to a seven-day breakdown. The other important limit of concern is the insurance period of indemnity. This period of indemnity can range from about three months to one or two years.

In order to simplify the calculations, as a first approximation of the exposure one should simply work on the basis that a certain item of machinery will be out of operation for a period of say six months and determine the exposure on that basis. If one can be reasonably sure that it is not probable that an out-of-operation period will last longer than six months, as in the case of a normal electric motor, then it is not necessary to be concerned with losses of long-term items such as a loss of the market share.

If the procedure for selecting a fixed period of outage is not adopted, loss-distribution curves must be developed for each asset. The analysis then becomes considerably more complicated.

By selecting a fixed period of outage, the MPL, EML can be derived, since the cost of outage is time related.

Failure frequencies

Considerable effort has been devoted by a number of organisations to the establishment of failure frequencies for a large range of assets. These can be used in the place of distribution curves as a first approximation in the evaluation of losses.

8.7.10 Engineering risk control

8.7.10.1 *Loss statistics of machinery breakdowns*

Since we are trying to determine the consequences of a loss or damage to assets and particularly machinery, considerable use is made of information relating to loss statistics which has been collected over the years. Various sources can be consulted but probably the best known is the course which is run by ICI in London.

Munich-Re, one of the world's (as well as one of South Africa's) largest reinsurance companies, has done extensive work in the field of insurance claims from machinery breakdowns. The following is an evaluation of cases which they have investigated:

> Altogether 16 005 cases of damage which occurred during the years 1969 to 1974 were evaluated. These cases were distributed amongst the various groups of machinery as follows:
>
> - 9 135 cases of damage to electrical machines
> - 1 045 cases of damage to steam generators
> - 1 215 cases of damage to fluid-flow machines
> - 1 000 cases of damage to piston machines
> - 3 610 cases of damage to mechanical handling and lifting machines.

Munich-Re found that as the proportions of the groups of causes of damage included vary widely with the type of machines considered, the key measures necessary for successful loss prevention also vary.[71]

Once a machine has broken down, it is necessary to identify the cause of the breakdown. To a large measure the classification system chosen is arbitrary and there are various ways in which causes can be classified. Munich-Re have classified causes into three categories, namely:

- product faults
- operational faults
- handling faults.

- **Product faults** include all causes of damage which are the result of manufacture. These causes include faults in planning and design, such as deficient layout calculation, incorrect choice of materials and unsuitable geometry; faults in processing, such as incorrect heat treatment, machining errors and assembly faults; and faulty materials.
- **Operational faults** include causes of damage which originate during the operation of the installation such as the loosening of components, failure or non-response of protective devices, servicing faults, damage arising from corrosion, ageing, etc., as well as causes that can be traced back to external influences, for example natural forces, foreign bodies, overvoltages from the grid and so on.
- **Handling faults** or attendance faults can be regarded as a sub-section of operation faults. In about 95% of the damage cases, external influences did not play any part.

We therefore see from the analysis that the vast majority of machinery failures which have taken place, have been as a result of aspects which could have been prevented.

71 *Machinery Loss Prevention – A Handbook for Engineering Insurers.* 1978, Munich-Re.

In designing risk control steps to prevent machinery breakdowns generalised steps such as a relevant management system could be specified, which is applicable to all types of machinery. However, once this has been done it is necessary to examine each type of machine to plan the desired risk control steps. In other words, there are specific steps that could be taken to prevent the breakdown of a transformer and to prevent the breakdown of a piston machine, for example.

8.7.10.2 *Risk control steps – machinery breakdown*

General steps

If the breakdown statistics are examined, the various ratios of the different types of faults can be determined. Therefore for electrical machines it is noted that product faults comprise some 41 %, whereas operational faults comprise 59%.

In their study Munich-Re came to some general conclusions regarding loss control steps for the different types of faults. The different faults and the relevant risk control steps that could be taken can be summarised as follows:

☐ **Product fault**

In terms of numbers and costs, the proportion of damage resulting from product faults is most pronounced in the case of fluid-flow machines and steam boilers. It is heaviest in terms of cost in the case of electrical machines and installations, but it is relatively low in terms of numbers, indicating high repair costs per individual case of damage.

With these three types of equipment the trend of technical developments towards larger and more powerful items of equipment is particularly noticeable. For example, 50 years ago a 50 MW electrical generator was regarded as a large generator, but today 960 MW units are routinely installed.

It is happening with increasing frequency that newly developed components which have not been sufficiently tested in a practical operation, are simultaneously installed in a large number of machines.

Munich-Re suggest the following:[40]

Methods of preventing damage as a result of product faults as primary cause, involve utilisation of knowledge from loss events regarding calculation, design and manufacture by way of:

- close co-operation with manufacturers in special cases
- early publication of experience in specialised journals
- open exchange of experience at conferences and seminars.

In this way, an important contribution can be made towards ensuring that, with different manufacturers, damage arising from identical causes will be prevented from happening again.

Further support for the prevention of damage is offered by purposeful inspection and replacement at the appropriate time of components which have lead to damage to similar machines, as well as a result of basic deficiencies.

☐ **Operational faults**

Munich-Re note that the proportion of damage from operational causes, in terms of numbers and costs, is highest in the case of piston machines, followed by electrical machines and installations. In the case of the latter the high number of cases of damage with relatively low costs is conspicuous, indicating that there are many causes and instances of fairly inexpensive types of damage.

Munich-Re suggest the following methods of prevention in connection with the operational faults:

- Optimum supervision of the installation, when not only sudden, but also gradual changes in operational data (pressure and temperature, deficiencies, power input, etc.) must be noted and their causes established without delay.
- Constant control and supervision of measuring, control and protective devices.
- Constant control of the condition of operational and auxiliary materials (lubricating, cooling, refrigerating media, etc.).
- Regular servicing, maintenance and overhaul.
- Overhauls and inspections at regular intervals so that the components which have reached the end of their lives through wear, corrosion, erosion or temperature influences can be replaced before failure occurs.

On the basis of systematic evaluations of damage and inspections, optimum levels between inspections have been established for most machines; or reliable supervisory and control systems have been introduced for the determination of the most favourable points in time for carrying out inspections.

☐ **Handling faults**

The largest portion of damage from faults arising from mishandling is found in a group of machines concerned with mechanical handling and lifting. However, in other groups of machines dealt with here, the cause of damage is also noteworthy.

For loss prevention, Munich-Re suggest the following:

- Selection of suitably trained personnel for operating, maintaining and servicing machines.
- Continual training and inspection of operating personnel, especially with regard to the action to be taken in the event of machine breakdowns, by means of courses, lectures, literature and pamphlets.

- Installation of easily operated fitting and control elements, warning notices and instruction plates.
- Provision of easily understood, detailed operating instructions.

General risk control measures for different classes of machines

In the study conducted by Munich-Re the machinery was classified into different categories. Munich-Re then summarised the general steps which could be taken for each class of machinery.

☐ **With electrical machines**, the key risk control with electrical machines points are the utilisation of damage experience for calculation, design and manufacture; revisions, if possible, at regular intervals; and the training of personnel.

☐ **With fluid-flow machines and steam generators** the utilisation of damage experience for the manufacture of machines and also inspection and overhauls are of utmost importance. It is essential to consider the distribution of the findings of damage causes which was the result of inspections carried out on turbines by Allianz and on steam generators by TUV.

☐ **With piston machines**, the key to loss prevention lies in the improvement of servicing and maintenance, as well as in inspections.

☐ **With mechanical handling and lifting equipment**, damage arising from handling faults predominates, as should be expected. In this case therefore, loss prevention lies primarily in training personnel by demonstrating examples of damage, as well as by pamphlets and instruction plates. In addition, nothing must be omitted in the attempt to reduce the proportion of handling faults by the improvement of man-to-machine interfaces.

Planned maintenance systems

☐ **Introduction**

We have already seen that the key element to the prevention of loss or damage to equipment and in particular production machinery is an adequate inspection and maintenance programme. These inspection programmes are best formalised in terms of what is known as a planned maintenance system. In terms of such a system, the maintenance requirements of machinery is defined beforehand and then executed in accordance with the programme.

Some of the elements which are required for a successful planned maintenance programme (which can be used to prevent the damage to assets that gives rise to consequential losses) will now be examined.

☐ **Responsibility for the planned maintenance programme**

If the programme is to function satisfactory, it is essential that responsibility for the programme be assigned to one person or one department. It is equally essential that this person or department should not form part of the production department, as the aims of planned maintenance and that of production differ. In large organisations a separate planned maintenance department should be established and responsibility for the planned maintenance programme be assigned to that department. This department should not fall under the responsibility of the production management either.

☐ **Work instructions**

At the heart of a successful planned maintenance programme is, what can be referred to, as work instructions or planned maintenance cards.

For each and every item of equipment or machinery, a separate planned maintenance card should be drawn up. The card cannot be a general card but must relate to the specific item which is being inspected.

This planned maintenance card should indicate the specific work which should be carried out on that particular item of equipment. A determination of the work requires that a detailed investigation should be undertaken of the types of failures and faults which can take place for that particular item. In this way, if a planned maintenance programme which would include the maintenance of an electric machine is to be instituted, it is necessary to determine what specific inspections must be carried out for that type of machine and once that has been determined, the maintenance card should deal with that specific item.

In determining the maintenance work which is required on the machine, one should take cognisance of the existing literature on the subject and particularly the insurance literature, as to causes of failures. The major causes of failures should be investigated and the steps which could be taken to avoid any further failures should be incorporated into the planned maintenance card.

It is not sufficient to simply define the project or work to be done in terms of the planned maintenance project; it is also necessary to ensure that only competent and qualified persons carry out that work.

Provision should be made on the card for comments and the signature of the person to indicate that the work has been done. Where applicable, the statutory requirements must be incorporated into the planned maintenance costs.

☐ **Inspection frequencies**

The various frequencies of inspection and other maintenance work should be determined by consultation of literature, the manufacturer's manuals and specifications. These requirements should be incorporated into the work instructions and into the control system for the planned maintenance system.

Spares policies

As we have already seen, a consequential loss is time-dependent. Therefore, the more quickly machinery can be repaired to get it back in operation, the lower the loss will be. It stands to reason that the programme should not only concentrate on preventing a machine from breaking down, but should also include contingency plans for locating spares.

A spares inventory should therefore be drawn up and kept up to date. Where high vulnerability is detected, spare equipment should be purchased.

8.7.10.3 *Risk control – suppliers*

As a general rule, it is not possible for a customer to tell a supplier how he should manage his own business or assets. Therefore it is not generally acceptable for a client to tell a supplier that his planned maintenance programme is not up to standard; although it is becoming acceptable in terms of SABS 0157 for a client to inspect and evaluate suppliers' premises.

The following risk control steps can, however, be implemented in this regard:

- ☐ identify key suppliers of goods, services and materials
- ☐ identify key markets
- ☐ investigate alternative suppliers and markets
- ☐ assess the vulnerability of the supplier and market to loss of assets
- ☐ assess the ability of the key supplier and market to recover from loss or damage to their assets.

8.8 Summary

The aim of this chapter has been to describe the risk management activity of risk control. Against the background of risk identification and evaluation, risk control is concerned with the physical treatment of risk. An important aspect which was considered was the meaning of risk control and its position within the overall discipline of risk management.

Risk control was established as a sub-discipline of physical risk management, which encompasses the overall process of risk identification and evaluation. In turn, physical risk management, when integrated with the activities germane to financial risk management, constitutes the entire discipline of risk management. Risk control was simply defined as a method of meeting risk, which definition recognised the broad aims of:

- ☐ eliminating or reducing the factors that may cause loss (loss prevention/control)
- ☐ minimising the actual loss that occurs when preventative measures have not proved to be fully effective.

The historical development of risk control, particularly in the areas of fire, explosion and industrial accidents, was sketched before describing the general principles and objectives of risk control. These principles included the important premises that:

- ☐ management principles be identified and applied to risk control
- ☐ the approach(es) to risk control be integrated with the other activities within the organisation so as to achieve optimal results.

The objectives of risk control programmes were stated as endeavouring to reduce the frequency and severity of loss costs resulting from risk exposures and, through emergency and contingency planning, to deal with and recover from loss-producing events.

Approaches to loss prevention were then described. These were categorised as engineering, human, educational and enforcement approaches. Risk control programmes and codes of practice relative to South Africa were enumerated and under the heading of assets programmes, general assets perils were listed, around which specific risk control programmes are designed. Finally, the more important acts which prescribe authoritative risk control measures were listed.

Mention was made early in the chapter that risks can be differentiated broadly as being assets (property) and liability related. The fundamental nature of liability risks differs from that of assets risks. This, together with the fact that there is in evidence a 'liability crisis', dictates that, with regard to risk treatment, separate examination of this subject is called for. Hence, Chapter Nine deals with the nature of liability risks and the liability crisis.

Bibliography

Allen, PM 1943. *The first hundred, 1843-1943*. Philadelphia: Germantown Mutual Fire Insurance Company.

Baket, M 1986. 'Legislation on occupational health in South Africa.' *Continuing Medical Education*.

Baker, M & Coetzee, AC 1983. *An introduction to occupational health nursing in South Africa*. Wits University Press.

Benatar, SN, Metz, JT & Elmes, PC 1983. 'Occupational health and safety in South Africa.' *SAMJ*.

Best's Review. 1970. Property liability edition. Vol. VII, No. 1, May.

Blake, RP 1963. *Industrial safety*. Englewood Cliffs, New Jersey: Prentice-Hall Inc.

Boberg, PQR 1984. *The law of delict*. Cape Town: Juta & Co. Ltd.

Bridges, RS & Jaros, GG 1986. 'Ergonomics: Ergosystems & occupational health.' *Continuing Medical Education*.

Budlender, D 1979. 'Industrial legislation in South Africa, 1924-1945.' Unpublished M.A. Thesis, University of Cape Town.

Budlender, D 1979. *Labour law bulletin*.

Carter, RL 1982. 'Risk management under changing economic conditions.' *The Geneva Papers on Risk and Insurance*. Vol. 7, No. 22.

Crockford, GN 1982. 'The bibliography and history of risk management: Some preliminary observations.' *The Geneva Papers on Risk and Insurance*. Vol. 7, No. 23.

De Jager, FJ 'Die grondslae van produk-aanspreeklikheid *ex delicto* in die Suid Afrikaanse reg.' *THRHR*. Vol. 41.

De Jager, FJ 1979. 'Products liablity.' *BML*. Vol. 9.

De Jager, FJ 1980. 'Products liability.' *BML*. Vol. 9; 10.

Denenberg, HS, Eilers, RD, Melone, JJ & Zelten, RA 1974. *Risk and insurance*. Englewood Cliffs, New Jersey: Prentice-Hall Inc.

Diacon, SR & Carter, RL 1984; 1988. *Success in insurance*. London: John Murray Ltd.

Dworkin, R 1986. *Laws empire*. London: Fontana Press.

Friedman, M & R 1980. *Free to choose*. Suffolk: Penquin Books Ltd.

Fuggle, RF & Rabie, MA 1983. *Environmental concerns in South Africa*. Cape Town: Juta & Co. Ltd.

Heinrich, NW 1950. *Industrial accident prevention*. New York: McGraw-Hill Inc.

Hood, J 1990. 'Let the market protect the consumer's safety.' *The Freeman*. April.

Hurley, RL 1962. 'Review of a paper on 'The probability of A – M/N'.' (by Henry K Duke). *Annals of the society of chartered property and casualty underwriters*. Vol. XV, No. 2.

Kulp, CA 1956. *Casualty insurance*. New York: The Ronald Press Co.

Leeb, O 1989. 'Environmental impairment.' *Cover*.

McDonald, DL 1966. *Corporate risk control*. New York: John Wiley & Sons.

McKerron, RG 1971. *Law of delict*. Cape Town: Juta & Co. Ltd., 7th Edition.

Metz, JT 1987. 'Reliability of industrial audiometry as a screening method for incipient noise-indused hearing loss.' *SAMJ*.

Metz, JT 1987. 'Hearing loss in white South African gold miners.' *SAMJ*.

Metz, JT & Benatar, SR 1987. 'Occupational health legislation – progress since 1983.' *SAMJ*.

Neethling, J, Potgieter, JM & Visser, PJ 1989. *Law of delict*. Durban: Butterworths.

Pascoe, LC (ed) 1981. *Encyclopaedia of dates and events*. London: Hodder & Stoughton.

Piek, PJ 1986. 'Occupational medicine in small and medium sized organisations – Today and tomorrow.' *Continuing Medical Education*. Vol. 4, April.

Pizza, PF 1982. 'Assess environmental risk.' *Hydrocarbon Processing*. April.

Rabie, A 1976. *South African Legislation*. IFCOL.

Ruegg, AH 1901. *A century of law reform*. London: MacMillan & Co. Ltd.

Russel, DL 1987. 'Understanding ground water monitoring.' *Chemical Engineering*. October.

Russell, DL 1985. 'Managing your environmental audit.' *Chemical Engineering*. June.

Russell, DL & Ward, SW 1987. 'Underground storage tanks – potential for economic disasters.' *Chemical Engineering*. March.

Skully, MT 1989. 'Ever-increasing circles.' *The Review*. February.

Spiegelman, M 1962. 'Significant mortality and morbidity trends in the United States since 1900.' *American College of Life Underwriters*. Pennsylvania: Bryn Mawr.

South African Labour Bulletin. 1984; 1983. Vol. 9, February, & Vol. 8, August.

Stuart, CE 1990. 'General administrative regulation 4 of MOSACT.' *Association of Legal Advisers of South Africa*.

Valsamakis, AC 1983. *The investment policies and practices of South African long and short-term insurers*. Unpublished M.Com. Dissertation, University of the Witwatersrand.

Van der Walt, JC 1979. *Delict: principles & cases*. Durban: Butterworths.

Vernon, D 1989. 'Risk management – an asset not a liability.' *Accountancy SA*. May.

Vivian, RW 1990. 'The smoking gun arrives in South Africa.' *Cover*.

Vivian, RW 1987. 'Risk management and fatality frequencies.' *Loss Control Survey*. February.

Vivian, RW 1985. 'The fundamental principles of risk management.' *South African Treasurer*. May.

Wallace, M 1982. 'The Thalidomide girls.' *Star*.

Endnotes

[1] Denenberg, *et al.*, 1974, 82-84.

[2] Denenberg, *et al.*, 1974, 84.

[3] Denenberg, *et al.*, 1974, 85.

[4] Blake, 1963, 34-36.

[5] Budlender, 1984, 27.

[6] Vivian, 1986, 44.

[7] Denenberg, *et al.*, 1974, 86.

[8] Denenberg, *et al.*, 1974, 87.

[9] Denenberg, *et al.*, 1974, 91.

[10] Friedman, 1980, 227-269.

[11] Denenberg, *et al.*, 1974, 92-94.

[12] Denenberg, *et al.*, 1974, 100.

[13] Best's Review, 1970, 48.

[14] Denenberg, *et al.*, 1974, 93.

[15] Denenberg, *et al.*, 1974, 105.

[16] Kulp, 1956, 85.

[17] Heinrich, 1950.

[18] Friedman, 1980, 227-269.

[19] Vivian, 1987, 7.

[20] Piek, 1986, 119.

[21] Bridges & Jaros, 1986, 39.

[22] Wallace, 1982.

[23] *The Star* (6 July 1989) and *The Star* (24 July 1987).

[24] *The Citizen*, 15 February 1985.

[25] *The Star*, 14 April 1987.

[26] Vivian, 1990, 10.

[27] *New Scientist*, 20 September 1984; *The Star*, 12 January 1989.

[28] *The Star*, 14 April 1987.

[29] Leeb, 1989, 14.

[30] Rabie (1976); Fuggle & Rabie (1983).

[31] McKerron, 1971, 246.

[32] *The Star*, 14 December 1987.

[33] *The Star*, 22 June 1989.

[34] *The Star*, 14 August 1989.

[35] *The Star*, 26 December 1986.

[36] *The Star*, 28 July 1988.

[37] Russell & Ward, 1987.

[38] *Government Gazette*.

[39] Atkins, 1981, 69.

[40] Munich-Re, 1978, 7.

9 LEGAL LIABILITIES

9.1 The need to study legal liabilities

It is usual to start a study of liability exposures by looking at the basis on which liability can attach to the insured. This is true of insurance[1] as well as the field of risk management.[2] This tradition will be followed in this text.

Law can be broken down into different compartments for specialised study.[1] One of these compartments is the law of obligations. This area deals with the grounds in terms of which one person can become legally obligated to another.[2] Two of the main areas of obligation is the law of contract and the law of delict. The law of delict[3] is referred to as the law of torts in British[4] and American[5] literature. In addition to these two areas of obligations, there are other miscellaneous areas such as the law of unjust enrichment. For our present purposes the main area of obligations is the law of delict. However, in the field of delict, the question of contractual liability also arises, as does the question of statutory liability.

9.1.1 Legal liabilities and the risk manager

There are a number of reasons why the risk manager should have a firm grasp on legal liability issues, including:

- ☐ Firstly, liability claims and the magnitude of awards are on the increase. These ever-increasing legal liabilities claims represent a serious threat to a company. Sometimes the claims threaten the very existence of the organisation. Individuals in their personal capacity within the organisation are also exposed to these increasing liability claims.[6] The phenomena of ever-increasing claims and awards is referred to as the liability crisis.
- ☐ Secondly, legal liabilities is the object of some insurance policies and these policies cannot be understood unless the basis on which liability is imposed, is also understood.
- ☐ Thirdly, in order to introduce risk control steps and thereby minimise exposures from liability claims, a clear understanding of how claims can arise is needed.

---

1 For one such breakdown consult Nagel, *et al.*, (1980, 273).

2 Historically, in terms of Roman law, only two grounds of liability existed, contract or delict. Gaius, Inst. 3.88, '*every obligation arises either from contract or from delict.*' Obligations can also arise in terms of a statute.

3 The leading South African textbooks are Neethling, Potgieter & Visser (1990), McKerron (1971), Boberg (1984), Van der Walt (1979), Van der Merwe & Olivier (1976).

4 There are numerous leading British textbooks including Heuston & Chambers (1981). Another influential book is that of Fleming (1987).

5 A leading American textbook is Keeton, *et al.* (1984).

6 Examples are directors, sued in Directors and Officers cases and employees being sued after industrial accidents. A number of these cases are on record.

9.1.2 The liability crisis

The liability crisis is most pronounced in America and therefore some of the developments in America should be considered. The world has in recent years witnessed the failure and threatened failure of a number of major American companies simply because of legal liability claims against them. These include the following:

- **Manville Corporation**, the world's largest manufacturer of asbestos, arising out of asbestos-related claims.[3]
- **Union Carbide**, the 37th largest American company, arising out of the Bhopal disaster.
- **AH Robins**, arising out of the contraceptive Dalkon Shield.
- **Texaco**, the third largest American oil company, filed for insolvency as a result of a civil judgement arising out of a takeover bid. Texaco was ordered to pay out an amount of $11,1 billion.[4]

Although these developments took place in America they have a direct impact on the South African business community, for the following reasons:

Liability insurance is of an international nature

If there is a major disaster resulting in extensive liability claims anywhere in the world, this has an immediate impact on the insurance cover available in the rest of the world. For example, after Bhopal liability limits were halved and premiums escalated, difficulties were experienced by South African companies in obtaining adequate levels of cover.[5]

Changes introduced into the South African common law

A much more serious development has been the changes introduced by the South African courts into our legal practice under the influence of American and British jurisprudence. The South African courts have made so many changes to our common law that in many instances it is hardly possible to distinguish South African law from American law. In some cases the South African courts have made judgements which were unacceptable to the American courts.[7]

9.1.3 The impact of legal liability claims on insurance

The liability crisis is not confined to America. The extent of the problem posed by legal liability claims in England to the insurance industry can be gauged by analysing Lloyd's global results in the table below:

7 The introduction of so-called faultless liability for the press *Pakendorf v De Flamingh* 1982 3 SA 146 (A) went beyond what the American courts accepted. In a judgement which introduced liability for 'wrongful life', the international cases referred to by the court were opposed to the introduction of this form of liability.

Table 9.1
Lloyd's of London five year summary (general liability)[8]

General liability (£ millions)				
Year	**Net premiums**	**Underwriting result**	**Investment return**	**Loss**
1985	415,14	(353,69)	123,79	(268,37)
1984	364,78	(256,94)	134,95	(169,74)
1983	312,43	(384,44)	143,57	(285,50)
1982	346,15	(425,13)	142,70	(314,39)
1981	260,82	(195,57)	111,37	(108,57)

Source: *Post Insurance Magazine*, September 1988

From table 9.1 it can be seen that the Lloyd's liability account has been running at a substantial loss for a number of years. The above table does not however present the full liability picture as it only shows the general liability results. Liability also appear in the results of other classes underwritten at Lloyd's, including *Aircraft – damage and liability, UK motor vehicle – damage and liability, Overseas motor vehicle – damage and liability, Ships – damage and liability.*

The position in South Africa is discussed below.

9.2 Definition of a delict

9.2.1 Definition

The basis upon which legal liability is imposed is now considered.

Firstly it must be noted that the basis on which liability is imposed is today almost exclusively determined by the courts; it is not the product of legislation. This fact makes the study difficult for the layman because it is necessary to study a large number of court cases to understand the basis of liability. A second important point to note is that the basis on which liability is imposed has changed considerably in recent years.

This text will approach the study of the law of delict by examining the fundamental definition of delict and illustrating the elements of the definition by examining various South African cases.

The definition of Neethling, *et al.*[6] of a delict is used to identify the elements of a delict.

> A delict is the act of a person which in a wrongful and culpable way causes harm to another.

8 The results in table 9.1 reflect only the General Liability account. Chairman David Coleridge announced that Lloyd's will report an overall loss of almost £1 billion for 1989, the first in 24 years.

9.2.2 The elements

From this definition it is clear that five[9] elements are required for a delict:

- ☐ wrongfulness
- ☐ an act
- ☐ fault
- ☐ harm
- ☐ causation.

All of these elements subject to the qualification of fault discussed below, must be present before the conduct complained of can be classified as a delict. If none of these elements are present the defendant[10] may still be liable but the liability is then not one of delict but some other form of liability.[11]

This study is concerned mainly with cases where the harm suffered is loss or damage to property or injury to people.

9.2.3 Illustrative examples

It is easier to understand these elements if illustrated by examples. A number of these are discussed.

9.2.3.1 *Case: Abimelech v Abraham*

Liability issues have existed for as long as recorded history has existed. One of the earliest examples is recorded in the Old Testament.[12] This was the case of Abimelech and Abraham.[13] The facts are set out below.

---

9 Neethling, *et al.*, (1990, 4), in note 9 the authors argue that six, not five, elements can be identified. For the purposes of this work five is adequate.

10 In situations where the defendant is covered by liability insurance, it is not in fact the defendant who pays the claim but the insurer. The liability of the insurer is often dependent on the delict of the defendant. The liability of the insurer is however not an example of vicarious liability, but is a consequence of its contractual obligation.

11 For example, an employer individually liable in terms of section 37(a) of the *Workmen's Compensation Act* (30 of 1941) to pay compensation to the injured workman, is liable despite the absence of a wrongful act, fault or causation. In this case the liability is imposed by statute and is by nature a form of welfare liability.

12 The example is used for a number of reasons. It illustrates the following:
- the distinction between wrongfulness and fault
- that the defence of absence of fault has been raised for as long as delict has existed. Many writers are under the impression that fault is of fairly modern origin.

13 Recorded in Genesis 20. Similar events are recorded in Genesis 12 v. 10-20. The specific delict concerned is the interference with one spouse's right to consortium. (McKerron, 1971, 168).

Abraham v Abimelech

Abraham and his wife Sarah went to live in a place called Gerar. Sarah was by all accounts an exceptionally attractive woman. Abraham felt that as the husband of an attractive wife his life would be in danger as he would be killed so that his wife could be taken by another man. He thus devised a plan. He and Sarah told the people in Gerar that Sarah was his sister. As Abraham suspected, the beauty of his wife was noted and Abimelech, the local king, believing Sarah to be the sister of Abraham sent for and took Sarah.

The question now is, under the circumstances did Abimelech commit a delict?

Genesis 20

In this case the issue is, is Abimelech liable to Abraham for interfering with his matrimonial rights? This must be answered in terms of the elements of a delict.

Wrongfulness

The first issue is thus: did Abimelech perform a wrongful act? If there is no wrongful act, there is no delict.

The wrongfulness of an act must be determined according to the objective standard of the law. To act wrongfully is to act unlawfully.[14] This point is made clear by Von Rad,[7] late professor of the Old Testament at the University of Heidelberg:

> One could almost say that our story has two faces, an ancient and a modern. Ancient is the emphasis on Abimelechs's guilt: the king infringed on another's marriage, which was absolutely protected by the divinity. This is an objective fact, quite apart from premeditation or ignorance, which severely incriminates him.

Judged objectively, Abimelech acted wrongfully because his act violated the rights conferred by the law of marriage.

Ignorance of the true facts does not remove the wrongfulness of the act. Von Rad[8] makes this point clear:

> That Abimelech had actually violated Abraham's marriage was not questioned by the ancients.

From the text, God appears to Abimelech in a dream and also makes this point clear:

> Behold, you are a dead man, because the woman whom you have taken; for she is a man's wife.

14 Thomas (1986, 119) discussing Roman law, lists the elements of delict as act, unlawfulness, harm, causation, *mens rea*. Unlawfulness is more accurate than wrongfulness.

Abimelech recognises the fact that although he is ignorant of the true facts, this does not mean he did not, objectively speaking, act wrongfully. He summons Abraham and says:

> What have you done to us? And how have I sinned against you that you have brought on me and my kingdom a great sin? You have done to me things that ought not to be done. What were you thinking of, that you did this thing?

Clearly the old testament society, in determining liability, placed great emphasis on the act. If this act, objectively speaking, was contrary to existing law, then consequences were attached. This case also emphasises two points made by Fensham.[9] Firstly, the laws during that period seemed to be uniform throughout the area. Abimelech recognised the sanctity of marriage, as did Abraham and, secondly the emphasis was on the act and its consequences.[15]

From this example a clear understanding of the concept of a wrongful act can be grasped:

> **The meaning of a wrongful act**
>
> A person acts wrongfully, when he acts contrary to the existing law. To act wrongfully is to act unlawfully.

The concept of wrongfulness has been of minor importance for the greater existence of mankind, since to act wrongfully is to act contrary to the law. This being so, the study of specific laws was important and dominated the study of delict, not conceptual principles such as wrongfulness.

The act

The mere existence of the law cannot result in liability. The conduct or act of the defendant must violate the law.

The mere fact that Abraham's marriage was protected by law did not make Abimelech liable for a delict. Liability could only attach once he took Sarah. Despite the existence of the law, no liability could attach until he committed an act which was prohibited by the law.

Fault

The next element is that of fault. Fault is today equated mainly to negligence. To understand the principle of fault the next issue to be discussed is, was Abimelech's conduct negligent? When Abimelech took Sarah did he do so negligently? Any reasonable man will make certain enquiries concerning his future bride, which is what he did. He enquired from both Abraham and Sarah if she were married. Both of them informed him that she was not married. No reasonable man would expect the husband of a beautiful wife to lie about this point and allow his wife to marry another

15 Fensham (1978, 285) points out '*In Arabic and Bedouin law intention plays a minor role. The act and its result are regarded as of the utmost importance*'.

man. There was no one else from whom Abimelech could make enquiries, nor would one expect him to do so.

In modern law one would say that Abimelech was not negligent and thus not liable.

Abimelech raises the same defence to God:

> Lord, will you destroy an innocent nation? Did he not say to me, 'She is my sister'. Did she also not say to me, 'He is my brother?' I have done this with a clear conscience and clean hands.

One should note that, in the Old Testament, fault does not appear to be a total defence. The emphasis was on the law and the act. If the act contravened the law, negligence could still be raised as a defence, as Abimelech did. Despite protestations about innocence Abimelech paid compensation.[10]

As time progressed fault was accepted as a complete defence and the onus rested on the plaintiff to prove fault.

Harm

For liability to attach there must be harm.

In the case of Abimelech the damage was not damage to property but both Abraham and Sarah suffered personal *injuria*, or insult; humiliation in having their matrimonial rights interfered with. This was recognised and Abimelech made reparations.

Causation

Causation requires a link between the wrongful act and the harm or damage suffered; the wrong and the loss must clearly be concatenated as cause and effect.

9.2.3.2 *Further examples*

Having defined a delict, a number of examples will illustrate how delictual liability can arise.

- ☐ Mr X takes his 9mm revolver and aims and fires at a crowd some considerable distance away. The bullet hits Mr Y, a spectator in the crowd. Mr X committed a wrongful act by aiming and firing at the crowd. Mr X is also at fault, since any reasonable man in his position will foresee the possibility that the bullet may strike someone. Mr Y is injured and thus suffers damage. There is a direct causal connection between the firing of the gun and the injury sustained by the spectator. All the elements of delict are present and accordingly Mr X is liable.
- ☐ Mr X, a contractor is employed by the local authority to install a water pipe across a public road. Mr X digs a trench across the road. The trench is to be open at night and the road will be used by the public at night. Mr X does not erect any barriers to prevent the public from suffering injury or damage because of the trench, nor does Mr X install any warning devices to warn the unsuspecting public (who have every right to use the road) of the existence of the trench. That night, a car driven by Mr Y is travelling along the road and is damaged when it enters the trench.

Continued

Continued

Mr X by opening the trench in the road (which he knows is used at night, knows that it is inevitable that any unsuspecting person will collide with the trench and be injured or suffer damage when using the road) commits a wrongful act. Because a reasonable man in the position of Mr X will foresee that the users of the road will suffer injury and a reasonable man in the position of Mr X will take precautions to warn against the danger that he has created and because Mr X did not take such action, Mr X is at fault because he is negligent. Mr Y does suffer damage and the damage is caused by the trench opened by Mr X. All the elements of delict are present and Mr X is accordingly liable. This example illustrates an important point. Often a delay exists between the wrongful act and the damage. Even in the firing of the bullet a delay exists, although it is not as obvious as the time between opening a trench and someone falling into the trench.

- ☐ An Australian case can be used to illustrate circumstances where liability cannot attach in delict. An employee who spent a great deal of his working life working under the sun contracted skin cancer. He sued his employer. In this case there is no wrongful act, no fault, no causation.[16]

9.2.4 Summary

The elements of the law of delict are illustrated by the case and examples mentioned above. An interesting fact is that the elements as illustrated by the case of Abimelech remained intact until about two decades ago – a period of nearly 4 000 years!

It is now necessary to examine the problematical areas of the definition of delict.

9.3 The historical development of the South African law of delict

The South African law of delict is Roman-Dutch in origin.

In Roman law there was no such thing as a general definition of a delict.[11] There were only a number of separate and distinct civil wrongs, each with its own rules and remedies. The most important were the civil laws delicts of *furtum*,[17] *rapina*,[18] *damnum injuria datum*[19] and *injuria*[20], and the praetorian delicts of *metus*,[21] *dolus* and *fraus creditorum*. In the

16 The employer cannot be liabile in delict. If liability attaches it is for social reasons.
17 Furtum is generally translated as theft, but the Roman concept was much wider than theft, as the pledgee or depositee who used the pledge or deposited committed furtum. (Thomas, 1986, 120).
18 Rapina, robbery, is theft with violence. (Thomas, 1986, 122.) Rapina was merely an aggravated form of furtum. (Lee, 1946)
19 Damnum injuria datum, is wrongful damage to property.
20 Injury to the personality, harmful to the body, honour or reputation of a free person.
21 The actio metus causa was available to a person who through duress entered into a legal transaction by which patrimonial loss had been suffered.

original Roman law, upon which our Roman-Dutch common law is based, there were therefore only specific delicts, each of which were enforced via their own specific and definitive rules.[12]

In modern law by far the most important delicts which survived are those of *damnum injuria datum* and *injuria*. The scope of these originally limited and particular delicts were extended to cover virtually the whole field of delictual liability.

9.3.1 *Damnum injuria datum*

The delict known as *damnum injuria datum*[22] is derived from the *Lex Aquilia*, a plebiscite attributed to the year 287 BC. The *Lex Aquilia* was divided into three chapters. The first chapter gave the owner a remedy for the wrongful killing[23] of a slave or four-footed beast (*pecus*).[24] The second chapter does not concern us, since it became obsolete early on in the Roman Empire. The third chapter gave the remedy to the owner for the wrongful damage caused to a corporeal thing by limited, specific positive acts. Damage was caused, for instance, by burning, breaking or fracturing. It is the wrongful damage to the corporeal thing which remains of importance to us today.

The *Lex Aquilia* thus provided a very limited remedy against the wrongdoer:

- ☐ to the owner, where there had been
- ☐ damage or lesion to a tangible thing
- ☐ caused directly by
- ☐ the specific positive acts.[13] [25]

Initially the liability was not based on fault but the law developed to the point where it became a requirement that damage must have been caused with fault. *Injuria datum* was so interpreted that it excluded liability where damage was not the defendant's fault. Thus the action was later allowed for every kind of wrongful damage to corporeal property, movable or immovable, which could be attributed to the *culpa* or fault of the defendant. The remedy, too, was no longer confined to the owner as in the earlier law, but was available to any person who had real rights in the property.

We see therefore that there were four clear and definitive requirements for liability to exist. The person who could claim the remedy for damages

22 Wrongful damage to property.

23 The verb used was *occidere*, which means to slay. At a later stage the verb was extended to mean the causing of death.

24 The noun used for beast is *pecus* which is a four-footed beast which grazes in herds. It was later interpreted to include pigs, elephants and camels.

25 Slaying, burning, breaking or fracturing. At a later stage any damage was included.

did not form an unlimited class, but was initially confined to the owner of the property which had been damaged.

By the time of Justinian, if not earlier, the action based on the *Lex Aquilia* had become a general remedy for damage wrongfully done to a corporeal thing and for physical injuries wrongfully caused to the body of a freeman; whereby compensation could be recovered not only for immediate but also for consequential loss.[14] The action was still, however, related to damage to the corporeal thing.

The law against causing injury or damage

As noted, to act wrongfully is to act contrary to the law. This fact imposes considerable constraints on the imposition liability; since there are literally millions of different acts which can cause loss or injury to other persons. If wrongfulness was solely a product of pre-existing law, millions of laws would be required. This is not practical. The position began to develop to the stage where wrongfulness was somewhat more universal than to violate existing laws.

> It can be accepted that unless exceptional circumstances exist,[26] a person acts wrongfully if by his act he causes loss or damage to property or injury to people.

9.3.2 *Injuria*

In the preceding section it was noted that the *Lex Aquilia* was used to recover damages to corporeal property caused by the direct application of force. There is another action however, used where the rights of people to their person, dignity or reputation are violated. This can happen for example in the case of assault or defamation. Rights to the human body and integrity are referred to as personality rights and when these are violated in such a way as to give rise to damages, it is known as the violation of personality rights. The delictual action is that of the *injuria*. The delict of *injuria* also has a long history. Certain wrongs against the person, probably all of them species of assault, were treated as *injuriae* by the Twelve Tables 450 BC. For each of these wrongs a fixed monetary penalty was prescribed, which the victim of the *injuria* was entitled to recover from the wrongdoer.[27] This crude system was superseded in the second century BC by a series of praetorian edicts.[15]

The first of these new remedies was known as the *actio injuriarum aestimatoria*, substituted in place of the old civil action which had a fixed

26 It is not possible to have an universal law against damage, to replace specific laws. Exceptions always exist. Thus in the case of *Greyvensteyn v Hattingh*, Hattingh and others drove locusts from their lands with the result that they crossed the land of a neighbour. Their positive act caused damage to their neighbour. Nevertheless, the court concluded that they did not act wrongfully.

27 These fixed penalties became ludicrous as a result of inflation.

monetary penalty. In terms of the new *actio aestimatoria* the penalty would be assessed by the *judex* or judge and levied according to the gravity of the offence. It is this second *actio injuriarum* which has come down to us as the remedy which is available for recovering damages from somebody who violates, what is known today as personality rights.

Before the time of Emperor Justinian the *actio injuriarum* had come to be regarded as a general remedy for any wrongful aggression upon a person, his dignity or reputation.

An important difference between the action based on the *actio injuriarum* and the *Lex Aquilia* is the requirement of intention. In the case of physical damage to property, fault or negligence was sufficient to succeed in a claim of damages but in the case of an action based on the *injuria*, negligence was not sufficient cause; intention (*animus injuriandi*) was required.

The subjective element of intention involved in the concept of an *injuria* is usually referred to as the *animus injuriandi* (or the intention to injure). The expression is used by the Roman and Roman-Dutch writers in a strictly literal sense, namely the intention of committing an *injuria*; the intention of subjecting another to *injuria*.[16] *Animus injuriandi* is therefore merely a species of *dolus* or wrongful intent.

It is clearly difficult to prove what the intentions of a person are. Since the law judges a man's intentions by his conduct, all that the plaintiff need prove at the outset in order to establish the existence of *animus injuriandi*, is that the act complained of constituted an aggression upon his person, his dignity or his reputation, and that the act was intentional. Solomon J expressed this as follows in the case of *Whittaker v Roos* 1912 AD 92:[17]

> ***Whittaker v Roos***
>
> It is not necessary in order to find that there was *animus injuriandi* to prove any ill-will or spite on the part of the defendants towards the plaintiffs; and it is quite immaterial what the motive was or that the object which the defendants had in view was a laudable one. It is sufficient that the injuries suffered by the plaintiffs were inflicted by the defendants, not accidentally or negligently, but with deliberate intention.

Or as Innes J[18] pointed out in the same case:

> When an unlawful aggression . . . has been proved, the law presumes that the aggressor had in view the necessary consequence of his conduct; that he had the intention to injure, the *animus injuriandi*.

The requirement of *animus injuriandi* as applied in the Roman law can be illustrated by the following example: If A intentionally strikes B he clearly commits an assault. Because he intentionally assaulted B, it is said he had the necessary *animus injuriandi*, which is a prerequisite for the delict of *injuria*. If on the other hand A believed that B was his slave – and according to the Roman law he was quite entitled to strike his slave – he could not be sued in terms of *actio injuria* because he believed he had the legal right to strike B and therefore did not have the *animus injuriandi*.

In modern law, it is considered to be unjust for a man to escape liability in cases where he injures another simply because he does not have the prerequisite *animus injuriandi*, and this requirement has been watered down considerably in recent years. In the case of liability of the press for defamatory statements it has disappeared.

9.3.3 Strict liability

In addition to the two main areas of liability which have been discussed, that is, claims based on negligence which results in damage to property and claims based on the intentional violation of a person's personality rights, various other miscellaneous actions existed.[19] Some of these restricted actions required neither negligence nor intention and are thus classified as strict liability.[28] These include:

- *actio de pauperie*, which is an action for damage caused by domestic animals acting from inward excitement or vice
- the so-called quasi-delicts, for which the remedy is the *actio de effusis vel dejectis*[29] or the *actio positi vel suspensi*[30]
- the disturbance of lateral support, which is well known in insurance policies[31]
- interference with the natural flow of water
- nuisance (except where the defendant did not create the nuisance or actively continue it).

In recent years strict liability has been imposed by statute in a number of instances. Strict liability is also referred to as risk liability.

9.3.4 Conclusion regarding the Roman-Dutch law of delict

The Roman-Dutch law of delict recognised that two main actions could be brought. One was for physical damage to corporeal property and the other for aggression against the personality rights of a person. In neither case did a general action for recovery exist.

---

28 For reasons which are not clear, the emphasis is on the absence of fault. In fact, liability can attach despite the absence of any of the elements.

29 Liability of the occupier of a building from which things were thrown or poured into the public road.

30 Liability of the occupier of a building when something suspended is a danger to a passer-by.

31 This risk is normally an exception to liability policies.

Apart from these two actions there were a number of miscellaneous and special actions which did not require fault, but were imposed on a strict liability basis.[32]

9.4 The elements of delictual liability

9.4.1 Introduction

It has been shown that in practice the law of delict moved from a very rigid system of specific laws towards the position where liability is established in terms of general requirements or elements. The purpose of this section is to examine these general elements in greater detail. These elements are:

- ☐ wrongfulness
- ☐ act
- ☐ fault
- ☐ causation
- ☐ harm.

As a rule, all of these elements must be present before a person is held liable. In practice however, it is very seldom that all are investigated in a single case. Historically, most cases that come before the court are concerned with the element of fault.

9.4.2 Wrongfulness

Wrongfulness as unlawfulness

To act wrongfully, as noted, is to act unlawfully. Because of this, historically,[33] wrongfulness as a concept has not been important, since the study of the law of delict was a study of the specific laws of delict. With the evolutionary move towards general principles of delict, the concept has become increasingly important.

Initial attempts to define the wrongfulness tried to link the concept of wrongfulness to the act and so the offending act was referred to as a wrongful act.[20]

More recently however, wrongfulness has developed into and been discussed as a separate element of liability.[21] What *exactly*, is meant by wrongfulness remains elusive. Wrongfulness has been considered to be the infringement of a right,[34] while another definition is the non-performance of a duty.[22][35] It has been defined as the legal convictions

32 Liability could be avoided, even for strict liability, if the damage was what is referred to as an act of God. Legislation has introduced forms of no-fault liability as in the case of the *Aviation Act, Nuclear Energy Act* and so on. The statutory actions, however, fall outside of the scope of the common law since they were created by statute.

33 Historically, is meant for the past 7 000 years or so. The idea of a general principle instead of law is an untried innovation of the past few decades.

34 Which is meaningless unless what is meant by a *right* is known.

35 Which is also meaningless unless what is meant by a duty is known.

of society. These are meaningless. It can be said, for example, that liability cannot attach for an omission unless the omission is wrongful, but unless wrongfulness is defined, the concept is most unhelpful. Indeed, even from a reading of numerous cases it is not clear exactly what is meant by the concept of wrongfulness and how it is to be objectively determined. The view of Boberg[23] that wrongfulness is determined by the gut reaction of the judge may well be true but it certainly is not acceptable in a society which believes in the rule-of-law.

If an act is *prima facie* unlawful, it does not mean however, that liability automatically attaches, as there are various grounds on which one could justify the seemingly unlawful act. These include grounds such as necessity,[24] self-defence, *volenti non fit injuria*, voluntary assumption of risk, etc.

If a man's life therefore is threatened by an attacker and the attacker is killed by him, the latter's action is *prima facie* unlawful but nevertheless justified. The element of wrongfulness has, so to speak, been neutralised.

Historically, as noted, the law of delict consisted of specific delicts. When these specific delicts which result in damage to property or injury are examined, it is clear that these are very restricted and that they all:

- ☐ require a positive act
- ☐ result in damage to property or injury to people.

A generalised delict would thus be any positive act, resulting in any form of damage to property or personal injury.

From this it can be seen that historically there was no wrongfulness on the part of the defendant for:

- ☐ mere omissions
- ☐ damage which is of a purely financial nature (pure economic loss)
- ☐ damage not caused by the defendant.

Wrongfulness as a duty of care

English law has a tort of negligence and has a twofold approach to determining negligence:

- ☐ did the defendant have a duty of care towards the plaintiff, and if so,
- ☐ was that duty breached?

This approach to negligence can confuse the elements of wrongfulness and fault or negligence. The determination of the duty of care should be dealt with as a test for wrongfulness and be divorced from the determination of fault.

Wrongfulness as the legal convictions of society

Wrongfulness is no longer confined to the violation of existing law. Since the common law only recognised liability where the defendant had performed a positive act, even if only in the form of prior conduct, liability could not attach for a mere omission. In order to impose liability for a mere omission the court had to create a new basis for wrongfulness.

In the *Ewels* case the court stated that an omission is wrongful where the omission evokes the moral indignation as well as where the legal convictions require that the omission be regarded as wrongful and the loss suffered be compensated.

In short, something is wrongful if the court thinks it is wrongful.

Modern developments

Wrongfulness deemed as performing a positive act which causes damage to property. In the closing decades of the last century and the early part of this century the scope of the delict began to be broadened by the courts, and wrongfulness became blurred. For example, in the case of *Cape of Good Hope Bank v Fischer* 1886 4 SC 368, De Villiers, the Chief Justice states that in the time of the Roman-Dutch writers Voet and Matthaeus:[25]

> [T]he Aquilian action had received an extension by analogy to a degree never permitted under the Roman law. The action 'in factum' was no longer confined to cases of damage done to corporeal property, but was extended to every kind of loss sustained by a person in consequence of wrongful acts of another, and, thus extended, bore a curious analogy to the action on the case in the English Law.

In the ***Cape of Good Hope Bank*** case Mr T Hudson sold his property to Mr H Hudson. The property was bonded to the Mutual Life Assurance Society for the amount of £500. Mr T Hudson lost his title deeds and the registrar provided him with a duplicate, which omitted to show the mortgage bond. When he sold the property, it was transferred as if it had no bond. Mr H Hudson borrowed £1 000 against the property from one Mr Armstrong and had a bond registered for the amount of £1 000 against the property. Mr Armstrong in turn ceded his debt to the **Cape of Good Hope Bank**. Mr T Hudson became insolvent, the Old Mutual recovered their amount of £500 because of the first bond registered on the property. The property had an inadequate value to satisfy the remaining bond. The bank lost its money. The bank then sued Mr Fisher, the registrar.

This was clearly a claim for a pure financial loss, the cause of which was an omission. The bank lost the case because it was unable to prove the loss was caused by the registrar.

To succeed, the law of delict would have to have been extended. It is also worth noting that in this case the Registrar's office had in fact registered both the deed of transfer and the bonds. He had complied with the duty imposed upon him by law.

This statement creates the impression that the Roman-Dutch law recognised a general principle of delictual liability and that liability was not confined to physical damage to corporeal property caused by a positive act.

Although the statement appears in the judgement, McKerron[26] points out than in fact 'no statement to that effect is to be found in the commentaries of the Dutch writers Voet or Matthaeus on the Aquilian action, nor any passage indicating the recognition of such a wide extension to the action.'

And so it can be seen that even at this early stage the judiciary was beginning to reshape the field of application of delict without any real authority for its statements. Therefore broad statements imposing liability began to appear in judgements and the scope of delict has been extended in this fashion.[36]

A further illustration of this approach is the case of *Perlman v Zoutendyk* 1934 CPD 151, where the judge said the following:

> Roman-Dutch law approaches a new problem in the continental rather than the English way, because in general all damages caused unjustifiably are actionable, whether caused intentionally or by negligence.
>
> In Roman-Dutch law the duty [namely the duty to exercise reasonable care] arises whenever the defendant whose act is complained of should reasonably have foreseen the possibility of harm being caused by his act to another person, except, perhaps, in those cases where the act complained of can be said to be justified or excused.[27]

It is clear that this view is incorrect, as McKerron[28] pointed out, that 'no such all-embracing principles can be laid down'. If this view were correct wrongfulness arises if harm is foreseeable.[37]

A manufacturer who manufactures rope can foresee that someone may well hang himself with the rope. He does not act wrongfully by making and distributing the rope.

If wrongfulness is that which is foreseeable, we could be in the same position as America where the USA Government was successfully sued because a weather forecaster did not forecast a storm. A weather forecaster can foresee that if he forecasts sunny weather, people may believe him and go fishing. If they do believe him and go fishing and a storm develops he can foresee they may be killed. All this is foreseeable. To forecast the weather is not wrongful, storm or no storm, liability does not attach.

The modern development has thus been for the courts to move away from defined grounds of liability towards a general principle of liability, and the requirement of wrongfulness became meaningless in the process.

The current position is stated as follows by Van der Walt:[29]

> The essential characteristic of the South African law of delict is that it is founded on general principles of liability. This is the product of a long historical evolution.

With respect, one cannot help but be cynical about the notion of liability

36 Recent research indicates that the English courts have at times extended the field of torts 'in a manner at times close to deceit'. (Jowell & McAuslan, 1984, 123.)

37 This view is clearly totally incorrect and finds no support in the common law.

being determined according to general principles.[38] In the absence of specific laws, decisions are made according to policy considerations.[39]

Despite general principles, liability was limited by the fact that our common law did not recognise liability for omissions, pure financial loss, and the person sued had to be the cause of the loss. The common law did not recognise vicarious liability. The common law kept the liability based on general principles in check.

9.4.3 Act or conduct

The concept of an act

Delict is concerned with responsibility for the detrimental consequences of wrongful conduct. Some form of conduct on the part of the defendant is therefore required in order to establish liability.[30] Originally liability only existed for damage caused *by the positive* conduct of the defendant. Liability for a mere omission which results in damage to property or injury is unknown in the common law.

In primitive systems of law animals and even inanimate objects such as the sea were 'punished' but in modern legal systems only the conduct of the human being is subject to the law of delict. Human activity constitutes conduct for legal purposes only if it is voluntary in the sense that at the time it occurred it was subject to the control of the actor's will. Control by the defendant's will implies the existence of the mental capacity to direct his physical conduct. Conduct by the will does not necessary imply the capacity to direct one's actions responsibly; it is sufficient if one has the minimal capacity of control in the sense of being able to choose or refrain from a course of conduct. Therefore persons who have no control over their conduct do not meet the requirements of a wrongful act or conduct. Therefore, generally, an insane person or an infant cannot commit a delict to the extent that they have no control over their bodily movements.

Liability for omissions

☐ **Omissions – unknown to the common law**

The historical position was that for liability to attach, the damage caused to property or injury to people must be caused by a positive act.[31] The Roman and Roman-Dutch law recognised liability only for the positive act of a person and not for omissions.[40] Theoretically, at present, liability attaches only to commissions and by exception as a consequence of omissions.

38 Van der Walt (1979, 4) draws attention to the cynicism. In view of the American liability experience the cynicism was well justified.

39 That policy considerations influenced the path of delict is admitted by Corbett (1987).

40 In order to avoid confusion it must be pointed out that the issue is not one of omissions and commissions but one of law. If the law imposed liability for a specific omission, then if the specific omission exists the matter is settled. The fact of the matter is, no law exists that imposes liability for an omission which results in damage to property. There is no known law requiring a man to act to prevent loss or damage to another.

This has often been stated as follows:[41]

> It must be noted . . . that mere omission did not under the *Lex Aquilia* constitute *culpa*; it only did so when connected with prior conduct.

Because the law did not recognise liability based on an omission, a school of thought developed around the problem of when a person could be liable for an omission. McKerron lists a number of circumstances for which liability could attach. The following are discussed as grounds for liability for omissions:

- Prior conduct
- Control over a dangerous thing
- The relationship of the parties
- Public office or calling
- Statute
- General grounds for an omission.

The general grounds for an omission is an addition to the list developed by McKerron.

The leading case on omissions is that of *Die Minister van Polisie v Ewels* 1975 3 SA 590 (A), where the concept of a general ground for liability for an omission was introduced. This is discussed below.

☐ Prior conduct

Some of the cases where liability can attach for prior conduct will now be examined. Although prior conduct is usually discussed as a ground on which liability can be imposed for an omission, this is incorrect. Prior conduct is a positive act and is therefore not an omission.

Liability may result from an omission where the person has, by prior conduct, created a potential risk of harm to others. For example, if a person starts a fire and does not control the fire and it spreads, he is liable for the damages.[42] He is not liable for omitting to control the fire, he is liable because he started the fire with the consequence of the fire, not being controlled, spreading and causing damage.

Earlier in the century a number of important cases occurred in which liability was based on an omission involving prior conduct.

In the case of *SAR & H v Estate Saunders* 1931 AD 276[32] the defendants, having delivered goods in a trailer, left the trailer inside the premises of a company called Crittal Manufacturing Company (SA) to be unloaded by its servants. After the trailer had been unloaded one of the consignee's servants pushed it outside the premises and

---

41 *Halliwell v The Johannesburg Municipality* 1912 AD 659.

42 This is a well established law, as old as recorded history.

> If fire breaks out and spreads into thornbushes so that it burns stacked grain or standing grain or the whole field, he who started the fire shall make restitution.
>
> Exodus 22 v 6

placed it on the opposite side of the road. The consignee then telephoned the SAR & H and advised them that the trailer was in the road and ready to be picked up. The reply was received that it would be picked up in due course, which was in accordance with the usual practice of the SAR & H. The SAR & H denied ever having been advised but the court accepted the view of Crittal. The trailer was not, however, collected but left in the road overnight and without lights. It constituted a danger to persons using the road after dark. During the course of the night the plaintiff's bus, which was being driven by his servant, collided with the trailer and was damaged. The SAR & H was held liable on the ground that since it knew and allowed the trailer to be placed in the street, there had been prior conduct on their part which imposed upon them the duty to ensure that the trailer, when pushed into the road, did not constitute a dangerous obstruction on the highway. The SAR & H both knew and allowed its customers to place its trailers in the street. Anyone who performs an act through the office of another is deemed to have done the act himself. The SAR & H was therefore responsible for the trailer being in the street, despite the fact that its own employees did not place it in the street.

Joffe and Company Limited v Hoskins 1941 AD 431 demonstrates the truth of the maxim: hard cases make bad law.

Joffe, a firm of engineers, contracted to design, supply and deliver on site, cut, bend and fix in position all steel reinforcement for a building project. They did all that was required of them in terms of the contract.

The steel went into a cantilever. It is absolutely essential that the steel should be near the upper surface of the cantilever. Unfortunately, while pouring the concrete, which was undertaken by the contractors, the steel was moved to the lower surface, making it quite useless. As can be expected, the cantilever collapsed killing a plumber named Hoskins, who was working under the cantilever.

His wife sued the engineers and the contractors. It is clear from the evidence that the steel was physically mishandled by the contractors and accordingly the contractors were in fact negligent, as pointed out by judges De Wet and Centlivres. The trial court should have given judgement against the contractors for damages. It did not, but granted judgement against the engineers and absolved the contractors.

The widow did not appeal against the finding of the court concerning the contractors, but the engineers appealed.

The appeal court had a hard case. If it ruled in favour of the engineers the widow would lose her case, despite the fact that all five appeal court judges were satisfied the contractors were liable! De Wet, the chief justice, agreed that the engineers were not negligent.

The majority judges found the acts of designing, supplying and placing of the reinforcing constituted prior conduct which imposed a duty on the engineers. This argument is forced.

The case of *Joffe and Company Limited v Hoskins*[33] also recognised that prior conduct was necessary for the imposition of liability.

☐ **Control of a dangerous thing**

This is applicable where a person assumes control over a dangerous thing such as a fire. When a person starts a veld fire, for instance the law imposes upon him a duty to take reasonable precautions to avoid harm being effected to others by that action. If a person takes over responsibility for a fire started by another and negligently fails to control the fire he could be liable. The omission to exercise proper control will therefore give rise to a liability.

Another example is a failure to exercise control over a wild animal kept in captivity. If the animal escapes and injures somebody else, the act is 'committed' by the animal and not the person. Nevertheless, the person who had control of the animal can incur liability for his failure to exercise control over the animal.[34][43]

☐ **Relationship of the parties**

In certain circumstances the relationship of parties may give rise to a duty to take affirmative action and failure to take such action can result in liability. Thus McKerron argues that the owner of a dynamite factory would have an obligation under common law[44] to procure prompt medical assistance and render help when employees are injured as a result of an explosion at the factory and would be liable for damages to any employee whose injuries were aggravated by his failure to do so.[35]

☐ **Public office or calling**

Positive duties may impose upon persons occupying certain offices, or those following certain callings of a public or quasi-public nature to perform specific acts. If these are not performed, liability could attach. Liability does not attach merely for holding a specific office. Thus in the case of *Cape of Good Hope v Fischer* 1886 4 SC 368 it was held that the registrar of deeds owes a duty to a creditor who has advanced money in consideration of bond, to duly register the bond when passed before him, and if he fails to do so and the creditor thereby loses his preference, the creditor will have an action for damages against him.[36] In the Good Hope case, Fischer, the registrar, did in fact register both the deed and the bond as required. He issued a duplicate deed which did not indicate that a bond was registered against the property. The property was sold.

43 *Buston v Lycett* 1971 4 SA 223 (SR).

44 This is in any event and has long been a statutory duty in terms of section 75 of the *Workmen's Compensation Act* and the regulations promulgated under the *Machinery and Occupational Safety Act*.

The new owner, H Hudson, borrowed money against the property and the money lender (Armstrong) was under the incorrect impression that the property was unbonded. Armstrong, in turn ceded his rights to the bank. The new owner (Hudson) was declared insolvent. The bank sued Fischer, the registrar, but lost the case for lack of proof of causation.

☐ **Statute**

Positive duties may be imposed by statute. Thus users of machinery are generally required by statute to put a guard on the moving parts of machinery which may be dangerous to persons. If the person fails to carry out the duties imposed upon him, it could constitute an actionable act of negligence, providing the requirements of negligence are met. As a general rule, however, the mere contravention of a statute does not lead to delictual liability in South Africa.[45]

☐ **General grounds of liability for omissions**

The original requirement for liability to attach was that there always had to be a positive act which resulted in damage to property or injury. If an action was brought involving an omission, it was necessary to show that omission fell within one of the exceptions. There were many cases where it was difficult to do so and therefore legally liability did not attach. A number of cases were heard where attempts were made to extend delict in cases where no prior conduct was present.[46]

Matters came to a head when in 1975 a case based on omissions, *Die Minister van Polisie v Ewels* 1975 3 SA 590 (A) went before the appeal court. In this case the Appellate Division introduced the concept of a general grounds for liability, in terms of a judgement handed down by Rumpff CJ.

> The facts of the ***Ewels*** case was that an off-duty policeman was assaulting the plaintiff outside a police station. The on-duty policemen including a sergeant omitted to prevent the assault. The minister was sued as a consequence of this omission.
>
> In this case there was no prior conduct on the part of the on-duty policemen causally connected to the assault. In terms of the common law the action could not succeed.[47] The off-duty policeman could have been sued but since he was off-duty the minister would not have

Continued

45 In the Kinross disaster, for example, the mine owners and operators were acquitted despite the conviction of an employee for contravening a mining regulation.

46 In particular, *Regal v African Superslate (Pty) Ltd* 1963 1 SA 102 (A), *Minister of Forestry v Quathlamba (Pty) Ltd* 1973 3 SA 69 (A).

47 The absolute need for prior conduct had been stated in more appeal court judgements than one cares to remember. See *Halliwell v Johannesburg Municipality* 1912 AD 659; *Cape Town Municipality v Paine; Joffe and Company Ltd v Hoskins; SAR & H v Estate Saunders.*

Continued

been liable (this was the case at that stage, but this was also changed a number of years later in the ***Rabie*** case).

Clearly the reason why the minister was sued is that he had a deeper pocket than the off-duty policeman who had assaulted the plaintiff.

Rumpff CJ expressed the test for wrongfulness of omissions as follows:

> Our law has developed to the stage where an omission can be regarded as wrongful also where the circumstances of the case are such that the omission not only evokes moral indignation, but also the legal convictions of the community require that the omission be regarded as wrongful and that the loss suffered be compensated by the person who failed to act positively.

Although liability is based on omissions in the vast majority of actions before the courts today, the test laid down in the *Ewels* case is generally not applied[48] and the court is prepared to hold persons liable despite the absence of any positive act whatsoever by the defendant. Men are no longer judged by their deeds. The present position is therefore that in practice very little distinction exists, if indeed any, between an act of commission and an act of omission.

9.4.4 Fault, mainly negligence

Introduction

As has been noted, the original *Lex Aquilia* did not require fault as an element of liability, but later interpreters of the *Lex Aquilia* required damage to have been wrongfully caused. Hence fault, in the form of *culpa* or negligence, has been an essential element to establish liability for several centuries.[49]

Fault has two main forms. One is intent (referred to as *dolus*) and the other negligence (referred to as *culpa*).

☐ ***Intent or dolus***

Intent is referred to as *dolus* and negligence as *culpa*. It is not intended to discuss the requirement of intent any further, since it is clear that somebody who intentionally causes damage or injury to somebody or to someone else's property, without justifiable cause, incurs liability. Where intention is present few problems in delict arise.

If a person intentionally, that is, with *dolus*, wrongfully, causes damage to a person, fault is established.

☐ ***Negligence or culpa***

The most important, and indeed most controversial element of delict and also the element which has undergone the most change in the last few decades is that of negligence.[50]

48 For a discussion on some cases involving omissions, particularly motor accidents, since 1975, consult Vivian (1986, 7 *et seq.*).

49 From the Abimelech case it appears that fault has always been a requirement for liability.

50 For a discussion on the changes note Vivian (1984, 67 *et seq.*).

Various definitions of negligence have been given. Once wrongfulness has been established, negligence is the failure, in given circumstances, to exercise the degree of care which the circumstances demand. It is thus a relative or subjective and not an absolute or objective concept and may consist of either omitting to do something which a prudent and reasonable man would have done in similar circumstances or in doing something which a prudent and reasonable man would not have done in the circumstances.

Negligence, the duty of care and wrongfulness

English law approaches the question of negligence from the position of a *duty to care*. Negligence will not be a ground for civil liability unless there exists in a particular case a duty to care. A man cannot be liable for negligence if he had no obligation to exercise diligence. The English approach to negligence therefore involves two elements, namely:

(i) the inquiry into the existence of a *duty to care*

(ii) the inquiry into whether there has been a breach of that duty.[37]

The first issue is really the issue of wrongfulness as discussed above.

The test of negligence

The test employed by South African courts to determine whether a person acted negligently or not, is that of the reasonable man. In the case of *Kruger v Coetzee* 1966 2 SA 428 (A) the test was formulated as follows:[38]

> For the purpose of liability culpa arises if –
>
> (a) a diligens pater familias [that is, the reasonable man] in the position of the defendant
>
> (i) would foresee the reasonable possibility of his conduct injuring another in his person or property and causing him patrimonial loss
>
> (ii) would take reasonable steps to guard against such occurrence.
>
> (b) the defendant failed to take such steps.

The test is the so-called *diligens pater familias* or reasonable man test. The above is known as the foreseeability test and presupposes that the defendant also acted wrongfully as discussed above. For example, a reasonable man may see that somebody has fallen into a swimming pool. He can foresee that without assistance the person may drown. A reasonable man will save the drowning man. The fact that a person does not jump into the swimming pool to rescue that drowning person does not mean he is liable. It must first be determined if it was wrongful not to rescue the drowning man. So mere foreseeability is not sufficient to establish liability. Fault is only one element.

The tragic case of *S v Bochris Investments (Pty) Ltd* 1988 1 861 (A)[51] is used to illustrate the test of the reasonable man.

51 For a contrary conclusion as to whether negligence was present in this case, see Boberg (1988, 167).

A public swimming pool was operated from at least 1957. In 1967 a filtration system was installed by a firm of water engineers specialising in the design of filtration plants. An opening of 25 cm diameter was installed but was not covered by a guard of any kind. From 1967 to 1984 it was estimated that 300 000 people used the pool without mishap.

In October 1984, a 9 year old boy drowned in the swimming pool when he was caught in the unguarded hole.

Charges of culpable homicide, which requires negligence, were brought. The court had to decide if negligence was present. The court ruled negligence was not present.

The fact that the pool had been used safely by approximately 300 000 people over a 17 year period showed that the opening did not constitute a danger in the ordinary course. The freakish condition that led to the accident had not been reasonably foreseeable. The reasonable man would not have appreciated the magnitude of the forces involved or the mechanism by which an accident could happen.

Fault and the breach of statutory duty

The fact that the defendant's conduct is contrary to an existing law does not mean he necessarily has the requisite fault toward the defendant. A connection must exist between the act complained of and the delict committed against the defendant.

9.4.5 Causation

As has been noted, the original Roman and Roman-Dutch law required that there had to be a connection between the positive act and the physical damage to property or injury. The damage had to result from the act. Today this requirement is studied under the concept of causation. Causation is an element in delict which has to be present to establish liability.

The claim by the bank in the *Cape of Good Hope v Fischer* over a century ago, failed because causation could not be shown. The court remarked:

> With all the assumptions I have made in the plaintiff's favour the proof would amount to no more than this, that but for the defendant's acts no loss would ultimately have accrued to the plaintiffs; but surely that is not enough. 'It were infinite for the law' says Lord Bacon 'to judge the cause of causes, and their impulsions one of another; therefore, it contenteth itself with the immediate cause, and judgeth of acts by that, without looking to any further degree.'

Modern practice, however appears, not to judge the cause, but the cause of causes. Liability is today imposed even if the defendant did not factually cause the harm. The harm could be caused by a third party.

An example of this is *Langley Fox Buildings Partnership (Pty) Ltd v De Valence* 1991 1 SA 1 (A). In this case the main contractor, the defendant, was sued after a subcontractor erected a wooden beam across a sidewalk and a person walked into the beam and was injured. No act was performed by the defendant, the act which caused the injury was performed by the subcontractor.

The causal connection between the injury and the act, existed between the subcontractor and the injured person, not the defendant. The main contractor was held liable despite the fact that he did not cause the damage. He was held liable because he failed to prevent the injury.

As a general rule however, for causation to exist, as quoted over a hundred years ago, the wrongful act and the loss must be clearly concatenated as cause and effect. In general, the establishment of a cause and effect or a relationship between the act and the loss is usually sufficiently close to justify the court holding the defendant legally responsible. Causation is thus generally not a problem.[52] The onus on establishing such a relationship, if it is in issue, is in every case on the plaintiff.[39]

Where it does arise however, the issues may be very complex indeed. A number of tests have been established to determine whether cause and effect exist. However, there is no totally acceptable test in practice and each case is still essentially treated on its own merits.

> The following three cases may demonstrate the complex problems which arise:
>
> - ☐ A man decides to murder a rival. He kidnaps the rival, ties him up next to a river and goes away to dig a grave to bury his victim. Having done this he returns to murder his victim. On return he finds a crocodile has killed his helpless victim. Is he guilty of murder?
> - ☐ A patient uses a drug which is defective. The patient does not know who manufactured the drug but it can only be one of two manufacturers. One manufacturer is liable, but the patient cannot prove which one.
> - ☐ A man stabs another. The stabbed man is rushed to hospital by ambulance. On the way the ambulance is involved in an accident and the stabbed man dies. Is the man who stabbed him guilty of murder?

9.4.6 Harm, loss or damage

The final element which must be present for delictual liability to arise is that of an injurious consequence following upon the wrongful act.

Not every form of damage is recoverable

Since originally only damage due to corporeal property was recognised, not every form of damage could be recovered. This may be illustrated with reference to the leading case concerning patrimonial damage, namely the *Union Government v Wanakee* 1911 AD 657.[40] In this case a man

52 The theoretical grounds of causation on the other hand present considerable problems in modern delict.

claimed a sum of money for the loss of comfort and society of his wife.[53] The court rejected this claim in the words of Lord de Villiers CJ:

> Whatever may have been the practice under Roman law, it is clear that under the Dutch law the practice was to confine the damages claimable by the Aquilian law action to cases in which a calculable pecuniary loss has been actually sustained. Such loss must be explicitly and specifically proved . . . The loss of comfort and society of a wife does not appear to me to be a pecuniary loss at all. It is a deprivation which in many cases transcends, in the grief, distress and discomfort which it occasions, any other loss which a man can sustain, but it is not a loss which, for purposes of compensation, as distinct from retribution, is capable of being calculated in money. [But] the loss by the husband of his wife's assistance in the care, clothing and upbringing of his children by her seems to me to stand on a different footing. It is quite conceivable that there may be cases in which the loss of such assistance entails an expenditure by the husband which, if the wife had lived, would not have been necessary for him to incur. Such loss might fairly be held to fall under the expression '*damnum rei familiaris*' which is used by Voet 47.10.18.

Pure economic loss

One of the recent developments is the recovery of liability for pure economic or financial loss.[54] As was noted in the discussion on the original requirements of Roman Law, there had to be physical damage to corporeal property. That was the only form of damage recognised under the action of *damnun injuria datum*.

A recent extension of delict is the recognition of liability for a pure economic loss.

Early attempts which extended delict to include claims for pure economic losses were *Perlman v Zoutendijk* 1936 CPD, *Cape of Good Hope Bank v Fischer*, and *Herschel v Mrupe* 1954 3 SA 464 (A). Whether or not the law permitted recovery for pure economic loss was hotly disputed.

The appeal court finally recognised liability for pure economic loss by, what it referred to as caesarian section in the case of *Administrateur, Natal v Trust Bank van Afrika Bpk* 1979 3 SA 824 (A). As predicted by Lord Denning, once the liability had been recognised, the actions and quantums escalated. Actions for damages of R14 million and even R25 million are being brought before the South African courts.[55]

Loss of support

The dependants of a person killed in a wrongful and culpable manner may claim as damages, loss of support from the wrongdoer.

This action developed from the Germanic customary law.[41]

Pain and suffering

A plaintiff may recover compensation for pain and suffering.

53 Not to be confused with loss of support, which is now recoverable.

54 *Greenfield Engineering Works v NKR Construction* 1978 4 SA 901 (N).

55 'Pik summonsed for R25 million – Jalc claims Foreign Minister failed to carry out 'duty of care' to SA citizens.' *Sunday Times*. 1 September 1991.

Emotional shock

The Roman law, recognising only liability for damage to property or injury to people, did not recognise liability for pain and suffering. The Dutch law allowed the plaintiff to claim for physical pain and disfigurement.[42] The courts have also recognised that the plaintiff may recover compensation for emotional shock.[56]

9.4.7 Conclusion

The five elements discussed above are today regarded as the elements necessary for establishing delictual liability. It is clear that the legal system has moved from specific requirements for each delict or tort to specific elements.

9.5 Risk liability

A new basis of liability is beginning to develop, which is known as risk liability. This form of liability is sometimes called strict liability or faultless liability.

It is not quite clear in what way it is determined who is liable, or which test is to be adopted to impose or limit liability based on risk.

In some cases, none of the requirements of delict need to be present, other possibly, than the requirement that the plaintiff has suffered some form of harm.[57] Excluding the examples of strict liability discussed above, the following are examples:

- ☐ **The *Rylands v Fletcher* rule (1868)**
  According to this rule a person who, for his own purposes, brings onto his lands and collects and keeps there anything likely to do mischief if it escapes, must keep it in at his own peril, and, if he does not do so, is '*prima facie*' answerable for all the damage which is the natural consequence of its escape.[43] This rule has never been applied, as such, in South Africa.
- ☐ **Liability of the press, editors and publishers for defamatory published material**
  In the case of *Pakendorf v de Flamingh* 1984 3 SA 146 (A) the appeal court imposed liability on a variety of persons on a risk basis. The editor can, for example, be liable for a defamatory article even if he did not write it (no act), or approve it (no causation) or could not know it was defamatory (no fault).
- ☐ **Liability of the Minister of Police for persons employed in the Department of Police**
  In *Minister of Police v Rabie* 1986 1 SA 117 (A), the court departed from the traditional test for vicarious liability and imposed liability on a risk basis. After this case, it is virtually impossible that a minister will not be liable.

56 *Bester v Commercial Union Versekeringsmaatskappy van Suid Afrika Bpk* 1973 1 SA 769 (A).
57 Huber (1988, 87) demonstrates that in America even this could be doubted.

9.6 Specific liability doctrines

Having stated that in order to impose delictual liability five elements are required to be present, it should be noted that cases exist where liability is imposed despite absence of all or some of the elements. There are a number of instances where actless, faultless, causeless and harmless liability was imposed despite the lawful activities of the person being sued. Vicarious liability is an example of where some of the elements may not be present.

9.6.1 Vicarious liability

Importance of vicarious liability to the risk manager

Vicarious liability is important to the risk manager because it is often encountered in practice. It deals with questions, such as the liability of a company for the delicts of its employees, a contractor for the delicts of the subcontractor, the principal for the delicts of the contractor, the owner of a vehicle for the delicts of drivers of the vehicle.

Insurance issues are also involved. If the insured lends his car to a friend, will the insurance cover accidents caused by the friend? If a motor vehicle is insured by the employer, is the employer exposed to liability and does his insurer cover the employer? These issues all concern the question of vicarious liability.

Prohibited in the common law

A recent development to the law of delict is the dramatic extension of vicarious liability.

Vicarious liability exists when one person is held liable for the acts of another. Historically, vicarious liability was virtually unknown in common law. It was initially strictly prohibited as indicated below.

> **The prohibition against vicarious liability**
>
> The soul who sins is the soul who will die. The son will not die for the father's sin; he will surely live. Yet you may ask, 'Why does the son not share the guilt of the father?' Since the son has done what is just and right and has been careful to keep my decrees, he will surely live. The soul who sins is the one who will die. The son will not share the guilt of the father, nor will the father share the guilt of the son. The righteousness of the righteous man will be credited to him, and the wickedness of the wicked will be charged against him.
>
> Ezekiel 18 v 20

Vicarious liability is in the first instance a question of fact not law. If one person is held liable for the acts of another, he is then factually said to be held vicariously liable.

The law may define the circumstances where liability is imposed. One of the first circumstances for which vicarious liability was imposed is in the case of master and servant. The grounds of liability were as stated below.

> **Vicarious liability of the master for the delicts of the servant**
>
> The test for the liability of the master for the delicts of the servant was laid down as follows:
>
> > A master is liable to a third party for the act of his servant, so long as the latter is about the business of his master and does the act in the course of his employment.

From this it can be seen that for vicarious liability to attach to the master the following must be present:

- ☐ an employee-employer relationship
- ☐ the servant must be delictually liable
- ☐ the servant must be about his master's business
- ☐ the act committed by the servant must be done in the course of his employment.

The development of vicarious liability

A number of cases are used to illustrate the development of vicarious liability.

> ***Colonial Mutual v MacDonald:* Principal-Agent**
>
> Dr MacDonald, a passenger in a car driven by Mr WE Brittain, was injured through the negligent driving of Mr WE Brittain. Mr Brittain was not an employee of Colonial Mutual but an independent agent. Dr MacDonald sued Colonial Mutual for the injuries sustained. Colonial Mutual defended the action on the grounds that it was not vicariously liable for the act of its agent.
>
> The appeal court dismissed the claim because the principal is not liable for the acts of the contractor, sub-contractor or the servant of the contractor or sub-contractor. No employee-employer relationship existed.

In the *Colonial Mutual* case the action had to fail because there was no relationship of employer and employee, between Mr Brittain and Colonial Mutual.

The next case was that of *Feldman v Mall* 1945 AD 733, the salient facts of which are set out below.

> ***Feldman v Mall*: Employer and employee**
>
> In the **Feldman** case an employee-driver deviated from his route and went on a drinking-spree. After drinking for a number of hours he decided to return to his place of employment. On the way back he was involved in an accident. The employer was sued as a result of the accident.
>
> The issue is: was the employee about his master's business?

It is clear that to drive to a place of drinking is not to be about the master's business, nor is drinking in the course of the business of the master. If the accident happened on the way to the drinking session, there is little doubt that the employer would not be liable as the law stood at that time. However, the court broadened the test for vicarious liability. Two of the judges made it clear that since the claim involved a motor accident and this type of liability was insured, no undue hardship would be created if vicarious liability was extended. The hardship which would have existed, had the extended form of vicarious liability been imposed at a previous age – in the days before insurance had developed – no longer existed. The master was held vicariously liable for the accident and the law was extended.

A more recent decision involving vicarious liability is that of *Minister of Police v Rabie* 1986 1 SA 117 (A).[58]

> ***Minister of Police v Rabie***
>
> In this case Van der Westhuizen, a motor mechanic, was employed by the SA Police. One evening outside of working hours, in order to gain access to a party from which he had been barred, he beat up and arrested an innocent person. He had hoped that his actions would impress the people at the party. He did not succeed in being re-admitted. He was clearly not about his master's business.

Clearly in this case the wrongful act of the off-duty motor mechanic had nothing to do with his employer. The facts of the case fall completely outside the scope of employment, as agreed by all the judges of appeal. To quote Jansen JA, who delivered the majority judgement:

> However, it is contended by the appellant that Van der Westhuizen at no stage acted in terms of the Police Act, that his conduct was unrelated to his employment and that in reality he was engaged upon a private and personal action that had nothing to do with police work, but flowed from malice and the furthering of his own interests. In view of the analysis by van Heerden JA, I am prepared to accept in favour of the appellant, that on the stated case and the evidence of the respondent the probabilities are that Van der Westhuizen, in committing the delict in question, was totally self-serving and ***mala fide***, and that he knew from the very beginning that the respondent was innocent and that there were no grounds for using his powers as a policeman.

One would have thought that that would have disposed of the case. Van der Westhuizen was not acting in the course of his employment. Thus it is inconceivable that Van der Westhuizen was about his master's

58 This case attracted considerable comment. (Vivian & Thompson, 1987) and Van der Walt (1988, 4) supported the judgement. Martin (1989, 273) concluded that the decision to base liability of the State on the creation of risk was unfortunate because no indication of the limitation of liability was given by the court.
Further discussion can be found in Stranex (1986, 190); Dendy (1987, 82); Dendy (1986); Otto (1986, 177).

business. The case should have been dismissed in accordance with the decision made by the dissenting judge.

The court however, created a new test for vicarious liability called a risk test. According to this new test, the Minister of Police (and hence the taxpayer) was liable. Commentators have pointed out that it is not at all clear what the ambit of the risk test is.

At present it is therefore unclear under what circumstances an employer will be liable for the delicts of his employees.

9.7 The liability crisis

9.7.1 The American liability crisis

9.7.1.1 *Introduction*

The next step entails an examination of the development which gave rise to the American liability crisis. A study of the theory of the law of delict such as the above seems to be logical and acceptable, but when one looks at the practice, warning bells begin to ring. The following examples of American cases will give an indication of some of the developments which have taken place in the legal liability arena.

9.7.1.2 *Examples of American liability cases*

There is little difficulty in understanding why America is experiencing a liability crisis if the following well-publicised judgements are taken into consideration:

- ☐ Milo Stephens, who has a history of psychiatric problems, attempted to commit suicide by throwing himself in front of a subway train. He then sued the New York City Transit Authority, contending that the driver of the subway train that had hit him, had been negligently slow in bringing the train to a halt. He won $650 000 in an out-of-court settlement.[44]
- ☐ A 32 year old doctor tried unsuccessfully to start a lawn mower. After pulling the cord 15 times he suffered a heart attack. A Philadelphia jury made a products liability award of $1,75 million against the manufacturer of the lawnmower.[45][59]
- ☐ A 19 year old man and his three friends tried, at night, to take a floodlight off the roof of a California High School as a lark. While trying to steal the floodlight, he fell through a skylight and was badly injured. He was awarded $260 000 plus $1 200 per month against the school because they did not paint the skylight in such a way that it could be seen at night.[46]

Continued

59 *Share v Sears, Roebuck & Co* 1984 Pa C quoted in Huber (1988, 39; 235).

Continued

- ☐ Four insurance companies repudiated a claim from the Occidental Petroleum Corporation. Because the claim was repudiated, the companies were sued for $125 million in punitive damages.[47]

- ☐ Mr Roger Boisjoly sued his employer and NASA for $1,1 billion alleging that the parties, amongst others, defamed and discredited him after he had testified against them before a panel investigating the space shuttle disaster.[48]

- ☐ Several manufacturers of aspirin, that household drug used by billions of people worldwide, were sued for $150 million when it was alleged that the manufacturers conspired to block a federal requirement warning that the drug is, under certain circumstances, dangerous.[49]

- ☐ Tobacco manufacturers were successfully sued by relatives of a man who died from cancer.[50]

- ☐ A man was injured in a motor accident. The person who injured him was inadequately insured. He then successfully sued the insurance company because, as a result of negligence on the part of the agent, it did not sell enough insurance cover to the man who had injured him.[60]

- ☐ A Chicago Osteopathic Medical Centre was sued after an accident occurred in a pool at a private party. The only connection between the accident and the hospital is that the doctor who hosted the party worked at the hospital and had advertised the party on the hospital notice board. The hospital's insurers are reported to have paid out $7 million.[51]

- ☐ A woman engineer was awarded R78 million against a church because, contrary to what it had said, she did not become more intelligent nor did her eye-sight improve.[52]

- ☐ A telephone company was ordered to pay $36 million to the children of a couple killed in a motor accident. The company had placed a telephone pole in a bean field. A farmer working in this field accidentally hit the guy wire supporting the pole. The pole snapped and the wires fell across the road. A passing truck struck the wires which resulted in the fallen pole flying like a missile into the van containing the couple.[53]

- ☐ The families of some fishermen who were killed in a storm, recovered a judgement against the United States weather service for negligently failing to predict the storm.[54]

- ☐ In the well-known case of *Sindell v Abbot* (1980), a drug manufacturer was held to be liable although it could not be proved that it had manufactured the drug thought to have caused the problem.[61]

- ☐ A woman was awarded $986 000 for the loss of psychic powers after a brain scan.[55]

---

60 *Flattery v Gregory* 489 NE 3rd 1257 (Mass 1986); See also *Journal of Risk and Insurance* (September 1986, 563).

61 *Business Insurance* (20 October 1980), followed in *Abel v Eli Lilly & Co* and *Collins v Eli Lilly & Co.*

It is quite clear that these judgements cannot be understood in terms of the law of delict as set out above. The reason for these judgements must be found elsewhere.

The judgements can be explained by the so-called *Deep Pocket Theory*. The party who is sued is liable because he has the most money or because he is a large company or is insured; he is for that reason liable.

It is not only the strange cases which are cause for concern but also the magnitude of the awards. The following are some of the better known awards:

☐ *Pinto* case: 'defective' design of a car	\$121 million
☐ *Texaco*	\$11.1 billion

9.7.1.3 *The failure of the rule-by-general-principles*

American law of torts started off with specific writs which defined the basis of liability. Clearly, the movement away from the definitive grounds or laws of liability to general principles has been a failure. Once the definitive grounds are abandoned, liability is determined on relative grounds; the rule of law becomes the arbitrary rule by the judicial system.

Further illustrations of the evolutionary nature of delict are the cases against cigarette manufacturers. In the USA, cigarette and tobacco manufacturers were unsuccessfully sued over a period of 20 years by relatives of smokers who died as a result of cancer.[62] As the judicial system became used to the idea that tobacco companies could be sued, it was inevitable that an action would eventually succeed and this did indeed happen in May 1988.[56]

Obviously, in the absence of clear and definitive laws in terms of which liability can be established, the rule-by-general-principles in practice degenerates into plain stupidity. One author has argued that some aspects of recent judgements are so wrong that they are contrary to natural justice.[57]

The ever-increasing liability judgements contributed to the insurance crisis of the early 1980s[58] and the rule-of-law began to be equated with the decision of the judge. This decision was no longer based on the law; the decision itself was the law . We therefore moved from the rule-of-law to the rule-of-judge and we had therefore once again moved to the rule of men from the rule of laws.

9.7.1.4 *Judicial activism – a cause of the liability crisis*

The liability crisis of the United States was in fact a judicial crisis. In the early 1980s liability awards were of great concern in the USA; the matter

62 See for example *Cipollone v Liggett* 387 NW2d 565, Iowa Supreme Court (1986). *Product Liability International* (February 1987); *Sunday Star* (11 August 1985).

was investigated by the Reagan administration and its finding can be accepted.

Richard K. Willard, Assistant Attorney General of the United States Department of Justice, was asked by the then Attorney General, Richard Meese, to chair an inter-agency committee to investigate and report on the causes of the liability crisis. Willard presented his findings to president Reagan and his cabinet at a series of meetings during 1986. The report of the committee was endorsed by the president and released as a statement of the administration's policy. The report found that two basic causes contributed to the crisis, namely, the insurance cycle and more fundamentally the expansion in the degree of liability imposed by the tort or civil justice system. Willard noted the following at a conference in London on 8 April 1987:[59]

> Most tort law in our country is a product of judicial decision-making rather than legislation, a phenomenon I sometimes refer to as 'judicial activism'. For many years our judges seemed to feel that tort liability doctrines should be liberalized.

Later that year Willard again made this point:[60]

> 'Judicial activism' – not a lack of regulation – is to blame for the liability explosion that caused the insurance crisis of the mid-1980s. . . . The explosion of liability is the result of activist judges whose penchant for social engineering has distorted beyond recognition the common law of torts.

Thus the American liability crisis was caused by judicial activism. Judicial activism may be defined as the action of judges who deliberately ignore the law, as it is, and make judgements according to their personal and hence political opinion. It is the substitution of the **rule-by-law** by **rule-by-judge**.

As is often said: hindsight is a very precise science, and with the advantage of hindsight the path of substitution of **rule-by-law** by **rule-by-judge** can be traced. At the turn of the century the rule-of-law prevailed. The American Congress made the law; the executive functioned according to the law and in situations of doubt as to the meaning or applicability of the law the courts were called upon to interpret the law. However, even at that early stage, lawyers began to realise that the power to interpret is actually the power to make to law. In 1897, Mr Justice OW Holmes, a famous American judge, wrote:[63]

> The prophecies of what the courts will do in fact, and nothing more pretentious, are what I mean by the law.

It was statements such as this one which gave rise to the theory of realism.

The abortion decisions of the American Supreme Court can be used to illustrate how the American judges abandoned the law in favour of their own personal opinions.

---

63 *The Path of Law*, quoted by Lord Lloyd. 1979. *Introduction to Jurisprudence*. 4th Edition. 477.

By 1973, with hindsight, any doubt that the American judges were substituting their personal political opinion for the law was removed. In what must rank as the single most astounding judgement in history, the case of *Roe v Wade* 410 US 113 (1973), the United States Supreme Court ruled that the entire democratically elected process of the United States may not make laws to prevent abortion-on-demand. That this decision was not a judicial, but a political act was pointed out in the dissenting judgement of Mr Justice Rehnquist, (later Chief Justice) as follows:[64]

> The decision here to break pregnancy into three distinct terms and to outline the permissible restrictions the State may impose in each one, for example, partakes more of judicial legislation than it does of a determination of the intent of the drafters of the Fourteenth Amendment.

The court then ruled that a 100 year old law preventing abortion was contrary to the constitution. Legislation **against** abortion can be traced back for 3 500 years! This decision caused a tremendous public outcry and as Wolfe has pointed out:[65]

> Even very activist legal commentators who admired and defended the Warren Court balked at defending this decision.

Mr Justice Bork of the United States also draws attention to the lack of legal authority for the *Roe v Wade* decision:

> 'In the years since 1973, no one, however pro-abortion, has ever thought of an argument that even remotely begins to justify *Roe v Wade* as a constitutional decision'.
>
> Justice Blackmum (who delivered the majority opinion of the court) frequently discusses the case in public, but the only justification he offers is not legal, but moral: the case he says, is a milestone on women's march to equality. There is certainly room for argument about that. There is no room for argument about the conclusion that the decision was the assumption of illegitimate judicial power and the usurpation of the democratic authority of the American people.[61]

The decision of the American Supreme Court in *Webster v Reproductive Health Services* (1989) to limit its *Roe v Wade* decision on abortion may well be an indication that the tide is turning in America. The original decision to prevent individual states from preventing abortion was an act of judicial activism; this point is accepted by American jurists.

It is interesting to note the attitude of the German Supreme Court on the issue of abortion. The German Parliament essentially passed an abortion-on-demand statute and the opposition party applied to the *Bundesverfassungsgericht* to have the statute set aside since it conflicted with article 2 of the *Grundgesetz*. The German court ruled that abortion-on-demand is unconstitutional since the constitution protected the life

---

64 An extract of the judgement is quoted in *The American Constitution and the Judicial Process*, 235.

65 *The Rise of Modern Judicial Review*, 307; the commentators were not opposed to abortion as such – see note 37 on 376.

developing in the womb as an independent *Rechtgut* (protected interest).[62][66]

9.7.2 The United Kingdom liability crisis

It is incorrect to believe that the *Deep Pocket Theory* exists only in America. It has taken root in the legal practice of most Western societies.[67] The development of the *Deep Pocket Theory* in the United Kingdom can be now traced.

If the British law of torts at the turn of the century is examined, basically the same position existed as that in South Africa. Liability was determined according to specific laws. At that time a leading writer in this particular field of law was Sir John Salmond. When asked under which circumstances liability can attach in the field of tort, he answered:[63]

> Just as the criminal law consists of a body of rules establishing specific offenses, so, the law of torts consists of a body of rules establishing specific injuries. Neither in the one case nor in the other is there any general principal of liability. Whether I am prosecuted for an alleged offence, or sued for an alleged tort, it is for my adversary to prove that the case falls within some specific rule of liability, and not for me to defend myself by proving that it is within some specific and established rule of justification or excuse.

So, at the turn of the century the British law of torts consisted of fairly well-defined grounds of liability or defined laws. As long as the people arranged their affairs to avoid those grounds of liability, they were safe from ruinous delictual liability.

However, the tendency evolved towards the judiciary determining whether liability exists, rather than the law. The United Kingdom law of torts expanded.

One can only agree with the view expressed by Lord Denning in the case of *Sparham-Souter v Town Developments* (1976) QB 858:

In recent years the law of negligence has been transformed out of all recognition.

Lord Denning, who is generally regarded as the most influential English judge of this century, in a book entitled *The Discipline of Law* examined the changes which took place in the various branches of the law during the years that he was on the bench. In discussing the law of delict (or torts), he noted that the courts had adopted a policy in these cases. He said in this connection:

---

66 As a further point of interest, it was also argued before the South African appeal court that abortion-on-demand was permissible in terms of SA law. The appeal court dismissed this as a proposition without merit in *S v Collop* 1973 2 SA, 163 (D).

67 See for example the view expressed by Mr Walter Diehl, Chairman of the Board of Directors Swiss-Re, Zurich, 22nd November 1985 at 3. 'It would be totally misleading to interpret these changes as characteristic of American society, since the same tendencies are visible in all highly-developed industrial nations.' The speaker, being the chairman of one of the large reinsurers was in a position to detect the influences throughout most of the world.

> The policy behind it all is that, when severe loss is suffered by any one singly, it should be borne, not by him alone, but be spread throughout the community at large.

According to Lord Denning the courts achieved this policy as follows:

> In most of the cases that come before the Courts today, the parties appear at first sight to be ordinary persons or industrial companies or public authorities. But their true identity is obscured by masks. If you lift up the mask, you will usually find the legal aid funds or an insurance company or the taxpayer – all of whom are assumed to have limitless funds. In theory the Courts do not look behind the masks. But in practice they do. That is the reason why the law of negligence has been extended so as to embrace nearly all activities in which people engage. That is the reason the awards of damages have escalated so as to exceed anything that even the wealthiest individual could pay.

This is of course nothing but an acknowledgement of the application of the *Deep Pocket Theory*. Lord Denning clearly saw that the British courts had begun to be biased towards the injured party in the case of a large institution being sued. It is because of this bias that the awards had escalated. This is the *Deep Pocket Theory*. The body with the deepest pocket is liable, not because it is the law but because he has the deepest pocket.

9.7.2.1 *The United Kingdom judicial activism*

The method of arriving at the Deep Pocket Theory in the United Kingdom is of particular importance since the British courts are conservative. The doctrine of precedent is particularly well developed in England. Unlike the USA, the various members of the judiciary would tend to rule against any judge who **openly** attempted acts of judicial activism.

The course of judicial activism can be traced through the decisions of Lord Denning since, it is doubtful whether any jurist would quarrel with Atiyah's[64] opinion that:

> Some of Lord Denning's greatest triumphs are to be found in the modern development of the law of negligence. In this area his willingness to innovate has, at least in recent years, struck a responsive chord with most of his colleagues who have found the conceptual apparatus of tort law less constricting than that of contract law. Indeed, it is not going too far to say that a large part of the modern law of negligence owes its origins to Lord Denning's judgements.[65]

That Lord Denning is responsible for the current state of the 'law' of torts is a point that indeed, few would care to challenge. Therefore when Lord Denning indicated a judicial tendency to the *Deep Pocket Theory*, he knew what he was talking about.

Lord Denning is a most remarkable judge. Within years after his retirement, his life's work had been analysed and a book on this research published. This, as the authors of the work freely acknowledge, was in itself without precedent.

How then did Lord Denning make these innovative judgements in the face of binding precedent? This question is too complex to be fully answered in this text, and the various works on Lord Denning's life needs to be studied. His approach can, however, be illustrated by the comments of Freeman:[66]

> Throughout the whole period of the Master of Rolls Lord Denning has taken a fairly cavalier approach to the doctrine of precedent. . . . He has a knack, **close at times to deceit, of paying lip service to precedent, while not really complying with it.**[67]

Atiyah makes a similar point as follows:

> That many judges feel their way intuitively to their conclusions, and then articulate their justification in terms of legal principle afterwards, is now a commonplace of legal theory. But in Lord Denning's case, the articulated reasons often seem forced and unacceptable; indeed, they are often couched as to enable him to depart from them almost at will in subsequent cases.[68]

The problem any modern jurist now has, is to know which reasons or judgements he can trust and believe in.

The doctrine of precedent is nowadays very unreliable and provides ample scope for mischief.

The United Kingdom with is strong traditions may yet withstand the drift to the American system; certainly the House of Lords has been a restraining influence and indeed Lord Denning himself understood the dangers of the United Kingdom system going too far, when he wrote:

> I sometimes wonder whether the time has not come – may indeed be already with us – when the Courts should cry Halt! Enough has been done for the sufferer. Now remember the man who has to foot the bill - even though he be only one of many.

It can be concluded that the British law of torts is in danger of moving towards the American situation, for the same reasons – judicial activism.

9.7.3 Summary of recent developments in South African delict

Without expressing any opinion[68] as to whether the liability crisis which has taken place in America and to a lesser extent in Britain will take place in South Africa it should be noted that the South African law of delict has in recent years undergone significant changes. These changes, as pointed out by Professor Kahn,[69] were as in America and Britain introduced not by Parliament but by the judiciary:

> The law of delict has seen considerable change for the better partly through legislation, but mainly through the decision of the courts . . . at the risk of over-simplification, one may say that the judiciary has to a degree extended the scope of the Aquilian action and the *actio iniuriarum* in favour of the injured party.

68 For a separate comment note Vivian (1984).

There are certainly grounds for debate as to whether the changes are for the better.

Table 9.2 indicates some changes which have taken place in South Africa in recent years.

Table 9.3 indicates the magnitude of claims or awards for personal injury claims.

Table 9.2
Changes to the common law

Change	Case
Liability for emotional shock	*Bester v Commercial Union* 1973 1 SA 769 (A)
Liability for omissions	*Die Minister van Polisie v Ewels* 1975 3 SA 590 (A)
Liability for mere words causing economic loss	*SA Bantoetrust v Ross en Jacobs* 1977 3 SA 184 (T)
Liability for pure economic loss	*Greenfield Engineering Works v NKR Construction* 1978 4 SA 901 (N) *Administrateur, Natal v Trust Bank* 1979 3 SA 824 (A)
Introduction to the Anton Piller order	*Roamer Watch Co v African Textile Distributors* 1980 2 SA 254 (W)
Liability for an opinion about future events	*Kern Trust v Hurter* 1981 3 SA 607 (C)
Liability based on speculation (law of evidence)	*MVA v Dubusane* 1984 3 SA 700 (A)
Faultless liability and liability for the independent actions of others (law of defamation)	*Pakendorf v de Flamingh* 1984 3 SA 146 (A). The case was subsequently applied to found faultless criminal liability, which in turn was limited on appeal.
Introduction of risk liability. Liability for the independent criminal actions of employees	*Minister of Police v Rabie* 1986 1 SA 117 (A)
Liability for wrongful life	*Edouard v Administrator, Natal* 1989 2 SA 368 (D)
Introduction of the legitimate expectation rule	*Administrator, Transvaal v Traub and others* 1989 4 SA 731 (A)

9.7.4 The *quantum*

As indicated by Lord Denning,[70] there is a tendency for awards to escalate in the face of the belief of limitless funds. The attached table of claims indicates the escalation which is taking place in South Africa.

Table 9.3 Recent personal injury awards in South Africa

Injury	Award	Status of injured person
Spinal damage	R14,8m (outcome pending)	Hyper store manager
Quadriplegic	R7 200 000	Motor accident
Brain damage	R2 500 000	35 year old computer systems analyst
Paraplegic	R1 350 000	21 year old university student (computer science)
Quadriplegic	R1 200 000	24 year old Polish immigrant; former trade union member
Loss of sight, bedridden	R1 000 000	11 year old child; injured in a motor accident
Quadriplegic	R 712 000	49 year old fitter
Quadriplegic	R 500 000	23 year old university student
Loss of eyesight	R 330 000	31 year old motor body builder
Brain damage	R 322 000	21 year old woman passenger, occupation not stated
Paraplegic	R 300 000	20 year old resident
Loss of a leg	R 225 000	29 year old carpenter
Loss of hearing	R 220 000	11 year old girl
Loss of a lower leg	R 240 000	40 year old welder
Loss of an arm	R 62 000	

9.7.5 Objections to the liability crisis

A number of objections can be raised to developments which have taken place in delict:[69]

The system is inefficient

Every year, in South Africa, about 25 000 third party motor vehicle claims are made and about 242 755 workmen's compensation claims. The judicial system which can take several years to resolve a single claim is not suited to deal with a large volume of claims. Legal costs to resolve a single dispute can run into millions of rands.[71]

In some cases, *Minister of Police v Mbilini* 1983 3 SA 705 (A) for example, a case which went to appeal, the final award was R175. In a case like this, one can expect seven supreme court judges, four advocates and a set of six attorneys to be involved – all for R175. This type of legal system simply cannot be afforded.[72] The transaction costs are simply too great.

69 For a more detailed discussion of the consequences of the liability crisis, see Huber (1988, 123).

The system is expensive to administer

The American experience of tort liability costs indicates that only 31.4% of loss expenses are paid to the injured party.[73]

The system is capricious

The American tort system has often been described as a roulette game, the outcome cannot be determined with any degree of certainty beforehand. If the cases set out in section 9.7.1 are examined, then this is not surprising.

The main beneficiaries of the system is the legal profession

It is estimated that 46% of the loss expenses are recovered by the legal profession. In the final analysis the tort system is a system designed by lawyers for the benefit mainly of lawyers.

The system promotes socialism not justice

Much of the literature portrays the system as promoting justice or an equitable result. However, any system which has as its basis a loss-spreading function, or 'premiumless' insurance, is simply a form of socialism.[74]

The system results in the substitution of rule-by-judge in the place of rule-of-law

For reasons discussed above, ultimately the decision to impose liability is not decided according to law but by the opinion of the judge. The approach is not based on the rule-of-law. In South Africa the rôle of policy considerations as opposed to the application of existing laws is admitted.[75] In America outright concern has been expressed about the same issue.[76]

The system destroys innovation

The reaction of businessmen who are faced with the prospects of being sued for millions of rands or having to spend millions of rands defending cases based on vague principles and not law, will be to retreat to less risky areas. Innovations are thus destroyed by the liability system.

The system undermines the fundamental notion of fault; justice and injustice is confused

Historically fault has been a requirement for liability. In order to impose liability where none exists, the court had to create fault where none existed. Innocence was thus equated to guilt, which contaminates the value system of society.

Bibliography

Boberg, PQR 1988. 'Foresight or hindsight.' *BML.*

Boberg, PQR 1985. 'From pecus to pecuniary loss – Aquilian liability in the twentieth century.' *Lesotho Law Journal.*

Boberg, PQR 1984. *The law of delict.* Cape Town: Juta & Co. Vol. I.

Bork, RH 1990. *The tempting of America.* Sinclair-Stevenson.

'Biggest asbestos producer seeks bankruptcy.' *Star.* 27 August 1982.

Corbett, MM 1987. 'Aspects of the rôle of policy in the evolution of our common law.' *SALJ.*

Dendy, M 1987. 'Ministerial liability for the focus of the force: Curbing the over-zealous policeman.' *SAJHR.*

Lord Denning, A 1979. *The principle of law.* Durban: Butterworths.

Fensham, FC 1978. 'Liability in case of negligence in the Old Testament covenant code and ancient legal traditions.' *Essays in honour of Ben Beinart.* Cape Town: Juta and Co.

Flemming, JG 1987. *The law of torts.* London: The Law Book Company. 7th Edition.

Heuston, RFV & Chambers, RS 1981. *Salmond and Heuston on the law of torts.* London: Sweet & Maxwell, 18th Edition.

Huber, PW 1988. *Liability – The legal revolution and its consequences.* Basic Books Inc.

Jowell, JL & McAuslan, JPWB 1984. *Lord Denning: The judge and the law.* London: Sweet & Maxwell.

Keeton, WP (ed.), Dobbs, DB, Keeton, RE & Owen, DG 1984. *Prosser and Keeton on THE LAW OF TORTS.* West Publishing Company. 5th Edition.

Kinsley, M 1986. 'Craziness in the court room' *Readers Digest.*

Lee, RW 1946. *An introduction to Roman-Dutch law.* Oxford University Press. 4th Edition.

Martin, BSC 1989. 'State liability for the delict of the police.' *THRHR.*

McKerron, RG 1971. *Law of delict.* Durban: Butterworths.

Mehr, RI 1986. *Fundamentals of insurance.* Homewood, Illinois: Richard D. Irwin Inc. 2nd Edition.

Mehr, RI & Hedges, BA 1974. *Risk management: Concepts and applications.* Homewood, Illinois: Richard D. Irwin Inc.

Mogg, WR 1990. 'Sorry-trial of Judge Bork.' *Star.* 6 June.

Nagel, CJ, van Niekerk, CG, Hosten, WJ Edwards, AB, Nathan, C & Bosman, F 1980. *Introduction to South African law and legal theory.* Durban: Butterworths.

Neethling, J, Potgieter, JM & Visser, PJ 1990. *Law of delict*. Durban: Butterworths.

Otto, JM 1986. 'Oorsig van regspraak.' *DR*.

Stranex, M 1986. 'Liability for the delict of the police; the underwriter state.' *SALJ*.

Thomas, J 1986. *Introduction to Roman law*. Digma Publications.

Van der Merwe, NJ & Olivier, PJJ 1976. *Die onregmatige daad in die Suid Afrikaanse reg*. Pretoria: Van der Walt. 3rd Edition.

Van der Walt, JC 1988. 'Die staat se aanspreeklikheid vir onregmatige polisie optrede.' *THRHR*.

Van der Walt, JC 1979. *Delict: Principles and cases*. Durban: Butterworths.

Vivian, RW 1990. 'Judical socialism in South Africa.' Unpublished *BERG* paper presented at the University of the Witwatersrand.

Vivian, RW 1986. 'Director's criminal liability.' *Newsletter*. Institute of Directors.

Vivian, RW 1984. 'South Africa is poised for a liability crisis.' *South African Annual Insurance Review*.

Von Rad, G 1972. *Genesis*. SCM.

Wall, FD 1987. 'A matter of attitude.' *Best's Review*. October.

Endnotes

[1] Mehr, 1986.

[2] Mehr & Hedges, 1974, 255 *et. seq.*

[3] *The Star*, 27 August 1982.

[4] *The Star*, 14 April 1987;
Business Week, 27 January 1986;
The Economist, 18 April 1987;
Sunday Times, 10 April 1988.

[5] Vivian, 1986, 22.

[6] Neethling, *et al.*, 1990, 4.

[7] Von Rad, 1972, 228.

[8] Von Rad, 1972, 228.

[9] Fensham, 1978, 285; 290.

[10] Genesis 20, v. 14.

[11] Thomas, 1987, 123.

[12] McKerron, 1971, 6.

[13] McKerron, 1971, 6.

[14] McKerron, 1971, 7.

[15] McKerron, 1971, 9.
[16] McKerron, 1971, 56.
[17] McKerron, 1971, 56.
[18] McKerron, 1971, 56-57.
[19] McKerron, 1971, 11.
[20] McKerron, 1971, 13.
Boberg, 1984, Chapter 2.
[21] Neethling, *et al.*, 1990. Chapter 3.
[22] Nagel, *et al.*, 1980, 470.
[23] Boberg, 1985, 338.
[24] Nagel, *et al.*, 1980, 471.
[25] McKerron, 1971, 8.
[26] McKerron, 1971, 8.
[27] Van der Walt, 1979, 119-122.
McKerron, 1971, 32.
[28] McKerron, 1971, 30.
[29] Van der Walt, 1979, par. 2.
[30] Van der Walt, 1979, 57.
[31] McKerron, 1971, 8.
[32] McKerron, 1971, 15.
[33] McKerron, 1971, 15.
[34] McKerron, 1971, 33.
[35] McKerron, 1971, 23.
[36] McKerron, 1971, 24.
[37] McKerron, 1971, 25-26.
[38] Nagel, *et al.*, 1980, 480.
[39] McKerron, 1971, 52.
Nagel, *et al.*, 1980, 485.
[40] McKerron, 1971, 51.
[41] Neethling, 1990, 237.
[42] Lee, 1946, 323.
[43] McKerron, 1971, 232.
[44] *Time*, 24 March 1986;
Star, 23 Dec. 1983;
Kinsley, 1986, 39;
Huber, 1988, 78; 239.
[45] *Time*, 24 March 1986, 32.

[46] *Time*, 24 March 1986.

[47] *Business Insurance*, 2 February 1987, 1.

[48] *Business Insurance*, 2 February 1987.

[49] *Products Liability International*, February 1984, 31.

[50] *Sunday Star*, 11 August 1985;
Fortune, 23 May 1988.

[51] *Forbes*, 11 August 1986, 79.

[52] *Star*, 19 May 1985; 21 May 1985; 17 July 1985; 2 June 1985;
The Economist, May 25, 1985.

[53] *Experiodica*, March 1988.

[54] *Foresight*, May 1987.

[55] *The Economist*, 2 December 1989, 79.

[56] *Star*, 14 June 1988.

[57] Vivian, 1986, 50 *et seq*.

[58] Vivian, 1986, 50 *et seq*.

[59] *Foresight*, May 1986.

[60] *Business Insurance*, 12 October 1987.

[61] Mogg, 1990;
Bork, 1990.

[62] *THRHR*, 1976, 72 *et seq*.

[63] Heuston & Chambers, 1981, 14.

[64] Jowell & McAuslan, 1984.

[65] Lord Denning, 1984, 54-55.

[66] Jowell & McAuslan, 1984.

[67] Lord Denning, 1984, 123.

[68] Lord Denning, 1984, 180.

[69] *SALJ*, 1989, 610.

[70] Lord Denning, 1984, 280.

[71] Vivian, 1990.

[72] Stagg, 1989.

[73] Wall, 1987, 12.

[74] Vivian, 1990.

[75] Corbett, 1987.

[76] Bork, 1990.

10 RISK FINANCING

10.1 Introduction

The earlier sections concentrated on the nature and definition of risk and the placement of pure risk within the framework of risk management. The introduction of a model facilitated a logic to be applied to the management of risk. The model dictated that after identifying and evaluating the risk, an 'action' point was reached when the practical aspect of risk control had to be considered.

Viewing this text as a progression of the fundamental logic provided broadly by the risk management model, means that a further turning point is now reached. Allowing a necessary digression to examine liability issues discussed in Chapter Nine, the model now prescribes that attention be drawn to the question of financial provision for fortuitous losses which may occur from risk exposures identified, evaluated and controlled to the extent possible.

The path that was followed and explored now requires some further clarification. By differentiating the risk management elements and arranging these sequentially for discussion, their significance in the overall process is highlighted. More importantly, the sequence aims to allow the integration of these aspects more easily into one encompassing model of risk management.

The purpose of this chapter is threefold. First, it is necessary to link the elements of the basic model so as to achieve an overall process of risk management, which includes the considerations of loss financing. It will be seen that not only is integration necessary **across** the model, but that effective risk management implies integration **within** the model.

Secondly, this chapter will provide a brief overview of risk financing mechanisms, the aim being to distinguish between pre-loss and post-loss financing. The intention is not to examine such mechanisms in detail, but rather to provide a framework within which the ensuing discussions of the financing techniques of insurance and self-funding can be placed.

Thirdly, the underlying rationale for risk management is investigated by viewing the risk management function in relation to the corporate objective of value maximisation. This criterion is then finally used as a base from which to critically assess the risk management model and ultimately adapt it to take cognisance of decisions concerning investment and finance – hence achieving the desired holistic approach to the management of pure risk.

10.2 Interrelationship between risk control and financial elements in the risk management process

10.2.1 The risk financing element within the basic risk management model

In Chapter Eight, section 8.2, it was stated that risk control[1] entailed any activity aimed at reducing the severity and frequency of losses that may arise from the pure risks facing an organisation. Through systematic identification, evaluation and control this objective is achieved by:

- ☐ eliminating or reducing the factors that may cause loss events
- ☐ minimising the extent of the actual loss that occurs when preventative methods are not fully effective.

The risk management process is incomplete however, until one also considers the element of financing (diagrammatically depicted in figure 10.1).

Figure 10.1
The risk financing element within the basic risk management model

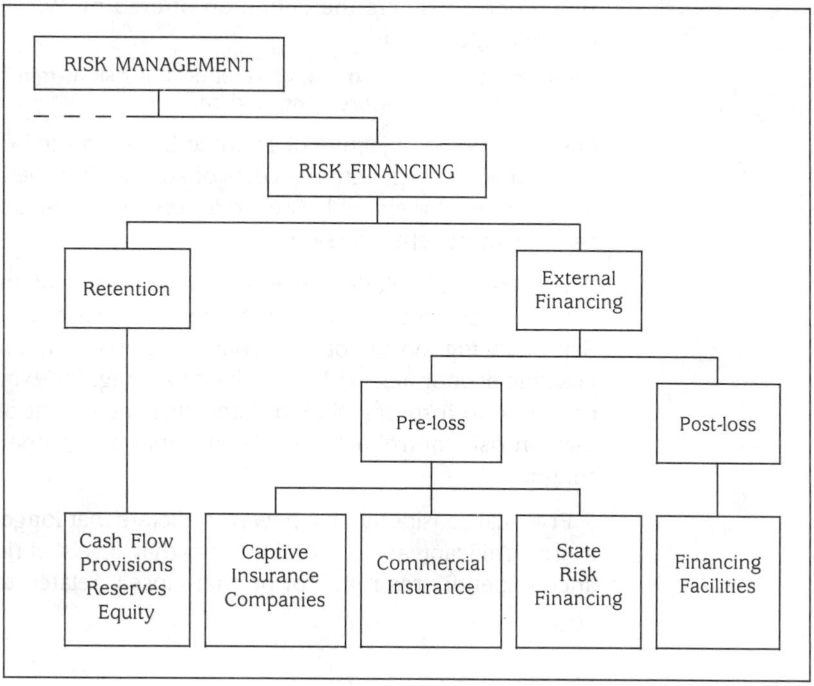

The risk financing function comes into view when consideration is given to the pursuit of minimising the 'total cost-of-risk' to an organisation.

1 The reader is referred to Chapter Four, section 4.4.1.

10.2.2 Cost-of-risk

Risk management professionals have for some time been concerned with the problem of measuring their effectiveness in controlling risk costs.[1] The 'cost-of-risk' concept was thus developed by Barlow[2] as a useful measurement device for reporting the results of the risk and insurance management function. As defined, the cost-of-risk is the sum of:

- ☐ net insurance premiums
- ☐ unreimbursed losses (self-insured, self retained)
- ☐ risk control and loss prevention expenses
- ☐ administrative costs.

The central issue becomes one of **optimal financing** (pre-loss),[3] so that while the risk control process is being addressed, the financing of risk and losses as they occur, does not introduce any inefficiencies.

Immediately evident is the preoccupation with an overall cost efficiency. When one considers the definition offered by Williams & Heins[2] that risk management is

> the minimisation of the adverse effects of risk at minimum cost through its identification, measurement, and control

one detects the objective of **balance** between the benefit from removal or reduction of risk with the costs of such action. Definitions afforded by other writers, for example Greene & Serbein,[3] also appear to reflect similar cost to benefit trade-offs.

The trade-off alluded to is the direct result of the interrelationship between risk control, on the one side of the risk management model, and risk financing, on the other. What manifests is that in the shorter term, possible economies evident in risk financing, for example a reduction in premium to insurers, should determine the extent of effort or expenditure on risk control activities – and that an optimal balance should be sought.

Practical considerations, however, dictate that **longer term** horizons are more significant, and this often means that 'levels' of risk control and insurance expenditures may not be that closely related to shorter-term cost

2 In 1960, Douglas Barlow, a former President of the Risk and Insurance Management Society and risk manager for Canada's Massey-Ferguson Ltd, developed the concept of *cost-of-risk* as a useful measurement device for reporting the results of the risk and insurance management function to senior management (*Cost of Risk Survey*, 1981, 1).

3 There exists a distinction between what is termed pre-loss financing and post-loss financing. This distinction is made later in the chapter. However, it is apposite to state here that insurance and deliberate self-funding are examples of pre-loss financing. The concern, when reference is made to financing optimisation, is with regard to pre-loss financing.

to benefit trade-offs.[4] This does not, nevertheless, imply that the concept of balance or optimisation is unimportant. On the contrary, once one qualifies that long-term horizons are contemplated, optimisation becomes again of paramount importance to risk managers.

It can be argued that risk control endeavours should not necessarily be a function of short-term cost to benefit trade-off *per se*; risk control should be undertaken within the limits imposed by **broader** corporate financial objectives and constraints, and once determined, the risk finance function should then be optimised.

The implication for financing through insurance following such desired optimisation, is interesting. When insurance is regarded as a transfer of risk cost,[5] and an insurer as a financial intermediary, then, in the long run, being more reliant on this type of intermediary financing must imply a higher cost than being less reliant.[6]

Even with long-term considerations in mind, there remains the close interrelationship between risk control and the financial elements that constitute the risk management process.

In assessing the interrelationship between risk control and financial elements there is, however, a most significant aspect that needs contemplating. Risk is identified, measured and handled on the implicit assumption that decisions relating thereto will affect both investment decisions (commitment of resources to productive use) and financing decisions (those concerning the funding of such investments).

Often, the reflection of the investment decision is ignored; with emphasis usually being placed on the insurance purchase alone, being a source of finance, without due attention being paid to whether such financing is indeed necessary at all[7] or necessary and prudent to support post-loss reinvestment.[8]

---

4 See Chapter Four, section 4.3.2.1, in which the point was made that often undue emphasis is placed on short-term cost to benefit relationships where there exists the danger of producing correct short-term answers that may yield disasters in the long run.

5 It is emphasised that insurance transfers risk cost, not risk. (Vivian, 1990).

6 Naturally, it is not contemplated that the ideal situation is where corporations achieve zero or close to zero insurance or third party finance. Pre-loss financial provision for catastrophe contingencies through insurance must be more efficient by virtue of the diversification and pooling achieved by the insurance sector.

7 If the concern is owned by diversified shareholders, it can be argued that the specific risk dealt with by the pooling effect of insurance has already been dealt with by the holding of a diversified portfolio. In this case the purchase of insurance merits closer investigation. (De Villiers & Vivian, 1991).

8 This consideration is most important. It is interesting that most insurance writers in the field ignore the investment consideration, which when included in the overall risk management process facilitates a more encompassing model for risk management *vis-à-vis* the operations of the business organisation as a whole. See Doherty (1985, 28-34). The risk management model developed in section 10.4.3 purports to incorporate the investment consideration.

The relevance of this distinction between investment and financing decisions becomes clearer once the corporate objective is defined to be maximising the wealth of shareholders in the long run, that is, the value derived from the firm's projected earnings stream.

The above factors lead to the conclusion that in pursuing the practical risk management objective of minimising the cost of risk, the following qualifications are necessary:

- a longer term view should be adopted when cost-to-benefit trade-offs relating to levels of risk control expenditure are considered
- risk control should be undertaken within the limits dictated by broad corporate financial objectives and constraints
- the risk financing decision-making should be taken with due reference to the investment decision.

It may be appropriate to simplify the model so as to illustrate the integrative path in the risk management process. If 'cost-of-risk' is defined as comprising three basic elements:[9]

(i) expenditure on risk control

(ii) expenditure relating to retained risk/self-funding (deliberate and non-deliberate)

(iii) expenditure on insurance cover

then, simplistically, one objective of risk management can be stated to be the long-run minimisation of the cost-of-risk to an organisation.

It is pertinent to describe the cost-of-risk in such a manner for it emphasises that effective risk management is based firstly on managing the physical risk situation through risk control and then directing attention to the most efficient method of financing. Given that the 'boundaries' that separate the three elements are not absolute or well defined, the challenge faced, is to combine or integrate these to achieve a long-run cost efficiency.

9 It should be noted, however, that by simply defining the cost of risk as the sum of three constituent elements, the associated costs should not be ignored. For example, in considering expenditure relating to self-funding and insurance, any administrative or procurement costs etc must be accounted for. There has also been considerable debate amongst risk management practitioners around the question of risk cost apportionment, particularly with regard to expenditure on risk control measures. The question is often asked as to whether all such expenditure should be regarded as risk costs as opposed to some element being regarded as operational expenditure. The problem is in fact of an accounting nature. Any expenditure deliberately intended to reduce frequency or severity of loss should be included in the 'cost-of-risk' equation.

Diagrammatically, the cost-of-risk can be shown as follows:

Figure 10.2
The cost-of-risk[10]

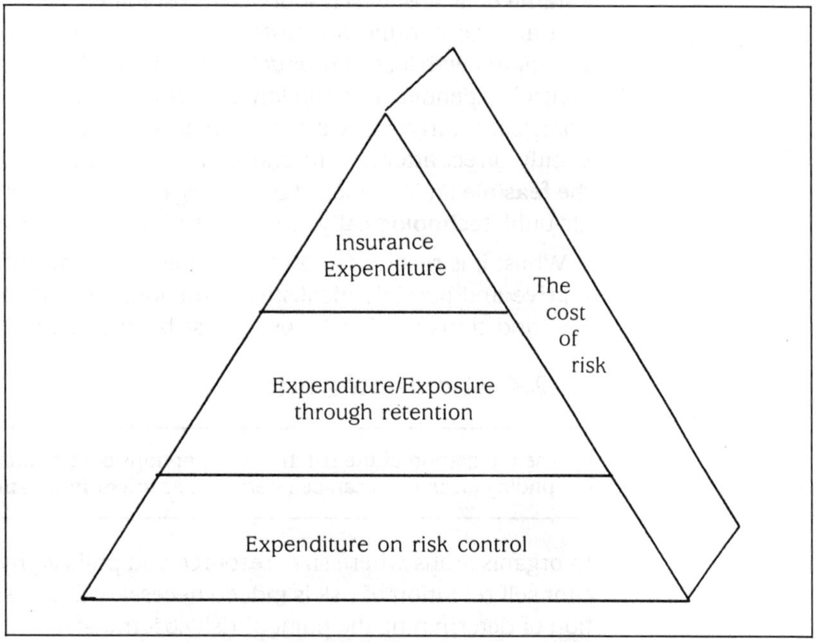

10.2.3 Macro-integration

The model also proposes a 'macro' and 'micro' integration process.

> **Macro-integration** refers to the optimisation of expenditure on risk control within the context of **long-run** benefit from the removal or reduction of risk.

In such context, optimising becomes somewhat of a misnomer: in the short term it may be possible to balance/optimise expenditure against benefit as measured against, say, a discount in premium, but longer term considerations, as mentioned earlier, introduce added difficulties.

---

10 Depicting the cost-of-risk elements within a triangular shape is of course arbitrary. The intention however is to illustrate that the foundation on which the minimisation of the cost of risk rests, is a deliberate policy of risk control. The apex of the triangle, where the purchase of insurance is housed, intends to signify the catastrophe element in risk situations – whilst the 'middle' part of the triangle refers to the element of risk where losses are reasonably predicted, and where self retention/self-financing is a more appropriate financing technique.

With regard to other incidental costs, such as costs of administration, agency fees, etc. and the debate around the apportionment of risk control costs, the reader is also referred to the previous footnote.

Recognising the very cyclical nature of the insurance market (one parameter against which short term cost-to-benefit analyses are conducted) and also accounting for costs other than risk financing, such as costs associated with loss of productivity and morale, it can be argued that risk control expenditure in the longer term is optimised once 'feasible technological saturation' has been achieved. That is to say, one should constantly direct attention to and make expenditure on risk control within the **feasible** limits imposed by the organisation's operations, shareholders etc until, **technologically**, the effects of risk can be **minimised no further**.

Whilst it is recognised that such policy may be criticised as being **normative** and possibly idealistic, in the long term its effects on self retention and transfer of risk costs must be seen as beneficial.

10.2.4 Micro-integration

> The integration of the risk financing options of self-funding and third party funding (insurance) can be referred to as **micro-integration** or optimisation.

In organisations where size, resource and philosophy dictate that significant self retention of risk is indeed necessary and cost efficient, the question of determining the point of risk cost transfer to the insurance market preoccupies risk managers and risk consultants considerably in practice.

It is also not surprising that most academic thinking has centred around this problem.[11] When one considers the insurance market as a mechanism or market that reallocates financial resource (supply and demand) with all its associated notions, such as, for example, capacity and transfer costs, the question of 'optimal mix' becomes an interesting economic conundrum.[12]

The intention thus far has been to link the elements of the risk management model. Reference to macro- and micro-integration aims at illustrating the earlier point that a holistic approach to risk management means integration across (risk control and financial) and integration within (insurance and self-funding).

10.3 Risk financing mechanisms

The concern, now, is with issues relative to financing risk. It is important to qualify that when consideration is given to risk financing mechanisms

11 See Chapter Fourteen, section 14.4, which discusses and makes reference to insurance purchasing optimisation models developed. A survey of academic writings indicates that risk control has received scant attention.

12 A comprehensive discussion of composite financing strategies can be found in Doherty (1985, 327-361).

it is not misconstrued that these refer only to insurance or self-funding. One may categorise finance mechanisms broadly into two strategies:

(i) **pre-loss financing** (through insurance, retention funding, and hence some form of composite funding or 'mix')

(ii) **post-loss financing** (through, for example, cash resources, debt, equity finance).

Whilst reference is made to two broad strategies, it should be noted, in practice, depending on the class of risk being financed, a **hybrid of pre- and post-loss financing** is used. The burning-cost insurance and retro-rating plans is an example of a structured hybrid where a deposit insurance premium is payable, the balance being calculated in accordance with a formula dependent on the loss experience.[4] Spreadloss insurance also represents this form of financing. Here, the loss is financed by the insurer, and the pay-back (in the form of additional premium) burden spread over a period of time.

It is true to state that in the context of risk management however, consideration is mostly given to pre-loss financing and particularly to insurance. Although there is often a logical case for adopting a post-loss financing strategy, particularly when it can be shown to be more suited to satisfying corporate objectives (shareholders' wealth maximisation), practical considerations which may have no cost foundation render pre-loss financing (principally through insurance) the most chosen alternative in practice.[5]

In the chapters which follow, attention is focused on issues related to pre-loss financing. Overall, what requires investigation is insurance, self-insurance and composite funding, which incorporates the question of self-funding/insurance integration.

10.4 Risk management within a financial decision structure

10.4.1 Corporate objective of maximising shareholders' wealth

In adapting the basic risk management model to take account of risk financing it is necessary to consider the setting within which risk financing and risk management as a whole, should be placed. This setting entails the understanding and agreement of corporate objectives or criteria to be satisfied when risk management decisions are taken.

Not only is this necessary for the purpose of adding direction, it also represents a point of criticism of the conventional thinking on the subject of risk management, which traditionally has been made from an insurance point of view rather than from that of the wider base of financial management.[13]

The development of financial management has prompted a very definite corporate objective. The firm is assumed to be a profit-seeking organisation owned by the holders of its equity. Owners' welfare is furthermore assumed to be measured by the value of ownership claims, thus making the appropriate corporate objective the maximisation of the total value of the firm.[14]

The use of value maximisation as the corporate objective is consistent with the agency-type relationship that exists between the shareholders and managers of the firm. Paid managers therefore have to satisfy the aspirations of shareholders, but may indeed have other personal objectives that exert forces in other directions.

This aspect is an important one when viewed in the practical context. When one considers invested human capital or the 'employment risk' faced by such managers (a risk which is not easily diversified away) managers do understandably adopt a more risk-averse attitude when taking corporate decisions.[15] This factor adds a further dimension to the

---

13 The practical application of risk management entails the integration of various subject disciplines. Some may argue that risk management should fall within the discipline of financial management, whilst others who adopt a more behavioural view stress the 'management' rôle in risk management. An alternative view is that risk management is technological in nature, losses being the side-products of the technological processes carried out by the firm. The view taken in this text is that regardless of orientation, projects are appraised against corporate objectives; financial management simply offers a decision framework with a perspective that does not compete with alternative subject areas in its claims on risk management. Rather, it should be perceived as complementary.
Most risk management thinking and writing has emerged from an insurance background, where respectfully little attention has been directed toward the motivating objective of risk management activity to maximise share value. However, this thinking is emerging in recent literature. See Doherty (1985) and Olson & Simkiss (1982).

14 It may be opportune to qualify that the value maximisation objective implies a risk adjusted longer term view. This is necessary in order to reconcile the value maximisation objective with micro-economic behaviour of the firm, where typically the firm is assumed to be a wealth maximiser. At first there may appear to be a conflict of objectives between the theory of the firm and financial management. The former seeks to maximise profit, and the latter, to maximise equity value. However, if one considers that, for the most part, micro-economic analysis has been static that is, concerned with maximising profit over a **single period**, and generally free of considerations of risk, then (Doherty, 1985, 17):

> it may be concluded that **value maximisation** is a multiperiod, risk-adjusted analogue of singleperiod profit maximisation.

Thus, the economic concept of profit maximisation is broadly compatible with shareholders' wealth maximisation.

15 Surveys indicate that risk managers adapt more risk-averse postures in making corporate decisions. (See Chapter Four, section 4.4.2.4).

reasons why insurance is purchased, and could also explain the more conventional orientation toward insurance as a financing technique.

Nevertheless, the shareholders' wealth maximisation objective does provide a measure of performance. The share price of the firm represents the capital market's assessment of its expected future earnings, given available information. Thus, the wealth maximisation objective implies that decisions are taken which will seek to maximise the size of the firm's future earnings stream or its corollary: to minimise its level of pure or specific risk.

Rationalising along these lines, and on the assumption that risk management is to be encompassed within a financial management decision structure, then the same objective can be adopted for risk management.

10.4.2 Financing and investment considerations

Defining the risk management objective thus, introduces the differentiation of the **financing decision** from the **investment decision**. Decisions concerning the **sources** of funds (insurance, self-insurance funds, etc) are referred to as financing decisions, whilst decisions involving the **use** of funds are referred to as investment decisions.

As with investment appraisal, well-developed criteria exist for comparing competing sources of finance (an evaluation that risk managers should logically effect in accordance with the finance decision introduced).[16] Recalling that the principal objective is to maximise the firm's share value, the source of finance should be that which leads to the lowest cost of capital.[17]

Consequently, this criterion introduces to the risk manager added sources of finance other than insurance or deliberately retained funds to

---

16 The criteria for making investment decisions refer to the class of techniques known as discounted cash flow (*DCF*). *DCF* criteria are not specific to any class of investment decisions and may be said to have equal validity for risk management decisions. Under *DCF*, the cash flows (both positive and negative) resulting from a project are capitalised at an appropriate discount rate. If the capitalised value is positive, acceptance of the project will increase the value of the firm. The project should not be accepted if the capitalised value is negative, since this decreases the value of the ownership claims. It can be accepted that EMV of the insurance purchase decision must be negative.

Application of *DCF* requires that costs and revenues are quantified. This is not an easy task, since in most instances perfect information is not available. It becomes even more difficult with risk management decisions because these are probabilistic in nature. Nevertheless, the point should be made that such difficulties are not unique to risk management.

17 Naturally, the cost of capital calculation must take into account any risk effects and spillover effects on the costs of other funds, as may be evident. Hence, debt financing may be nominally cheaper than insurance for example, but debt may introduce added **financial leverage risk** that in turn increases required rates of return to shareholders and therefore the cost of equity.

finance the self-insured exposures. The use of fund sources such as for example, new issues of debt or equity, term loans or lines of credit can be termed post-loss financing, since the funding arrangement is set in place *ex post*.

Conversely, the purchase of insurance, or the establishment of an internal reserve fund from which potential future losses can be met, is termed *pre-loss financing*.

Interestingly, apart from 'undeliberate' post-loss funding resulting really from 'undeliberate' self retention of risk, most risk management financing strategies are pre-loss in nature.[18] It is doubtful, in fact, whether in practice meaningful deliberation as to the optimal source of finance is made. It is suggested that this is partly due to the non-integration of the risk management objective with that of the firm – and partly, because of inherent objectives and security considerations evident in risk managers (a point that was made earlier).

Turning now to the investment decision, as it pertains to risk management, consideration should be given to three scenarios.

The first concerns investment in the replacement of destroyed assets. To illustrate this, a concern working at surplus capacity would view the reinvestment decision in different light to a concern which, for example, was working at full capacity. The latter firm would be more adversely affected by a loss of output (hence revenue and profits) if a resource were destroyed.

Parallel to the finance decision, the reinvestment decision is often ignored. As Mehr & Hedges[7] point out, the omission may be explained[19] under the assumption of survival and continuity of operations being corporate objectives.

Nevertheless,

> even when continuity is not assumed explicitly, a high emphasis on insurance to finance losses has a similar effect . . . the goals of survival and continuity are not necessarily compatible with **value** maximisation, and the decision to reinvest is not necessarily a rational economic one.[8]

Yet, the decision to invest is not inconsequential if the firm is to pursue a strategy based on value maximisation.

---

18 Self retention of risk is often as a result of risks not formally identified or evaluated. Under these conditions, firms accept the risks for own account, perhaps non-deliberately. In the event of losses arising from such risk sources, finance is sought and hence the term '*undeliberate*' post-loss financing.

19 Another explanation could be the principle of indemnity. The very intention of insurance is to restore the asset to its pre-loss value. The investment decision is made almost by default as part of the decision to purchase insurance.

The second scenario concerning investment decisions involves the evaluation of risk control expenditure. It can be argued that such risk reduction investments have identifiable cash flows and that therefore the investment decision can be assessed along the same lines as one would any investment project or proposal.

With risk control investment, the pay-off takes the form of a reduction in the cost of contingent losses; if the capitalised values exceed the capitalised costs, the expenditure is warranted.

Here it is necessary to make certain important qualifications, however. Firstly, an investment decision assessed under the wealth maximisation criterion assumes implicitly that a long term horizon is being contemplated. Thus, with such time horizon, for the assessment to be of value, all benefits and costs, including indirect costs (and savings) arising from such factors as, for example, employee consciousness of work hazards and worker morale need to be accounted for. This in itself becomes a difficult task.

Secondly, if this type of valuation criterion is accepted, the investment should also, logically, be evaluated in the light of other competing[20] and most often, mutually exclusive investments. This is particularly relevant with risk control investment proposals, where the capital outlay is quite significant and hence comparable with alternative possible investments.

Often, this evaluation renders risk control investment sub-optimal. Yet, in the long-run such investments could safeguard the firm from disaster. Hence, the statement made earlier in this chapter that firms should ordinarily achieve an 'operating efficiency' level through investment in risk control; such level to be within feasible bounds dictated by overall organisational and financial constraints.

A third investment consideration refers to decisions regarding contingent liabilities. Liability losses do not relate to the destruction of assets of the firm, but rather, damage is suffered by third parties. The firm however, acquires an obligation to pay compensation.

Nevertheless, such contingent liabilities summon investment decisions similar to those involving destruction to corporate resources. Investments may be made with the purpose of reducing expected accountability and burden of such losses. The benefit of such investments lies in the reduction of financing costs of the liability payments.[21]

---

20 In some instances, as when legislative reasoning is applied, the investment may be compulsory.

21 If, for example, liability insurance is in place, the benefit may take the form of reduced premiums, given a sensitivity of premiums to expected loss value.

The more difficult problem is whether a liability loss questions the continuation of the firm's operations. In this regard it is not dissimilar to the reinvestment decision that arises following the loss or destruction of the firm's resources.

Although a liability claim does not directly affect the ability to generate future earnings, it can affect the firm's ability (and indeed willingness) to continue with its operations or part of its operations.[22] Dependent upon the source of finance, the value of ownership claims may reduce substantially; should retained earnings be used for example, the value for shareholders would reduce by the quantum of the liability claim.

There are however also indirect costs. For example, product defect and community resistance may cause the demand for the firm's product to subside; employee consciousness of work hazards and morale may cause production costs to increase. Such effects may prompt the firm to cease operations after a loss, although production was profitable before the event.[23]

10.4.3 The risk management model within a financial management decision structure

Risk financing has been evaluated in the light of corporate objectives. The discussion advanced considerations of investment and finance decision-making. The primary reason was to obviate the danger of distancing risk management, or risk financing, into a position of isolation from the general finance and investment disciplines.

It is opportune to summarise the caveats drawn from this evaluation, since discussions in the ensuing chapters must be seen in relation to such evaluation and subject (where applicable) to these caveats. Moreover, these caveats form the basis for adapting the basic risk management model to the one depicted in figure 10.3:[24]

---

22 A number of American firms have withdrawn perfectly safe products from the market as a result of ever-increasing, but unsuccessful liability claims.

23 This argument comes significantly into focus when viewed against the backdrop of Chapter Nine, which discusses the liability crisis. Even though liability claims may be financed by third party funding through insurance, which arguably may have a cost of capital lower than, for example, retained earnings, insurers' results have forced such increases in premiums, that continuation of operations is still nevertheless being jeopardised. The questioning by firms of continuation of operations, along the same lines as with the destruction of physical resources, may indeed be the catalyst needed to effect appropriate change in the legal system and in the litigious nature of some societies.

24 These caveats follow closely the critique by Doherty (1985, 35-38) of the so-called *Traditional Risk Management Structure*. The model is a slight adaptation of that proposed by Doherty (1985, 32).

- ☐ Any risk management structure should not support an inappropriate measure of the costs of loss events. The cost should not be assumed to be replacement value necessarily, but considered against the impact of any loss of earnings stream.
- ☐ The productivity of resources employed by the firm is central to the reinvestment decision. Emphasis on corporate risk aversion and supposed desire for continuity of production should be evaluated in this light.
- ☐ The distinction exists between those decisions that involve investment and those that involve the funding of such investments, that is financing decisions. Insurance is a source of finance and failure to identify the nature of financing and investment decisions leads to alternative sources of finance not being considered.
- ☐ The approach to the handling of risk should be an integrative one. Considerations relative to risk control and its management, bears on risk financing. Furthermore, risk should not be considered simply as 'additive'; possibilities for diversification exist, risks being spread over various risk management exposure units, for example, and even by the firm's shareholders through portfolio investment diversification.[25]

Given the caveats drawn from the evaluation of risk management against the corporate objective of value maximisation, figure 10.3 represents the final adaptation to the risk management model as first depicted in figure 10.1. The differentiation between investment and financing decisions further clarifies the process of integration:

- ☐ on the **macro-level**, investment in risk control activities is considered with due reference to the (long-term) financial investment decision – that is, whether post-loss reinvestment or abandonment should take place
- ☐ should investment in risk control be decided upon, the model then directs attention to the financing decision (post-loss reinvestment option) and to the question of **micro-integration** of the pre-loss financing means of insurance and self funding.

25 The caveats imply the existence of non-efficiency should the suggested decision structure not be adopted. To the extent that these inefficiencies exist, then, theoretically, such **opportunity costs** should be incorporated into the total cost of risk equation. The lack of discussion of opportunity costs in risk management texts and articles on 'cost of risk' is suggestive of the non-finance orientation of traditional risk management.

Figure 10.3 Risk management model within a financial management decision structure

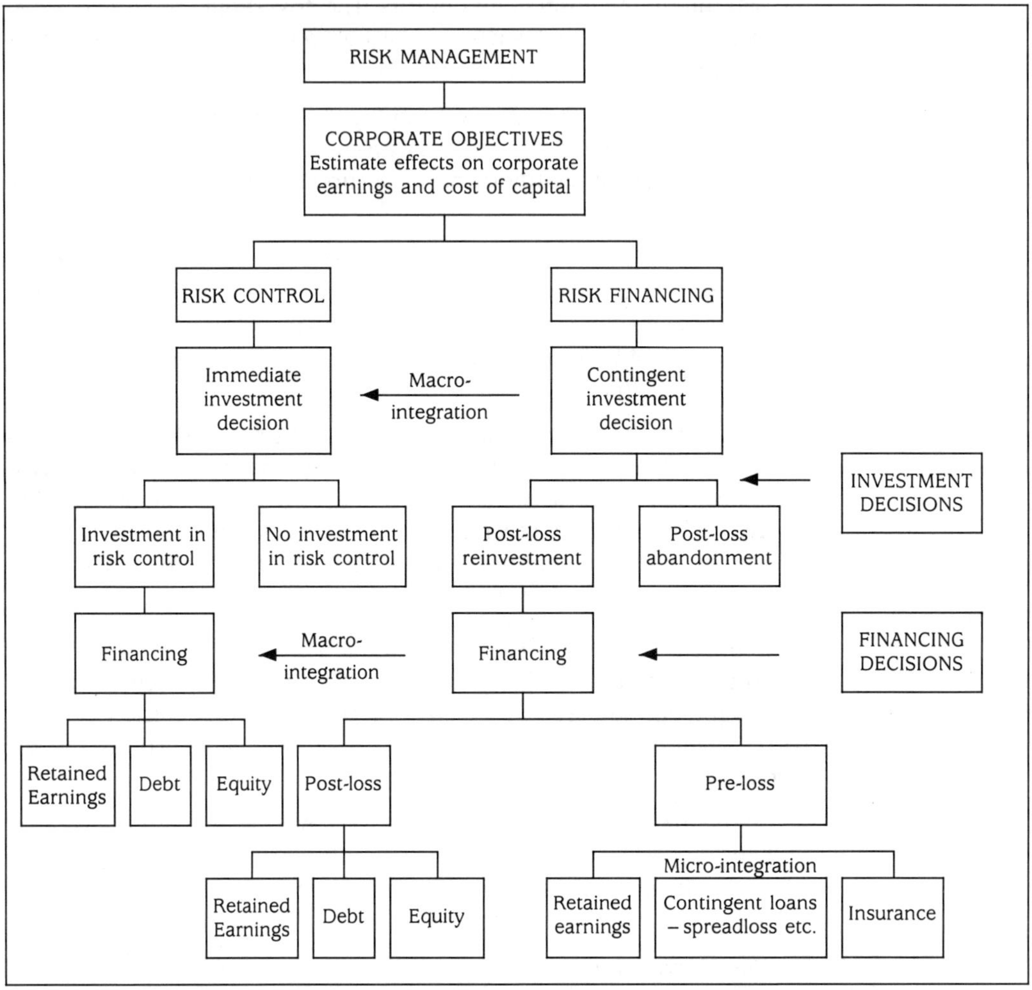

Source: *Adapted from Doherty* (1985, 32).

10.5 Conclusion

This chapter dealt with the element of risk financing in the risk management process. The major objectives were to describe the inter-relationship between the physical and the financial elements of risk management and to investigate the underlying rationale (financial) for risk management – with the view to modifying the risk management model by placing it within a financial framework of decision-making.

By introducing the concept of 'cost-of-risk', attention was focused on the aspects of integration and optimisation. It was held that these could be approached from a macro- and micro-basis. Relevant conclusions reached, with regard to cost-of-risk optimisation were that:

- ☐ a longer term view is necessary when determining levels of loss control expenditure
- ☐ risk control should be undertaken within the broader corporate financial objectives and constraints
- ☐ decisions should be taken with due reference to investment considerations.

The broad categorisation of risk financing mechanisms into pre-loss and post-loss financing, was discussed. It was concluded that in a practical context, micro-integration entails the optimum use and mix of pre-loss financing sources/strategies, namely, insurance and self-insurance.

The placement of risk management within a financial decision structure necessitated the adoption of the corporate objective of maximising shareholders' wealth. An important differentiation was drawn between the financing and investment decision. These discussions lead to a summary of risk management caveats which formed the basis for adapting the risk management model to one which now reflects risk financing considerations.

Bibliography

Cost-of-Risk Survey. 1981. Connecticut: Risk Planning Group Inc.

De Villiers, JU & Vivian, RW 1991. 'The need for insurance by large corporations: An economic analysis of some observations made by the Melamet Commission.' *BERG*. University of the Witwatersrand.

Duncan, CA 1990. 'Using cost-of-risk to measure performance.' *Risk Management*. February.

Doherty, NA 1985. *Corporate risk management – A financial exposition*. New York: McGraw-Hill Inc.

Elliott, JW 1972. 'Control, size, growth and financial performance in the firm.' *Journal of Financial and Quantitative Analysis*. Vol. 7.

Greene, M & Serbein, O 1983. *Risk management: Text and cases*. Virginia: Reston Publishing Co. Inc.

Mehr, RI & Hedges, B 1974. *Risk management: Concepts and applications*. Homewood, Illinois: Richard D. Irwin Inc.

Murphy M 1984. 'Can you construct a truly effective paid loss retro plan?' *Risk Management*. December.

Olson, DG & Simkiss, JA 1982. 'An overview of risk management.' *The Geneva Papers on Risk and Insurance*. Vol. 23.

Williams, CA & Heins, RM 1981. *Risk management and insurance*. New York: McGraw-Hill Inc.

Endnotes

[1] Duncan, 1990, 28-33.

[2] Williams & Heins, 1981, 16.

[3] Greene & Serbein, 1983, 3.

[4] Murphy, 1984, 24-34.

[5] Doherty, 1985, 272.

[6] Elliott, 1972, 1309-1320.

[7] Mehr & Hedges, 1974, 2.

[8] Doherty, 1985, 28-29.

11 RISK RETENTION

11.1 Introduction

Apart from insurance as a pre-loss means of financing risk, the risk management model as depicted in figure 10.1 also makes reference to retention funding. The object of this chapter is to discuss and evaluate this pre-loss means of financing. To do this, it is necessary first to examine what is meant by risk retention.[1] The mechanism of retention funding is then appraised using the customary *value of the firm* criterion.

Practical vehicles for retention range from a retention fund [at the one end of the continuum] as an accounting provision or reserve in the books of a firm, to captives [as the continuum moves towards external financing] which may be defined as capitalised insurance companies that underwrite the risks of a parent organisation (refer to Chapter Twelve for a detailed discussion). Along this continuum, there have also developed insurance programmes, such as structured insurance programmes and *cell-captives/rent-a-captive*, which represent facilities offered by established insurance companies.

11.2 Unfunded risk retention

> Unfunded, or non-deliberate risk retention is defined as the failure to take any positive or deliberate action to provide for the financial consequences of a risk.[1]

Such retention takes place when a risk-cost is ignored, or even when the risk situation is identified, evaluated but the decision is taken not to provide for it.

Based on this definition and bearing in mind the number of risks faced by business organisations, non-deliberate risk retention can be seen to be the most common risk financing method adopted. Naturally, economic or speculative risk is included in the array of risks facing the organisation. If one accepts the descriptive parameters of *end* and *intermediate* economic risk proposed in Chapter Thirteen, then, obviously the provision for *end* economic risk would serve no purpose. If such risk could be provided for, there would exist no justification for profit as the latter presupposes the assumption of risk by the risk bearer.

1 It is more correct to refer to risk-cost retention. The question is not whether the risk per se is retained or transferred. The reader is also referred to section 11.3, footnote in paragraph 5. Most of the literature in insurance makes reference to risk retention. This text will follow the convention but subject to the qualification made.

Commonly, the kinds of risks *assumed* by business firms can be divided into two broad categories:

(i) risk exposures which are insurable, but left uninsured

(ii) risk exposures which are uninsurable.

Generally, the first category includes exposures characterised by high frequency/low severity losses. The second category would include speculative risks.

There are numerous reasons why unfunded risk retention is practised. Often the cost of treating a risk in a positive manner, say through insurance, may far exceed the benefit to the insured. In such cases, although insurance coverage is available, the cost-to-benefit relationship prompts the risk bearer to effectively ignore the risk exposure, as is the case, say with the earthquake-risk where a firm might take no positive action as regards provision internally, nor purchase external insurance.

Another reason for non-deliberate retention is that some risks are simply not responsive to any other treatment. The risk of loss of property from war on land, being fundamental by nature, is not, for example, insurable, and would not ordinarily call for any deliberate financial provision by the organisation.

On many occasions however, risks are not funded through lack of knowledge, carelessness, or poor judgement. Since there does not exist a ready source of information regarding the kinds of risks that are uninsurable, organisations should investigate risks that are not covered or excluded from insurance contracts, and compile a list of their uninsured/uninsurable risk exposures.

11.3 Funded risk retention (FRR)

A firm may find that a particular type of risk that it faces meets with such requirements, as for instance, that the exposure units are independent and homogeneous and displaying a well defined loss distribution over time. In such situations aggregate losses can be fairly accurately predicted and can be deliberately provided for, under a retention plan. This, then, represents another form of pre-loss financing, that is, the establishment of an internal fund into which contributions are made periodically and from which withdrawals can be made following loss.

In risk management terminology it is usual to define losses as retained if they are not insured. Deliberate retention is sometimes referred to as self-insurance;[2] it is preferable to equate deliberate retention to funded

2 In this text the term *self-insurance* is not favoured: insurance is a contract between two parties and thus it is not possible for one person to contract with himself and provide himself with insurance.

risk retention (FRR). Consequently, under this definition FRR is considered to be any plan of risk retention in which a programme or procedure has been set up to meet the adverse results of a financial loss.

The use of the term *self-insurance* gives rise to a number of controversial issues in the field of risk management. It is argued that the definition of insurance determines the definition of self-insurance, but, whereas insurance has been defined by some in terms of the technique of pooling,[2] others[3] define insurance in terms of 'transfer', and still others[4] require both pooling and 'transfer'. Thus, for those who define insurance in terms of pooling, the term self-insurance is an accurate description of deliberate pre-loss retention funding. Those who contend that 'transfer' is a prerequisite for insurance, hold that the term *self-insurance* is a misnomer.

These arguments confuse the concept of insurance and the mechanism of insurance. In concept, insurance is an enforceable contract. Pooling is the mechanism which explains how and why insurance can succeed in replacing uncertainty with certainty.

The association of funding and self-insurance might also lead to the illusion that the process of funding of retained losses operates similarly to insurance with regard to the 'reduction' or 'elimination' of risk.[3] As Doherty[5] points out, this misconception arises from the observation that any contingent loss will be offset exactly by a payment from the fund, leaving the firm immune from risk.

However, on a postloss basis, insurance has the effect of maintaining value to the firm; with retention funding the firm will lose value following payment from the fund, since the fund is regarded as an asset of the firm. The negative cash flow caused by the loss is simply afforded a different accounting label.

The practice of retention funding should not be regarded as self-insurance, notwithstanding that the properties of pooling may be indeed evident – and particularly where the retention fund is considered an asset in the books of account of a firm.

Cognisance should however be taken of the development of insurance programmes or facilities offered by commercial insurers where there is 'transfer' and risk assumption to a limited degree by the insurer, who facilitates the financing of risks retained by the firm.[4]

---

3 In actuality there can be no real reduction or elimination of risk through the medium of insurance. Reference can be made to discussions concerning this issue in Chapter Thirteen. Insurance does not reduce or eliminate risk, there is no risk transfer to the insurer *per se*, but rather the obligation to pay for the financial consequences arising from losses incurred.

4 These facilities are briefly discussed in section 11.7.2 which examines retention and insurers.

These insurance programmes, as will be seen later, are quasi retention funds and do entail a payment of premium to a commercial insurer. Whilst it may be argued that the premium is somewhat transparent, the firm does not regard the fund or any residual value that accrues to the firm, as an asset.

It is difficult to estimate the extent of retention funding as there is little current available information. Although the results of a survey conducted by Goshay[6] revealed that the majority of firms did not fund retained risks, with the passage of time and the changes in risk management policy it is doubtful that the results would hold true today.[7] It is an accepted fact that retention levels by firms have generally increased, (following the more focused and scientific approach to risk management adopted by firms generally) and that these might require more attention to be directed toward loss financing. In addition, the growth in the captive insurance industry has been significant since Goshay conducted his analysis.[5]

Interestingly, there appears to be no clear agreement in the literature as to the purpose of funding, and in general, funding is associated with financial stability and planning. The motivation for retention funding can be seen to be similar to that applying to unfunded retention.

Basically, the incentive for retention funding and self-insurance arises from two sources.[6] First, it may not be possible to fully 'transfer' the risk through insurance or any other device. The situation arises frequently because there is no market available to take the risk. The second is that it may be less expensive than conventional 'risk transfer' techniques. This reasoning applies particularly to what has been termed *high frequency/low severity* risks where conventional 'transfer' devices, such as insurance, can prove to be relatively expensive given the cost structures of commercial insurance companies. In these circumstances, retention funding

---

5 Although captive insurance companies will be discussed separately (see Chapter Twelve), the issues of retention funding debated in this section, do also apply to captives.

6 Although reference is made to two basic incentives, there are of course other incentives to retain risk. It may be worthwhile to mention that on occasion, especially with national strategic industries, there might be a reluctance to divulge to an insurer the information necessary to allow underwriting and premium setting. Also, one finds that government and quasi-government organisations have little incentive to finance losses other than through retention funding. If the motivation for such approach is based on sound risk financing cost criteria, such as for example lower costs associated with self-funded frequency losses, then the approach has obvious merit. However, if the motivation is based purely on the fact that substantial liquidity is available or accessible to finance losses as they occur, then some inefficiency could be evidenced. An evaluation of the insurance technique (particularly for catastrophe exposures) should therefore be conducted even by large organisations that have the availability of substantial reserves or an accessibility to such.

permits substantial savings in insurance premium, with a good opportunity to reduce loss costs.[7]

11.4 Considerations in developing a retention programme

11.4.1 Practical steps in developing a retention programme

Given the various incentives for risk retention, several practical steps are usually specified for developing any retention programme. These considerations revolve principally around the following:

- ☐ determining the opportunity and feasibility of funding
- ☐ analysing the statistical properties of the risk exposure one proposes to retain
- ☐ evaluating the retention strategy.

The discussion of these considerations at this point is intentional. As mentioned in the introduction to this chapter, retention as a pre-loss financing mechanism will be appraised based on the effect that funding may have on the value of the firm. It becomes opportune to list the various considerations (*ex ante*) and to review these once the conclusions of the 'value added' analysis have been drawn.

11.4.2 Determining opportunity and feasibility of funding

The first step in developing a retention programme is to determine the risk financing techniques available to the risk bearer. Although in the wider sense, this would entail an analysis of post-loss financing techniques as well, generally what is implied is that the risk should be evaluated from an insurance availability standpoint. The risks with which the firm is faced should therefore be classified in terms of the categories mentioned earlier, namely insurable or uninsurable risk. This will naturally elucidate the feasibility and opportunity of retention funding *vis-à-vis* financing through insurance, and will facilitate any evaluation of the retention strategy.

7 Although there can be a saving in loss costs, the exposure to the firm is greater – so that in the event of a bad loss experience, the firm may indeed witness a higher cost than would have applied under conventional insurance. It is customary therefore to combine a retention programme with insurance, whereby cover is purchased to cater for the catastrophe risks and to insure against some aggregate level of the fund being surpassed. In insurance parlance such cover would be termed *excess loss* and *aggregate stop-loss* protection, respectively.

When embarking on a course of deliberate risk retention, the firm accepts, for own account, the responsibility for the financial consequences of (pure) risk. As a second step in the process therefore, an evaluation of the firm's risk retention capacity is essential. The risk retention capacity, or the limit of loss bearing capacity of the firm should be gauged by the degree to which the firm's cash flow can be diverted from its usual uses to meet losses without significantly disrupting normal operations.[8]

11.4.3 Analysing the statistical properties of the risk exposure retained

The characteristics of risk retention are not dissimilar to those of insurance, so that many of the risk management choices facing the firm are analogous to choices facing an insurer. Among these is the issue concerning the extent of funding for the firm, or the size of reserves for an insurer. This entails as a the third step in the process, an analysis of historical loss patterns and the estimation of possible future loss costs. The statistical analysis revolves around loss distributions established with reference to both frequency and severity of losses with the objective of predicting the likely future costs of losses.

As a general rule, risks that display high loss frequency with a potential for relatively low severity permit predictability, and hence are amenable to retention.[9] For the risk manager it is of interest to also know how a retention fund will stand up in the face of claim demands and therefore, the probability that the fund will be insufficient to meet these demands needs to be addressed. This involves computation of, what has been described as, the *ruin probability* of the retention fund.[10] Similar to protecting insurance reserves, the objective of risk managers is to minimise the retention fund's probability of ruin.

---

8 In practice, one finds various risk retention capacity formulae in use. One view is that risk retention capacity should be measured largely in terms of creation and availability of liquid reserve funds – maintaining that prudent policy requires assets to be immediately available to meet loss costs. Others assign weights to financial ratios (liquidity, profitability and even leverage) and arrive at a weighted average computation which then determines the absolute risk retention capacity level (Gibson, 1983, 1-5).

9 The high degree of predictability also means that in effect the pooling advantage otherwise evident with insurance becomes 'redundant'. The relatively low risk allows the firm to retain and internally finance these losses without incurring the higher costs of administration of the insurer.

10 The ruin probability of a retention fund may be defined as the probability that the aggregate retained losses in a given period exceed the value of the fund in that period (Doherty, 1985, 306).

Collective risk theory, a branch of actuarial mathematics that analyses the ruin probabilities of insurance reserves (retention funds), is well developed and provides a sophisticated framework within which the analyses referred to, may be conducted. In Chapter Fourteen the statistical methodologies used presently in risk financing (forecasting models, and ruin probabilities) are discussed.

11.4.4 Evaluating the retention strategy *vis-à-vis* alternative financing techniques

The third step is to evaluate the risk retention strategy *vis-à-vis* the alternative risk financing techniques. Basically, this process begins at one extreme by comparing the total cost-of-risk under a retention strategy with conventional cover. The intention is to explore the risk-return trade-off between risk retained and risk 'transferred'.

The risk-return element in the total process, albeit a difficult one is possibly the most important consideration. The final decision based on whether the retained strategy is optimal for the firm needs to be taken. It must be recognised that notwithstanding a high degree of loss predictability, it is obvious that the retention fund will not cater for catastrophic losses. In this area of risk, the characteristics (severe but infrequent) are by nature more amenable to insurance where the large exposure base will ensure that the pooling will facilitate financing. Hence, a retention strategy does not, in the main, imply non-insurance, but rather selective insurance probably on the basis of excess of loss and stop loss protection. Encompassed in the objective of total risk cost minimisation therefore, lies the question of optimum integration of retention with insurance following a risk-return analysis.

Determining the optimal trade-off between insurance and retention faces certain difficulties. Firstly, the cost of retention can only be predicted; it can never be known in advance, and only the passage of time can determine the exact cost and hence possible benefit of retention. By then the decision regarding retention will already have been made.

Secondly, for many risks it may be difficult to determine insurance costs under varying assumptions of retention, and indeed more difficult to determine future insurance costs.

Nevertheless, it may be possible to analyse insurer costs broadly in order to estimate possible opportunities for savings. Given that retention is considered for those risks or sections of risk, where loss predictability is reasonably accurate, insurer **expenses** become a major factor and might be accurately assessed; under assumptions of required profit to insurers it is possible to construct 'what-if' scenarios and direct a risk-return trade-off analysis.[11]

Finally, the last consideration revolves around the choice of appropriate fund retention vehicle. Earlier, in section 11.1, it was indicated that

---

11 Considerably sophisticated models have been developed to assist in trade-off analysis. One such technique uses simulation theory to arrive at expected costs of self-insurance and expected values of pure premium likely to be charged by insurers, assuming varying levels of risk retention. Reference can be made to Chapter Fourteen, section 14.2.5.2, where this technique is discussed.

one could consider at one end the implementation of a simple internal retention fund, and, at the other, the setting up of a captive insurance company. Various factors exist which influence firms' decisions regarding the level of sophistication required of their retention programme – this aspect is reviewed under section 11.7.

11.5 Evaluation of retention funding using the value of the firm criterion

Funding is simply a means of providing finance (from operational cashflow) for loss events; in contrast to debt and equity financing, the opportunity costs for financing with retention funding are incurred before a loss rather than after a loss has occurred. Therefore, contributions to a retention fund are akin to the interest or dividend payments for post-loss financing, and more directly comparable with premium payments under the pre-loss means of financing through insurance. As with other forms of financing, the method of analysis is based on the effect funding may have on the value of a firm's existing equity. The criterion dictates that should funding have a more positive effect on value than do other forms of financing, it is to be preferred.

It is necessary however to clarify certain issues that are central to the understanding of the rôle of funding. Firstly, the interrelationship between the fund and other sources of post-loss financing is such that a reduction in the contribution to the fund implies a shifting of burden toward external financing (for example, debt) with an associated increase in the cost of such finance, and transaction costs. Conversely, an increase in any contribution to the fund would entail an opportunity cost in terms of any investment opportunity foregone due to the added contribution being directed towards specifically providing for contingent losses. The implication here is that there should be, ideally, a level of fund coverage that maximises value.

Secondly, there is the issue concerning transaction costs. Possibly this is the most significant aspect to be considered when evaluating the case for retention funding. Raising new external debt or equity gives rise to issue and underwriting costs, and may also be associated with time delays and hence interruption costs – these delay costs should be regarded as part of the transaction costs.

The effect that funding may have on the firm's cost of capital is the third issue to consider. Funding merely shifts the cost to another accounting label, and the firm is exposed to the same riskiness of the retained losses. Since the investor will discount the cash flows at the rate determined by the systematic component of the risk, the loss beta value is important in determining the cost of equity.

In evaluating retention funding the analysis as has been conducted by Doherty[8] [12] provides significant conclusions under the following assumptions:

- ☐ that the firm carries no debt and that alternative sources of finance command no transaction costs
- ☐ that alternative sources of finance do command transaction costs.

11.5.1 Evaluation of retention funding under the principle assumption of no transaction costs

Under the principle assumption of no transaction costs, the value of the firm can be depicted in equation form where the firm's value appears as the sum of:

- ☐ the commercial non-risk management activities of the firm
  and
- ☐ the value of the retention fund
  reduced by
- ☐ the value of the firm's loss exposure.

It is shown that the **case for establishing a fund** depends exclusively on the relationship between the risk-adjusted **return** on the fund assets and the risk-adjusted **cost** of the fund. Only in the event of the risk-adjusted return on the fund surpassing the risk-adjusted cost will there be value added to the firm.

The significant conclusion[9] is that

> the case for establishing a fund is entirely independent of the firm's loss exposure – hence, there is no **risk management case** for establishing a retention fund under the assumption (principally) of no transaction costs.[13]

---

12 For a detailed mathematical evaluation the reader is referred to Doherty (1985, 297-303). The conclusions provided under this section are taken from such analysis.

13 The firm may of course choose to hold financial assets in the form of a fund, but it will be rational to do so only on the basis of the investment return on those assets.

The spurious argument put forward for the establishment of a fund is that it represents an orderly method for financing the capital demands induced by a loss, and that therefore the firm is not exposed to any sudden financial demands. The argument, however, ignores the economic costs or opportunities facing the firm. Should the fund opportunities induce investment, the investment would ordinarily be made. The investment decision would be taken independently of any risk management motive. The fund itself does not protect a firm from the random incidence of loss. When such a loss occurs, the firm will lose value, the result being identical to that where the loss was 'unfunded'.

The position can also be seen in the following light. The establishment of a retention fund is no more than bringing forward the date on which financing is raised for the purpose of reinvestment following a loss. The case for bringing such date forward rests purely on whether the investment of the fund assets yield a return in excess of the cost of capital. Again, the firm's risk exposure and risk management motive has no bearing on the investment decision.

Revisiting, for a moment, the considerations for establishing a retention fund, outlined in the previous section, these findings give rise to the following modifications:

- ☐ The first step of determining the opportunity and feasibility of retention funding assumes a more significant profile. The investment of resources in fund assets transcends the mere comparison with insurance; the feasibility of funding is dependent on the funds expected return *vis-à-vis* the firm's hurdle rate, or cost of capital.
- ☐ The statistical analysis, shown as the second step retains its significance only in so far as it purports to provide an estimate of expected loss costs to be borne by the firm. Since the case for establishing a retention fund is not influenced by the value of losses, the statistical estimate will not be a factor in determining the value of the fund. Should the criteria dictate that investment in fund assets be favourable, it would be other factors that determine the fund's assets value.
- ☐ The process of evaluating the retention funding strategy remains, in concept, an important consideration. However, rather than evaluating the funding strategy, the process hinges upon evaluating **risk retention** as a risk management strategy, *vis-à-vis* alternative risk financing mechanisms (usually insurance).
- ☐ Finally, under the assumption of no transaction costs, the results show that retention funding has no risk management case for it. Hence, in a strict sense, it should not be 'formally' identified or defined as an alternative pre-loss vehicle or means of financing risk. The implication is that the firm, in adopting a risk retention strategy, should finance losses in the ordinary way and not create a vehicle designed to match expected loss costs.

11.5.2 Evaluation of retention funding under the assumption of transaction costs commanded by alternative sources of finance

As mentioned earlier, post-loss sources of finance may have associated costs, such as underwriting and issue fees, and/or cost of delays.

Introducing transaction costs to the question, the value of the firm emerges as the sum of:

- ☐ the value from commercial (non-risk management) operations
  and
- ☐ the value of the retention fund (value of establishing the fund and investing its assets net of the cost of raising capital to finance the fund)
  reduced by
- ☐ the loss exposure contribution
  and

☐ the contribution arising from the prospect of incurring transaction costs for unfunded losses.

It can be seen that with the likelihood of transaction costs, *the value of the fund is dependent upon the loss exposure – thus there is a* ***risk management case*** *for the establishment of a retention fund.*

11.6 The case for retention programmes

A case can be made for risk retention on risk management grounds if retention avoids the costs imposed by other forms of financing. Included in these costs is the delay factor in securing alternative forms of risk finance,[14] which aspect may become significant when one considers the effect of interruption loss. The establishment of a liquid fund specifically earmarked for reinvestment may facilitate recovery. In addition, the existence of a fund following a sizeable loss may obviate any market nervousness and hence unfavourable issue terms which might have prevailed had the firm required to raise new external finance.

Transaction costs arise when the loss exceeds the assets of a retention fund and the firm is forced to consider alternative sources of finance for the purpose of reinvestment. It follows that the larger the retention fund, the smaller the probability that an unfunded loss will occur and thus the smaller the probability of incurring a transaction cost. However, this benefit needs to be balanced against the opportunity costs of maintaining the fund. Probably, since these funds are subject to certain constraints in so far as their investment is concerned (for example they may demand a high liquidity condition) the return is less than the cost of capital. Consequently, a retention fund must be viewed in a similar light to the management of the firm's general liquidity, where an optimal level implies a trade-off between the cost of maintaining liquid resources and the benefit of avoiding cash embarrassment (or transaction costs in the case of pure risk retention funding).

Maintaining an optimal fund level introduces two further important qualifications. The first, concerns the fact that, generally, retention funds are regarded as being separately earmarked for the purpose of providing for losses. Indeed, this would facilitate recovery from losses, particularly if interruption losses are a feature. In a sense, the immediate availability of corporate liquidity implies a form of *de facto* risk management.

However, if retention funds are to be separately regarded from the firm's general funds, and if no transfers are permitted between the funds, then

14 Delays can occur when insurers rely on purely technical defences to claims such as lack of insurable interest or non-disclosure of material facts.

the funding requirement to maintain a given probability that either or both funds will be ruined, is generally higher than the requirement to maintain a composite fund at the same probability of ruin.[15] The contention now is that any demand for liquidity should be met jointly with other demands for corporate liquidity, and the risk manager should co-operate with the other managers, each recognising the composite nature of demands likely to be made on those liquid resources.

The second qualification concerning optimisation of the fund level involves the integration of the fund with the purchase of insurance. The dynamic nature of funding must be recognised:

- Fund level optimisation criteria dictate that the level should be reviewed (usually in tandem with the insurance covers which relate to a particular period), and not be merely allowed to accumulate asset balances that are more than required as estimated by any statistical methodology. The latter strategy would, probably, introduce inefficiencies from the point of view of opportunity cost of holding the fund.
- Earlier mention was made of the fact that the fund's objective is not to provide for catastrophic risks, and for this purpose selective insurance would ordinarily be purchased. Since the insurance market is itself dynamic in nature, the optimal fund level would also be influenced by the risk-return trade-off between retention and 'transfer'. Liquidity optimisation considerations must therefore not be isolated from those which concern the **integration** of retention and insurance. The composite nature of the fund *vis-à-vis* the other demands on liquid resources should be recognised, as should the composite nature of the fund *vis-à-vis* any insurance coverage.

11.7 Other practical considerations and retention programmes

11.7.1 Practical considerations with regard to retention funding

An evaluation of risk retention would be incomplete without a discussion of certain practical considerations which, as will be seen, do exert influence on the way funding is regarded in practice. In the main, these

15 Consider this statement in general. If two separate funds were established, with values X and Y which were then combined into one fund X + Y, the ruin probability cannot rise, since each opportunity that was available before the funds were combined, still exists. The combining of the funds in fact achieves a 'pooling effect' – the combination of funds has only given additional opportunities for inter-transfers. Hence, the probabilities must either remain the same, or fall.

considerations revolve around the issue of taxation and the personal objectives of risk managers.[16]

Amounts raised to establish a provision in the books of account of the firm for the financial consequences of pure risk are generally not deductible for company tax purposes. Premium paid to an insurance company on the other hand, is regarded as a tax-deductible expense. It can be argued that where the retention fund is depleted, the net after tax position is identical since the losses would be claimed as tax deductions.[17] The situation therefore affects the firm only in so far as it implies an **accumulation** of fund reserves in a non tax-efficient manner. The counter argument of course is that the accumulation of 'excess' fund assets is in itself undesirable from an optimisation standpoint, as debated earlier.

The objectives of risk managers, however, can often be seen to be personalised. It should be recalled that there exist various other factors which ultimately modify the firm's objective, but more importantly from a risk management perspective, the risk manager's function is most often interpreted in the narrower sense. Aspects of security, job evaluation and human capital considerations effectively focus their attention on the specifics of funding and insurance.

This means that the motive to accumulate fund assets is strong as is the tendency to design retention funds in a manner whereby the fund is not labelled or perceived as an asset.

Any dichotomy of the risk management activity from the general financial management activity of the firm is disappointing. A central viewpoint expressed in this text is that the function should be 'elevated' and integrated with the other activities, which not only include finance activities, but all those which by nature influence the risk profile of the firm. In the final analysis, it is exactly this aspect with which the risk manager is concerned. A general appreciation of the risk management function and the integration (as suggested by the risk management model) must have the effect of tempering any isolationist motives and reduce any associated inefficiencies.

The question of taxation raises further interesting debate. Establishing a retention fund should not be inspired by any favourable tax effects *per se*, since this motive has no underlying foundation in risk management. But, this is not tantamount to saying that risk managers should take no account of tax-efficient means of retention funding that may be available.

---

16 There can be seen to exist an agency-type relationship between shareholders and managers of a firm. Paid managers need to satisfy the aspirations of shareholders, but may indeed have other personal objectives that exert forces in other directions.

17 This holds true on the assumption that, following a loss, the reinvestment or expense relates to a revenue producing asset, that is, an expense actually incurred will be allowed as a tax deduction if incurred for the purpose of production of income.

For a discussion of the tax implications of retention see Divaris (1988, 131).

This question prompts a discussion of retention facilities/plans that have developed to facilitate risk retention through the medium of an insurance company.

11.7.2 Retention and insurers

The origins of these programmes may be found in retention facilities defined as *cell captives*. The terminology is somewhat unfortunate, as these facilities cannot be regarded as captives (or mutual captives) – there is no requirement for the firm to capitalise as is the case when a firm establishes its own captive insurance company. The cell-captive is not a subsidiary of its parent. The intention, rather, is to make use of the facilities of an established insurance company to achieve the objectives of a captive insurance company. Hence, this type-facility has also been named *rent-a-captive*.

The rationale is simply to pay as a premium the amounts required to satisfy the level of risk-retention to an insurer which is identified as a separate cell or participation unit – in the overall premium receipts of the insurer.[18] Instead of the firm's internally held retention fund financing the losses as they occur, the insurance company would settle the losses as insurance claims when presented to it.

Before describing the features of such self-insurance programmes it is desirable to examine the rationale and motivation for insurers to offer such facilities.[19] The appropriate starting point is the realisation that with

18 It is easy to perceive why such a facility has been termed a *rent-a-captive*. In essence, the firm rents the insurance company's/captive's license to transact insurance business. There is naturally a facility fee payable to the insurer, which, theoretically, compensates the insurer for the strain on solvency resulting from its writing the self-insurance premiums.

Kloman & Rosenbaum (1982, 135) describe such *rent-a-captive* facilities as non-owned captives. The advantages of such a scheme are:

- the unrelated company does not have to capitalise its own captive
- the unrelated company does not have to go through the formalities associated with the setting up of a captive
- the rent-a-captive (related company) obtains unrelated insurance business (which in the USA context is good for its tax defence position)
- the rent-a-captive (related company) receives fees for the service, and usually some of the investment income as well.

19 There is controversy surrounding the issue of self-insurance facilities. For instance, the tax implications of self-insurance premiums are not all clear; some argue that effectively there is no real 'transfer' of risk to the insurer, and that therefore the 'veneer' of insurance is inadequate to allow payments into the facility to be regarded as insurance premiums. In the end analysis, the insurer may bear some risk, but the extent of risk bearing that would allow eligibility for insurance, is a debatable point.

From an economic standpoint, one could argue that insurers have adapted their cost structures to maintain their competitiveness in this niche market and have diversified their portfolio by writing relatively low risk/low return business. To the extent that the inclusion of this business improves overall results which in turn might lead to the creation of insurance capacity and the provision of other insurances at a more competitive price, this activity (self-insurance facilities) is advantageous.

the development of risk financing (coupled with other factors), firms have begun to retain higher levels of risk for own account. All the reasoning as described in prior sections has encouraged a more active involvement by insureds, and particularly with the larger organisations, this has resulted in the restriction of insurance purchase to catastrophe-type covers.

As a general statement then, this has caused premium incomes to conventional insurers to drop as firms more efficiently finance those risks or sections of risk where, because of their nature (predictability and severity) the advantages of pooling offered by insurers becomes more redundant .

Interpreted in a slightly different fashion, insurers' inherent cost structures disqualify them from providing an efficient pre-loss means for financing risk under these conditions.

Such realisation has prompted certain insurer organisations to differentiate risks according to similar risk retention criteria, and to regard such high frequency/low severity risk situations as 'niche market' opportunities. Tailoring their risk financing involvement in these situations, insurers are able to offer such facilities at an economic price or premium.

Most self-insurance facilities are composite programmes. The optimal integration of retention with insurance implies the 'transfer of risk' at some point. Thus, where the insurer facilitates the retention programme and writes the residual risk, the policy may be seen as a composite mechanism encompassing both the relatively predictable, low severity portion, and the relatively unpredictable high severity exposure.

The facility as a whole may alternatively be regarded as 'layered';[20] the first layer caters for the retained portion of the risk, whilst the second provides excess loss cover for the more catastrophic element.

This does not imply that the insurer bears no risk whatsoever in the retention or first layer. Generally, in competing for such premiums (or retention funds), the insurer grants cover in excess of what has been provided for in terms of total premium. Depending on the contractual agreement between the parties, a portion of any excess of premium over actual losses may be refundable to the insured, or utilised to fund the following period's risk financing requirements. Thus, the hybrid nature of these programmes becomes apparent. There exists the element of 'transfer' and pooling and there is an assumption of risk by the insurer.

---

20 Layering can be described as an arrangement whereby two or more insurers each provide an absolute monetary amount of insurance coverage, or layer. The insurer of the first layer is primary, thus responding first in covering a loss. Insurers of subsequent layers respond in sequence, as necessary, to cover any larger loss. See *Risk Management Glossary* (1985, 42).

Apart from cell-captive or rent-a-captive facilities there has also developed recently a facility whereby underwriters assist the insured to spread a particular loss over a period of time thus smoothing the impact of a large loss on the financial statements of the insured.[21] These facilities or programmes have been termed *Structured Insurance Programmes* (SIP) and have mainly also materialised as a response to the sophisticated risk financing needs of today's risk managers who are seeking to achieve effective asset and balance sheet protection.

Structured Insurance Programmes enable the insured to manage losses in a structured manner through the following characteristics:

Risk transfer

In a SIP risk transfer can take the form of:

- ☐ an **underwriting risk** (actual aggregate loss incurred exceeds the projection)
- ☐ a **timing risk** (actual claims payments occur faster than projection)
- ☐ **interest rate risks** (earnings on invested assets fall short of projection)
- ☐ **credit risks** (uncertainty surrounding the collection of future premiums).

Risk spread/ risk combination

Risk spread/combination can take various forms. For example, one could spread the impact of large losses over time through a multi-year policy or to combine several exposure years into a single policy term. It is also possible to provide coverage for different lines of business on a combined basis.

Aggregate limits

In order to limit the total exposure an overall aggregate limit is normally applied for the contract period, and if necessary annual payout limitations are set which define the maximum amount available in any one given year.[22]

Commutation

This last feature is of particular importance in a Structured Insurance Programme. Commutation is a system whereby any excess premium (surplus), plus interest is returned to the insured.[23]

---

21 The interested reader is referred to Cheng (1990).

22 The underwriter first determines the expected loss. Then, based upon assumptions concerning pattern of loss payments and interest rates for the individual risk(s), the discounted losses will be established.

The difference between the expected loss and the discounted loss represents the area where the timing and interest rate risk is assumed. The difference between the expected loss and the aggregate limit represents the underwriting risk assumed by the insurer.

23 Typically commutation is achieved in the following manner. Upon receipt of the premium, a pre-agreed percentage is deducted to cover underwriting expenses including a charge for insuring the risk. Loss payments (if any) will also be deducted. Then, to the remaining amount interest earnings are credited (such is usually calculated on the basis of a predetermined interest rate factor).

Finally, the influence of these practical considerations on the implementation of a risk retention strategy is not difficult to perceive. The introduction of transaction costs resulted in a risk management case for retention funding; the practical considerations of tax add a further dimension to the risk manager's evaluation criteria and provide further choice as concerns the retention vehicle. Depending on the size of the organisation and the intended sophistication surrounding its risk retention, the firm may even consider the incorporation of its own captive insurance company.

Bibliography

Bickelhaupt, DL & Magee, JH 1970. *General insurance.* Homewood, Illinois: Richard D. Irwin Inc.

Cheng, W 1990. 'Structured insurance programmes as part of risk management.' *Zurich Group International Division – Speeches.* Interlaken. September.

Cummins, D 1976. 'Risk management and the theory of the firm.' *Journal of Risk and Insurance.* Vol. 43.

Divaris, C 1988. 'Internal self-insurance.' *Tax Planning.* No. 4.

Denenberg, HS, Eilers, RD, Melone, JJ & Zelten, RA 1974. *Risk and insurance.* Englewood Cliffs, New Jersey: Prentice-Hall Inc.

Doherty, NA 1985. *Corporate risk management – A financial exposition.* New York: McGraw-Hill Inc.

Gibson, JP (ed) 1983. 'Calculating the risk retention capability of an organization.' *Risk Financing: A Guide to Insurance Cash Flow.* Texas, Dallas: International Risk Management Institute Inc. February.

Goshay, RC 1964. *Corporate self insurance and risk retention plans.* Homewood, Illinois: Richard D. Irwin Inc.

Kloman, MF & Rosenbaum, DH 1982. 'The captive insurance phenomenon: A cautionary tale.' *The Geneva Papers in Risk and Insurance.* Vol. 7, No. 23.

Kulp, CA & Hall, JW 1968. *Casualty insurance.* New York: The Ronald Press Co.

Mowbray, AH, Blanchard, R & Williams, CA 1969. *Insurance.* New York: McGraw-Hill Inc.

Report of the Commission of Inquiry into the Flow of Short-Term Insurance Premiums out of the Republic and the Operations of Captive Insurers. 1990. Pretoria: Government Printer. April.

Risk management glossary. 1985. New York: Risk Management Society Publishing Inc.

Sharpe, WF 1981. *Investments.* Englewood Cliffs, New Jersey: Prentice-Hall Inc.

Endnotes

[1] Denenberg, *et al.*, 1974, 122.

[2] Kulp & Hall, 1968, 10.

[3] Mowbray, Blanchard & Williams, 1969, 62.

[4] Bickelhaupt & Magee, 1970, 62.

[5] Doherty, 1985, 293.

[6] Goshay, 1964, 126.

[7] Doherty, 1985, 292.

[8] Doherty, 1985, 297-303.

[9] Doherty, 1985, 300.

12 CAPTIVE INSURANCE COMPANIES

12.1 Definition

> A captive[1] insurance company is defined as an insurance company that is owned by a parent company (or companies) and which writes the insurance business (in sum or in part) of its parents.[2]

Bawcutt[1] provides a similar purist definition of a captive and states that

> the key factor is that the insurance company [captive] is owned by the parent and therefore has its own captive business.

Defining captives becomes difficult however, for there have developed a number of captive types,[3] and as one moves away from the pure captive that insures only the parent's business, one is attracted to the suggestion that:

> it would probably be more helpful to accept the origins of captives and move towards a situation where the word 'captive' disappears and where . . . [it] is referred to as an insurance affiliate of a corporation.[2][4]

There is considerable debate and unnecessary confusion over the nature of captive insurers, basically resulting from the American concept that insurance requires risk shifting, risk distribution or risk transfer.[5]

Although 'transfer' of risk is substantiated by the fact that captives adopt rating and reserving procedures, it was initially argued that the risk does not in fact leave the corporate group and that therefore there is no real

---

1 Credit for the name 'captive' is given to Fred Reiss, who coined the name 40 years ago. (*Melamet II*, 1990, 61.)

2 Some captives, specifically US captives write non-parent related risks. This has largely occurred because of tax considerations.

3 Kloman and Rosenbaum (1982, 137) divide captives into the following categories:
- Pure captive (writing only or predominantly the risks of the parent)
- Senior captive (whose portfolio includes a significant, although not overwhelming portion of external risks)
- Profit centre captive (where the parent's risk represents a small portion of the total risks underwritten)
- Group captive (which are jointly owned by two or more parents and underwrite the risks of the parents).

4 It has been suggested that the term *dedicated insurance company* be considered to describe a captive insurer.

5 For a discussion of tax issued relating to USA, see Pine, *et al.*, (1978, 11) which was published after the IRS issued its ruling but before the Carnation case and gives a clear explanation of the IRS position.

Further reference is found in Pine & Wright (1979, 37) and Wright (1979, 1), and in the following court cases:
Helvering v Le Gierse 312 US 531 (1941)
Peter Theodore v Commissioner 38 TC 1011 (1962)
IRS Revenue Ruling 77-316
Carnation Company v Commissioner 71 TC 400 (1987), affirmed 640 F. 2nd 1010. Cert. Denied 454 US 965 (1981)
Humana Inc v Commissioner F. 2d WL (1989).

'transfer' of risk to a third party – the captive may be seen to be a member of the same 'economic family'.[6]

The same economic family concept however cuts across the well established principle of the corporate entity, or *juristic persona*, and it is not surprising that the American courts have begun to reject this concept.

It is submitted that the correct test to determine whether a particular transaction or scheme is one of insurance or not, is not to enquire whether risk transfer[3] or loss spreading[7] is involved, but to determine whether an enforceable insurance contract is present, obliging one party (the insurer), for a consideration (usually a premium), to indemnify another party (the insured) in the event of a defined loss-producing event materialising.[8]

Thus, the test is whether, when an **individual** loss occurs, the claimant, in exchange for a consideration, has an enforceable right to indemnification, say from a captive insurer. If such right exists, it is argued that the party obliged to provide such indemnification is indeed an insurer. Moreover, it is requisite that an insurance contract/policy exists before any reinsurance can be arranged and hence it is only when a captive is a legitimate insurer that reinsurance of the captive is possible.

As concerns the circumstances in which a captive insurer can be used, it would appear that the earlier conclusions relating to retention funding would apply equally to captives. This section provides certain facts and estimates about the captive industry and examines the features of captive insurance, and the motivations for forming a captive. The section concludes by discussing certain issues relative to South African owned captives.

12.2 The captive insurance industry

A convenient starting point is to offer some facts and estimates about captives which will show how pervasive this form of risk financing has become. It should be mentioned that exact details concerning captives

6 The 'economic family' concept was specifically rejected in a number of cases including *Mobil Oil Corporation v United States* F.2d Cl Ct (1985) and *Humane Inc v Commissioner*. See *Business Insurance*, 7 August 1989, for a discussion of the issues. In the *Humane* case the court said 'under no circumstances do we adopt the economic family argument advanced by the government.'

7 It can be shown that the pure premium to insurers equals $p = \Sigma p_i . x_i$, or the expected monetary value of the claims. Each insured theoretically pays his own expected annual claims costs. Theoretically, the pooling effect then allows the insured to spread his own expected claims costs over a period of time.

8 Clearly, this makes reference only to short- term insurance contracts and not to long-term (life) assurance.

are difficult to ascertain because of the difficulty of extracting information in many captive locations. Also, captives' operations are considerably dynamic, experiencing rapid growth in a wide variety of domiciles. The following summarises the captive environment.

Table 12.1 Total number of captives by domicile[9]

Location	Estimate (Number)
Bermuda	1 225
Cayman	350
Barbados	175
Bahamas	32
Guernsey	190
Luxembourg	140
Isle of Man	97
Ireland	26
Singapore	44
Vermont	189
Colorado	32
Other US domiciles/states	213
All other non-US	165
US public entity pools	272
Total	3 150

Source: *Offshore Finance*. 1990.

- ☐ The industry is dominated by captives of US parents; it has been approximated that 200 of the 'Fortune 500 companies' have captive insurance companies.[4] It is reported[5] that some two-thirds of the biggest companies in the UK are thought to own captive insurance companies.
- ☐ The largest captive is thought to be the insurance subsidiary of Exxon[6] which, it was estimated, had an asset value approaching $1 billion.
- ☐ Total world premiums of captives were estimated in 1990 to be $10 billion and investable assets to be $19 billion[7] – in view of the rapid growth in the industry these figures are probably underestimates today.
- ☐ Some preliminary evidence[8] suggests that the incorporation of captives has had a positive and meaningful effect on the value of some parent companies.

9 Other captive locations include Cyprus, Hong Kong, Nauru and Netherlands Antilles. A comprehensive table comparing various locations can be found in Bawcutt (1982, 73-76).

The captive concept is not a new one.[10] Its origins may be found in the early efforts by industrial groups to join together to establish organistions for which the principal objective was the provision of mutual indemnification against loss.[11] In today's terminology, such an establishment might be called an industry or association captive.

12.3 Features and motivations for forming captives

Although mention was made that a captive insurer can be viewed in the same light as a retention fund, certain features distinguish it from other sources as a means of pre-loss funding. Some writers, for example Kloman and Rosenbaum[9] refer to the feature of risk reduction through **adequate reserving** to be a distinguishing and meaningful function, suggesting too that the instability and unpredictability of modern economic life be a major factor encouraging the growth of the captive industry. In attempting to cope with such conditions, Kloman & Rosenbaum,[10] state that:

> Within this environment, prudent managers seek to insulate the organisation against the unexpected through larger contingent reserves.[12]

Most of the writings on captives maintain that captives have certain advantages relative to commercial insurance, and these, as cited by Lenrow, Brainerd, Hall & Heitz,[11] are summarised hereunder. It should be noted that although these points do provide insight into captives, they address rather the inadequacy or disadvantages of insurance more than the advantages of captives. It is opportune to recall that the case for establishing a captive requires that it be shown to be preferable to all competing forms of post-loss reinvestment financing rather than simply less expensive than commercial insurance.

---

10 Bawcutt (1982) describes that captive insurance companies have become popular and a major topic of discussion in the insurance world over the last 25 years. Their history goes back at least 100 years and arguably, many centuries before that when one regards, for example, trade guilds as a method of mutual financial protection. In tracing the history of some of today's major insurers it is interesting to discover that companies such as Guardian Royal Exchange and General Accident were established by small groups of people with the object of providing financial protection for each other, or to improve on the insurance offered by the then-established insurance companies.

11 The *Protection and Indemnity Clubs* which insure marine liabilities are examples of industry mutuals which have been in existence for some time.

12 This might be accurate in describing one motivation for forming a captive. But, as Doherty (1985, 442) points out: this reasoning may not be valid for managers seeking to increase the value of the firm. As usual, the effect of diversification on the ultimate risk borne by shareholders is ignored, as are the other potential sources of finance (post-loss) for reinvestment. However, as will be seen, captives do have certain relative advantages when compared to commercial insurance as a pre-loss means of financing.

Investment income earned on reserve funds accrues to the captive as opposed to an unrelated insurer

Reserve funds and paid-up capital form a pool of investable funds; such investment income serves to reduce the overall cost of operating a captive. In the case of purchasing commercial insurance, the investment income accrues to the insurer, but in a competitive environment, this income might be reflected in premium rates. However, imperfections may restrain insurers from fully passing on the investment income to the insureds in the guise of lower premium rates. Also, the investment regulations of the domiciles of captives may be more liberal which, given that the captive has access to skilled and effective portfolio managers, may result in superior performance. Finally, the investment income from offshore locations often is treated more favourably, from a taxation viewpoint, than is domestic investment income.[13] Naturally, value will be created if the after-tax yield is in excess of the cost of capital.

Captives may offer certain tax advantages over commercial insurance or other forms of retention

As in, for example, the US, commercial insurance premiums in South Africa are deductible for purposes of calculating tax. If insurance is not purchased the firm may deduct (most) uninsured losses as they are incurred. These provisions are not neutral in their impact on the decision to purchase insurance if time value of money is considered; the payment of premiums precedes the occurrence of losses and hence the tax benefit from premium payment arises earlier than the tax benefit from deduction of losses uninsured. This creates a bias in favour of insurance over other methods of financing losses, but consideration needs to be given to the recognition of a captive as an insurer and the tax treatment of a captive's underwriting and investment income.[14] These aspects will be dealt with briefly under the section that examines the operations of South African owned captives.

Cover may be difficult or expensive to obtain

A popular argument has been that captives have been established because the commercial market has failed to satisfy the needs of insureds by failing to provide premiums that fairly reflect the risk exposure or the insured's loss record. The foundation of this argument lies in the imperfection, or cross-subsidisation (over different types of insureds) that may arise in the commercial market. A captive provides the opportunity to use its own data and set its own rates.[15] This function is only of value

13 The question of taxation on investment income as well as underwriting income as pertains to South African captives is examined later in this section.

14 It should be noted that the taxation of captive insurance transactions is complex for various reasons. Tax law is imprecise in defining insurance and, therefore, the circumstances under which a captive will be recognised as an insurance company for tax purposes. Also, captive transactions are often international in nature, thus subject to the jurisdictions of more than one tax authority.

It is not intended to provide an in-depth analysis of taxation pertaining to captive insurance. This would entail a separate and intensive study in its own right.

15 It may be fair to state that the liability crisis (discussed in Chapter Nine) has prompted a considerable number of firms (some non-profit organisations) to establish their own captives that provide liability related insurance covers and that also act as expedient vehicles in risk/claims/litigation management. See Otto (1989, 1-9).

if the firm is able to produce a more reliable estimate of the probability distribution of future losses than that produced by the commercial market.

Underwriting costs often lower

Commercial insurance is expensive relative to the expected value of loss. Kloman and Rosenbaum[12] claim that with commercial insurance the expense ratio is 0,3 and higher as compared with expense ratios of captives that range from 0,05 to 0,1. Part of these savings arises from the exclusion of marketing costs (including commissions) and insurer profits

The captive has access to the reinsurance market, which by virtue of its wholesale nature is thought to be more competitive than the direct (retail) market

By forming a captive, a firm is not restricted to placing its insurance in the direct market, but has access to the more competitive reinsurance market. Advantages that are advanced are that the firm will enjoy more flexibility in negotiating deductibles with commensurate premium discount. In the direct market insurers are often reluctant to issue policies with high levels of deductibles or to offer significant premium reductions.

Several reasons have been proposed to explain the difference in intensity of competition between the reinsurance and the direct market. These may be briefly itemised as follows:[13]

- ☐ Direct writing is usually more regulated than is reinsurance. Regulation is not aimed at keeping rates low, but rather at protecting solvency and protecting local markets from international competition.[16] Moreover, often such regulation is protectionist in nature resulting in inefficiency and added expense.
- ☐ The market for direct insurance is nation-wide in its dimensions; reinsurance is often transacted on an international basis, and this exposes firms to more intensive competition.
- ☐ Typically, direct insurers incur higher costs of production and marketing than do reinsurers.

Incentives for risk control stronger

It can be thought that insurance leads to moral hazard (in its correct definition), where losses are transferred to an independent third party. With commercial insurance, the higher total claims costs resulting from moral hazard factors will ultimately be borne by policyholders as a group; if the loss is transferred to a related third party, this moral hazard cost is nonexistent. With a captive therefore, incentives to formulate effective risk control programmes are sustained.

---

16 The degree of protectionism varies. An extreme example is the *Swaziland* legislation which allows insurance to be placed only with the *Swaziland Royal Insurance Corporation* and makes it a criminal offence in terms of section 3 of the *Control of Insurance Order*, 1973, to insure elsewhere.

The features described in the preceding section provide the motives for establishing a captive. When observed in an overall sense, these can be condensed into two broad motives:

(i) **A captive may be formed with the object of obtaining insurance on more advantageous terms**
The intention here is to establish the captive as a conduit to the reinsurance market which is perceived to offer more favourable terms and conditions.[17] Thus, there is the motive to obtain meaningful pre-loss financing from an unrelated reinsurer, although this does not imply that the captive will not retain some risk for itself.

The perceived advantages of directing the risk premium to reinsurers through the medium of the captive are also 'qualitative' in nature. Since the cession of premium is in effect a cession from direct insurer (the captive) to the reinsurer, there may be the opportunity to disguise the risk source. This is not to suggest that captive parents generally wish to maintain anonymity, but rather, that the opportunity to do so exists. A major motivation for South African organisations to form a captive has been that it could allow more concealed accessibility to the international markets. A captive could therefore facilitate the marketing of certain risks in, say, politically sensitive or nervous markets.[18]

(ii) **A captive may represent a genuine pre-loss financing alternative to insurance**
Where there is the intention to retain risk within the organisation the captive competes with alternative methods of reinvestment financing, such as internal retention funding, new debt issues, new equity and commercial insurance. In such cases the captive may or may not be heavily reinsured. It is probable that in the early years there will be substantial reinsurance of the captive until its retention capacity grows to allow it to carry more of the parent's exposure. There may also be the opportunity (and willingness) for the captive to write unrelated third party risks, in which case the captive assumes a wider responsibility and acts as, what has been termed, a senior captive.

---

17 This belief, as mentioned earlier, arises from the differences in the intensity of competition in the direct and reinsurance markets. Although the arguments put forward are plausible, it should be mentioned that there exists no scientific study to support the hypothesis.

18 This issue was seen by South African insureds as being of strategic importance. Captives were seen to facilitate transfer to markets willing to write the business so long as the risk source was disguised. It is not possible to appraise the effectiveness of such a mechanism (*ex ante*), as it is dependent in part on the strength of economic motives of (re)insurers under imposed conditions of trade restrictions.

Unlike other methods of retention, the captive may provide certain tax benefits; this and other issues relative to South African owned captives are now discussed.

12.4 Considerations pertaining to South African owned captive insurance companies

Inquiry into the operations of South African owned captives

This section examines specific issues relative to offshore captives owned by South African parent organisations. In recent years there has been a considerable growth experienced in the establishment abroad of captive insurance companies by South African organisations. There is record of 21 South African owned off-shore captives [and one on-shore captive] at the offices of the Registrar of Financial Institutions and The Exchange Control Department of the South African Reserve Bank. It has been estimated that in 1988, premiums to captives totalled over R300 million.[14]

Following the recommendations of the *Melamet Commission (Melamet I) of Inquiry into the winding-up of the short-term insurance business of the AA Mutual Insurance Association Limited* (April, 1988) the South African government appointed, in April 1989 the *Commission of Inquiry into the flow of short-term insurance premiums out of the Republic and the operations of captive insurers (Melamet II).*[15][19]

Some of the terms of reference of the Commission [with regard to captives] are:

To inquire into and report and make recommendations on:

- ☐ the operations of captive insurers and the necessity for South African insureds to use their services inside or outside the Republic
- ☐ the extent to which the services of captive insurers are currently being used by South African insureds and the effect on inter alia –
  - the insurance industry
  - the outflow of funds
  - the loss of taxation
  - the investment of the funds of captive insurers
- ☐ the advantage gained from captive insurers as genuine risk carriers for the South African insurance industry as to *inter alia* –
  - an awareness of risk management by the local personnel, and their training therein;
  - the promotion of entry into international reinsurance markets;
  - the practice whereby local insurers act as a front for foreign captive insurers.

It is not the intention here, to offer commentary on the wider issues and effects of captives as per the terms of reference given to the Commission,

19 The Melamet Commission of Inquiry (1988, 102) following the collapse of the AA Mutual Insurance Association Limited recommended that:

> The operations of and necessity for captive insurers, should be investigated by the Registrar of Financial Institutions, the Commissioner for Inland Revenue and the Exchange Control authorities.

nor to debate the recommendations proposed by the Melamet Commission Report (1990); this section, rather, provides a summary of the Melamet Commission's recommendations with regard to off-shore captives, and an insight into the specific aspects of taxation, and exchange control as they pertain to South African owned captives.

Table 12.2
Summary of the Melamet Commission's recommendations

- ☐ A committee consisting of representatives from Excon, Registrar and Revenue be formed to control off-shore captives. (5.8.1)
- ☐ The recommendation by the committee of what funds, if any, and in what form, accumulated in the captive be returned to the parent. (5.8.2.1)
- ☐ The investigation by Revenue of any unjustified deductions of premiums for income tax purposes. (5.8.2.2)
- ☐ Investigation of possible contravention of section 60(2) and section 75 of the Insurance Act. (5.8.2.3)
- ☐ Annual returns to be submitted to Excon and to Registrar, as prescribed. (5.8.3)
- ☐ Revenue to investigate premium deductions to rent-a-captives. (5.8.4)
- ☐ Deduction for premiums remitted to off-shore captives should not be allowed for income tax purposes, except amounts spent on reinsurance less commissions received thereon. (5.8.5)

12.5 Taxation

The establishment and operation of captives raise a number of tax issues.

12.5.1 Taxation on interest income

A South African owned captive, registered outside South Africa, may be liable in South Africa for tax on interest accruing on loans and deposits made in South Africa.[20] Some confusion appears to exist as to whether or not interest accruing to a non-resident is liable for taxation. The confusion arises following the announcement by the Minister of Finance concerning the repeal of non-resident tax on interest and the subsequent changes to the legislative position. When the repeal of s 64A-F was announced, the minister is reported to have said, 'it is proposed that from tomorrow interest accruing to foreign lenders will no longer be taxed'. It thus appears that when Parliament abolished s 64A-F it also intended to abolish tax on non-resident interest. It is however not clear that this is what in fact has happened since fundamentally in South Africa, tax is determined by source.

The issue hinges around the concept of source. Source is notoriously difficult to determine as it is a function of factual circumstances. In terms

20 The position of non-resident taxation on interest was governed by section 64A-F of the Income Tax Act, which was repealed by Act 90 of 1988.

of case law, the source of interest on a loan (or deposit) is the provision of credit, so that if the supply of credit (or making the deposit) takes place in the Republic, the source of interest is in the Republic.

To determine the interpretation of source as used in the *Income Tax Act*, one must rely on case law. Such case law is largely based on the case *CIR v Lever Brothers and Unilever Ltd*, 1946 AD 441 SATC 14 1, where it was held that:

(a) The source of receipts, received as income, is not the quarter whence they come, but the originating cause of their being received as income.

(b) This originating cause is the work which the tax payer does to earn them the *quid pro quo* which he gives in return for which he receives them.

The case authoritatively lays down that by 'source' is meant 'the originating cause'; determination of the originating cause involves enquiry into two matters, namely:

- ☐ What is the originating cause of the income?
- ☐ Is the originating cause in the Republic?

In the case of employment and services rendered, the special income tax court has consistently laid down that the source or originating cause of income from employment and other services rendered, is the services, irrespective of the place where the contract is made or the remuneration is paid.

If interest accruing to a non-resident does indeed attract tax, this implies therefore that an off-shore captive which earned interest in the Republic, should register with the Inland Revenue Department as a tax payer and furnish returns reflecting as South African income all interest accrued on deposits which have been made in South Africa.

Furthermore, if the off-shore captive were a domestic company for tax purposes, that is, one that is managed and controlled in South Africa, then it would also be subject to tax in South Africa [S. 9(3) of the *Income Tax Act* (58 of 1962 as amended)] on interest derived from loans to or deposits in a bank anywhere in the world, except where the loan or deposit was made out of foreign funds derived entirely from sources outside South Africa, with a foreign bank for the purposes of a business carried on outside South Africa. To avoid being classified as a domestic company in terms of the *Income Tax Act*, the risk manager should ensure that the captive is not managed and controlled in the Republic.

12.5.2 Deductibility for tax purposes of premiums paid to captives

The *Income Tax Act* does not specifically deal with expenditure for insurance purposes. The deductibility of these amounts for tax purposes is thus determined in terms of the general deduction formula. It has been the practice, quite correctly, to allow the deduction of insurance premiums to commercial insurance companies for tax purposes. There does not appear to be any reason why deductibility in respect of genuine risk-related premiums paid to captives should not also be allowed for tax purposes. It has been the practice of companies to claim such deduction (as noted by *Melamet II*, 72).

It has been suggested that a strong motive for the formation of captives is tax-related, but in view of the extensive use of captives where tax deductibility does not exist, the correctness of this view cannot be sustained. Should a captive insurance company be formed solely for the purposes of avoiding, postponing or reducing tax liability then it would run the risk of falling foul of section 103 of the *Income Tax Act*, summarised as follows:

(a) any transaction, operation or scheme,

(b) has the effect of avoiding, postponing or reducing liability for the payment of tax, and,

(c) the transaction, operation or scheme was carried out in an abnormal way or has created abnormal rights or obligations (that is, those that would not normally be created between persons dealing at arm's length), and,

(d) the sole or main purpose of the transaction, operation or scheme, was the avoidance, postponement or reduction of liability for the payment of any tax,

the liability for tax shall be determined as if the transaction, operation or scheme had not been entered into, or in such other manner as deemed appropriate.

12.5.3 Taxation of underwriting profits

The question now of whether the underwriting income represents South African sourced income for purposes of tax, needs to be examined. It should be noted that different tax regimes exist – USA, for example, follows a worldwide tax base. In South Africa, on the other hand, the operability of tax laws are confined to income derived from a source within the Republic, unless specifically extended as in the deeming provisions through legislation.[21]

Section 28(2) of the *Income Tax Act* deals with the determination of taxable income of a taxpayer carrying on short-term insurance business in the Republic of South Africa.[22] An offshore captive would be liable in

21 A Commission of Enquiry 'Taxation in South Africa' (RP86) in 1970 recommended a worldwide tax base be implemented. This has not been followed, to date.

22 In terms of section 1 of the *Insurance Act* (27 of 1943 as amended) a 'Domestic Policy' means

> any policy issued anywhere upon an application made or presented to a representative of the insurer concerned, (or to any person on behalf of such representative) at a place in the Republic, . . .

In terms of section 1(2)(c) of the Act, a person is deemed to be carrying on insurance business in the Republic if he is liable under a Domestic – Policy. Getz & Davis (1983, 26) relying on *R v Buchanan* 1914 AD 509 state

> For business to be carried on in the Republic, the premiums must be received within it and there must be a manager, secretary or agent here.

terms of this section for tax in South Africa if it were carrying on short-term insurance (or reinsurance) business in South Africa (the basis of taxation being as set out in this section).

For the South African tax legislation not to be applicable to an off-shore captive insurance company, any discussions, negotiations and the determination of cover to be underwritten by it, require to be made outside of South Africa.

12.5.4 Summary

In summary, South African-owned offshore captives may be liable for tax on interest income earned on deposits made in South Africa. In order not to attract South African tax in terms of various other sections, the following principles should apply:[23]

- ☐ **Management and control** must be outside of South Africa
- ☐ The offshore captive must be operated on the **principles and practices** of a **normal** Insurance Company, transactions being conducted at arm's length
- ☐ **Premium to risk** relationships should be **normal** and in accordance with the market place.

12.6 The Insurance Act

The applicability of a number of the provisions of the *Insurance Act* (27 of 1943) should be considered. Three sections in particular, of the *Insurance Act* (27 of 1943) must be considered in relation to captives. These are section 5, section 60(2) and section 75.

Registration as an insurer

Section 5 prohibits the captive, as an insurer, from carrying on insurance business in South Africa unless it is duly registered. The relevant portion of section 5 reads as follows:

> Unregistered person may not carry on insurance business . . . no person shall carry on any class of insurance business in the Republic unless he is registered as an insurer under this Act for the purpose of carrying on that class of insurance business, . . .
>
> Section 5

In order not to contravene this section the risk manager should ensure that the captive does not carry on insurance business in the Republic. Thus all negotiations, transactions etc should not be carried out in the Republic. The captive should not have an office, secretary, manager or agent in South Africa.

23 These requirements need also be met so as not to contravene section 5 of the *Insurance Act* which requires registration of those carrying on insurance business in the Republic of South Africa.

Placing insurance with the captive

Section 60(2) is the closest that the *Insurance Act* comes to prohibiting the placing of insurance business with an overseas insurer without permission from the South African authorities. The relevant portion reads as follows:

> Except with prior written approval of the registrar, no person who is deemed for the purposes of subsection (1) to be carrying on insurance business in the Republic shall effect or renew any insurance business (other than reinsurance business) through a broker at Lloyds which is not underwritten by an underwriter at Lloyds.
>
> Section 60(2)

Clearly this section only applies to insurance business effected through a Lloyd's broker not underwritten at Lloyds and does not prohibit the risk manager from placing the risk directly with the captive.[24]

Offence to secure application for insurance on behalf of unregistered concern

A further provision of importance to the placing of insurance with a captive is section 75, which reads:

> Any person who induces or attempts to induce any person to enter into a contract of insurance with a person who is not registered as an insurer under this Act, or to make an application to enter into such a contract with such last mentioned person shall be guilty of an offence and liable to a fine . . .

Clearly this provision only applies to a person who induces or attempts to induce; it does not apply to a company who decides itself to place its risk with a captive.[25]

12.7 Exchange control

A further aspect of concern to the authorities is the extent to which captives facilitate the outflow of funds from South Africa.[26] It is necessary therefore to briefly describe the requirements with regard to the remittance of premiums to captives.

The placement of insurance outside the Republic is governed by the *Insurance Act* and the Exchange Control Regulations.[27] It is explained (Registrar of Financial Institutions Circular R.V. 55, 18 February 1981), *inter alia*, that

> no person may place his insurance outside the Republic unless – if not placed in accordance with the provisions of section 60(1) or 60(2) of the Insurance

24 See *Melamet II*, par. 2.6, par. 2.7 and par. 3.7. *Willis Faber Enthoven (Edms) Bpk v Receiver of Revenue and The Registrar of Insurance* (unreported TPD 3456/88). (*Melamet II*, 47.)

25 This is the interpretation applied to section 75 as derived from the wording of the section as correctly noted by *Melamet II*, 47 and 95. Any broader meaning will require an amendment by Parliament.

26 *Melamet II* estimated the between R200-R300 million leaves the country as premiums to captives. Unfortunately the commission did not estimate the inflow from captives.

27 Details of the foreign exchange rulings covering insurance and premiums are set out in *Melamet II*, par 7.1-7.2.

> Act, the placement abroad has previously been approved by the Exchange Control Authorities.[28]

This therefore means that:

> South African Reserve Bank permission for the formation and capitalisation of a captive and for the remittance of the establishment capital is required. It is also required that on an on-going basis the renewal programme of the captive, including the captive's reinsurance and expense requirements be approved by the authorities, from the standpoint of remittance of funds.[29]

Since the captive's liability would ordinarily be in the designation of the local currency, the retained portion of the risk could ordinarily be held by the captive in a non-resident's banking account in South Africa.

Finally, it is inopportune and beyond the scope of this study to speculate on the recommendations of the Melamet II Commission of Inquiry. Suffice to say, that its appointment is indeed relevant to the issue of South African captives as a means of risk financing, and that pending any action following its findings and recommendations, the South African captive environment must be seen to be in a state of flux.

---

28 As noted section 60(2) does not prevent the risk manager from placing the risk with the captive for which no permission is required. (*Melamet II*, 47).

29 Although not a legal requirement, in practice, it is also necessary to seek and obtain the approval of the South African Registrar of Insurances to form a captive and to place insurances with it.

It has been recommended by the Melamet Commission that a committee consisting of representatives from Exchange Control, Registrar and Inland Revenue be formed to monitor off-shore captives (1989, 80).

Bibliography

Bawcutt, PA 1982. *Captive insurance companies – Establishment, operation and management.* Cambridge: Woodhead-Faulkner Ltd.

Cooney, R 1990. 'Bermuda triangle.' *The Review.* March.

Cross, M, Thornton, J & Davidson, D 1984. 'Impact of the captive insurance company's foundation on the parents firm's value.' Paper presented to the *American Risk and Insurance Association.*

Doherty, NA 1985. *Corporate risk management – A financial exposition.* New York: McGraw-Hill Inc.

Getz, WS & Davis, DM 1983. *The South African law of insurance.* Cape Town: Juta & Co. Ltd.

Kloman, MF & Rosenbaum, DH 1982. 'The captive insurance phenomenon: A cautionary tale.' *The Geneva Papers in Risk and Insurance.* Vol. 7, No. 23.

Lenrow, GI, Brainerd, JH, Hall, J & Heitz, MG 1982. 'Captive insurers: Pitfalls and practicalities.' *Best's Review.* Vol. 82, No. 12.

Loy, D & Pertl, M 1982. 'Why do Fortune 500 companies form captives?' *Risk Management.* January.

Otto, WM 1989. 'Basic ingredients and principles for a comprehensive programme for liability insurance and risk/claims/litigation management.' 'One captive group's experience over the first 10 years, 1976-1985.' Papers presented at Cayman Islands Captive Insurance Conference, May.

Pine, SR & Wright, PB 1979. 'The Carnation case: How will captives be affected?' *Risk Management.* March.

Pine, SR, Stanger, AM & Wright, PB 1978. 'IRS revenue ruling 77-316: Avoiding its consequences.' *Risk Management.* April.

Porat, MM 1982. 'Bermuda captive insurers: An analysis of underwriting exposure ratios.' *CPCU Journal.* Vol. 35, No. 2.

Report of the Commission of Inquiry into the Flow of Short-Term Insurance Premiums out of the Republic and the Operations of Captive Insurers. 1990. Pretoria: Government Printer, December.

Report on the Commission of Inquiry into the winding-up of the AA Mutual Insurance Association Limited. 1988. Pretoria: Government Printer, April.

Vivian, RW 1990. 'Insurance – risk transfer, fact or fancy?' *Cover.*

Wright, PB 1979. 'Tax issues for captives.' *Risk Management Reports.* Vol. 13.

Endnotes

[1] Bawcutt, 1983, 1.

[2] Bawcutt, 1983, 1.

[3] Vivian, 1990.

[4] Loy & Pertl, 1982, 32-36.

[5] *Financial Times*, 1990, March 29.

[6] Kloman & Rosenbaum, 1982, 132.

[7] *Offshore Finance*, 1990.

[8] Cross, Thornton & Davidson, 1984, 5.

[9] Kloman & Rosenbaum, 1982, 130.

[10] Kloman & Rosenbaum, 1982, 130.

[11] Lenrow, Brainerd, Hall & Heitz, 1982, 82-84.

[12] Kloman & Rosenbaum, 1982, 136.

[13] Doherty, 1985, 445.

[14] *Report of the Melamet Commission of Inquiry into the Flow of Short-Term Insurance Premiums out of the Republic and the Operations of Captive Insurers*, 1990, April, 24; 62.

[15] *Government Gazette*, 14 April 1989.

13 PRE-LOSS FINANCING THROUGH INSURANCE

13.1 Introduction

Insurance represents an important formal method of meeting the financial consequences of risk. It has been traditionally defined as the business of transferring pure risk by means of a two-party contract.

Whilst the intention is not to dispute the definition afforded, it is as well to realise at the outset that insurance provides a mechanism for the transfer of the **cost** of risk rather than the transfer of risk *per se*. This is a primary criterion for regarding insurance as a mechanism of risk financing within the overall model for risk management. The conviction here is that there can neither be a transfer of risk nor the responsibility therefor, and this fact places a greater emphasis on an imposition of a discipline on risk management, which in the final analysis is the focal point of this text.[1]

With this distinction being made, it follows that the concern of this text is primarily with the analysis of the rôle that insurance plays in the model for risk management. An examination and evaluation of insurance as a method for treating risk is required. It is recognised, however, that the subject of insurance is indeed a wide one which in itself dictates a study in isolation.

The purpose of this chapter is to consider particular aspects pertinent to insurance thus providing an insight to insurance as a method of financing risk costs. As a starting point, macro-considerations of insurance are briefly examined followed by the reasons why an insurer 'assumes risk'. The requisites of an insurable peril are then discussed. An interesting development has been the extension (limited) of insurers' activities into areas of speculative or business risk. The treatment of speculative risk through the medium of insurance is thus debated. A discussion of insurance pricing follows. A brief overview of the various short-term insurance policies concludes this chapter.

---

1 It should be noted that although this difference is advanced with a view to correlating the insurance function with the underlying philosophy of acceptance and management of risk as proposed in the text, it must not be considered as being merely one of convenience. There exist, in addition, legal considerations which support this view. See Chapter Four, section 4.4.2.4.

The concept of pooling is considered in section 13.3. An insurer's risk can be described as the risk that aggregate **claim payments** exceed the appropriate premium and claim reserves, which would bring about a reduction in the insurer's surplus. Moreover, the statistical properties of an insurance portfolio suggest that, theoretically, the larger the number of independent risks or exposures, the smaller the relative variability in aggregate claim payments. This argument would imply therefore that, given a large portfolio of exposures, the insurer's risk is in fact very limited – that the premium charged would in the long run prove sufficiently large to cater for the expected aggregate claims. Hence, theoretically, insurance could be seen as a financing mechanism *per se* – with little or no risk attached.

13.2 Macro-considerations of insurance

> If I had my way, I would write the word 'Insure' over the door of every cottage and upon the blotting book of every public man because I am convinced that, for sacrifices which are inconceivably small, families be secured against catastrophes which otherwise would smash them up.
>
> ***Winston Churchill***

In a macro-economic sense, the essential benefit accruing to society from the institution of insurance is the reduction of the uncertainty of losses in the aggregate. In as much as the pooling effect, inherent in insurance, represents an efficient risk financing or loss transfer device, this mechanism reduces the impact of pure losses, aids economic progress and is thus a valuable contribution to the well-being of society.

Insurance allows the prospective entrepreneur to more easily secure and commit risk capital to the purchase of plant, equipment and other factors of production and business facilities. Without insurance, the entrepreneur would be exposed to pure risk in addition to speculative risk. Anticipating the possibility of the destruction of his property, he would necessarily reserve part of his funds for the purpose of financing such losses to remain in business. This accumulation of individual reserve funds could be seen as restricting output, and presumably also affecting other economic units, such as for example, lending institutions which would require a greater liquidity position.

The availability of insurance on the other hand permits the entrepreneur to more fully commit assets to the intrinsic operation of the business, and premiums accumulated by the insurer would represent the reserve assets of the many individuals or business units. In a sense, insurers could be regarded as a clearing house which alleviates the impact of pure risk. Such action, on a large scale suggests a more efficient utilisation and allocation of resources.

It is reasonable to assume that the availability of insurance also permits a reduction in the prices of consumer goods and services. Firstly, the expansion in output made possible through insurance should create economies of scale which should have a positive impact on prices. Secondly, in the absence of insurance, the entrepreneur, when faced with greater risk would presumably require a greater return, recoverable through higher prices. The entrepreneur's loading for this factor of risk would undoubtedly exceed the premium cost, since insurance economies of scale through pooling would not be possible.

Turning, finally, to the social costs of insurance, much of the premium payments represent transfer payments among the insureds (with a zero gain in the long-run), and as such are not a cost to society. The social cost of insurance is determined by the amount of productive factors consumed in the process of providing the service, such costs relating mainly to insurers' general overhead costs and costs of operation.

Losses themselves, although a loss to society, do not represent a social cost of insurance, as they are not attributable to the existence of insurance.[2]

13.3 Limits of insurability

> Insurance, n. An ingenious modern game of chance in which the player is permitted to enjoy the comfortable conviction that he is beating the man who keeps the table.
>
> ***Ambrose Bierce, The Devil's Dictionary (1881-1911)***

The function of the insurer is to diversify the claims cost of individual insureds (exposures) over a wide base of policyholders who are commonly exposed to the possibility of loss. To make this function feasible there are several prerequisites, from the insurer's perspective, to be satisfied. The question is: Why and how is the insurer able to accept the risks, (the costs of which) the insureds are willing to transfer?

The most relevant aspect is that the combination of many similar exposures, (the practice of pooling) brings into operation the law of large numbers. Through pooling there is an increase in knowledge which then enhances one's ability to predict the range of probable losses from a risk exposure.

The statistical properties of the insurance pool have already been described in Chapter Three. It was stated that the insurer faces a risk, described as the variation within the pure premium distribution. Mathematically, this is the standard deviation

$$\sigma_{pp} = \sqrt{\frac{\Sigma(pp - \mu)^2}{n}} \qquad 13.1$$

where

σ_{pp} = standard deviation of the pure premium distribution
pp = all possible pure premium values
μ = mean pure premium
n = number of pure premiums.

There is also the added risk resulting from the fact that insurers cannot insure the entire population of exposures but only a sample of it. There exists the risk that the underwriter's sample of exposures is not identical to the population of exposures from which the pure premium was estimated.

2 It follows, however, that if the presence of insurance invites moral hazard (in the literal sense) with consequent increases in the frequency or severity of losses, then the additional losses do become a social cost of insurance.

Similarly, it can be argued that if the existence of insurance encourages the insured to engage in loss prevention activities through the lure of premium reduction, then society benefits.

Thus, if the insurer decides to charge as its pure premium, it is faced with the risk that its sample of insureds will have an actual average pure premium, defined as $\bar{X}_s$, which differs significantly from μ. This element of risk to the insurer may be termed sampling error, and is a function of the size of the sample.

It can be recognised that as there exists a pure premium distribution, there exists also a distribution of sample means, each sample being composed of a number of exposures from the underlying pure premium distribution.

The mean of the distribution of sample means ($\bar{X}_s$) has the same value (μ) as the underlying distribution from which the sample is selected. The Central Limit Theorem justifies approximating (when n is sufficiently large) the distribution of sample means ($\bar{X}_s$) with a normal distribution whose mean is and whose variance is:[3]

$$\frac{\sigma\ pp}{\sqrt{n}} \qquad 13.2$$

Diagrammatically, the relationship can be depicted as follows:

Figure 13.1 Relation of pure premium distribution to distribution of sample means

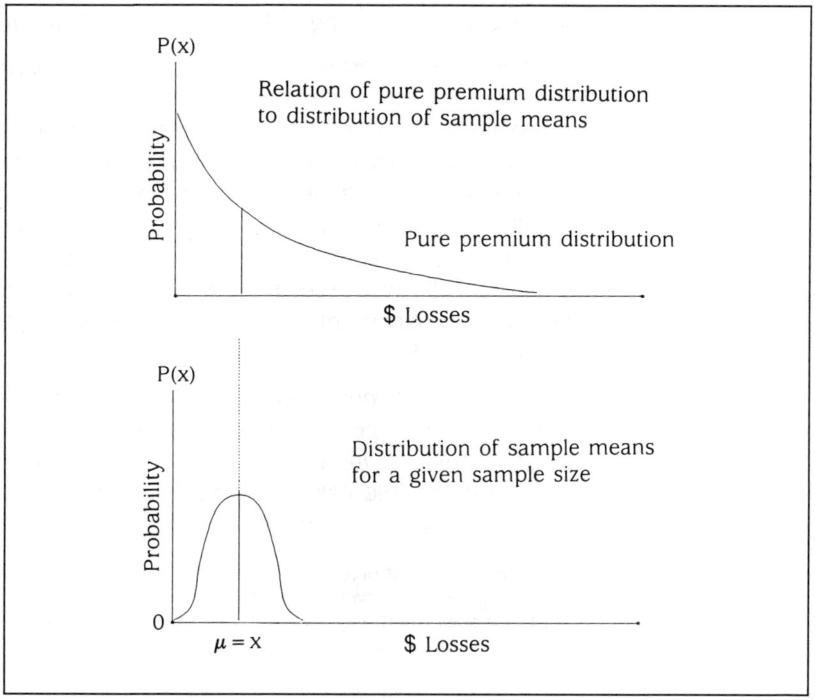

3 The Central Limit Theorem states that:
The distribution of the mean value of a set of n independent and identically distributed random variables each having mean μ and variance σ^2 approaches a normal distribution with mean μ and variance σ^2/n as n tends towards infinity (Freund, Williams & Perles, 1988, 299-301).

Thus, there is a relationship between the standard deviation of the pure premium distribution σ_{pp} and the standard deviation of the distribution of the sample means $\sigma_{\bar{X}s}$:

$$\sigma_{\bar{X}s} = \frac{\sigma_{pp}}{\sqrt{n}} \qquad 13.3$$

It will be seen that where the insurer has but one exposure or insured, that is, when $n = 1$, the risk is equal to σ_{pp} and the insurer faces the same risk as the insured prior to transfer. Only when the insurer combines more than one insured does the risk reduction process become evident, that is, the advantage of pooling is reaped. Indeed, the insurer's risk varies inversely with the square root of the number of exposures insured (equation 13.3).[4]

In sum, an insurance portfolio can be seen as a collection of insured exposure units, each represented by a contract with an external party – and the insurer's interest lies in the aggregate claims to be paid under the portfolio. The insurer's portfolio risk, as measured by the standard deviation of the average loss, tends towards zero as the number of exposure units in the portfolio tends towards infinity.

Furthermore, according to the Central Limit Theorem, the distribution of the average loss tends towards a normal distribution as the number of exposure units increases. This latter tendency permits the employment of the normal- approximation method to estimate the probability (probability of ruin) that the average loss for the portfolio will exceed some critical value, determined for example, by the insurer's reserves. As the number of exposure units increases, the probability that the average loss for the portfolio will exceed some critical value in excess of the mean, falls. As *n* approaches infinity, the ruin probability approaches zero (equations 13.1 & 13.3).

Thus, both risk measures, the standard deviation and the ruin probability, reveal that portfolio risk is inversely related to the size, or number of exposures in a portfolio.[5] These properties therefore make insurance a feasible risk financing means or mechanism.

---

4 The contributions of probability and sampling theory toward the theory of insurance is well recognised. However, note should be made of the many limitations of these statistical techniques when they are applied to insurance situations. One such limitation, for example, is the assumption that conditions in the future will exactly duplicate those of the past. In the case of insurable risk, this is seldom the case since deviations in actual experience are not necessarily due to randomness alone. Thus, these theoretical concepts are used solely for the purpose of calculating first approximations of the expected outcomes of future events – other adjustments, often of a qualitative nature, are usually required.

5 It should be noted that these properties relate to a portfolio of risks or exposures that are independent but similar (homogeneous).

Continued on page 195

There are also instances where insurers do not enjoy the statistical advantages derived from pooling but where they nevertheless accept such unique risks. In these cases it may be said that perceived **differences in uncertainties** exist surrounding the risk: the insurer's subjective valuation of the risk may be lower than that of the insured.

It may be possible too that the insurer may have greater knowledge regarding the outcome of the event, based on factors other than the law of large numbers, or that the reward for assuming the risk is sufficient to overcome the uncertainty of the insurer. Naturally, the insurer's knowledge may indeed be inferior to that of the insured, and there may be a moral hazard involved. Insurers may anticipate this situation, commonly referred to as **adverse selection**, and make adjustments to their premium calculations.[6]

An insurer may also be willing to accept the risks of the insured on account of its **greater financial capacity**. Because of the decreasing marginal utility of money, the difference in the relative value of risk to the insurer and the insured may permit a mutually acceptable contract.

Finally, an insurer may accept risk even when faced with concentrations of value in a particular exposure, geographical location, or line of insurance, because it may reduce its uncertainty by **transferring** part or all of the **risk to another insurer**. This process is termed reinsurance, and represents a very important facet of the business.[7]

13.4 Requisites of an insurable peril

In Chapter Three the distinction was drawn between the terms *peril* and *risk*. Peril was defined as the **source** causing the financial loss, as opposed to risk which was defined as the **uncertainty** surrounding the event and

---

Broadly, similar results are evident when the insurer's portfolio is composed of heterogeneous but independent exposures. Risk tends to disappear as the number of policies becomes very large, but, this is on the assumption that the relative **composition** of the portfolio is independent of its size.

When the risks are not independent – hence policies are correlated, the distribution of average loss does not tend toward normal as the number of policies increases. More importantly, the riskiness of the distribution of the average loss does not tend toward zero as the number of policies tends towards infinity. Such portfolios exhibit a minimum level of risk which cannot be diversified away. The risk of earthquake, which displays a rather high degree of geographical interdependence, is an example of such risk category.

6 See Chapter Three, section 3.10.

7 In the process of reinsurance, the ceding insurer may be viewed as the marketing intermediary to the reinsurer. Treaty reinsurance arrangements (surplus and quota-share) often imply that a relatively small part of the risk is retained by the direct insurer, and that, thus, the ultimate carrier of the risk is in fact the reinsurer. The pricing interrelationship between insurer and reinsurer can be considerably complex, but on the premise that the ultimate risk carrier is the reinsurer, it is not surprising that changes in market pricing (the hard and soft market cycle) are reinsurance led. (Valsamakis, 1983, 6-14.)

its possible financial outcome. The rationale for purchasing insurance hence becomes to negate or reduce the financial consequences arising from the uncertainty surrounding a given peril.

Perils that give rise to the risk of financial loss are, for example, fire, thefts, and motor collisions. Such perils create the types of risk that have been termed pure risks, for which insurance provides a feasible risk financing mechanism. Of course, not all perils that give rise to pure risk situations are insurable.

The requirements of an insurable peril are governed by the statistical and administrative factors discussed earlier, and are associated with the practical operation of the insurance technique.

The qualifications offered below are not to be seen as exhaustive, but are presented rather with the aim of identifying the types of problems that must be considered in deciding upon the insurability of a particular peril.[8]

- ☐ There must be a large number of homogeneous exposures. In order to permit the operation of the theory of probability, the requirement of large numbers is necessary. Homogeneous exposures are those that display similar expectations of loss – reliance can be placed on statistical probabilities only if the sample to which the probability is applied is similar to the one from which the probability was derived.[9]
- ☐ The insured group (exposure units) must be independent and hence not exposed to a catastrophe, the consequences of which cannot be estimated. From a statistical perspective the estimated probability of loss will only apply if the units that are exposed to loss, are independent. Exposures that are not independent, that is, risks that are correlated, exhibit a minimum level of risk which cannot be diversified away. Such risks are therefore difficult to underwrite. Examples of such risks include earthquake and unemployment.
- ☐ The occurrence of the event insured against must be fortuitous. Strictly interpreted, this means that the timing and severity of the loss should be entirely out of the control of the insured. Of course, this requirement is not met literally, since most perils are subject to some degree of control by the insured. Indeed, the fact that many losses are within the control of the insured provides the underlying assumption of risk management and risk control activity.

---

8 It is recognised that a peril may theoretically fail to meet one or more of the requirements, but that insurers overcome such 'disqualification' through practical controls found in underwriting, policy provisions, and rating techniques.

9 Reference should be made to section 13.3 which discusses the statistical properties and results where risks are heterogeneous but independent, and where the risks are not independent, ie, where they are correlated.

However, what the requirement contemplates is the following: That the outcome of the event is not known in advance by the insured;[10] that moral hazards[11] are not the subject of insurance; also that underwriters are reluctant to insure in situations where there may be an incentive by the insured to exploit a loss, as is the case where amounts of insurance in relation to say property values or income levels, is excessive.

- ☐ If the peril insured against produces a loss, this must be definite in time and quantum. This requirement can be seen as a statistical and administrative one: in order to correctly adjust claims and accurately reflect liabilities, the insurer must be capable of substantiating losses.

  In practice, insurable perils meet this requirement only in varying degrees. The timing and severity of loss is often not easily determinable (such as for instance in cases involving health and fidelity guarantee insurance). This indefiniteness of loss in time and quantum introduces an element of moral hazard, which makes the underwriting of such covers more difficult.

- ☐ The premium must be reasonable in relation to the potential financial loss. This requirement has implications relative to both insurer and insured.

  From an insurer's viewpoint, there must be economic sense in providing insurance; an economic premium to risk relationship implies that there exists some minimum premium, hence risk exposure, which the insurer requires to make insurance viable. Thus, in the case of covers relating to individuals or households where the potential financial loss is small (relatively), the insurer would require an aggregation of exposures, or simply stated, sufficient volume of business.

  From an insured's perspective, it is also not sound financial management to insure against perils that have a high probability of occurrence. The suggestion here is that where perils display high probability of loss (and usually are accurately predictable), the insurance mechanism represents a weak method of financing.

  What is entailed, in essence, is 'dollar-swapping', and given the insurer's inherent costs of administration, these, added to the high frequency claim costs, result in a premium that approaches (and may even surpass) the value of the potential loss. It is, in part, such rationale that has prompted the consideration and growth of 'self-insurance' mechanisms as a means of providing for such category risks.[12]

---

10 With regard to life insurance, the outcome of death is certain and indeed known in advance by the insured. However, the risk to be considered is not **whether** the insured will die, but rather **when** the insured will die.

11 See Chapter Three, section 3.5.

12 The question of risk retention is examined in Chapter Eleven.

The implication is not that the advantages of pooling are not in evidence, but that infra-structurally, insurers 'disqualify' themselves from providing a cost efficient means of financing.[13]

13.5 Financial treatment of speculative risk through insurance

As discussed in Chapter Three, section 3.4, risk can be classified into pure and speculative. The distinction is made since it is generally accepted that insurance applies to pure risk situations. There are cases however where insurance applied to speculative-type risks is evident. An example of such a case is the availability of mortgage guarantee arrangements to indemnify the mortgagee for losses through mortgage default.

The following reasons are cited for the non-insurability of speculative risk.

- ☐ **Firstly**, there is limited availability of adequate statistics to enable one to predict probability of loss. It can also be argued that even if there were such statistics available, events may not evidence a satisfactory degree of regularity to permit accurate prediction.
- ☐ **Secondly**, the probability of loss may be too high to make insurance a practical mechanism, given an inherent administration cost and requisite return for the risk assumed. Whilst this argument is presented in the context of speculative risk it does also often apply in the realm of pure risk. As discussed earlier, where the probability of loss is high (even in pure risk situations) economic or cost constraints may render insurance unsuitable, when compared to other forms of financing risk, such as self-insurance mechanisms, for instance.
- ☐ **Thirdly**, the most important reason for not insuring speculative risk, is that the process would be self-defeating. The assumption of risk by individuals is based mostly on the expectation of gain; to insure against the possibility of loss would substantially reduce or eliminate the extent of gain since the premium required would in theory approximate closely the expected return. Paradoxically, the insuring of speculative risk, or say business risk, would in this instance represent real transfer of risk from the individual or business unit to the insurer.

Thus, from an economic standpoint, insurance of speculative (business) risk is questionable. The substantial premium required would lead to uneconomical output and the reduction of profit. Also, it may be argued

13 Regrettably, insurers sometimes do not appreciate the rationale offered and are opponents and critics of 'self-insurance' mechanisms. There exists in South Africa a small minority of insurers who have recognised these cost constraints (in so far as this category of risk is concerned) and who have developed 'niche-market' insurance products.

that transfer of such risk is superfluous, for, if it were the intention to transfer risk to the insurer, then this could otherwise be achieved by the insurer purchasing the business unit's shares or stock.

This being the case with speculative risk, the question may still be asked as to why in the progression of insurance contract sophistication, more and more economic-type risks are sought to be insured.

It is accepted, for example, that when insuring the value of an asset, not only the material value is considered but also the economic value attached to such asset. Loss of profits insurance resulting from a pure risk event is commonplace.

But further along the spectrum there is evidence of insurers being requested to consider insuring risks considerably detached from the definition of pure risk with the view of facilitating the operations of business units. An example that could be cited is residual value insurance which would guarantee some minimum economic value attaching to an asset after a determined period of time.

The answer to this question or phenomenon lies within two broad interpretations. First: one should be circumspect in defining economic or speculative risk. There exists a wide spectrum of economic risk where one could, for example, perceive **resultant economic loss** from a predefined **pure risk** at the one extremity and business risk proper (the speculative risk assumed because of possibility of gain) at the other.

Often therefore, there is loose definition of the risk in question. The point made earlier is that the 'extreme' case of speculative risk displays no economic rationale in favour of insurance. Stated in a different way, if one introduced further descriptive parameters to economic risk – being **end** risk and **intermediate** risk, then the extreme case of pure business risk represents an *end* economic risk for which risk elimination or diversification through insurance becomes futile or superfluous.[14]

The second interpretation offered stems in fact from the descriptive parameter of *intermediate* economic risk. One could define such intermediate risk as a series of risks which in the aggregate constitute or result in end economic risk. Such intermediate risks are *de facto* speculative in nature but do not represent the *de jure* economic risk taken by the business unit in its attempt to procure gain.

---

14 The conceptualisation of end and *intermediate* economic risk arises from an attempt to define those economic risks that can, theoretically, be insured against, and the setting of fundamental principles upon which any request for such insurance may be founded. In the final analysis, the conclusion which is sought to be motivated is that:
- if the risk is classed as *intermediate* economic risk, then insurance is theoretically possible, given the normal criteria for risk diversification through pooling etc. that apply to insurers
- if the risk is identified as *end* economic risk, then there exists no economic rationale for risk elimination through insurance. The insurer would in effect be diversifying horizontally by virtue of his investing in the 'insured' business.

The choice of the word *intermediate* in this context is not without design. The modern-day interpretation of the business of an insurer is that it acts as a financial **intermediary**: in exchange for a pre-paid fee [the premium], the cost of financing reinvestment is transferred to a financial intermediary [the insurer].[1]

With such a broad based financial approach to the definition of insurance, it can be argued that the class of **intermediate economic risk** may be added to the class of risks for which insurance is a feasible risk elimination or reduction technique (given, of course, the requisite criteria for the insurer to assume risk in the first place). Hence, this viewpoint suggests and encourages a more penetrating participation by insurers in the wider spectrum of risks facing the business environment.

Given the necessary information, knowledge and spread of risk, insurers could consider insuring (or part-insuring) intermediate economic risk (which would have the effect of reducing end economic risk to some extent) without refuting the basic economic rationale for a business accepting business risk. So long as the economic risk is **incidental** there may be opportunity for insurers to **intermediate** and to thereby offer business units a further risk management possibility or outlet.[15]

13.6 Insurance pricing (rate-making) theory

13.6.1 Scope of discussion

This section discusses the theory behind the rate-making process - a 'rate' being defined as the price an insurer charges for each unit of risk accepted (or, from the standpoint of the insured, the price per unit of protection afforded). Particular attention is given to the following areas:

- ☐ the nature and principles of rate-making
- ☐ problems in deriving rates
- ☐ general methods of calculating premium rates.

13.6.2 Nature and principles of rate-making

> The premium that an insured pays for coverage is simply derived by multiplying the appropriate rate by the number of homogeneous exposure units (units of risk).

15 The broadening of insurers' rôle along the lines stated represents a novel and significant area for research in the future. Using the argument presented above, a most recent market has been developed, where the insurer accepts the intermediate economic risk of currency fluctuation to which, importers for example, are subjected. This aspect was also discussed in Chapter Four, section 4.2.

Hence, the premium reflects both the likelihood of occurrence of loss and the size of the potential loss. Viewed in such a manner, it follows that a lower premium will result from both a reduction in exposure value, and, say, from a superior quality of the risk insured.

The rate-making function, from an insurer's standpoint is seen as the process of predicting claims and expenses following the assumption of risk, and then apportioning the estimated claims and expenses, including the required profit margins to the various classes of policyholders.[16] In practice however, this process is not so precise and refined that it can readily justify the rate to the parties involved with the insurance arrangement.

This apportionment applies across various classes of policyholders, and therefore, prior to computing a rate it is necessary to select and group the types or classes of risks for which the rate will apply. **Rate-making classifications** are required both in predicting claims and in allocating costs. Such risk classification attempts to identify homogeneous risks where loss characteristics are similar, and which then make possible the allocation of costs (including profit) to the risk as a function of its profile and size.

Earlier, under the section that examined the circumstances under which an insurer will accept risks, the question of **loss predictability** was reviewed. Obviously, this factor in the rate determination process is the most significant.[17] Suffice it to say that the procedure relies principally upon the operation of the law of large numbers. Given the caveats mentioned earlier, it is possible to estimate within reasonable accuracy the ratio of losses to total exposures.

A problem with premium rates is, of course, that they apply to a period of time subsequent to the time they were calculated. In so far as conditions of the past (reflected in the loss experience and used to predict future losses) differ from those expected in the future, adjustments to the

---

16 In the case of certain methods of rate determination, such as for example retrospective plans, the process is somewhat different. Retro-plans may be described as a partly post-loss financing technique and hence the rate utilises the experience of the **past** period to determine the rate for **that period**.

17 People's perception of this aspect of loss predictability, may range from intrigue to disbelief, and the operations of insurers have often been likened to gambling.

It may be opportune at this juncture to draw attention to the fundamental differences between insurance and gambling. Both transactions require the payment of a relatively small amount in exchange for the return of a much greater amount upon the occurrence of a chance event. However, with insurance, should the event occur, the recovery under the contract does not (purport to) enhance the participant's (insured) asset or wealth position. Gambling, on the other hand, is a speculative risk where the participant has a chance of gain or loss. Moreover, the risk is non-existent until the gambler creates it. An insured, though, is exposed to the risk whether he chooses to insure or not; the insurance transaction reduces the possible financial impact resulting from the uncertainty.

statistics and hence to the rate must be made. Such adjustments will necessarily introduce an element of subjectivity to an otherwise objective basis of predictability. But, as Hurley[2] writes:

> . . . This is no denial of the value of statistics . . . It is solely a reminder that improper rates can result from statistics – when the statistics are an imperfect representation of future loss expectancies.

In addition to the determination of risk categories and the prediction of claims, the **prediction and allocation of expenses** is a constituent of rate-making.

In most lines of insurance the expense component is smaller than the component used to cover the cost of losses. Claims predictions of many insurer organisations are similar for several lines of insurance or risk, and the competitiveness therefore of a particular rate most often depends on the element of costs and margin for surplus and profit.[18] One should also note that expenses often constitute a proportionate addition to the pure premium, as many expense items vary somewhat directly with the size of the basic premium. There is naturally the fixed cost element which is not a function of the pure premium.

As concerns the margin element, this includes a contingency allowance and a provision for profit (or for surplus in the case of the insurance mutual). The allowance is designed to provide funds to offset adverse claims experience by the insurer. In the event of the contingency not materialising, such allowances may become additions to profit or surplus. Although the profit factor can be considered and accounted for in various ways, insurance companies tend to use realistic assumptions with respect to claims and expenses and then add an additional margin as a provision for profit.[19]

13.6.3 Problems in rate derivation

It may be said that insurance pricing involves problems not ordinarily encountered in the setting of prices for other services and products. As has been shown, the price-setting in the insurance market demonstrates

18 The expenses that an insurer would need to typically consider are marketing (acquisition) costs, office administrative expenses (infrastructural) and claims settling costs. When one considers total costs per the classical economic definition, then included in these is the normal profit element required to be in the business of insurance.

19 One other significant element accounted for in the rate is the investment income element. Although strictly speaking it may be argued that investment income accruing to insurers should fall outside the factors which determine rates, since such factors should reflect only the underwriting considerations facing the insurer, in practice one finds that the investment climate plays an important rôle. Investment underwriting has been identified as having a contributing influence on insurance pricing cycles.

The point of view taken in this section covering the nature and principles of rate-setting is a purist one, which divorces the influence of investment income from the underwriting activities of insurers. However, the reader is referred to Valsamakis (1983, 6-8; 120-65).

a myriad of subjective and anticipatory facets. Apart from these problems associated with the statistical and anticipatory nature of insurance, there are a few specific issues which warrant inspection and which are now discussed.

The nature of insurance and particularly the social responsibility attached to insurers affording protection to society in general has encouraged regulation to some extent, or at least public inspection which often requires detailed justification of the internal composition of a rate structure. This is difficult in most businesses, even with developed cost-accounting techniques and in insurance the problem is more pronounced.

Notwithstanding this difficulty, in a sense there exists the objective of reconciling on the one hand the fiduciary responsibility of insurers (implying an **adequacy** in pricing/contingency provision) with **reasonableness** and **equity** (as relates to the fair treatment of individual insureds), on the other.

A trade-off represents a problem in its own right, but it becomes exaggerated when applied to the insurance market. Whilst the strength of the underlying statistics of large insurers usually lends considerable accuracy to loss predictions, in many cases the experience of one company is insufficient in volume to facilitate a close prediction. As a result, one finds a form of price co-operation being practised, and even cartelisation, especially in a hard market cycle when insurers attempt to recover from losses incurred and restore their solvency margins. This can be seen as being contrary to economic philosophy and even statute.

It is of course difficult to measure, let alone ensure, acceptable degrees of reasonableness and equity. The nature of the problem is apparent by the excessive fluctuations in insurance pricing and availability of capacity as the market moves through its cycle. This implies that the market swings from a position of fierce price competition (when underwriting principles are often ignored) to a position of 'extreme' price regulation. When one adopts the definition of an insurer as being a financial intermediary facilitating transfer from supply to demand, this problem then comes further to the fore. One can only conclude that the price instability denotes an intermediary mechanism that at present is imperfect and undeveloped. It is interesting that price instability has been a factor encouraging self-retention of risk which is evidence of the market's inability as a mechanism to efficiently facilitate transfer.

In Chapter Three economic considerations for treating risk were discussed. As such, the rationale and requirements necessary for market formation were advanced. The possible sources of market failure were also examined and particular attention was directed at the question of adverse selection resulting from asymmetrical information between supply and demand.[20] With respect to the question of rate derivation, asymmetrical information introduces the problem of *moral hazard*, which is now appraised.

> Moral hazard is the behavioural effect that insurance might have on the level of effort or expenditure devoted to loss-reducing activities.[3][21]

Given that the value of individual and corporate wealth (property value) is reduced by risky events and by claims from employees, third parties, defective products, and the like, any expenditure effected with a view to reducing the probability or severity of loss will benefit the owner and increase value. There is thus an incentive to protect ownership rights and to undertake forms of protection which yield benefits in excess of costs.

An insurance policy, however, which transfers the cost of losses from the owner to the insurer reduces the pay-off to any expenditure on loss reduction and removes the incentive for the owner. In order to restore such incentive, the insurer may modify the pricing structure or the conditions of cover. Hence, rate reductions may be allowed for installation of preventative devices, and premium increases may be considered for adverse risk features.

The problem, though, arises from the inequality in the information on loss reduction available to the insured and insurer. Although the insurer may be able to distinguish some form of loss-reducing activity or feature in the insured's operations, it may not be possible to observe everyday housekeeping and work practices that may give rise to perils insured against. These unobserved practices cannot be controlled or rewarded by pricing adjustments or contract conditions. Consequently, insurers may not be able to charge the correct rate or premium.

From the insured's or risk manager's viewpoint, moral hazard is simply rational economic behaviour. The rational risk manager would take account of any premium incentive in designing a risk control programme since the premium saving offered to the insured may represent a major part of his expected benefit.[22]

20 Adverse selection of insureds poses a problem to insurers with regard to rate derivation. Basically, the heterogeneity of insureds as concerns their utility curves and indifference premiums may mean that insurance is offered at premium levels which cannot support profit to underwriters. There is asymmetry in the information which may disallow differential pricing, so that the better risks no longer buy cover leaving a higher proportion of relatively poorer risks to share the costs of benefit payments.
Reference can be made to Chapter Three, section 3.10.2.

21 Unfortunately the term **moral hazard** has emotional connotations which often confuse the understanding of the issue in question. It should be pointed out that activities categorised under the label moral hazard are neither unethical nor illegal.

22 It is not suggested that the risk manager should become unconcerned about risk control or try to deceive the insurer about loss expectancies. Rather, the rational risk manager should take account of the economic issues involved following expenditure on any risk control programme.

This argument supports the view that premiums, sensitive to changes in the expected value of loss, will serve the purpose of conveying to the insured information on the effectiveness of different forms of loss reduction. To the extent that asymmetry of information remains a feature in the market, then the efficient dissemination of loss prevention information will be frustrated.[23]

13.6.4 General methods of calculating rates

Fundamental approaches

There are two fundamental approaches that may be taken by insurers in setting rates and premiums. Paradoxically, the two approaches exemplify somewhat conflicting philosophies. The two approaches are **class rate-making** and **individual risk rating**. The latter approach takes more direct cognisance of the individual's loss experience and risk characteristics when setting premium rates.

☐ **Class rates**

> A class rate is obtained by apportioning the anticipated losses and expenses for a given class of peril or coverage across all the exposure units.

This procedure incorporates, naturally, the pooling or averaging principle which is the foundation of insurance. It implies that the losses of the less fortunate are subsidised by the premium payments of the more fortunate. Hence, losses of a particular policyholder affects the rate only to the extent that such losses generate a change in the **class** rate.

The derivation of class rates involves all of the problems associated with selection of risk categories, and the prediction of losses and expenses; judgement too plays a determinant rôle in class rate calculations. As few risks fall into distinct categories, or classes, judgement is required to set class boundaries and ensure homogeneity of risk.

☐ **Individual or experience risk rating**

With the growing concern by organisations over the management of risk and the expenditure toward insurance, the class rating method has come under criticism, as it is seen to be discriminatory. Policyholders who have better than average loss experience argue that the

23 As Doherty (1985, 71) points out, there are several features of the insurance market that lend support to the view that insurers disseminate appropriate loss-prevention information:
- Competition tends to lead to premium rates/structures that discriminate among risks according to loss expectancies.
- Insurers often pool their information to refine their data base.
- Insurers, and typically Reinsurers, employ technical experts to survey risks in order to convey information to underwriters and insureds.

broad classes should be restructured into more homogeneous groups which further distinguish 'better' risks from others.

> Individual risk rating is based on the principle that the number of exposure units of some insureds is sufficiently large to conclude that losses that are (or are not) incurred reflect to some degree the actual characteristics of the risk of the particular insured.

Hence, individual risk rates reflect more directly the actual loss experience of particular policyholders. The nature of this approach has prompted the usage of the term *experience rating.*

The application of individual risk rating raises, however, a broad question concerning the function of insurance. In the extreme, every insured will pay his own losses and the pooling function of insurance is destroyed. It can be assumed, on the other hand, that some form of pooling is involved, because those losses that exceed expectations (under experience rated situations) are subsidised by those with fewer losses than anticipated.

It follows that as predictability of loss becomes more certain, so is the pooling effect minimised. Under these conditions insurance becomes a non-efficient method of treating the financial consequences of risk – a point made earlier in the chapter.

From the point of view of equity, the technique is seen as appropriate, although some argue that the general result of individual rate-making has probably been to increase class rates.[4] It is felt that insurers have disquietly adopted the approach, as a result of competitive necessity. All observers recognise, nevertheless, that individual risk rating will continue to grow in use.

There are basically three methods of individual risk rating to be considered, namely:

(i) experience rating

(ii) retrospective rating

(iii) schedule rating.[24]

– **Experience rating**

This technique utilises the **past** loss experience of a particular insured to determine, at least in part, the rate to be paid in the

24 It should be noted that the generic definition of individual rating does not explicitly include schedule rating, which most observers would categorise as more of a class rating technique. However, since this was one of the earliest forms of individual rating, purporting to identify physical characteristics for a given type of exposure, it is listed under the form of individual rating.

future.[5] The experience rates are **prospective**, where the basic formula used is

(A – E)/E 13.4

where

A = the actual losses, and

E = losses expected to be incurred.

The experience rate derived as shown above would then be applied to the basic formula used.

> For example, if a firm incurred actual losses of R50 000 in a given period, when it was expected to incur losses of R100 000, then the rate for the following period would be reduced by fifty percent. To the resultant rate must be added the expense element and consideration must be given to the size of risk. Thus, the rate of an insured may not be determined entirely by his past experience.

– **Retro-rating**

> A retrospective rate utilises the experience of the **past** period to determine the rate for **that period**.[6]

Usually, retro-rating requires the payment of a deposit (often minimum) premium at the inception of the policy protection period, and then the policyholder's experience for the period determines whether he receives a partial refund or pays an additional amount. There is also a maximum premium provision.

This method is the closest possible approach to self-rating, where the insurance would be merely a service contract that provided no real protection against the risk. The maximum premium, however, does ensure that the insured's payments will not exceed a given amount even in the light of inordinately high losses.

In essence, the technique provides cover only above the maximum premium, with the insurer providing a claims service below that level, which cost is catered for in the minimum premium paid by the insured.[25]

25 There has been a considerable amount of concern by insurers over the use of retro-plans, since the technique largely dismisses their major function of risk handling. Again, viewing an insurer as an intermediary mechanism for financing risk places this argument in a different light. In any event, the increased use of self-insurance has forced insurers to offer retrospective-rated contracts.

- **Schedule rating**

> Schedule rating uses a schedule which enumerates supposedly average physical characteristics for a given type of policyholder, and each insured is compared with the schedule, for rating purposes.

This comparison then determines the extent to which the appropriate class rate is modified.

The technique requires the actual inspection of the property being insured, and tends to place emphasis on the physical characteristics, although some non-physical aspects (for example safety programmes) are also considered. The process does, however, rely on judgement particularly when a physical feature varies from the average.

Schedule-rating was first developed for fire insurance, and is still used today in this field of insurance. In this connection its use as a technique has been rationalised on the following basis by Hurley:[7]

> It is generally accepted that over-all rate levels and classification relativities . . . must take into consideration the actual loss statistics. However, there are many students of the business who believe that final individual risk rates on an important segment of the fire insurance business are most equitably distributed by the schedule rating approach . . . It may well be that fire loss expectancy for other than trivial losses may be of such a low order of magnitude that a fire rating system based solely on loss statistics may prove not feasible within the normal tolerances for credibility standards.

13.7 Specific policies

13.7.1 Insurance and the risk manager

Insurance remains the single most important method of financing the consequences of pure risk and the risk manager needs to have a firm grasp of a number of insurance issues.

In particular he needs to understand the law of contracts and how this law applies to the insurance contract, the law of insurance,[26] specific insurance contracts, insurance practice, insurance regulation,[27] cover

26 The leading South African textbooks on the law of the insurance contract are Getz and LAWSA.

27 Regulation includes the *Insurance Act, Medical Schemes Act, Co-operatives Act.*

provided by the various statutory funds,[28] various insurance markets.[29]

It is not intended to deal with all of these at this point but only to review the more common types of insurance policies available.

13.7.2 Specific markets and insurance policies

13.7.2.1 *The marine and the aviation markets*

Marine[30]

The oldest class of insurance is marine insurance. Persons involved in a marine venture are exposed to what is referred to as the *perils of the sea*,[31] *perils on the sea* and extraneous risk. These perils operate to cause loss or damage. Ships are lost at sea; cargo is lost at sea. The cost of transporting the cargo (freight) is paid, but since the cargo is lost, the expenditure is lost. Lives are lost at sea. Liability claims can be instituted as a consequence of a marine venture.

The marine policy is in the first instance assets policy.

The most famous form of marine policy was the so-called Lloyd's SG policy[32] which was phased out in 1982 with the introduction of the *Lloyd's Marine Policy* (the MAR Form) and the *Companies Marine Policy of the Institute of London Underwriters*. It is however the Institute Clauses that are important. The first of these, the '1888 Time Clauses' were accepted by the Institute of London Underwriters in 1888, and were subsequently issued annually. Each complete set of Institute Clauses to be used with the Lloyd's policy, constitutes a self-contained insurance cover.

English Marine Insurance Law was codified at the turn of the century in terms of the *Marine Insurance Act* (1906). This Act is very important since essentially it is a codification of not only marine insurance law, but insurance law in general.

An unusual risk to which the person who uses marine transport is exposed, is the risk of 'general average' being declared. General average loss is described as follows in the *Marine Insurance Act*.

28 Workmen's Compensation, Third Party motor insurance, Insolvency legislation.

29 The South African market, the United Kingdom market, to a lesser extent the American market and Lloyd's.

30 Many insurers produce easy-to-read publications on the various classes of insurance. See for example Mellert (1989) for an explanation of marine insurance.

31 The term *perils of the sea* lacks precise definition but has been in use for several centuries. It has been traced back to Walford Insurance Encyclopedia (1541).

32 A copy of the policy, referred to in terms of section 30 of the *Marine Insurance Act* (1906), is annexed to the Act as the First Schedule. This same form of policy was affixed to the *Stamp Act* (1795). The wording is far from easy to understand, and as far back as 1791 it was called 'an absurd and incoherent document'. Nevertheless the document was in use for 200 years.

- ☐ A general average loss is a loss caused by or directly consequential on a general average act. It includes a general average expenditure as well as a general average sacrifice.
- ☐ There is a general average act where any extraordinary sacrifice or expenditure is voluntarily and reasonably made or incurred in time of peril for the purpose of preserving the property imperilled in the common adventure.
- ☐ Where there is a general average loss, the party on whom it falls is entitled, subject to the conditions imposed by maritime law, to a rateable contribution from the other parties interested, and such contribution is called a general average contribution.
- ☐ Subject to any express provision in the policy, where the assured has incurred a general average expenditure, he may recover from the insurer in respect of the proportion of the loss which falls upon him; and, in the case of a general average sacrifice, he may recover from the insurer in respect of the whole loss without having enforced his right of contribution from the other parties liable to contribute.
- ☐ Subject to any express provision in the policy, where the assured has paid, or is liable to pay, a general average contribution in respect of the subject insured, he may recover therefore from the insurer.
- ☐ In the absence of express stipulation, the insurer is not liable for any general average loss or contribution where the loss was not incurred for the purpose of avoiding, or in connexion with the avoidance of, a peril insured against.
- ☐ Where ship, freight, and cargo, or any two of those interests, are owned by the same assured, the liability of the insurer in respect of general average losses or contributions is to be determined as if those subjects were owned by different persons.

Persons engaged in a marine venture are exposed to legal liability claims. However, the usual marine cover provided by the *Institute Time Clauses (Hulls)* (1/10/83) does not provide full protection against liability claims, but only limited cover in terms of the so-called *3/4 Collision Liability Clause*.[33] The liability of the insurer is limited to three-quarters of the amount paid by the insured as a consequence of liability claims. The obligation of the insurer is limited to three-quarters of the insured value of the insured vessel and the clause does not cover the costs of the insured for the removal of wrecks, loss of life, personal injury or pollution.

It is clear that very limited marine liability cover is provided.

☐ **Protection & Indemnity Clubs** (P&I Clubs)
Since the marine policy only provides limited liability cover, a need exists to provide a more comprehensive protection. In the marine market this need is filled by the P&I Clubs.[34]

33 Some writers refer to this as the *Running Down Clause* (RDC).
34 For a discussion of the P&I Clubs consult Dillon & Van Niekerk (1983).

Aviation insurance

Aviation insurance is a modern addition to the insurance industry. However, since both the marine and aviation markets concern forms of transportation, the tendency in modern theory is to deal with marine and aviation jointly.

Aviation gives rise to a number of risks: loss or damage to the aircraft (hull), loss or damage to cargo; cost of search for missing aircraft; extensive liabilities attached to people on the ground; liability to crew and passengers.

Some forms of aviation liability are governed by legislation and international treaties.

13.7.2.2 *Fire insurance*

The next comprehensive short-term insurance market to develop was the fire market. This policy provides indemnification against loss or damage of assets from a specific peril, namely fire. A fire can be caused by a number of factors. An earthquake can be preceded (sometimes by a mere few seconds) or followed by fires. Other perils such as explosions can precede the fire or be caused by the fire.

In such cases confusion arises as to the cause of or the proximate cause of the loss incurred: fire, explosion or earthquake. The tendency was either to exclude fire as a result of the other natural perils or to extend the fire policy to provide indemnification against a variety of natural perils.

The fire-fighting process could entail a variety of expenses as the fire department may levy a charge for their services. After the fire, indirect costs such as the employment of accountants to quantify the cost of the loss can be incurred. In order to rebuild the damaged asset, the service of architects may be required. If a factory has to be rebuilt, the municipal regulations may have changed and increased costs may be incurred to meet the higher standards. It may be desirable not to replace the building in exactly the same manner as it was before the fire, but to make use of the opportunity of the rebuilding of the factory to carry out capital improvements. It may also take some time for the building to be rebuilt, by which time inflation has reduced the value of the money. It may also be necessary to make provision for infraction in the policy.

After centuries of experience, the modern fire policy is a very sophisticated policy designed to cater for a wide range of costs associated with fire and natural perils.

13.7.2.3 *Accident market*

The development of railtransport and factories led to the desire to be compensated for an accident. This gave rise to a number of accident policies: railway accident, employer's liability (which initially was not actually liability-based but accident-based and gave rise to the workmen's compensation movement and employee benefits), personal accident policies. It was customary for large insurance companies to have accident departments.

The following is a list of covers listed by the Liverpool & London & Globe in 1936:

- Accident (Personal) and Disease
- Aviation (Personal Accident)
- Boiler
- Cash in Transit
- Combined Domestic
- Commercial Motor Vehicles
- Court and Government Bonds
- Defects of Title
- Driving Accidents
- Farmers' Public Liability
- Gas Engines
- Golfers' Indemnity
- Householders' Comprehensive
- Innkeepers' Liability
- Live Stock (Horses and Cattle)
- Machinery
- Missing Documents
- Motor Cycles
- Oil Cabinets
- Personal Accident
- Petrol Pump Installations
- Private Cars
- Public Liability
- Refrigerating Plant
- Securities in Transit
- Sports Club Indemnity
- Third Party (Farmers)
- Tourists' and Travellers' Personal Accident
- Traders' Collective
- Travellers' Baggage
- Workmen's Compensation
- 'All Risks'
- Boarding Housekeepers' Liability
- Burglary, Private House and Business Premises
- Contingency
- Cycle
- Domestic Servants
- Electrical Plant
- Fidelity Guarantee
- Goods in Transit
- Gun Risks
- Hold up
- Lifts, Hoists and Cranes
- Lost Document Indemnity
- Missing Beneficiaries
- Money, Insurance of
- Motor Traders' Road and Garage Risks
- Personal Liability
- Plate Glass
- Property Owners' Indemnity
- Redeemable Securities
- Schools' Public Liability
- Sickness and Accident
- Steam Engines
- Third Party (Schools)
- Tractor
- Time Loss (Power Plant Breakdown)
- Wireless

The modern motor, liability and consequential loss policies developed from the accident markets that were created at the turn of the century.

It is still usual today for companies to retain the 'accident' structure in reporting and controlling results. To a degree it is necessary because of reinsurance treaties.

13.7.2.4 *Motor policies and markets*

Because of the magnitude of business in the motor class, modern practice tends to treat motor policies as a separate class.

The operators of motor vehicles are exposed to a number of risks. Firstly they are exposed to the loss or damage of the motor vehicle itself. This is normally covered in terms of section A of the motor policy, which is essentially an assets policy. Certain assets associated with the vehicle or risks cannot be covered because of their nature. Damage to tyres and springs not associated with an accident is not covered, nor is wear and tear on the vehicle. Generally consequential losses are not covered, except possibly the cost of towing and transportation of the damaged vehicle.

The operators are exposed to legal liability claims and provision to indemnify the insured and other persons is catered for in terms of section B of the policy. Finally, persons may be injured and limited provision is made to pay for medical costs associated with the motor accident in terms of section C of the policy.

13.7.2.5 *Consequential loss market*

It has always been realised that when people are injured or assets are damaged, consequential losses of a financial nature arise. Thus an injured person who is unable to work loses his income. A building destroyed by fire cannot produce the rent income for the landlord. Without a specific extension these losses are not covered by an asset policy such as the fire policy. Consequential loss policies developed during this century to cater for the losses which arise as a consequence of loss-producing events.

Consequential losses can be treated as part of the market that deals with the major perils. Thus consequential losses arising as a result of fire can be treated as a part of the fire market, while conseqential losses arising as a result of machinery breakdown is part of the engineering market.

13.7.2.6 *Liability policies*

Liability developed as part of the accident market but is today regarded as a separate form of insurance. In addition to the general liability a number of specific forms of liability cover exists. As noted, the marine hull cover provides a measure of liability cover. Section B of the motor policy provides liability cover and the aviation policy also provides liability cover.

The purpose of the liability policy is to indemnify the insured against amounts that he becomes legally liable to pay, usually (except in professional liability policies) arising from accidental loss or damage or injury to persons. The cover is essentially in line with the damage to property or injury to people. Liability for pure financial loss is not covered, nor are claims for violation of personal rights such as defamation, without special extensions.

Bibliography

Biger, N & Kahane, Y 1978. 'Risk considerations in insurance ratemaking.' *Journal of Risk and Insurance.* Vol. 45.

Brigham, EF 1985. *Financial management: Theory and practice.* New York: The Dryden Press.

Cummins, JD & Nye, D 1980. 'The stochastic characteristics of property liability insurance company underwriting profits.' *Journal of Risk and Insurance.* Vol. 47.

Cummins, JD & Harrington, S 1985. 'Property liability insurance rate regulation: Estimation of underwriting betas using quarterly profit data.' *Journal of Risk and Insurance.* Vol. 52.

Denenberg, HS, Eilers, RD, Melone, JJ & Zelten, RA 1974. *Risk and Insurance.* Englewood Cliffs, New Jersey: Prentice-Hall Inc.

Dillon, C & van Niekerk, JP 1983. *South African maritime law and marine insurance – selected topics. Durban: Butterworth.*

Doherty, NA 1985. *Corporate risk management – A financial exposition.* New York: McGraw-Hill Inc.

Freund, JE, Williams, FJ & Perles, BM 1988. *Elementary business statistics. The modern approach.* Englewood Cliffs, New Jersey: Prentice-Hall Inc.

Hurley, RL 1962. 'Review of a paper on 'The probability of A – M/N'.' (by Henry K Duke). *Annals of the Society of Chartered Property and Casualty Underwriters.* Vol. XV, No. 2.

Mellert, WM 1989. 'Marine insurance.' *Swiss Re.*

Valsamakis, AC 1983. *The investment policies and practices of South African long and short-term insurers.* Unpublished M.Com. Dissertation, University of the Witwatersrand.

Endnotes

[1] Doherty, 1985, 248.

[2] Hurley, 1962, 188.

[3] Doherty, 1985, 69-70.

[4] Denenberg, *et al.*, 1974, 519.

[5] Denenberg, *et al.*, 1974, 520.

[6] Denenberg, *et al.*, 1974, 520.

[7] Hurley, 1962, 187.

14 STATISTICAL ANALYSIS IN RISK MANAGEMENT AND COMPOSITE STRATEGIES: TRANSFER OPTIMISATION

14.1 Introduction

The two preceding chapters dealt with insurance and retention respectively as a pre-loss means of financing the consequences of pure risk exposures. Evident in the discussions is the interrelationship between these strategies. Both financing means were evaluated from the point of view of the firm's objective of maximising value which entailed the consideration of alternative sources of finance and their associated costs.

Although not ignoring the post-loss alternative sources of finance, the discussion has centred more around the problem of a composite retention/insurance strategy, given that certain practical considerations modify the value maximisation and risk management objective. The aspect of risk finance integration or optimisation now needs to be explored.

From the standpoint of risk retention, the firm acts as its own underwriter. In so doing it becomes imperative that the statistical properties of the risk (retained) are understood. If there is to be optimal transfer to the insurance market, for example, this cannot be achieved without the process of statistical analysis – the two aspects thus become interlinked in the risk management discipline. Hence, this chapter considers and combines both the area of statistical analysis in risk management and the question of optimal composite financing strategy.

Statistical analysis in risk management entails the accurate estimation of loss costs and probabilities. In exhibiting its importance the following should be considered:

- ☐ such estimates are essential for decision-making in risk retention and self-funding plans, providing dimensions such as estimates of maximum probable yearly aggregate loss
- ☐ the analysis enables by a risk-return exercise, to identify economies of risk retention
- ☐ the analysis is useful in designing and placing insurance packages because of the need for accurate statistics when 'marketing' the firm's risk to potential insurance markets.[1]

In Chapter Three, an introduction to the theory of probability and its application to risk measurement was provided. The intention was only to afford

1 This point is becoming increasingly significant. The rôle of statistics in the marketing of risk to potential insurance markets is now being regarded in a more serious light. Increasingly, attention is now being paid to data quality and the numeric ability of risk managers, consultants and insurance brokers. It is possibly fair to state that considerable asymmetry in information has arisen in the past because of unclear lines of responsibility as concerns the collation and dissemination of loss statistics and a general lack of appreciation of the importance of loss experience statistics. The dynamic nature of insurance coupled with the more deliberate and scientific approach to risk management has altered perceptions about statistics considerably.

an initial outline which could assist in the development and understanding of such concepts as long-term expected costs, and pure risk (premium) to insurers; to which reference would be made in the subsequent chapters. The chapter also introduced the concepts of regret and utility to explain decision-making under conditions of risk.

The section in this chapter which covers statistical analysis must be seen, therefore, as an extension of the statistical theory developed earlier; and deals with the more sophisticated aspects surrounding the prediction of loss costs and associated probabilities.

The section that follows, covers composite financing strategies. The concern here, is with the prospect of the optimal form of financing requiring a package drawing on two or more competing sources; for example, the use of debt, internal liquid resources and insurance. The primary consideration however, is the partial use of insurance, that is, the integration of insurance and retention funding as an optimal composite financing strategy. The integration of insurance and retention funding requires a statistical analysis to be conducted. This provides the reasoning for combining, in one chapter, the subjects of statistical analysis as applied in risk management and transfer optimisation.

14.2 Statistical analysis in risk management

14.2.1 Maximum probable yearly aggregate loss (*MPY*) and estimated maximum loss (*EML*)

In statistical analysis, the concern is primarily with data inputs which describe prospective losses and their associated probabilities. The quantity and quality of the information available to the risk manager is not fixed, yet the assembly of such information into a form which is usable for making financial decisions is critical to the quality of such decisions.

The end objective is the estimation of a particular risk management statistic, termed the *maximum probable yearly aggregate loss (MPY)*.

> *MPY* is defined as that value which will equal or exceed in a stated proportion of all cases, the **total** loss amount during a one-year period from a specified peril.[1]

Since it represents the largest total loss amount which an exposure or group of exposure units is likely to suffer during the one-year period, the value requires an implicit or explicit choice of a probability or likelihood level. By implication, if the probability or likelihood level is say α, then $(1 - \alpha)$ represents the probability of ruin.

To illustrate, a 90% *MPY* of say, R1 million implies that aggregate losses will in 90% of the cases equal or be less than R1 million. Doherty[2] defines the probability of ruin as:

> the probability that the aggregate losses in a given period exceed the value of the fund in that period.

Hence, if a retention fund of R1 million is established, the probability of ruin, assuming a 90% *MPY*, is (1,0 – 0,90), or 10%.

Therefore, that which is sought is an estimate of the probability distributions for losses of various types that face the firm and which can then be aggregated to estimate the distribution of total loss costs facing the firm.

Concepts such as maximum probable yearly aggregate loss (*MPY*), estimated maximum loss (*EML*) and maximum possible loss (*MPL*) are mentioned frequently in the risk management and insurance literature, and it may be opportune to briefly clarify the difference between the *EML* and the *MPY*, after also defining what is meant by *EML*.[2]

The estimated maximum loss (*EML*) is that value which will equal or exceed, in a stated proportion of all cases, the amount of loss from a specified peril or perils.[3]

In less technical language it is the 'largest loss which can occur under the worst conditions which are likely to occur'.

EML is a **severity** concept, that is, it does not consider the probability that a loss will occur.

The *EML* does not apply to a group of exposure units, as it is valid only for individual exposure units, and, in fact for individual losses. The *MPY*, on the other hand, applies to one exposure unit or a group of exposure units and is that value which will equal or exceed, in a stated proportion of all cases, the **sum** of all losses sustained by the group of exposure units during a one-year period.[3]

2 Discussion of these terms can be quite confusing because analysts have not been able to agree fully on standard definitions for EML, MPL and other terms. The definitions adopted here may be seen as having a statistical bias, as they are intended to clarify differences of a statistical nature. See also Friedlander (1977, 26), McGuinness (1969, 31-40) & Williams & Heins (1981, 67).

3 For a stated probability value, the MPY for one exposure unit is less than the EML for that unit. This is because MPY is based on the total loss cost distribution which incorporates the no-loss case, while EML is obtained on the condition that a loss has occurred. Due to the large probability attaching to the no-loss case, any specified cumulative probability level will be reached at a smaller value for MPY than for EML.

14.2.2 Applications of estimated maximum loss (*EML*)

EML is often used by insurers in deciding whether their capacity permits the acceptance of particular exposures.[4] For example, in the field of commercial fire insurance, underwriters use the concept of line limits which indicate the maximum exposure to loss that the company will accept on any given property.

> In risk management, although the *EML* could be used to determine and limit the amount of insurance to purchase, thereby reducing the premium outlay, such reduction should rather be achieved by increasing retention through increased deductibles, but maintaining coverage limits equal to the total exposure.[4]

Insurance is most valuable for large infrequent losses, which, when they occur are most likely to cause the firm severe financial problems.

14.2.3 Applications and limitations of maximum probable yearly aggregate loss (*MPY*)

Whilst it is useful for the firm to know its *EML* values, the *MPY* has greater applicability, especially when an increase in retention limits is being considered. Naturally, the possible losses to individual exposures will influence the aggregate loss distribution, and different deductibles will lead to different *MPY* values. It is, however, the *MPY* and not the *EML* which is of primary relevance to risk management decision-making; knowledge of the *MPY* can for example, assist in decisions concerning the trade-off between higher risk following further retention and resulting savings in premium.

The principle function of the *MPY* in situations where the firm may have the opportunity to choose between different levels of retention, is to provide additional information about the alternative loss cost distributions; that is, information to supplement the usual summary statistics, such as the mean and variance. Its use is not without problems, however. The choice of *MPY* loss values and probabilities is somewhat arbitrary, there being little guidance (theoretical) to indicate how and what levels should be chosen. Consequently, a careful analysis of the firm's financial position, coupled with informed judgement is also necessary before selecting the loss level.

Establishing the probability value is possibly more difficult since management is generally unaccustomed to thinking in terms of probabilities, especially small probabilities. There is also the related problem that the

4 Of course, the decision increase the deductible level implies the support of sound analyses of costs, probabilities and other relevant factors.

MPY represents only one single point on the probability distribution of total loss costs. Hence, in complex situations, the selection of the best alternative necessitates a more thorough analysis of the distribution; management might react very differently to a 0,90 *MPY* of R500 000 and a 0,995 *MPY* of R1,5 million. Evaluation of the entire probability distributions, or even multiple *MPY* points is, however, a very challenging task.

14.2.4 Sources of data

Before proceeding with the discussion of estimating techniques, it is appropriate to look at the sources of data available to the risk manager. The most obvious source of data is the past loss experience of the firm (and other firms engaged in a similar activity). The historical data may be presented as a frequency distribution, and given the fact that the underlying factors producing the losses have remained unchanged over a period of time, the frequency distribution could be used to estimate the distribution of future losses – a process known as statistical inference.

Unlike an insurance company which usually has at its disposal a much more comprehensive statistical base, the individual, non-insurance, firm typically does not hold a diversified or large portfolio of risk exposure units. Therefore, a point to consider is that its historical loss experience may be a limited and random selection of events that is not representative of entire possibilities. The quality of data will depend much on circumstance, but it is generally related to the size and quality of the sample from which the experience is drawn. The quality of internal data depends on the number of exposure units and the length of experience.[5]

The internal data may of course be supplemented by the use of external data, but its use requires firstly, accessibility and secondly, presupposes relevance. The relevance of information depends on whether the firm is representative of the industry. Although statistical testing may render aid in establishing whether samples of loss experience for two firms may be drawn from the same probability distribution, if internal data is limited, the issue of relevance of external data becomes a matter of subjective judgement.

A second source of information comes from subjective, non-statistical sources, which include, for example, technical, organisational and economic judgements made by the firm about the probabilities surrounding an event happening and the economic consequences of the event.

5 Together these factors determine the size of the statistical sample from which data are drawn. Thus, if a firm has owned 100 vehicles for a period of 10 years, it would have 1 000 vehicle-years of experience from which to estimate probabilities, and would be regarded as having a sample size of 1 000 comprising 100 exposure units, each covered for 10 years.

Often, statistical and subjective data can be combined, whereby statistical inference is tempered with subjective judgement – a process which resembles the use of credibility formulae by insurers.[6]

14.2.5 Estimation of maximum probable yearly aggregate loss (*MPY*) from loss data

There is a number of different *MPY* estimation procedures in existence – this section examines several of the more prominent approaches.

In estimating the *MPY*, an attempt is made to locate a particular point or points on the probability distribution of total losses. One way to develop such information is to observe total cost of losses (of the particular peril) over a time period and to develop an empirical distribution from the observed values. The observations can be divided into convenient ranges and the relative frequency (the number of losses within each range divided by the number of observations) and the cumulative frequency (indicating the proportion of losses lying within the range in question or below that range) can be calculated. The frequency values may be used as probability estimates. The *MPY* would then be selected from this empirical distribution.

An alternative approach is to use the available data to develop two probability distributions, one relating to the **frequency** of losses, the other, to the **severity** of losses. The combination, mathematically, of these distributions would derive the total loss distribution, a process known as convolution. The process is somewhat richer than direct estimation of the distribution of aggregate loss, since use is made of the additional information on frequency and severity, but the computation of an *MPY* estimate is relatively difficult. In consequence, other procedures have been developed which estimate the *MPY* without determining the total loss cost distribution, but rely instead on certain statistics (sample mean and variance) which can be computed from the data.

There are, thus, two groups of estimation methods for *MPY* – one contains the methods which require the estimation of the form and shape of the underlying loss distributions, the other contains the procedures that base the *MPY* on statistics developed from the loss data.

14.2.5.1 *Methods based on loss distribution statistics*

The *MPY* calculation methods based on loss distribution statistics utilise the **mean**, **variance** and, in some cases, the **skewness** of the total loss cost distribution.[7] Skewness indicates the extent of departure of the loss distribution from symmetry.

6 A credibility formula can be defined simply as a weighted average of say, a statistical estimate and a subjective judgemental estimate (Doherty, 1985, 79).

7 The mean and variance have been discussed in Chapter Seven, section 7.5.

Suppose that there are n number of possible out comes for total annual losses, that x_i denotes the possible outcomes ($i = 1,2,3, \ldots, n$), and, that the probability of the ith outcome is denoted by $Pr(x_i)$, (x represents the random variable: total annual losses), then, the following equations can be used to determine the mean, variance and skewness of the total loss distribution:[8]

- ☐ The mean or expected value

$$E(x) = \sum_{i=1}^{n} x_i Pr(x_i) \qquad 14.1$$

- ☐ The variance $\sigma^2(x)$

$$\sigma^2(x) = \sum_{i=1}^{n} [(x_i - E(x)]^2 Pr(x_i) \qquad 14.2$$

- ☐ The standard deviation is the square root of the variance $\sigma(x) = \sqrt{\sigma^2(x)}$
- ☐ The skewness, $\alpha_3(x)$ is developed by using the formula:[9]

$$\alpha_3(x) = \frac{\sum_{i=1}^{n} [(x_i - E(x)]^3 Pr(x_i)}{\sigma^3(x)} \qquad 14.3$$

In order to calculate a value for the *MPY* from one of the approximation formulae, three basic steps must be followed:

- ☐ a probability level must be selected

8 These formulae are given in most basic statistics texts. See, for example, Freund, Williams & Perles (1988).

It must be noted that the formulae apply when all the required probability distributions are known. If the total loss distribution is unknown, its mean, variance and skewness must be **estimated** from the available data. The equations cannot be used since the probability values $Pr(x_i)$ are not known. Subject to certain assumptions, the estimates of the mean, variance and skewness can be obtained using the following formulae:

$$y = \frac{1}{n}\sum_{i=1}^{n} y_i \qquad s^2(y) = \frac{1}{n-1}\sum_{i=1}^{n} (y_i - y)^2$$

$$a_3(y) = \frac{\frac{n}{(n-1)(n-2)}\sum_{i=1}^{n} (y_i - y)^3}{s^3(y)}$$

where n denotes the number of years of data, y_i the observation in the ith year and where the symbols $s^2(y)$ and $a_3(y)$, stand for the sample estimates of the true parameter values, $\sigma^2(y)$ and $\alpha_3(y)$.

9 The denominator is obtained by taking the square root of the variance (the standard deviation) and cubing the resulting value. The numerator is called the third moment about the mean. For almost all pure risk loss distributions, skewness is positive, meaning that the loss distribution has a long right tail.

- ☐ the loss distribution statistics calculated
- ☐ these statistics inserted into the approximation formula of the method chosen.

Three methods of approximation are discussed hereunder.[10]

The normal approximation

This approximation assumes that the distribution of total losses can be approximated by a normal probability distribution. Given that an *MPY* probability of α is chosen [ruin probability is $(1 - \alpha)$], the *MPY* estimate is that value on the total loss distribution which is equal to the mean plus a multiple of the standard deviation. The number of standard deviations is indicated by z_{α}, which is a point from a standard normal probability distribution (the value of z_{α} is obtained from a table of the standard normal probability distribution).[11]

The formula for obtaining the normal approximation of the *MPY* estimate is the following:

$$MPY_N = E(x) + z_{\alpha}(x) \qquad \text{14.4}$$

where

MPY_N = the maximum probable yearly aggregate loss estimator utilising the normal approximation
E(x) = the mean of the distribution of total losses
σ(x) = the standard deviation of the distribution of total losses
z = the standard normal random variable
z_{α} = the value of the random variable z where $\Pr(z \leq z_{\alpha}) = \alpha$.

If the actual values of the parameters, mean and standard deviation of the total loss distribution are not known, and estimates are used instead, then the formula must be adjusted for sampling error. There are two adjustments – one is to replace z_{α} with a comparable value from a *student t probability distribution* (because the standard deviation is not known); the

---

10 A good discussion of *MPY* estimation techniques using loss distribution statistics can be found in Cummins & Freifelder (1978, 18-27).
Cummins and Freifelder also include in their discussion the Allen-Duvall Method which follows an intuitive estimation procedure. This method is not reviewed here, but the abovementioned publication and a publication by Allen & Duvall (1971) can be referred to in this regard.

11 These tables usually give the cumulative probability that a standard normal random variable will assume a value that is less than or equal to a certain number. The interpretation of z_{α} is that a standard normal random variable will be less than or equal to z_{α} with a probability of α. To illustrate, suppose a 90 percent *MPY* value is desired; then α equals 0,90 and from the table one can determine that z_{α} is 1,64.

other change adjusts for using an estimate of the mean rather than its actual value.[12]

The problem with this method is that the probability distribution of total losses may not closely approximate a normal distribution. Although the Central Limit Theorem can be used to show that the distribution of total losses will approach normality as the number of losses increases, for many types of perils the individual loss (severity) distribution is so highly skewed that this causes the total loss distribution to be skewed too. By ignoring the skewness, this method will produce an underestimate of the true *MPY*.

The Chebyshev method

The *MPY* calculation formula for the Chebyshev method is similar to that for the normal approximation, except that the standard deviation is multiplied by a different number. The formula is as follows:

$$MPY_C = E(x) + k\sigma(x) \qquad 14.5$$

where

MPY_C = the maximum probable yearly aggregate loss estimator based on Chebyshev's theorem, and

k = the solution to the equation $k = \sqrt{1/(1-\alpha)}$, where α is the *MPY* probability level.[13]

This method is based on a result from statistics which is called Chebyshev's theorem.[14] Since the theorem is valid for all probability distributions, there is no need to be concerned with the actual form of the total loss distribution. The Chebyshev method produces an estimate of *MPY* that is larger than the true *MPY* value.

The normal power method

The normal power method is similar to the normal approximation technique, but purports to correct the skewness of the distribution. The procedure requires the estimation of only one more statistic from the observed

---

12 In order to adjust for sampling error, the following formula should be used to produce a normal approximation *MPY* which applies at the α level:

$MPY' = x + t_{\alpha, n-1} s(x)\sqrt{1 + 1/n}$

where

MPY' = the normal approximation *MPY* estimate adjusted for sampling error

n = the number of annual total loss observations utilised to estimate x and s(x)

t = the student t random variable

$t_{\alpha, n-1}$ = the value of t for a student random variable with n – 1 degrees of freedom where $P(t \leq t_{\alpha, n-1}) = \alpha$.

As in the normal distribution case, tables of the *t* distribution are available in most statistics books.

The multiplier, $\sqrt{1 + 1/n}$, recognises the fact that x is being used in place of E(x), while the substitution of $t_{\alpha, n-1}$ for z_α recognises the replacement of $\sigma(x)$ by s(x).

13 As an example, suppose $\alpha = 0{,}99$; the value of k is 10.

14 Chebyshev's Theorem states:

The probability that a random variable will take on a value within k standard deviations of the mean is at least $(1 - 1/k^2)$.

See Freund, William & Pearles (1988, 234).

loss data than either of the methods previously discussed. The formula for the *MPY* calculation using this method is:

$$MPY_{NP} = E(x) + [z_\alpha + (1/6)\alpha_3(x)(z_\alpha^2 - 1)]\sigma(x) \qquad 14.6$$

where

MPY_{NP} = the maximum probable yearly aggregate loss estimator utilising the normal power method

$\alpha_3(x)$ = the skewness of the total loss cost distribution

and where the other terms have the same interpretation as those provided earlier.

For skewed distributions, the normal power method is the most accurate for estimating *MPY*, but one limitation is that it tends to overstate the true *MPY* if the loss distribution is highly skewed.[15]

14.2.5.2 *Methods based on loss distribution estimation*

The objective of *MPY* analysis is to estimate the true *MPY* value accurately. The methods described above utilise approximation formulae to accomplish this task, and in some cases this task is accomplished adequately. However, since the value of the *MPY* depends on the form and shape of the total loss distribution, methods that estimate the actual distribution of aggregate losses are the most accurate way to calculate *MPY*.[16] There are two principal methods of estimating loss distributions: analytical tabulation, and simulation.

The analytical tabulation approach

This approach involves the use of estimated frequency and severity distributions. These distributions are then combined mathematically (convolution) to develop the estimated total, or aggregate loss distribution. The process of combining the frequency and severity distributions can be performed in two ways.

The first is to use **empirical** distributions, whereby the development of the total loss distribution is essentially a counting problem. The actual process is to 'count' or list the various total loss amounts that can arise and then to determine the probability of each outcome.[17] Although this process is the least complex, it may be practical only when the frequency and severity distributions have a fairly small number of classes. Suppose the maximum frequency shown in the frequency distribution is p, and

---

15 Accurate results have been reported for $\alpha_3 <= 2$.
See Beard, Pentikäinen & Pesonen (1977).

16 With these approaches, it is possible to approximate the true *MPY* value at least as accurately as with any of the statistical approximation methods.

17 A readable presentation of this method, supported by an example is given by Cummins & Freifelder (1979, 26-37).

the number of severity classes is q,[18] the number of possible loss sequences is:

$$S = \sum_{i=0}^{p} q_i \qquad 14.7$$

Without much difficulty one can gauge how quickly tabulation can become unmanageable: for instance, if a firm had, say, 20 losses in a single year, combined with, say, a severity distribution of 20 classes (to give some precision to defining loss values), then one is left with sequences or outcomes in excess of $1,1 \times 10^{26}$.

The other approach is to use **theoretical** probability distributions to describe the empirical frequency and severity data. Obviously, the theoretical distributions must be chosen carefully to ensure that the data is accurately described. One limitation is that only certain combinations of probability distributions will yield a workable mathematical expression for the probability of aggregate losses – one such combination being a Poisson frequency and a gamma severity distribution.[19]

Once the mathematical expression for the total or aggregate loss distribution is obtained, the *MPY* value can be computed. The cumulative total loss distribution can be tabulated using the mathematical formula that describes the distribution; this involves calculating the probability of different total loss amounts and then summing these numbers. The *MPY* value is the smallest total loss figure of which the cumulative probability equals or exceeds the *MPY* probability level.[20]

---

18 In the practical situation the empirical severity of loss data is condensed into a set of intervals. By using the interval midpoints to represent all the values in the interval, the severity distribution may be simplified to permit the computation without the use of a computer. However, the use of intervals can produce inaccuracies, and it is usually better to obtain the precise results.

19 The Poisson or Negative Binomial probability distribution is likely to describe the frequency of loss distribution accurately. In addition to the Gamma distribution, other distributions that might be used to describe the severity distribution are the Lognormal and Pareto distributions. In order to choose amongst these, various statistical tests which measure the 'goodness of fit' are available, for example the Chi-square test. Risk management consultants often ignore the goodness-of-fit problem by making an assumption about the proper theoretical distribution. The selection of the incorrect theoretical distributions can lead to substantial errors in the calculated values of *MPY* and other statistics.

For combinations of theoretical frequency and severity distributions that do not yield workable mathematical expressions for the aggregate loss distribution, numerical analysis methods could be employed. This approach involves 'integration' of the component distributions, whereby the numerically tabulated total loss distribution is then summed or cumulated to permit the *MPY* value to be estimated. The development of such processes requires some mathematical sophistication.

20 It is sometimes also possible to derive a mathematical expression for the cumulative distribution of aggregate losses, and in such cases the *MPY* can be estimated directly from this function.

The simulation method

In contrast to analytically tabulating the distribution of total losses, an alternative approach is to perform a computer simulation of future loss experience. The results of the simulation can then be used to estimate the total loss distribution. This technique, like the analytical tabulation method, requires the development of separate frequency and severity distributions of the actual loss experience.

Simulation is a mathematical procedure which aims to provide synthetic loss experience. Each replication represents the simulated loss experience for a period of one year, with the occurrence of loss determined by a random process. A simulation has two principal steps. First, a random number is generated. Using the frequency of loss distribution, this number determines how many losses have occurred in the simulated year.[21] Second, additional random numbers are generated, one for each of the simulated losses. These numbers and the severity of loss distribution are used to determine the size of the simulated individual losses.[22] The total loss figure for the simulated year is the sum of the values of the simulated individual losses.

To develop a simulated total loss distribution the process is repeated many times and the results of these replications are tabulated to produce a probability distribution.[23] The simulated cumulative probability distribution is then developed and the *MPY* estimate is determined from this distribution.

14.2.6 Standardisation of data

To conclude this section on statistical analysis in risk management, it is useful to include a discussion of what is termed the *standardisation* of data. The use of historical loss data implies that the economic and hazard conditions prevailing in the period over which the data was generated will continue into the future. However, the firm may have grown in size, and even if its operations have not altered to an extent that might give it a some what different hazard profile, the effect of size implies that it will

21 The random number selected has a value between zero and unity, which will be compared with the cumulative probabilities shown for the loss frequency to determine how many losses are assumed. If, for example the cumulative probability of no loss occuring is 0,5 and the cumulative probability of one loss occurring is 0,8 and the random number lies in the range 0,5-0,8 then one loss is assumed to have arisen.

22 This is undertaken by a procedure similar to the one described for the assumption of loss frequency. The value of the loss is chosen by selecting another random number between zero and unity and comparing that number with the cumulative probabilities for loss severity. If appropriate (that is, if the simulation process assumed two losses) a second loss will be chosen by making another random number selection and comparing it with the cumulative probability for severity. This procedure will generate the simulated loss experience for that replication.

23 Accuracy increases with the number of iterations (n), although reasonably good results are usually obtainable with iterations, n = 500. Probably, when using the simulation technique one should plan to run the simulation at least 5 000 times to achieve a sufficient level of accuracy. However, computer and time costs are factors ,which must be taken into consideration with this technique.

generate a higher frequency of losses.[24] Also, the effect of inflation will magnify the cost of the given losses.

These considerations mean that the basic historical data must be standardised so that the probability estimates will relate more correctly to the firm's current level of operations, and reflect the present price levels. This standardisation can be conducted separately on both the frequency and severity distributions.

The adjustment to loss frequency can simply be achieved by multiplying historical values by the ratio of the real value currently at risk to the real value at risk in year *i*:

$$f_{a,i} = f_{r,i}(V_c/V_i) \quad \text{.......... 14.8}$$

where

$f_{a,i}$ = the adjusted loss frequency
$f_{r,i}$ = raw frequency for year *i*
V_c = the real value of the property currently at risk
V_i = the real value of property at risk in year *i*

The adjustment will provide a basis for estimating the loss frequency distribution, given the current size of the exposure.[25] However, this type of adjustment may not always be appropriate. Liability claims, for example, may not bear a close relationship to the value of the firm's assets, so that methods for size adjustment depend to a large extent on the **nature** and **properties** of the individual risk. Nevertheless, some appropriate form of size standardisation is usually necessary.

Adjustment of the loss severity values for the effect of inflation simply entails the selection of a suitable price/cost index. The adjusted severity level for a loss arising in year *i* is:

$$S_{a,i} = S_{r,i}(P_c/P_i) \quad \text{.......... 14.9}$$

where

$S_{r,i}$ = the raw severity value for loss in year *i*
P_c = an index value for current prices
P_i = an index value for prices in year *i*

Adjustment of the loss frequency data for growth in exposure, and adjustment of the loss severity data for inflation often removes the most significant distortions that could arise from the use of historical data. But these adjustments do not address the effect of any underlying trends that may be evident. It could be, for example, that the risk has become more hazardous over recent years on account of, for example, poor risk control (maintenance), or increasing moral hazard. Tests for these distortions

24 Most often when the firm undergoes a change that is believed to alter the hazard conditions, the effects are subjectively assessed and the data modified judgementally.
25 The adjustment may result in fractional values of losses per year; if curves are to be fitted these fractional values should be used to estimate the distribution.

can be undertaken by searching for trends in the data series, and where separate loss frequency and loss severity data are available, each should be tested and adjusted for trend, before proceeding with convolution or curve fitting.[26]

Another problem that arises when using frequency and severity distributions is that events that have not arisen are ignored and events that have arisen are often given too much importance. The question that arises is whether the distributions have 'a missing tail'? These could present severe problems, particularly if the loss data are drawn from a small number of exposure units and/or cover a relatively few number of years. A method of addressing these issues is the consideration of the actual loss data, frequency and severity as constituting a sample that is drawn from an **underlying distribution** having a definite form. If the form is known, then curve fitting techniques can be used to estimate the parameters of the distribution from the sample data to 'smooth out' the distributions and fill in the missing tail.[27]

14.3 Composite financing strategies: Transfer optimisation

14.3.1 Introduction

Chapters Eleven, Twelve and Thirteen examined the mechanism of insurance and the aspect of risk retention, as separate means of pre-loss financing the financial consequences of risk. With retention funding, it was shown that there does exist a risk management case for funding under the condition of transaction costs associated with the alternative sources of finance. In separating the investment from the financing decision, both pre-loss means of financing need to be evaluated against each other and in turn against the post-loss alternatives. The concern now is with the question of integration, particularly with regard to the integration of insurance and retention funding.

For various reasons the firm may not wish to purchase full insurance. The fact has already been mentioned that expenses incurred in settlement

26 Trend analysis methods are widely used and discussed in most statistical texts. Several statistical methods are available. For instance, there is the Daniel-Spearman's rank correlation test (a non-parametric test) which tests for a trend but does not provide an appropriate adjustment factor, and there are regression techniques which fit a trend line to the data and thus provide an adjustment factor to enable projection of value for a future year. In interpreting the results of simple regressions, the correlation coefficient and the student's t-value will determine the 'goodness of fit' and whether the trend detected is statistically significant.

27 See section 14.2.5 on the use of theoretical probability distributions to describe empirical frequency and severity data.

of relatively low severity claims may be disproportionately high when settled by insurance. Because the regularity of such losses often permits the firm to budget accurately for their settlement, the insurance alternative would imply a 'trading of dollars' for these small losses. The prospect of larger losses, however, does present the firm with a substantive risk exposure and the attendant financing problems.

The solution, it would seem, is to insure high severity losses but retain the predictable low severity losses. Leading from this argument is the related question of costs; rationally there should be a balance such that risk sharing can be optimal. Although optimisation has been viewed traditionally from the standpoint of expected utility, where the problem is defined as deriving the optimal level of risk retention (through co-insurance or deductibles) so as to maximise expected utility of wealth, the optimisation question may also be more simply regarded as one of economic order quantities.[28]

14.3.2 Risk sharing through partial insurance

Before considering composite financing strategies however, it is important to consider first the available forms of insurance and partial insurance. Full insurance provides compensation for the full value of loss as defined in the insurance contract or policy. The compensation is for the cost of replacement, or repair of destroyed or damaged property with similar materials and within a reasonable time.[29] For interruption loss, the methods for calculating loss follow rules designed to measure the reduction in profitability from the level that might have prevailed had the loss not occurred. The insurance settlement is thus led by the principle of indemnity: the insurer will restore to the insured the financial loss from the insured event, and will usually limit recovery to the 'actual cash value' (*ACV*) of the loss.

The actual cash value is not, however, equivalent to the economic loss suffered by the owners of the firm, for economic loss relates to the loss of the value of equity as a result of the loss.[30] Ownership claims of share holders represent the rights to income generated from corporate investment and the rights to share in the residual value of the firm. The valuation

---

28 Optimal insurance models based on utility theory are discussed later in this chapter. Certain considerations limit their use in practical risk management decision-making; this limitation has prompted the consideration of the problem from a different perspective – one based on an economic order quantity model.

29 In the case of liability insurance, full insurance implies that the full value of the liability settlement against the insured, together with associated legal costs incurred in defending the claim, will be made good by the insurer.

30 Equity loss is not determined by the actual cash value of the property, but by its capacity for generating wealth in productive use. Similarly, in the case of a liability claim the equity value may not be related only to the cost of defending and satisfying litigation. Litigation may affect the firm's ability to successfully market its product, raise capital etc.

of these rights is determined by capital market activity, and this fact is not considered in the design of an insurance policy.

Full insurance does not necessarily imply therefore, that shareholders are indifferent as to whether a loss arises, and nor does insurance exactly compensate the firm's owners for loss in the value of their ownership claims.[31] However, full insurance serves as a yardstick for identifying the other strategies, or risk sharing (partial insurance) options.

Various forms of risk sharing are encountered in insurance contracts; this examination is limited to the most common forms, namely, deductibles, co-insurance and policy limits.

A **deductible** is a provision for reducing the insurance settlement on any loss by a specified sum. These may be arranged on a 'per loss' basis or may be related to the accumulated losses within a period of the policy (cumulative deductibles) which permit the firm to establish a clear upper limit of its retained liability within any accounting period.

Deductibles are often used to avoid the disproportionately large settlement costs for small claims. Depending on the risk characteristics of higher retentions, the premium discount for an increased deductible, and the costs of competing forms of finance, a firm may even consider very substantial deductibles.[32]

Co-insurance implies that the insurer pays an agreed proportion of the actual cash value of the loss leaving the insured to bear the residual proportion. The premium for proportional co-insurance is usually scaled proportionately to the full insurance premium. Unlike the case of deductibles, the firm faces a somewhat open-ended retention liability, but opportunities may be explored by balancing the risk characteristics of the retained distribution, the premium discount, and the costs of alternative financing methods.

The imposition of **policy limits** means that the basis of indemnity under the insurance contract limits the liability of the insurer to a value which is less than the actual cash value of the property. In the case of liability

31 The implication of this statement as regards the risk management activity of the firm is not difficult to perceive. It places further emphasis on the risk control activity and identifies a **further** element of cost to be 'accounted' for in the total cost of risk equation, as discussed in Chapter 10, section 10.2.2. The notion of cost, resulting from the possible difference between actual cash value and economic loss, should be added to the cost of risk.

32 Traditionally, insurers have been reluctant to offer contracts with substantial deductibles. This may be partly because of the difficulty in pricing such contracts (requiring an estimation of the tail of the loss distribution), and because of a reluctance to part with a substantial portion of their premium income especially when there is the intention of restoring incentives for the insured to undertake loss prevention/reduction measures. Recently, however, there has been evidence of firms increasing their retention levels. (Doherty, 1985, 331).

insurance, although the suits brought against the insured are open-ended, the liability policy will invariably specify an upper limit to the settlement. Policy limits are generally considered unattractive for the business firm since the retained loss is open-ended, difficult to budget for, and the uninsured component of the loss lies at the tail of the loss distribution – which is where insurance is most beneficial.

The effects of the abovementioned forms of risk sharing can be graphically depicted as per figure 14.1. A specimen distribution of actual cash value (*ACV*) is shown, which represents the distribution of *ACV* suffered by a firm if no insurance were in place. The distribution could then be segmented into the distribution of retained loss for the firm and the distribution of contingent payments, made by the insurer with the various forms of risk sharing.

Figure 14.1 Effect of deductible, proportionate co-insurance, and policy limit on hypothetical actual cash value distribution

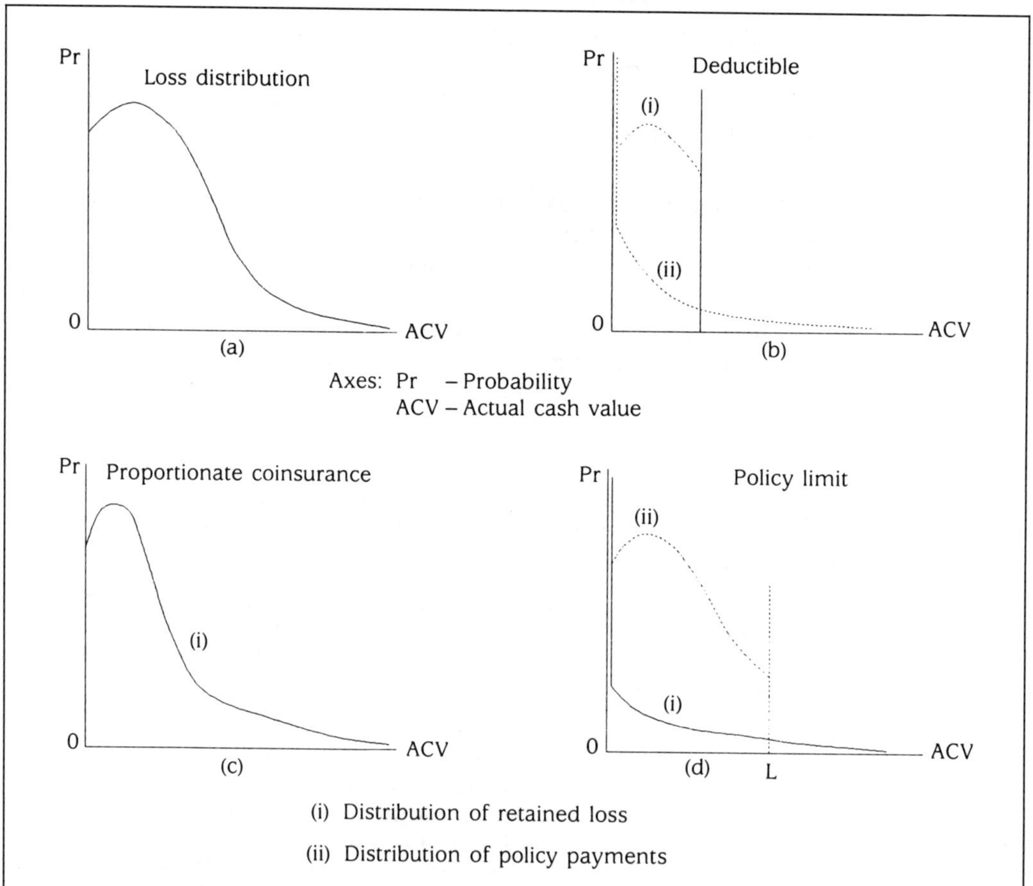

Source: Doherty (1985, 330).

The effect of a **deductible** is illustrated in figure 14.1(b). Losses below the deductible (D) are retained [dotted line(i)]. The dotted line (ii) shows the distribution of insurance payments for contingent losses; this distribution follows the vertical axis showing a probability close to zero, of insurance payments that arise if prospective losses turn out to be no greater than D.

Figure 14.1(c) shows that **co-insurance** compresses the range of potential values of retained loss toward the vertical axis. The distribution of policy payments would also be compressed toward the vertical axis in the same fashion. If a 50% proportionate co-insurance were arranged, the distribution of policy payments would be identical to that of retained loss.

The impact of a **policy limit** (OL) is illustrated in figure14.1(d). The limit considered in this illustration is a cumulative limit on payments made by the policy in a specified period. The distribution of retained loss shows:

- ☐ a high probability of no retention [shown by line (i) following the vertical axis]
- ☐ the open ended nature of prospective losses whereby the distribution converges but does not reach the horizontal axis.

Conversely, the distribution of policy payments [dotted line(ii)] shows the limited value of the insurer's payments, OL.

In comparing the forms of retention, it is commonly held that deductibles are more efficient devices for reducing risk than are proportionate devices such as co-insurance (or quota share reinsurance). Although this case has been motivated simplistically, evidence shows that a risk averter would prefer a policy with a deductible to another policy with the same expected payout but having the risk divided on a proportionate basis.[5]

14.3.3 Evaluation of alternative financing sources

In considering a composite financing strategy, which could include retention (through deductibles), insurance and outside finance, one would have to consider and appraise the associated relative costs. In respect of outside financing (debt and equity) allowance must be made for the transaction costs which would include issue expenses and underwriting costs. In respect of internal liquid funds one would have to consider the opportunity costs of maintaining these funds for risk management purposes.

The inclusion of such transaction costs brings a greater opportunity for satisfying the condition for insurance and retention. In order to explore the possibilities of a composite programme the competing sources are separated and their cost structures considered.

Table 14.1 summarises the financing costs from different sources.

Table 14.1 Examples of financing costs from financing sources[33]

	Actual cost (AC)	Present expected value (EC)
1. New insurance	$(1 + a)E(L)$	$(1 + a)E(L)$
2. New issue	$b + (1 + c)L$	$[P_{LA}b + (1 + c)E(L)](1 + k_1)^{-1}$
3. Internal liquid resources	L	$E(L)(1 + k_2)$

Source: Doherty (1985, 348).

The following can be noted:

- Financing losses from internal sources avoids the issue costs of external funding, and the premium loadings associated with insurance. Assuming losses of size L, the cost of financing such losses internally is L, and the present value is the expected financing cost discounted at the appropriate risk-adjusted rate (k_2).
- The insurance premium is represented by $(1 + a)E(L)$, where E(L) is the expected value of loss and 'a' represents the markup or transaction cost. This form of premium is implied by rating methods which calculate premium at a constant rate applied to some measure of exposure. Since premium is paid in advance, no discounting is required.
- For new debt and equity, the main transaction costs are incurred with issue, (shown as b), and since issue costs typically increase modestly with the size of the issue, the cost is represented as a linear function of the loss, where $c < a$ revealing the realistic situation where insurance transaction costs are higher than the variable costs of a new issue. The present value of expected financing cost is obtained by discounting at some rate k_1 that is appropriate to the riskiness of the contingent financing costs. For the sake of simplicity, this rate could be the (opportunity) rate used for internal financing which is calculated, in the usual way:

  $$k = r_f + b[E(r_m) - r_f] \quad \text{14.10}$$

  The respective costs of each form of financing are represented in figure 14.2. Each diagram shows the total actual **present** value of financing cost at different levels of loss L. It is clear that internal liquid resources represent the cheapest form of financing when losses are relatively low (avoiding transaction costs). However, it is also evident that not all losses can be financed internally; only regular and predictable losses can be accommodated within a cash management programme.

33 a, b, and c are positive constants with $a > c$, k_1 and k_2 are risk-adjusted discount rates, and P_{LA} is the probability that a loss that is above some threshold level of A will arise.

Liquidity limitations would cause the firm to access either the insurance market (which enjoys the advantages of pooling) or outside sources of debt/equity in order to finance losses of relatively high severity values.

Figure 14.2
Present value of financing costs from alternative sources

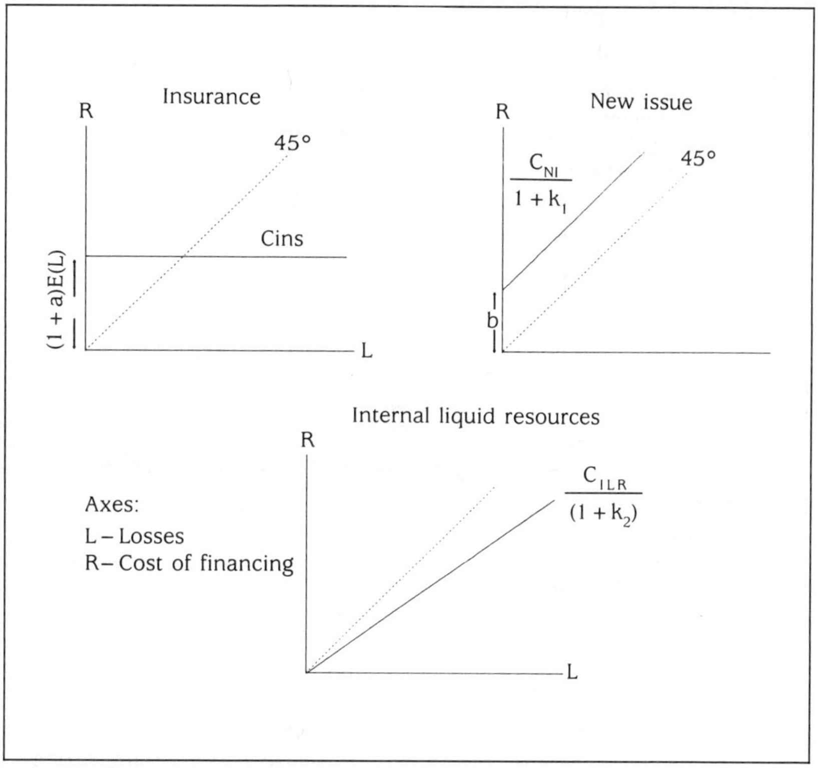

Source: Doherty (1985, 348).

Supposing that small losses, below some value $L = d$ can be financed from liquid sources (that is, the adoption of acumulative deductible d), one could combine the sources into a composite financing scheme, where the financing is layered. Losses above d are funded by insurance or by the new issue of debt or equity. If insurance is purchased, the premium would be $(1 + a)$ times the expected value of the insured loss, which can be represented as follows:

$(1 + a)E(L - d)$ 14.11

Figure 14.3 shows the total cost for different values of loss, as OADG, when small losses are retained internally and losses in excess of d are insured – and OABF, when small losses are retained internally but losses in excess of d are funded through new issues. The total cost of financing through new issue is shown by the continuation along line BF; the difference in gradient between BF and 45° represents the variable transaction cost.

Figure 14.3 Composite two-layer financing programme

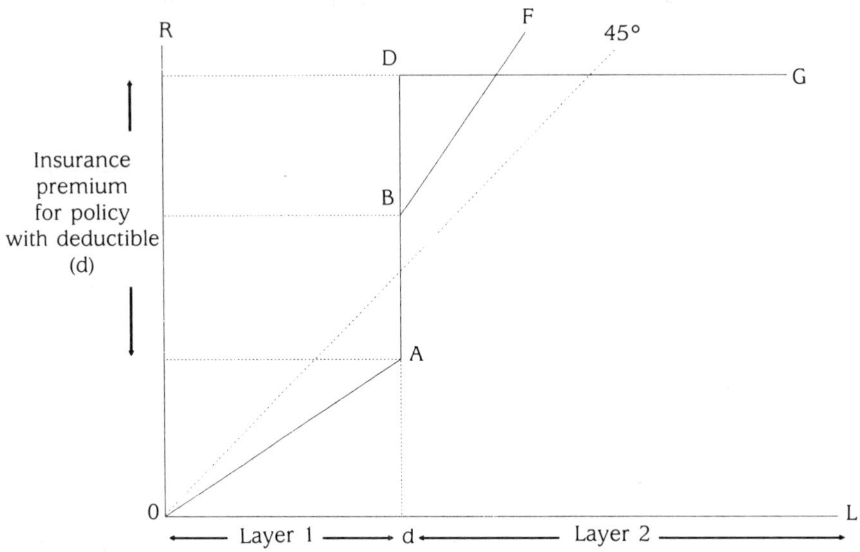

OABF: Total cost with deductible (d) financed by internal liquid resources and residual of larger losses financed by new issue

OADG: Total cost with deductible (d) financed by internal liquid resources and residual of larger losses financed by insurance policy subject to deductible (d)

Source: Doherty (1985, 349).

14.3.4 Conclusion

A comparison of approaches may be undertaken by means of risk-adjusted present values, where the decision-making process could adopt the following sequence:

- ☐ select a first layer of deductible to be financed by internal resources.
- ☐ choose between insurance and new issues on the basis of the expected value of financing costs.

Naturally, this process presupposes that the aggregate loss distribution is known, or accurately estimated by statistical techniques discussed in the earlier section; and that the statistical properties of the loss distribution, namely the expected value, the standard deviation and the measure of skewness are computed. With these parameters, and with knowledge of respective transaction costs and risk-adjusted discount rates, the financing strategy can be evaluated and a decision made on the form of the second layer of funding, given a first retention layer in the form of a suitable deductible.

There remains, however, the selection of the retention portion or deductible level, which as the decision process indicates, should be given first consideration. The size of this layer will be determined by its risk characteristics. More specifically, this layer should finance only losses or portions of losses which arise with sufficient predictability so that they can be accommodated within the firm's liquidity, or cash budget.

The method to be used may be developed by using the characteristics of the loss distribution. The deductible *d* can be chosen at some level (say a probability level of 0,25) where the probability of surpassing *d* (ruin probability) is acceptably low. If the probability is fixed too low, implying that losses might well fall below this level ($L < d$), the firm will find itself with surplus cash, which is costly in terms of investment earnings foregone. Finally, to gauge whether payments financed in this manner (that is, under the deductible at the appropriate probability level) are stable, the expected value and standard deviation of the prospective payments can be determined.

The comparison of the risk-adjusted costs of financing will determine whether the optimal strategy dictates the integration of retention with insurance (OADG), or the integration of retention with new issue financing (OABF).[34]

14.4 Optimisation models based on expected utility

The above-mentioned methodology, used to provide guidance for deductible selection (risk retention level) implied selection in a way which contains the riskiness of the retained risk at some acceptable level. There do exist several other types of insurance-purchasing models which may be found in the risk management literature.[35] These models mainly use expected utility to derive the optimum level of retention through the adoption of co-insurance or deductibles.

Utility theory has been theoretically recognised as a decision-making technique to facilitate the evaluation of probabilistic alternatives. The method assigns a single value, the expected utility, to each probability outcome. The expected utilities are compared and the largest expected utility is the preferred alternative.[36]

In order to compute the expected utility, each possible monetary outcome in the probability distribution needs to be converted to a utility value. These utility values are numbers that express the preference of the decision maker for various amounts of money. Since the decision maker is assumed to be risk averse, large losses would be assigned lower utilities than smaller losses; the utility curve therefore displaying diminishing returns.

34 The methodology is well illustrated by Doherty (1985, 351-355) by means of a case study.
35 See Smith (1968, 68-77), Mossin (1968, 553-568), Doherty & Schlesinger (1983, 555-565) and Cozzolino (1978, 499-471).
36 Reference can be made to Chapter Three, section 3.9.5, where the concept of utility was introduced and a utility-based decision for the purchase of insurance was illustrated by means of an elementary example.

In the case of risk management, utility values could be assigned to each possible outcome of a loss distribution, and would then be weighted by multiplying them by the probabilities of occurrence of the associated outcomes. The expected utility for the distribution is obtained by the summation of the weighted utility values. In considering an optimal level for insurance, the expected utility typically takes the following form:

$$\text{Expected utility} = \Sigma P_i U[W_i(INS)] \quad \text{......} \quad 14.12$$

where

W_i = the decision maker's wealth if a loss of size L_i occurs (the wealth level is determined by the level of insurance [INS])

P_i = the probability that a loss of size L_i will occur

U = an index of the decision maker's utility

The problem (optimisation) is therefore to maximise expected utility of wealth; where wealth depends on loss experience(which is random), and the purchase of insurance (which is a decision).[37]

The expected utility approach can clearly be useful in helping to identify broad risk management choices consistent with aversion to risk, and may help to eliminate specific choices from a decision. The approach presupposes that two fundamental requirements are satisfied:

(i) the probability distribution of losses must be known or at least accurately estimated and

(ii) the decision maker's utility function, that is, the rule which assigns utility values to monetary loss outcomes according to his preferences, must be available.

In the latter requirement, lies a major limitation.

Although most of the theoretical problems involving utility functions have been solved, utility theory has not been applied in many practical situations; theorists have been unable to convince practitioners that the method has merit: to them, the theory seems abstract and even abstruse.[6]

37 The propositions concerning the purchase of insurance derived from this type of model assume aversion to risk by risk management decision-makers, so that the example:
- if the premium is equal or less than the expected value of loss, (rationally) insurance will be purchased.
- if the premium is a constant multiple, greater than 1 of the expected value of the insured loss, the rational risk averter will retain part of the risk; a deductible will be preferred to coinsurance.
- if individual *A* is more risk averse than individual *B* – *A* will purchase more insurance than will *B*.

In sum, the following problems limit the use of utility theory for risk management purposes:

- ☐ To identify precise risk management strategies means full identification of the decision maker's utility function. It is extremely doubtful that the firm (its board) can expound a utility function or an attitude toward risk which satisfies the propositions of utility-decision models developed.
- ☐ Even if the utility function were available, the appropriate utility is that of the firm's shareholders who regard their equity holdings as financial assets traded in a capital market according to market-determined risk-return relationships. Since the risk is clearly priced in the market (assuming a widely held firm), it is consistent to impose the market price of risk on risk management decisions, that is, risk preferences are measured by capital market activity.
- ☐ Virtually all the utility based models formulate the insurance decision as one in which insurable risk is the only source of risk. Hence possible portfolio effects within a firm are ignored. The risk reducing effects of insurance may lose some value if shareholders are able to diversify away this risk in their personal portfolio holdings.

14.5 Summary

Having discussed in Chapters Eleven, Twelve and Thirteen the risk financing means of insurance and retention funding respectively, the objective of this chapter has been to describe composite financing strategies. As this approach requires a statistical analysis to be performed, it was necessary to begin the chapter by exploring further the use of statistical analysis in risk management.

The section covering statistical analysis concentrated particularly on the estimation of the maximum probable yearly aggregate loss (*MPY*), but also drew a distinction between the *MPY* and the probable maximum loss (*PML*) measure. Two broad methods of estimating the *MPY* were discussed. One is based on loss distribution statistics, which incorporates the methods of normal approximation, Chebyshev and the normal power. The other is based on loss distribution estimation, where the analytical tabulation approach and simulation method were examined.

The chapter proceeded by considering composite financing strategies. Firstly, attention was paid to risk-sharing through partial insurance, and the effects of a deductible, proportionate co-insurance and policy limits on hypothetical actual cash value distribution, were graphically depicted. It was stated that a risk averter would commonly prefer a deductible as a device for reducing risk, to having the risk divided on a proportional basis.

Secondly, alternative external financing sources, namely new issues of debt and equity, were evaluated against insurance and internal liquid resources. The present value of financing costs of these sources were separately depicted and then combined, to show the total cost of financing under a composite two-layer financing programme which entails financing losses though internal liquid resources and insurance, or internal liquid resources and a new issue of debt or equity. It was concluded that a comparison of the risk-adjusted costs of financing will determine whether the optimal strategy dictates the integration of retention with insurance, or the integration of retention with new issue financing.

In determining an optimal risk financing strategy involving risk retention and insurance, utility theory has been recognised as a decision-making technique to facilitate the evaluation of probabilistic alternatives. The chapter briefly describes the problem of maximising expected utility of wealth, the fundamental requirements it presupposes, and enumerates limitations of this theory. From a practical risk management decision-making point of view, it is concluded that it is extremely doubtful that the firm (its board) can expound a utility function that satisfies the propositions relative to the decision models developed.

Bibliography

Allen, TC & Duvall, RM 1971. 'A theoretical and practical approach to risk management.' *American Society of Insurance Management.*

Beard, RE, Pentikäinen, T & Pesonen, E 1977. *Risk theory.* New York: John Wiley & Sons.

Cozzolino, JM 1978. 'A method for the evaluation of retained risk.' *Journal of Risk and Insurance.* Vol. 45.

Cummins, JD & Freifelder, LR 1978-1979. 'Statistical analysis in risk management.' *Risk Management.* September-April.

Doherty, NA 1985. *Corporate risk management – A financial exposition.* New York: McGraw-Hill Inc.

Doherty, NA & Schlesinger, H 1983. 'The optimal deductible for insurance policy when initial wealth is random.' *Journal of Business.* Vol. 56.

Freund, JE, Williams, FJ & Perles, BM 1988. *Elementary business statistics. The modern approach.* Englewood Cliffs, New Jersey: Prentice-Hall Inc.

Friedlander, AW 1977. 'Assessing fire loss potentials.' *Risk Management.* October.

Friedman, M & Savage, LJ 1948. 'The utility analysis of choices involving risk.' *Journal of Political Economy.* Vol. LVI, No 4, August.

Holton, RB 1973. *Underwriting: Principles and practices.* Cincinnati National Underwriter Co.

McGuinness, JS 1969. 'Is 'Probable maximum loss' a useful concept.' *Proceedings of the Casualty Actuarial Society.* Vol. 56.

Mossin, J 1968. 'Aspects of rational insurance purchasing.' *Journal of Political Economy.* Vol. 76.

Smith, V 1968. 'Optimal insurance coverage.' *Journal of Political Economy.* Vol. 68.

Williams, CA & Heins, RM 1981. *Risk management & Insurance.* New York: McGraw-Hill Inc.

Endnotes

[1] Cummins & Freifelder, 1978, 59.

[2] Doherty, 1985, 306.

[3] Cummins & Freifelder, 1978, 58.

[4] Holton, 1973, 192.

[5] Doherty, 1985, 339-342.

[6] Cummins & Freifelder, 1978, 44.

INDEX

J

K

L

M

S